Worldwide Science and Technology Advice

to the Highest Levels
of Governments

Pergamon Titles of Related Interest

Brooks/Cooper SCIENCE FOR PUBLIC POLICY
Golden SCIENCE ADVICE TO THE PRESIDENT
Golden SCIENCE AND TECHNOLOGY ADVICE TO THE PRESIDENT, CONGRESS, AND JUDICIARY
Hart THE PRESIDENTIAL BRANCH
Spanier CONGRESS, THE PRESIDENCY AND AMERICAN FOREIGN POLICY

Related Journals
(Free sample copies available on request.)

LONG RANGE PLANNING
SOCIO-ECONOMIC PLANNING SCIENCE
TECHNOLOGY IN SOCIETY
WORLD DEVELOPMENT

Worldwide Science and Technology Advice

to the Highest Levels
of Governments .

edited by

William T. Golden

Pergamon Press

New York • Oxford • Beijing • Frankfurt •
São Paulo • Sydney • Tokyo • Toronto

Q 125
.W6
1991
Copy 2

Pergamon Press Offices:

U.S.A.	Pergamon Press, Inc., Maxwell House, Fairview Park, Elmsford, New York 10523, U.S.A.
U.K.	Pergamon Press plc, Headington Hill Hall, Oxford OX3 0BW, England
PEOPLE'S REPUBLIC OF CHINA	Pergamon Press, 0909 China World Tower, No. 1 Jian Guo Men Wei Avenue, Beijing 100004, People's Republic of China
FEDERAL REPUBLIC OF GERMANY	Pergamon Press GmbH, Hammerweg 6, D-6242 Kronberg, Federal Republic of Germany
BRAZIL	Pergamon Editora Ltda, Rua Eça de Queiros, 346, CEP 04011, Paraiso, São Paulo, Brazil
AUSTRALIA	Pergamon Press Australia Pty Ltd., P.O. Box 544, Potts Point, NSW 2011, Australia
JAPAN	Pergamon Press, 8th Floor, Matsuoka Central Building, 1-7-1 Nishishinjuku, Shinjuku-ku, Tokyo 160, Japan
CANADA	Pergamon Press Canada Ltd., Suite 271, 253 College Street, Toronto, Ontario M5T 1R5, Canada

Copyright © 1991 Pergamon Press, Inc.

All rights reserved. No part of this publication may be reproduced, stored in a retrieval system or transmitted in any form or by any means: electronic, electrostatic, magnetic tape, mechanical, photocopying, recording or otherwise, without permission in writing from the publishers.

Library of Congress Cataloging in Publication Data
Worldwide science and technology advice to the highest levels of
  governments / edited by William T. Golden
      p. cm.
    Includes index.
    ISBN 0-08-040406-5 (hard : alk. paper). -- ISBN 0-08-040407-3
soft : alk. paper)
    1. Science and state. 2. Technology and state. I. Golden,
William T., 1909-
Q125.W84 1991
338.926--dc20   90-7942
                                                                    CIP

Printing: 1 2 3 4 5 6 7 8 9 10   Year: 1 2 3 4 5 6 7 8 9

Printed in the United States of America

∞™ The paper used in this publication meets the minimum requirements
    of American National Standard for Information Sciences—
    Permanence of Paper for Printed Library Materials, ANSI Z39.48-1984

Dedication

I take the liberty of dedicating this book, on behalf of all its authors, to the future of Homo sapiens, our endangered species, in the hope that our efforts will contribute to the survival and betterment of humankind through the encouragement of education and international cooperation.

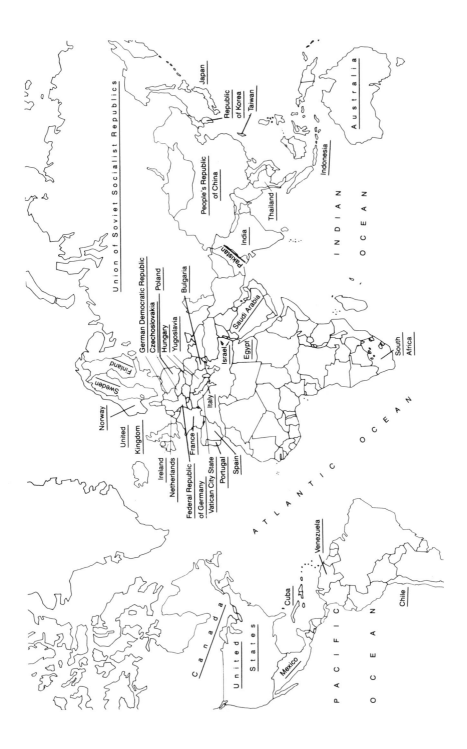

Contents

COUNTRY CHAPTERS

Contents

Acknowledgments

My gratitude goes first to the authors of these original essays, colleagues in a truly international project.

Then, I thank the friends who have been encouragers and helpers. Notable among them are Helene L. Kaplan, David A. Hamburg, J. Thomas Ratchford, D. Allan Bromley, Frank Press, the late I. I. Rabi, Helen Rabi, and the late Mack Lipkin.

And I thank the many others who have helped me in special ways. They include William O. Baker, Harry Barnes, David Z. Beckler, Justin Bloom, Sandra Burns, Robert Cutler, Kerstin Eliasson, Antonio Ruiz Galindo, Patricia Garfinkel, William E. Gordon, Allen Hammond, Ralph E. Hansmann, Ryo Hirasawa, Anne Keatley, George A. Keyworth II, Charles V. Kidd, Rustam Lalkaka, Liu Zhao Dong, Jan Oort, Richard F. Pedersen, Gunnar Randers, David Z. Robinson, Maarten Schmidt, Frederick T. Sai, Frederick Seitz, Kalman Szende, Cyrus Vance, Alberto Vollmer, Henry G. Walter, Jr., Jerome B. Wiesner, and Gabriel Fernandez de Valderrama.

This book would not have reached fruition but for the devoted and resourceful participation of my assistant, Christie Van Kehrberg, and of my other staff members, Ellen Rosenblatt and Eugene R. Gorman. My very special gratitude goes to Martha Miller Willett, finest of editorial ancillaries.

On a more deeply personal basis, I think of my grandparents, steerage immigrants little more than a century ago, who found refuge, freedom and opportunity in the United States of America, as did countless others, and I think of my late parents, S. Herbert Golden and Rebecca Harris Golden; my late brother, Barry; my late wife of forty-five years, Sibyl, ever loving and supportive; my cherished and admired daughters, Sibyl Rebecca and Pam; and certain friends. They are my inspiration and my reward.

William T. Golden
New York, March 1990

Worldwide Science and Technology Advice

to the Highest Levels
of Governments

Introduction: Science and Technology Advising in a Dynamically Changing World

William T. Golden

Tempora mutantur nos et mutamur in illis.

The only permanent condition is change.

—Heraclitus, c. 500 B.C.

We must, indeed, all hang together or, most assuredly, we shall all hang separately.

—Benjamin Franklin

As this is written, much of the world's political, economic, societal and governmental structure is in flux. Progress in science and technology has been accelerating. Information and advice about relevant issues have become exquisitely important to the highest levels of governments. The times are changing, and we are changing within them. It is a truism, but nonetheless true that science and technology affect increasingly the lives of all of us (and of other living creatures, including animals, plants and microorganisms) and of govern-

William T. Golden designed the first Presidential Science Advisory organization for President Truman in 1950. He is Chairman of the American Museum of Natural History and Past Chairman of the New York Academy of Sciences, and is Co-chairman (with Joshua Lederberg) of the Carnegie Commission on Science, Technology, and Government. He has served in the US Navy (World War II), the Atomic Energy Commission, the Department of State, and the Executive Office of the President. He received the Distinguished Public Service Award of the National Science Foundation (1982). Mr. Golden is an officer and trustee of the American Association for the Advancement of Science, the Mount Sinai Hospital and Medical School, and the Carnegie Institution of Washington; and is a member of the National Academy of Public Administration, the American Philosophical Society, and of the American Academy of Arts and Sciences.

ments and, indeed, the conditions and prospects of the earth itself.

These original essays, by distinguished and well-qualified authors, provide brief descriptions, with relevant commentary, of the science and technology advisory organizations to the highest governmental levels of all major countries of the world and a representative selection of smaller ones, a total of more than thirty-five countries. The United States advisory organization is described briefly in this volume and *in extenso* elsewhere.[1] These countries are diverse in many characteristics, including area, geography, population, economic and political systems, language, religion, culture, and stability. All are linked by a growing interdependence.

This collection considers an aspect of modern life that influences its entire fabric and quality: the role of science and technology in governments throughout the world—in the comity of nations, in peace and in war. It aims to be helpful to government officials, to politicians, to political scientists, to the media, and to the concerned public. The improvement of public understanding of science, worldwide, is ''a consummation devoutly to be wished.''

This volume is the first attempt at such a comprehensive organizational atlas. It aims at moving targets which are actively evolving. As recent and ongoing political events in Europe, Asia, Africa and Latin America demonstrate, the high road from dictatorship to democracy may digress, from time to time, through the bog of chaos.

The initiation of modern science and technology advising organizations in the United States (making a multi-millennial leap from the Serpent as adviser to Adam and Eve),[2] starting with President Truman's action of early 1951 and fortified by President Eisenhower after Sputnik in 1957, was chronicled definitively in 1974 by Detlev Bronk,[3] former President of Rockefeller University and former President of the National Academy of Sciences.

Perhaps evolving from these early US origins and other stimuli, many nations of the world have developed their own organizations and methods for introducing knowledge and ideas of science and technology into their governments' policy formulation and execution for both internal affairs and international relationships. The Truman science advisory emphasis was on national defense issues, spurred by the outbreak of the Korean War in mid-1950; and Eisenhower and the American people were galvanized by the success of the Soviet Sputnik. But over the years, as science and technology have become integral parts of everyday life, the involvements have broadened and deepened to comprise virtually all human concerns, including economic, societal, educational, political, health, population, ecological, space, and cultural issues— as well as matters of armaments, defense, and arms limitations.

THE ESSAYS

The essays which follow, on individual countries, were written in response to my request that each author (a) describe the science and technology advising organization to the highest levels of his or her government; and (b) comment on its effectiveness and how it actually influences policy formulation and action.

The authors, from some thirty-five countries, have done well, each in his or her own style and each independent of the writings of the others. I am grateful to them. They are of diverse political and cultural backgrounds, and are immersed in different cultural and political environments. Many of them occupy or are recent occupants of official positions more or less comparable to that of the Science Adviser to the President of the United States, and some of the authors are presidents of their national academies of sciences. All are well qualified by status, experience and wisdom.

In addition to the articles on individual countries, a number of broad overview articles, also especially written for this volume, are presented to fill *lacunae*, to stimulate thought, and to provide inspiration and guidance for the decades ahead in our interdependent world. Special attention is paid to the prospects for Europe after 1992 (Henry Durand, Vincent J. McBrierty) and to the needs and aspirations of the developing countries (Abdus Salam, Thomas Odhiambo).

D. Allan Bromley, Science Adviser to President Bush, and Frank Press, President of the National Academy of Sciences of the US, have graciously written prefatory essays of wisdom and scope.

An article by Shalheveth Freier is a distillate of the presentations and discussions at a remarkable four-day international Forum on Science and Government held in December 1989 at the Weizmann Institute of Science at Rehovot, Israel, in which some forty-five distinguished scientists, engineers, government officials, political scientists, sociologists, humanists, and journalists from eighteen countries participated. The co-chairmen of this extraordinary conference were Cyrus Vance, former Secretary of State of the United States, and Sir Zelman Cowen, Provost of Oriel College, Oxford, and former Governor-General of Australia.

David Z. Beckler's essay, "A Decision-Maker's Guide to Science Advising," is a practical, how-to-do-it manual by a practitioner of unique experience. It will repay careful study.

A recent novel development in the United States that may inspire creation of counterparts in other countries is the Carnegie Commission on Science, Technology and Government, conceived by David Hamburg, President of the Carnegie Corporation of New York, and organized in 1988. Its activities are described and its membership enumerated by its Executive Director, David Z. Robinson, in his article on the United States.

Another American innovation which may be deemed worthy of attention by other countries is the Congressional Science and Engineering Fellows Program initiated by the American Association for the Advancement of Science in 1973. Described elsewhere,[4] it has brought more than 400 scientists and engineers into federal government service for one-year staff terms. Many have remained in government service; others have returned to industry and universities better informed, as concerned citizens, on the practical workings of the government. The program flourishes, now bringing annually some twenty-five men and women, generally achievers of advanced degrees or at mid-level status in industry, into one-year Congressional staff service through a highly competitive selection process. A small comparable program of Westminster Fellows is now being initiated in England.

Caveat lector. Reader beware. This book is offered as a pioneering effort. The salutary trend toward globalization, encouraged by the acceleration of progress in science and technology and in communications, creates a need for such a compendium. It is hoped that it will encourage international cooperation and stimulate discussion in many countries, each of which can learn from others. From diversity may come progress. As Kipling put it, in a very different context, "There are nine and sixty ways of constructing tribal lays,/ And every single one of them is right."

CONCLUSION

Stimulated by these papers, I conclude with a question and a proposal. Where do we go from here? Would an informal, unofficial organization of science and technology advisers to the top levels of governments of the major countries— or of all countries—of the world be useful and viable? Such an organization could be a forum for discussion, for cross-pollination, and for exchange of ideas. It would have influence, but not authority. If it flourishes, it will mutate as conditions change.[5] If it does not prove useful, it will atrophy and disappear.[6] *Primum non nocere.*

The success of the Weizmann Institute conference, with its participants from diverse countries, encourages this idea. Consideration is being given by the Carnegie Commission on Science, Technology and Government and by the American Association for the Advancement of Science to inviting science and technology advisers of the top governmental levels of a few selected countries to a preliminary meeting to explore the merits, impediments and practicalities of establishing such an organization that might later be open to all countries of the world. Its informality and flexibility might confer advantages not available to existing official intergovernmental agencies, such as those of the OECD[7] and the UN.

Such a forum, with its cross-fertilization and peaceful interchange of ideas, would tend to broaden and intensify governmental and public awareness of the role of science and technology in national and international policy formulation and in everyday life. Whether or not such an organization is convened and flourishes, it is hoped that this book—the work of many heads and hands—will enrich the international gene pool of alternatives, and stimulate progress toward the betterment of life throughout the world.

NOTES

1. William T. Golden, ed., *Science Advice to the President* (New York: Pergamon Press, 1980) and *Science and Technology Advice to the President, Congress and Judiciary* (New York: Pergamon Press, 1988).
2. "Science advising has a long history. According to Genesis, 'In the beginning God created the Heaven and the Earth.' In due course, Adam appeared and then Eve. The Serpent was waiting for them. The Serpent, much maligned disturber of complacency, aroused Eve's curiosity and resistance to authority. Eve's example and persuasion spurred Adam to the quest for knowledge and understanding—which equates with science. Thus Adam and Eve became the first scientists—co-investigators, one might say—thanks to the Serpent who was clearly the first science adviser."—William T. Golden, "Science Advice to the President: Past, Present, Future," *Proceedings of the American Philosophical Society,* Vol. 130, no. 3 (1986), pp. 325–329.
3. Detlev W. Bronk, "Science Advice in the White House: The Genesis of the President's Science Advisers and the National Science Foundation," *Science,* Vol. 186 (October 11, 1974), pp. 116–121; reprinted in *Science Advice to the President, supra,* pp. 245–256.
4. Michael L. Telson and Albert H. Teich, "Science Advice to the Congress: The Congressional Science and Engineering Fellows Program," *Science and Technology Advice to the President, Congress and Judiciary, supra,* pp. 447–452.
5. ". . . from so simple a beginning, endless forms most beautiful and most wonderful have been, and are being, evolved."—Charles Darwin, *The Origin of Species,* concluding paragraph.
6. ". . . Natural Selection, entailing Divergence of Character and the Extinction of less improved forms."—Charles Darwin, *op. cit.*
7. Reference is made to the series of informative Reviews of National Science and Technology Policy in individual member countries of the Organization for Economic Cooperation and Development prepared in recent years under OECD auspices.

Foreword: Science Advice in a Global Context

D. Allan Bromley

There is no need to underscore the unique potential of science and technology for improving the human condition. Yet it is easy to forget just how rapidly and dramatically science and technology are transforming the world. Our knowledge of the physical universe and of the chemical and biological basis of life is expanding exponentially. And, in consequence, the importance of this knowledge and the technologies built upon it has risen to the point that science and technology are decisive factors in determining the international competitiveness of national economies, in establishing military advantage, and in a vast array of endeavors that speak to the quality of human life and the health of the planetary environment.

Given this growing importance, it is obvious that governments have a great need to make wise decisions about science and technology. These decisions are of two kinds: what kind of science and technology to support, how much support to give, and how best to provide it—in effect, policy for science and technology; and how best to tap the world's storehouse of scientific knowledge to help solve the myriad problems and challenges that governments and nations face—science and technology for policy. This second task is by far the more challenging aspect of science advice, and yet it is precisely the molding of the best available science and technology information into the policy-making process that holds the greatest hope of mobilizing the potential of science for helping humankind.

What makes the task of policy-making in science and technology so challenging today is its increasingly global context. The world is changing at an astonishing and accelerating pace, politically and in science and technology, so much so that it sometimes seems hard to adjust to, much less to identify and seize the new opportunities that it presents.

Nonetheless, it is clear that the fundamental new economic alignments underway in Western Europe and the even more fundamental political and eco-

D. Allan Bromley, physicist and educator, is Assistant to the President of the United States for Science and Technology ("Science Adviser to the President") and is Director of the Office of Science and Technology Policy and Chairman of the President's Council of Advisers on Science and Technology (PCAST). He has been Director of the A. W. Wright Nuclear Structure Laboratory and Henry Ford II Professor at Yale University. Born in Canada in 1926, Dr. Bromley is a former President of the American Association for the Advancement of Science, and has been a member of the White House Science Council (1981–89). He has received many honors and awards and is the author of many publications.

nomic changes taking place in the Soviet Union, in Eastern Europe and, inevitably, in China will reshape our options and our priorities away from defense issues and toward other pressing international and domestic problems, for example.

The nature of the science and technology issues that we face on an international level is changing, too. Global environmental problems, for example, can only be studied and resolved by concerted joint effort on an unprecedented scale. Increasingly, the key issues are science-based or science-related. Let me mention a few examples.

GLOBAL CHANGE

Science and technology are intimately related to the health of the environment, both locally and globally. There is great public concern in many countries about global change, the pollution of the earth's oceans, long-term disposal of hazardous wastes, too much ozone near the earth and too little far above it. People are increasingly making known their demands for clean air and water and for a halt to activities that threaten to degrade natural resources or destroy unique species and the genetic heritage that they represent.

These concerns focus attention on the state of human knowledge of both the sciences and the technologies involved. In the United States, we are expanding our research efforts in global change. But the problem is, indeed, global, and will require an international effort, both to reduce the substantial scientific uncertainties that surround our understanding of global warming and to stabilize or reduce emissions of the greenhouse gases that are changing the composition of the atmosphere. In this regard, the work of the Intergovernmental Panel on Climate Change, under the auspices of the United Nations Environmental Programme and the World Meteorological Organization, is an excellent model that is leading to a consensus set of information on which international policy-making can be based.

Francis Bacon wrote that "We cannot command nature except by obeying her." His meaning was clear: We must observe and understand the world to live within its bounds. If we fail to protect the environment, we will inevitably undermine the very conditions that make a technological civilization possible. Thus science and technology have a very special role—and a very special obligation—in improving our stewardship of Spaceship Earth.

PUBLIC HEALTH AND THE QUALITY OF LIFE

Health and an improved quality of life are universal aspirations. In the next half century, the world's population is likely to double. Most of these five billion new humans will be added to the developing nations of the world, and most of them to already crowded urban areas. Just to address the basic needs of adequate health care, food, shelter, and energy for these expanding populations will be an enormous task. Yet the developed nations have a number of reasons, quite beyond very real humanitarian concern, for taking on these serious problems. These include the desire to develop new markets for goods and services and the fact that we live in an era of rising expectations, when global communications bring into stark relief the disparities between rich and poor.

Relieving these disparities by enabling developing nations to improve their economic growth and meet their citizens' basic needs will require a sharing of the basic toolkit for industrial civilization. That means not only the transfer of technology, but also building, in developing nations, both an educational and a science and technology infrastructure. We will need wisdom, generosity, and perhaps new mechanisms to accomplish this task.

The developed nations also share with the rest of the world such serious problems as the growing prevalence of AIDS, drug abuse, and the burgeoning costs of medical care, as well as having to face the health challenges associated with an aging population. Again, as the AIDS epidemic makes all too clear, the context for policy is a global one.

INTERNATIONAL COOPERATION IN RESEARCH

Science has always been a truly international community, with members often having closer relationships with colleagues on the other side of the planet than with those on the other side of the hallway; technology was less so, but it is rapidly catching up. In a world that is increasingly interdependent—economically, militarily, environmentally—it is not surprising that even basic science projects must be considered in an international context. In particular, the time is right for expanded international cooperation on large science projects (megaprojects) whose beneficiaries are, in truth, the entire family of man. The cathedrals of science must increasingly be international—or, at least, multinational—ones.

A number of current world-class projects, such as the superconducting supercollider, the space station, and the human genome project are, in fact, being planned and supported on a multinational scale. Cooperation such as this, even when difficult, needs to become far more common, both to make better use of scarce resources and because cooperation builds human communication links that are valuable far beyond the confines of the science and technology involved. Such links, built through cooperative projects, scientific exchanges, and enlightened self-interest, speak to every nation's direct interest in remaining or becoming technologically competitive in a peaceful and cooperative—rather than a confrontational—world.

Because basic science—and, to a lesser degree, technology—are relatively neutral in a political sense, it is frequently possible to establish communication bridges and cooperation in matters of science and technology that would not be possible in other fields. Once established, however, these bridges can—and usually do—expand to encompass a much wider range of topics. And the person-to-person and institution-to-institution bonds that are forged under such international agreements are lasting ones and are at the heart of international science.

CONCLUDING REMARKS

In conclusion, I should like to pay particular tribute to the editor of this volume, William T. Golden. For more than forty years, Bill Golden has been one of the truly central figures in the establishment of formal channels for authoritative science and technology advice to American Presidents. It was also largely according to his plan—and as a result of his persuasion—that President Truman selected Alan Waterman to be the first Director and initiated the program of the National Science Foundation in 1950. And, in the intervening years, he has been a consistent and effective advocate for a strengthened White House science advising presence—in addition to all his many other leadership activities on behalf of American science.

The collections of papers in the earlier books, *Science Advice to the President* and *Science and Technology Advice to the President, Congress and Judiciary,* that Bill Golden edited in 1980 and 1988, in a very real sense are manuals for my position and provide very perceptive insight into the many dimensions of science and technology advising.

The present volume is a pioneering and unique companion volume in illuminating the broad range of approaches taken around the world to the challenge of providing national leaders with the scientific and technological advice that is essential to participation in an increasingly technological world. Bill Golden again deserves our congratulations and thanks for this important contribution to the growing literature in this field.

Preface: International Cooperation in Science—A New Agenda

Frank Press

In a volume dedicated to comparing differing national approaches to providing science advice to government leaders, it is appropriate to discuss a common issue faced by all governments, one that is a matter of continuing concern for scientists everywhere: that of global cooperation in science. It is an old issue, but one for which the time has arrived for serious consideration at the highest levels of governments. This follows from the changing relations between nations, the unprecedented pace of scientific discovery, and the new strategic roles of science in connection with transnational issues, such as health, hunger, population growth, global environmental change, and economic development.

The issue, then, is not so much whether international cooperation is a good thing. It is moving beyond its acceptance to constructing beneficial arrangements and having these arrangements survive the chronic political and economic frictions that occur—and will re-occur—among nations. The challenge—the art of scientific diplomacy—is to identify the points of intersecting interests, and then construct frameworks for national cooperation pivoting on such interests.

The bare bones of those intersecting interests, of beneficial arrangements, can be quickly stated. One is when nations recognize that they simply do not have sufficient resources to execute a desirable scientific or technological goal, and that international help is needed. That imperative is evident in the programs in space science between East and West. It animates the international role of CERN.[1] And it most certainly is responsible for the transEuropean scientific institutes from EMBO[2] to EUREKA.[3]

A second intersecting interest of nations, making for international cooperation, is that the scientific or technological goal is implicitly international—that it is feckless for one nation to go it alone, even making the dubious assumption that it has sufficient resources. Such recognitions drove the creation of the International Geosphere Biosphere Program, and it is driving the International

Frank Press, educator and geophysicist, is serving his second six-year term as President of the National Academy of Sciences, and is a former Science Adviser to the President of the United States (President Carter, 1977–80). He was a member of the President's Science Advisory Committee (PSAC) from 1961 to 1964 and of the National Science Board. Dr. Press has been on the faculties of Columbia University, the California Institute of Technology, and the Massachusetts Institute of Technology. Born in 1924, he has served on many government and scientific boards and has been the recipient of awards and honorary degrees. Dr. Press is a member of the American Philosophical Society and of The Royal Society (UK) and the French Academy of Sciences.

Decade for Natural Disaster Reduction and the Global Change Program, both under the auspices of the United Nations.

A third reason why nations cooperate is that they need concrete expressions of mutual regard that go beyond words. International agreements to cooperate in science and technology serve that need very well. The symbolism that nations can work together in an area as strategic as science is an important message.

SMALL SCIENCE/BIG SCIENCE

Another factor promoting cooperation is the fact that more and more fields of science that nominally have been small science are taking on the semblance of big science. By that I mean they require ever more costly instrumentation, large facilities, and large teams of personnel. That is true of materials science, of a widening list of chemical fields—from laser chemistry to homogenous catalysis, and of many sectors in modern biology, such as sequencing the genome.

This expanded need for resources is amplified by the increasingly transboundary nature of science. Thus, the fact that sciences increasingly depend on each other inevitably requires international collaboration.

I believe firmly that, in this next decade, we will move forward with much enhanced cooperation. International organizations like UNESCO[4] and ICSU[5] will undoubtedly play major roles, as well as regional organizations. We do not lack for things to do. We need cooperation in basic science, in the tools that will enable all nations to make substantial scientific advances in this decade. And we need cooperation to cope with the common problems pressing in upon all nations, such as installing networks of instruments to monitor global change or developing new, safe, non-polluting energy sources.

In all our elaborations of the problems and possibilities of scientific cooperation, we mustn't forget that the simplest, that of scientists of different countries being given opportunities to talk and work together—may be the most powerful of all. It would be a historic error if concern over national economic or military security prevents scientists from being scientists, with all that that implies for free and easy communication.

President John F. Kennedy said it well in an address to the members of the US National Academy of Sciences when they gathered for their centennial celebration:

> Recent scientific advances have not only made international cooperation desirable, but they have made it essential. The ocean, the atmosphere, outer space belong not only to one nation or ideology, but to all mankind, and as science carries out its tasks ahead, it must enlist all its own disciplines, all nations prepared for the scientific quest, and all men capable of sympathizing with the scientific impulse.

The world had been torn by wars on virtually every continent in recent decades. We raised our children amidst the foreboding of a nuclear holocaust.

Concern about food grips the majority of the world's population. We have witnessed recent decades of economic and political turmoil. A constant that remains is the dedication of scientists to understanding the universe, the world, and humankind.

We do not face the question of cooperating in science; rather, in the shadow of the dangerous forces about us and the opportunities for doing good, we must cooperate.

NOTES

1. The Conseil Européen de Recherche Nucléaire (European Council for Nuclear Research).
2. The European Molecular Biology Organization.
3. EUREKA is an organization concerned with competitiveness and productivity in European industry.
4. The United Nations Educational, Scientific and Cultural Organization.
5. The International Council of Scientific Unions.

OVERVIEWS

Report on the International Forum on Science and Government

Shalheveth Freier

A forum of forty-seven senior scientists, engineers, political leaders and journalists from eighteen countries[1] met at the Weizmann Institute of Science in Rehovot, Israel, from December 9 to 13, 1989.[2] Co-chairmen for the forum were Cyrus Vance, former Secretary of State of the United States, and Sir Zelman Cowen, Provost of Oriel College, Oxford University, and former Governor-General of Australia. The forum was organized by the author as Director of the Science and Government Forum of the Weizmann Institute. (A list of participants can be found in the Appendix.)

The group met in order to reappraise the role and structure of science and technology (S&T) advice to the highest level of government and to suggest improvements in the interaction of S&T and governments on the strength of their varied experience.

The forum agreed that a reappraisal was called for in view of the changing issues on the science and technology agenda and the resulting new challenges. Improvements were suggested in three areas. First, the institutional means and functions at the disposal of government are of crucial importance in generating the climate in which science and technology and government can consummate their mutual responsibilities and endeavors. Second is the manner of facing up to the ever-growing international interdependence brought about by advances in science and technology. Third is the role of education and the media and the need for publicly available information and open debate as essential for the enlightened appraisal of S&T issues.

There was agreement on most of the proposals made, and this included the character and functions of science and technology advice to governments. There were, however, differences of opinion and experience on the appropriate institutional arrangements, which resulted naturally from the different types of governments. Among these, the most prevalent were the presidential system, in which the president and the legislature derive their powers separately from the

Shalheveth Freier was Director of the International Forum on Science and Government at the Weizmann Institute. Born in Germany in 1920, he has been Director of the Arms Development Authority, Deputy Director of the Weizmann Institute, Head of the Israeli Atomic Energy Commission, and Chairman of the Presidential Council for Science Policy. Dr. Freier established the first electronic music studio in Israel, wrote the British part of the official history of the war of independence, and is a member of the Pugwash Council, the Academic Committee of the Jerusalem Academy of Music, and the Committee for Youth Activities in the Sciences.

electorate, and the parliamentary system, in which the government's authority derives from parliamentary support.

It was manifest also that the size of the country matters. Institutional arrangements are more critical in the bigger countries than they are in smaller ones, in which communication is easier.

But, most importantly, there is the difference between the industrialized countries, which have succeeded the most in integrating science and technology into their social and economic well-being, and the majority of countries where this is not yet the case for widely dissimilar reasons.

The forum registered these differences. It saw merit in this mutual exposure, and felt that all stood to benefit from studying the diverse experiences which had accumulated.

THE NEED FOR REAPPRAISAL: CHANGING ISSUES

In previous decades, the science and technology agendas of the industrialized countries gave prominence to military, nuclear, and—in varying degrees—space research and development.

Of late, place of priority is being claimed by science and technology issues relating to the following:

- Global environmental threats, such as greenhouse warming, ozone depletion, and the destruction of genetic diversity;
- Biomedical topics, such as the prevention and cure of AIDS, the development of new drugs, the sequencing of the human genome, and biotechnology and its implications, in general;
- Sustainable economic development, including sustainable energy supplies and agricultural systems;
- Improved manufacturing technologies, less demanding of energy and materials and sensitive to the environment; and
- The appropriate association of countries which differ in their attainments in S&T or its beneficial applications, or both.

It is in the character of these emerging areas that they are more international and interconnected, and cut across many traditional disciplines. They involve and affect more members of society, and are less tolerant of delays in diagnosis and response. The ten-year delay between the first warning of the pollution of the environment and the official recognition of these hazards, as requiring concerted action, shows how damaging such delays can be.

SPECIAL CHALLENGES ARISING FROM THE NEW AREAS OF PROMINENCE

The new areas of prominence demand a departure from traditional attitudes, as follows:

- More thought needs to be given to the anticipation of hazards and their prevention than to remedies alone. This is not easy in an environment which rallies to the cure of an actual affliction more readily than to the prevention of one which is perceived. The former has high visibility, and the latter has none.
- Governments need to embark on long-term policies for the benefits of which they will not be credited during their terms of office. Such policies will require broad parliamentary and public support in order to be credibly sustained.
- Timeliness is of the essence in making decisions, and decisions will have to be made also on the bases of uncertain premises, especially when potential hazards need to be forestalled.
- Forethought and anticipatory studies and assessments will be increasingly important in order to meet the requirements of timeliness in decisions.
- Science and technology should become as intelligible to the citizen as are, nowadays, economic or societal situations also to the non-initiated. This is essential for enlightened public debate in matters which, as was said, affect everybody.
- More of the formerly hidden agendas, meaning those that are at the back of one's mind, will need to be spelled out and discussed nationally and internationally. It will not be sufficient for societies to adapt or react to the applications of sciences or to the advances of technology, but they will have to try to grapple with the social and ethical problems so raised. The uses to which biotechnology should or should not be put illustrates the new type of dilemma.
- Concerted and harmonized international thinking and action on the issues under discussion is not a matter of volition, but of necessity. There was a stark reminder of our interdependence in the observation that most of the oxygen on which our lives depend is produced in the less-developed, debtor nations than elsewhere.
- The emerging areas of science and technology endeavor, some of which are set out above, do not supplant the traditional ones, except in prominence. In assessing budgetary requirements, account needs to be taken of this circumstance and not only of the urgings of the practitioners.
- Without science, it was said, there is no application. Even in the most advanced countries, there are ambivalent attitudes with respect to basic science, which is the origin of most insights. There needs to be clear government support for its pursuit. The solution to many of the problems under discussion depends on the ingenuity of the basic scientific endeavor, which often begot them in the first instance.
- All these challenges also commend the international discussion of institutional arrangements for science and technology administration and ad-

vice. These need to measure up to their tasks, and the forum brought into relief how much countries could learn from one another.

These challenges place additional burdens on the role of S&T in policy and policy in S&T, on education for S&T, and on the role of the media in enlightening the public on the critical issues with which it is confronted. They necessitate science and technology advice to governments that is more comprehensive in scope, more directly involved in all major policy decisions, and of more immediate access to the decision-making body than ever before.

These themes will now be addressed.

SCIENCE AND TECHNOLOGY EDUCATION

More attention needs to be given to all aspects of science and technology education, improving the teaching of S&T in schools and colleges, offering more and better worker training in S&T skills, increasing the S&T literacy of other citizens beyond the regular school years, and providing better training of scientists and engineers in the nontechnical aspects of the science/technology/society interaction, which includes economics, politics, the social sciences, and moral value judgments.

Practical proposals made included a greater emphasis on mathematics, the potential and limitations of organizing and processing information, and the natural sciences. Curricula and textbooks in these subjects should not only be written by educators, but should—at all levels—be jointly prepared by teams of educators and practicing scientists.

On the mutual exposure of scientists and engineers with governments and legislatures, an infusion of scientists and engineers into both was considered of paramount importance in view of their minimal representation in both, except where their professional expertise is required. Indeed, it was suggested that more scientists and engineers be trained than are required for teaching and professional work.

The scientific and technological backgrounds of scientists and engineers were considered assets, no matter what positions they occupy. The practice of fellowships, of inviting young scientists and engineers to spend time in government service was recommended for adoption.

Students and citizens should be taught *the nature of science* and not only its findings. They should be told that science progresses not smoothly, but in fits and starts, with errors and corrections, controversies and paradigm changes. They should also learn that science and technology are not cure-alls for society's ills and that the potential of S&T for good or ill depends on how well or how foolishly society uses them (wherein ethics as well as education and competence play roles).

There is an *international* dimension to S&T education. More emphasis is needed in all aspects of education on comparisons and contrasts in characteristics of societies, natures of problems, and approaches to solutions. Increased international mobility of students and mid-career professionals through fellowships and exchange programs would be highly desirable. It is the universal nature of science and technology that commends exchanges in these areas, which also hold promise for eventual cooperation.

Communication skills should be taught to S&T students and polished by practice and further training during their professional lives. Making S&T relevant and intelligible to the public, to decision-makers, and to legislators is important. Scientists and engineers who take the time to do this well should be rewarded and not derided by their peers as is often the case. Academies of science and other professional societies could help by honoring good performance in this sphere.

The role of the media is as crucial in presenting science and technology issues as it is on any other matter. The primary responsibility of the media is to their audiences, not to government, the scientific community, or any other constituency. To engage and retain these audiences, the media must present information in ways that make it interesting and understandable, and clear positions are expected on issues which are, in fact, attended by a large degree of uncertainty. This is especially true in science and technology reporting which dwells on scientific findings rather than on the nature of the scientific endeavor or its societal implications.

Since society is less familiar with S&T issues than with others, the public, administrators and legislators seek clear guidance from the media in these areas. These circumstances and the time pressures inherent in media work necessitate close collaboration between scientists and journalists to make complex material simple and entertaining without making it *too* simple or wrong.

The media require ready access to scientists and engineers. Without such access, they cannot fulfill the aim of responsible and accurate coverage that scientists and journalists alike prefer. This aim can be facilitated by the increased use of referral services that link journalists with willing scientists and engineers (such as, in the US, the Scientists' Institute for Public Information—SIPI), fellowships for journalists in S&T-oriented organizations, and scientist-journalist workshops and minicourses on particular topics. It was emphasized that referral services or expert panels could help the media especially in separating agreed facts from differing surmises or biases. Such practice would set in train discriminating reporting and public discussion of science and technology issues.

ADMINISTRATION OF S&T BY GOVERNMENT AND S&T ADVICE

The various systems of government represented at the forum differed in the way science and technology are administered by them and the way science advice is obtained.

They all, however, have a head of government (President or Prime Minister), who makes the ultimate decisions or associates his or her authority with decisions made by the Cabinet. They all assure themselves of the functions and services of a chief adviser for science and technology (described below), whether such a position exists or not. They all have legislatures to which they are either answerable or by which they can be challenged. All use the services of independent professional panels for science and technology advice.

Some have ministers for science; some have not. Some have chief scientists in the various ministries (or Assistant to the President, as in the case of the US), who are or need to be coordinated, while, in the West German instance, the Minister for Science and Research attends to the research needs of his colleagues. Some have ministerial councils for science and technology, chaired by the Prime Minister, to which, in some instances, scientists, civil servants, and industrialists are co-opted.

All countries have coordinating committees—some highly effective, and some less so—in order to ensure an overall perspective. While the relative merits of these various systems will not be discussed here, two practices deserve mention, decoupled from any particular paradigm.

In West Germany, the head of state convenes periodically a National Council for Science (Wissenschaftsrat) on which all sectors of society are represented and for which an agenda is prepared on topics on which an exchange of views among the different competences and interests may set the course for major policy decisions. This council is supported by a permanent secretariat, and it has no permanent membership. This institution is deemed to be eminently useful.

In The Netherlands, it is mandatory that government react officially to reports and recommendations submitted by the Scientific Council for Government Policy within three months, whereupon Parliament discusses both report and reaction and invites the views of independent professionals before taking a stand. This appears to be a good example of the interaction of government, Parliament, and independent advice, and is so seen by the Dutch.

In the following comments, only that part of the discussion will be reviewed which pertains to the head of government, the legislature, and the chief adviser for science and technology.

POLICY AT THE TOP

Despite the differences in systems of government, it was agreed that the head of the government (President or Prime Minister) should have—and should be seen to have—a policy for science and technology, either on his or her behalf or on that of his or her government. (It was welcomed that only two genders were eligible for these offices, and no "it" could stand for election!) It was recommended that a policy for S&T statement be included in the yearly presentation of his or her overall program. This is a practice in many countries, but it should be universal. A statement constitutes a commitment.

In most systems, the need was felt for a chief adviser on science and technology (CAST), who should be appointed by the head of government and supported by an advisory committee. It is the functions of the CAST, rather than the appellation which matter, and these will be detailed later. Irrespective of institutional differences, it was felt that the highest decision-maker or body should be assisted by the functions of a CAST.

The head of government should be placed in the situation of having to decide, and should be presented—where appropriate—with more than one policy option for a given problem.

He should ensure that his judgment benefits from public debate, and not depend only upon the advocacy of his appointees. In particular, he should insist that studies be solicited and unsolicited ones be considered from professional institutions or committees competent in the problem posed.

Open debate for the benefit of the decision-maker is especially necessary if the head of government is unfamiliar with science and technology issues. He may then be inclined to abdicate judgment to a trusted individual or permit the civil service alone to control the science and technology advice he receives.

In all systems of government, it was thought only natural that the legislature have not only a committee for science and technology, composed of its own members, but also enjoy an independent analytical capability on S&T matters. The Office of Technology Assessment of the US Congress was mentioned as a successful example. The point was made that the increased capacity of the legislature to ask pertinent questions needs to be paralleled by a commensurate ability on the part of government to stand up to scrutiny, *i.e.*, to have sufficiently qualified people in government. An analytical service for the legislature has the advantage that its credibility rests on the presentation of established facts, which cannot be disputed from the floor.

THE NEED FOR A CHIEF ADVISER

In most countries, it was felt, there is a need for a chief adviser on science and technology (CAST), reporting to the head of the government and supported by an advisory committee. The CAST and his committee should consist of individuals of high stature and credibility with their peers, who represent diverse expertise (including life sciences, as well as physical sciences and technology; social sciences, as well as natural scientists; and generalists, as well as disciplinary specialists). Members of the committee should be engaged part-time, and be able to return to their parent institutions at the conclusion of their appointments. The committee should include a mix of ages, and should undergo a mandatory staggered rotation of its members.

The CAST must have the confidence of and excellent access to the head of government, should be privy to all major policy issues before the government (including those which have no evident S&T component), and should have the resources to form special expert panels beyond the regular advisory committee as required.

For the CAST's effectiveness, his office should be adjacent to the offices of the head of government and his immediate staff, for nothing substitutes for physical proximity and awareness. The CAST should co-opt for his deliberations government officials germane to the issue being discussed. Mutual recognition and appreciation are necessary.

The functions of the CAST should include assisting the head of the government in the formulation of questions to be addressed; advising on science and technology policies funded by the public purse; informing the head or the government about needs, opportunities or hazards which require decisions and present policy options; monitoring the implementation of any major science and technology policy decisions, and intervening when necessary; initiating or advising on standards and regulatory procedures; and, finally, having on his agenda the appraisal of contingencies which might arise in the future and require study, but no immediate policy decision. The forum discussed whether science for policy and policy for science should be addressed by different advisory bodies. It concluded that the CAST should deal with both.

The CAST should bring his authority to bear on the stimulation of open debate and the education of the public and the media, as set out in detail previously.

The CAST and his advisory committee must have no institutional axe to grind. This is why the CAST was invested, in the forum discussions, with far-reaching responsibilities in addition to those mentioned here.

Where no CAST exists, it was still felt that this was a generic term for the kind of function and service which should be at the disposal of a head of government and answerable to him.

The question of confidentiality was examined. The relations between the CAST and the head of government require that the CAST enjoy and respect the confidence of the head of government. These relations may, of course, be strained if the CAST's advice is not accepted for reasons extraneous to S&T logic or, worse, if policies are engaged which run counter to the CAST's professional conscience or impair his credibility with his peers.

In such circumstances, the CAST can, of course, resign in protest or he can acquiesce. On defense issues, which cannot be adequately addressed in public debate, there are no apparent alternatives. On nonclassified issues, on which information is available and if professional bodies, the legislature, and the public join the debate, it is not principally with the CAST that the head of government need argue. It was agreed that the CAST should not be statutorily compelled to give evidence and air views which could undo his relationship of confidence with the head of government.

INTERNATIONAL COOPERATION

International cooperation does not come naturally, except in basic research. Competition which seeks superiority on the market or in defense is not disposed to share. The need for international cooperation has long been professed as desirable, but sharing of knowledge was practiced in the past mainly by allies in times of war or perceived threat of war. In more recent times, there have been transfers of knowledge across national boundaries and the joint generation of knowledge by way of transnational corporations and national associations in economic blocs, of which the European Common Market is an outstanding example. These associations, of course, have also come about in order to compete successfully.

It would seem, however, that we might be on the threshhold of change. The hazards and scarcities which were reviewed in the beginning of this essay and which have been recognized as global in character—such as those pertaining to the environment, disease, and the finiteness of resources—are threats which compel genuine international cooperation in science and technology. This is, of course, partly acknowledged, but it has not penetrated into public and governmental consciousness as the powerful inducement for a change in attitude that it is.

It was suggested, therefore, that meetings of heads of governments take stock, visibly and prominently, on their agendas, of existing common hazards which can be forestalled.

It was further recommended that periodic meetings of the chairmen of advisory boards on science and technology to heads of government be instituted. In these meetings, common hazards—actual or potential—would be identified, necessary national or concerted action would be discussed, and the agenda would be set for the meetings of the heads of government. It was recognized that, even by itself, the very institution of regular meetings of chief advisers on science and technology would create a new and vital constituency, attuned to the needs of the times.

International cooperation in science and technology between the countries which have been more successful in raising their living standards by the successful application of S&T and those which have been less fortunate—and the reference here is mainly to the countries of Eastern Europe—was touched upon.

In the area of S&T, there did not seem to be impediments to cooperation. On the contrary, motivations for pooling knowledge abound. The formation of competitive blocs favors this accretion of knowledge and markets.

Much thought was given to the ways in which international cooperation could benefit countries which have scientific and engineering bases that are too small to successfully exploit the potentials of their countries and combat its afflictions. These countries again can be divided into those in which the political leadership accepts the importance of S&T and those in which S&T does not figure as a priority item on the national agenda at all.

In the former case, beneficial changes were foreseen. The genuine need to face up together to the new hazards could serve as a powerful incentive to also put international money into education, training, and the establishment of indigenous research capabilities.

It was further suggested that the scientific communities in these countries pull together, as they have already done in some instances, and establish viable regional research centers, which would equally attract international support and interest in the knowledge created there.

Finally, it was thought that the proposed meetings of heads of government and chief advisers on science and technology would bring into prominent focus the need to support S&T in the less-favored countries and integrate them into the joint effort.

The forum was, of course, aware of the beneficial activities of the specialized agencies of the United Nations and other international organizations, but realized that these are not enough. There was no dearth of proposals on bilateral exchanges, fellowships and associations. These have been and are being equally beneficial. But they, too, do not do justice to the scope of the problems.

TWO UNRESOLVED ISSUES

Two proposals were discussed for which there was not much support. They are mentioned because they were made in answer to problems which were acknowledged to be valid. The Challenger disaster and the delay in taking up environmental hazards at the government level prompted the first proposal. It was felt that there should be a statutory repository to whom the Challenger engineers could have appealed against the launch, rather than appealing to their superiors alone. With respect to the delayed response to environmental hazards, it was proposed that the same statutory body should challenge governments on science and technology of which they were not taking timely cognizance.

The second proposal tried to address the vast amount of pertinent information at the disposal of the decision-maker, which could not simply be disregarded. It was suggested that a special position be created, attached to the head of government, which would be able to provide information to him in a concise fashion.

This was deemed especially important in view of the technical ability for presenting the decision-maker with the possible influence that any major decision in one realm might have on others.

Anyone who would so serve the decision-maker would occupy a position of undoubted influence. The proposal was rejected by some and relegated by others to the CAST, but the problem of providing information to the head of government and giving him also the benefit of contemporary technology in this area was acknowledged as one which needed to be solved.

A brief summary of the forum's reasoned recommendations on the above and other themes will be published, and will be sent to governments, legislatures, academies of sciences, industries, and the media. Edited proceedings will be published subsequently, as will an instructional package on compact disc in CD-ROM format.

NOTES

1. The countries participating in the forum were Argentina, Australia, Brazil, Canada, France, the Federal Republic of Germany, Israel, Italy, Japan, Kenya, Mexico, The Netherlands, Portugal, Spain, Sweden, the United Kingdom, the United States, and the USSR.
2. The forum was co-sponsored by the International Federation of Institutes for Advanced Study (IFIAS).

Appendix

LIST OF FORUM PARTICIPANTS

Willem Albeda, Chairman, Scientific Council for Government Policy, The Hague, The Netherlands

Moshe Arens, Minister of Foreign Affairs, Israel

Hanan Bar-On, Vice President, Weizmann Institute of Science

David Z. Beckler, Associate Director, Carnegie Commission on Science, Technology and Government, New York

Sir Hermann Bondi, Master, Churchill College, Cambridge

João M.G. Caraça, Director, Science Department, Calouste Gulbenkian Foundation, Lisbon, Portugal

Ashton B. Carter, Associate Director, Center for Science and International Affairs, J.F. Kennedy School of Government, Harvard University

Sir Zelman Cowen, Provost, Oriel College, Oxford; former Governor-General of Australia

James W. Curlin, Office of Technology Assessment, US Congress

John M. Deutch, Provost, Massachusetts Institute of Technology

Israel Dostrovsky, former President, Weizmann Institute of Science

Aryeh Dvoretzky, former President, Israel Academy of Sciences; former President, Weizmann Institute of Science

Kerstin Eliasson, Chairman, Committee on Science & Technology Policy, Organization for Economic Cooperation & Development (OECD), Paris, and Adviser, Scientific Affairs, Prime Minister's Office, Stockholm

Yehuda Elkana, Director, Van Leer Institute, Jerusalem; Director, Institute for the History & Philosophy of Science & Ideas, Tel-Aviv University

Michael Feldman, Head, Department of Cell Biology, Weizmann Institute of Science

Shalheveth Freier, Director, Forum on Science and Government, Weizmann Institute of Science

Virginia Gamba-Stonehouse, Visiting Professor, Department of War Studies, King's College, London; former Director, Buenos Aires Institute for Strategic Studies

Richard L. Garwin, IBM Research Division

William T. Golden, Chairman, American Museum of Natural History; Past Chairman, New York Academy of Sciences; Co-chairman, Carnegie Commission on Science, Technology and Government

Peter Grose, Executive Editor, Foreign Affairs, Council on Foreign Relations, New York

Victor Halberstadt, Leyden University, Leyden, President, International Institute of Public Finance

H.H. Haunschild, former Secretary of State for Research & Technology, Federal Republic of Germany

John P. Holdren, University of California, Berkeley; Chairman, Executive Committee, Pugwash Conferences on Science and World Affairs

Barry Jones, Minister Assisting the Prime Minister for Science & Technology; Minister for Science, Customs and Small Business, Australia

Ephraim Katzir, former President, State of Israel; Institute Professor, Weizmann Institute of Science

Alex Keynan, Special Adviser to the President, Hebrew University, Jerusalem

Giuseppe Lanzavecchia, Scientific Adviser to the Chairman, National Commission for Nuclear & Alternative Energy Sources (ENEA), Rome

Federico Mayor, Director-General, UNESCO, Paris

Charles J. McMillan, Faculty of Administrative Studies, York University, Toronto

J. Fraser Mustard, President, Canadian Institute for Advanced Research

H. Moyses Nussenzveig, Pontificia Universidade Catolica, Rio de Janeiro, Brazil

Thomas R. Odhiambo, President, African Academy of Sciences, Nairobi; Chairman, Kenya National Academy of Sciences; Director, International Centre of Insect Physiology and Ecology (ICIPE), Nairobi, Kenya

Michio Okamoto, Senior Member, Council for Science & Technology, Prime Minister's Office; former President, Kyoto University, Japan

Juriy A. Osipyan, Vice President, USSR Academy of Sciences, Moscow

David Owen, MP, Leader of the Social Democratic Party; former Foreign Secretary, United Kingdom

Baruch Raz, Director, Interdisciplinary Center for Technological Analysis & Forecasting, Tel-Aviv University, Israel

Francis Rosenstiel, Director of Political Affairs, Council of Europe, Strasbourg, France

Avram Schweitzer, Senior Editor, *H'Aretz,* Tel-Aviv, Israel

Michael Sela, Deputy Chairman, Board of Governors; former President, Weizmann Institute of Science

Guillermo Soberón, Executive President, Fundación Mexicana para la Salud; former Minister of Health, and Rector, University of Mexico, Mexico City

Gerald M. Steinberg, Political Science Department, Bar-Ilan University, Israel

Victor L. Urquidi, Member, National Science Advisory Council; Research Professor Emeritus and former President, El Colegio de Mexico

Cyrus R. Vance, former Secretary of State, United States of America

John Vereker, Deputy Secretary, Department of Education and Science, United Kingdom

Susan Watts, Technology Correspondent, *The New Scientist,* London

Ezer Weizman, Minister of Science & Technology, Israel

Andrew Wiseman, Media Consultant, London

A Decision-Maker's Guide to Science Advising

David Z. Beckler

In all countries, there are significant rewards to the government policy-making processes in reaching outside government for the best available scientific and technical advice. The increasing complexity of science and technology-related policy issues is such that, in many situations, there is no sound alternative to seeking outside advice. Scientists and engineers outside government, if mobilized and properly utilized, can bring a range of competence and experience to governmental decision-making that constitutes an enormous source of strength.

This essay is concerned with the interaction between part-time science and technology advisers and government decision-makers. It suggests a set of principles to guide this interaction that reflects the experience of the United States with the science and technology advisory process from the vantage points of both the decision-maker and the science and technology adviser. This experience may be applicable to other governments, although its relevance may vary in different political, organizational and decision-making contexts.

THE DECISION-MAKING ENVIRONMENT

Outside science and technology advisers should be aware of the decision-making environment in which they are advising, insofar as it affects the nature and receptiveness of science and technology advice. In this context, it is instructive to view the performance of the President's Science Advisory Committee prior to President Nixon's decision to terminate the White House science and technology advisory mechanism in 1972.

Although the decision reflected strains between the White House staff and the academic community engendered by the Viet Nam conflict, there were underlying factors that affected the committee's effectiveness during its entire lifetime, with periods of strengths and weaknesses. (See Beckler, D., "The Precarious Life of Science in the White House," *Daedalus*, Summer 1974.) They included:

David Z. Beckler was Executive Officer of the President's Science Advisory Committee and assistant to six Science Advisers to the President from 1957–1972. He served as Special Assistant to the President of the National Academy of Sciences of the US from 1973–1976. From 1976–1983, Mr. Beckler was Director for Science, Technology and Industry at the Organization for Economic Cooperation and Development in Paris. He is currently Associate Director of the Carnegie Commission on Science, Technology, and Government.

- The President's perception of science and technology as an instrument of national policy contributing to the solution of critical national problems;
- The effectiveness of channels of communication between the President and the science and technology mechanism, which tend to close unless positive pressure is exerted to keep them open:
- The potential threat posed by the science and technology mechanisms to other sources of advice and decision-making in the Executive Office of the President, such as the National Security Council, the Office of Management and Budget, and the heads of departments and agencies;
- The credibility and confidentiality of the science and technology mechanism in terms of its members and institutional loyalties, as perceived by the President and his staff;
- The relationships of the Presidential science adviser and his professional staff to key personnel in other White House units and in the federal departments and agencies;
- The level of the White House "generalists'" distrust for specialists on the President's staff, and fears of being pressured from within by narrow expertise and advocacy; and
- Budgeting as it is affected by political demands for short-term decisions that tend to drive out long-term thinking and planning, and by the extent of budgetary authority over program and policy decisions.

Situated between officialdom and outside interests, the performance of science and technology advisory groups is especially sensitive to the tides of political change, as was seen in the politicization of the Science Advisory Committee to the Environmental Protection Agency in the early 1980s. There are hazards to the inside science and technology adviser, as well, when linked to an outside advisory group that has fallen out of political favor.

Despite the steady growth of outside science and technology advisers, there have been no general ground rules for their utilization by the government. Although the ways in which science and technology advisers are selected and used affect their performance, there has been no systematic effort to distill from past experience the conditions influencing success or failure. Rules can be invigorating as well as stultifying. It is the object of this essay to chart a path for strengthening the science and technology advisory process, recognizing that— without cautionary road signs—public pressures and political controls might deny the decision-maker a valuable resource. There is already a perceptible trend in this direction in the United States. To stem or reverse this trend, the science and technology adviser and the policy-maker alike must understand each others' perceptions and preoccupations.

The following principles for science and technology advising have been drafted with the foregoing cautions in mind. The principles are expressed in simplistic terms. They are indicative, rather than definitive, since it is not possible within the confines of this essay to make them sufficiently comprehensive and nuanced. It is hoped that they provide a systematic way of viewing the science and technology advisory process from a management standpoint, particularly in identifying questions the decision-maker should have in mind in calling on outside science and technology advisers.

PRINCIPLE 1.
RECOGNIZE WHEN OUTSIDE
S&T ADVICE IS NEEDED

Government decision-makers should recognize the circumstances when they should consider calling on outside science and technology advisers. Advice can range from narrow technical questions to broad policy issues, for example, in the following circumstances:

- Where the problems raise science and technology questions that exceed the range and depth of expertise of the in-house staff (math and science education);
- Where the importance of the issue suggests the desirability of an independent assessment (failure of the space shuttle);
- Where the problem to be addressed cuts across lines of jurisdiction within or among departments and agencies (priorities of R&D);
- Where it is desired to have an authoritative, longer-range view and early warning of future science and technology developments (climate change);
- Where independent science and technology analyses can strengthen public confidence (nuclear reactor safety); and
- Where the character of the issue calls for science and technology competence that can be provided only by those working at the cutting edge of their fields (superconductivity).

With the growth of in-house staff capabilities, decision-makers may mistakenly feel self-sufficient in their abilities to handle science and technology questions. Even in the cases in which the need for outside advice is clear, time constraints, political sensitivities, and concerns over confidentiality and loss of control over the final decision may press the decision-maker to avoid the use of outside science and technology advisers. Countervailing pressures may be imposed by staff members who do not want their views challenged by outside advisers.

> **Guideline:** Decision-makers should recognize the circumstances where they should call on outside science and technology advisers and devise procedures for their proper selection and use as an integral part of their managerial function.

PRINCIPLE 2.
THERE IS A SPECTRUM OF VIEWS ON MOST S&T QUESTIONS

For most science and technology questions, there is a range of expert views, with their distribution represented by a bell curve. When the curve is steep, it is easy to distinguish between mainstream and outlier views (cold fusion). When the curve is relatively flat, the difficulty in resolving differences in science and technology views is correspondingly greater (advising on the effects of potential carcinogens based on animal tests). While the decision-maker reaches for certainty, he will often face scientific uncertainty, and will need to take into consideration the distribution of scientific views and the risk factors involved.

Rejecting the views of the outlier at the extremes of the bell curve is not without concern, as they may subsequently prove to be correct (should cold fusion be found to have scientific validity). Depending on the nature and importance of the scientific question, the outlier paradox can be partially addressed by designing the advisory process to give fair hearing to the outlier. Conversely, the views of the outlier should be put to the test of theory and data.

> **Guideline:** The decision-maker should recognize the inherent nature of science and technology uncertainty and design science and technology advisory and decision-making processes to assure that differences in S&T views are given appropriate weight in decision-making and in the composition and procedures of S&T advisory groups.

PRINCIPLE 3.
QUALITY CONTROL IS NEEDED IN THE S&T ADVISORY PROCESS

The quality of science and technology advice depends upon the competence of the S&T advisers and the completeness and reliability of the data, information and analysis used. This requires careful attention to the selection of advisers and the provision of qualified professional staff support. Even with the best effort, there may be information, data and viewpoints that are not adequately reflected in advisory reports. On important questions, it may be desirable to have such reports critically reviewed by external reviewers who did not participate in the original study, a procedure regularly employed by the National Research Council. This precaution also recognizes that outstanding experts, not available as original advisers, may be willing to review the final draft report.

> **Guideline:** Procedures for quality assurance should be built into the S&T advisory process: in the selection of advisers, the provision of high-quality S&T information, data and analysis and, where appropriate, the use of external reviewers of the final draft report.

PRINCIPLE 4.
PURELY OBJECTIVE S&T ADVICE IS NOT ACHIEVABLE

Non-S&T values are inevitably embedded (consciously or unconsciously) in judgments of "fact," particularly where there is S&T uncertainty. The resolution of that uncertainty may be biased by individual perceptions and values concerning the underlying issue in question (*e.g.*, environment, health, national security, arms control). Within science, the outlook of an expert in one field can affect an assessment of other fields.

Although it may not be possible to separate value judgments from findings of scientific fact, distortions in decision-making can be reduced by differentiating the various categories of science and technology advice and by using panels of advisers. On narrow questions of S&T fact-finding, panel membership that is balanced from an S&T standpoint should suffice. For public policy issues and regulatory decision-making, scientific backgrounds need to be balanced with other expertise and institutional backgrounds (academia, industry, government, public interest, political inclinations, etc.). The use of open meetings and public hearings can further promote balanced findings on broad issues.

The definition of the questions to be examined should minimize value-laden formulations. Should the decision-maker phrase the question put to the advisers in order to achieve a particular outcome or convene an advisory group with biased orientation, the results may be perceived in this light and discounted along with the decision-maker and the advisers.

Decision-makers should refrain from asking S&T advisers to address the ultimate answer to a question that transcends S&T considerations (*e.g.*, the probability of detecting underground nuclear tests versus the degree of probability required to protect national security).

> **Guideline:** In the selection and use of science and technology advisers, care should be taken to separate S&T fact from value judgment in formulating the question to be addressed. The composition of membership should be matched to the nature of the issue and the breadth of judgment required. In addressing policy issues, S&T advisory panels should be carefully balanced in S&T fields, sectoral involvement, and political inclinations.

PRINCIPLE 5.
THE S&T ADVISER SHOULD RECOGNIZE THE LIMITS OF S&T ADVICE IN DECISION-MAKING

Science and technology advisers should not presume that the decision-maker will faithfully follow their conclusions and recommendations. Although the ultimate decision should be based on the latest available S&T information and expertise, it will often depend on other factors (whether an SST should be built if it is shown to be economically and environmentally unsound, or whether SDI should be pursued in the face of critical assessments of S&T feasibility). Despite what they may perceive to be lack of S&T rationality, S&T advisers must accept that other considerations (political, economic, international, etc.) may impose limits on the acceptance of their advice.

On the other hand, it has been argued that S&T advisers can legitimately go beyond the confines of S&T considerations. For example, some believe that members of the General Advisory Committee to the Atomic Energy Commission had the right—if not the duty— to recommend against the development of the hydrogen bomb, since they were in the best position to understand its destructive power. This is a dangerous proposition. Although science and technology are essential considerations, they are not necessarily controlling.

Science and technology advisers are no more expert than others in dealing with nonscientific aspects and values. At times, such as in environmental issues, the general public may place too much credence in scientific authority when weighing their public policy positions. On the other hand, as indicated above, scientists and engineers should be included in broader groups of advisers when advising on policy questions because of their special S&T insight. By the same token, S&T advisers should be informed of non-S&T considerations that might influence their judgment concerning relevant S&T facts and assumptions.

> **Guideline:** Science and technology advisers should be aware of the limits of S&T advice in government decision-making. They should not be called upon to make recommendations calling for judgments that transcend S&T considerations, and should be joined with advisers competent in other areas of public policy when addressing S&T-related public policy issues.

PRINCIPLE 6.
S&T ADVICE MUST BE COUPLED TO THE DECISION-MAKING PROCESS

The coupling between science and technology advisers and decision-makers is critical to their performance. It was a central consideration in the decision by President Bush to establish a Presidentially appointed science and technology advisory committee, the President's Council of Science and Technology Advisers. This positive step by the President signifies his personal desire for outside S&T advice. For an S&T advisory committee to be effective, there must be an indication by the decision-maker that its advice is needed and that a close and continuing relationship will be maintained, including face-to-face meetings.

The validity of this principle was demonstrated by the changing fortunes of the President's Science Advisory Committee between the time of its establishment in 1957 (after its creation in a different organizational setting by President

Truman in 1951) and its termination in 1972. The peaks of its performance were reached during the Eisenhower and Kennedy Administrations, when the first three Presidential Science Advisers enjoyed strongest access to the President. There was a decline in effectiveness during the Johnson and Nixon years when the Presidential linkage of the Science Advisers and the Science Advisory Committee was weak.

Some observers have argued that the President's Science Advisory Committee was weakened because it offered unwanted advice, that the decision-maker does not welcome unsolicited advice where, for example, the problem to be addressed is beyond the political horizon or may not be in line with political objectives or realities. This difficulty is illustrated by Congressional testimony of former members of the President's Science Advisory Committee contrary to the President's position on the development of an anti-ballistic missile system, and by the advisory report in opposition to the President's stand on the development of the SST.

S&T advisory committees that have well-defined mandates seem more effective than committees with diffuse mandates. The mandates should permit flexibility in reformulating the question asked and in examining issues on the committee's initiative, rather than being confined to passive responses to requests for advice, provided it is with the concurrence of the decision-maker. Such flexibility can be valuable in performing an early warning or alerting function, as well as in suggesting alternative approaches to problem-solving.

Some tension between S&T advisers and decision-makers should be expected and accepted as the price to be paid for obtaining objective and sound advice. Despite possible drawbacks, the decision-maker is better served by a science and technology advisory committee that has the possibility of taking initiatives, particularly in addressing long-range problems (such as the first comprehensive report on environmental pollution prepared on the initiative of the President's Science Advisory Committee in the mid-1960s).

The coupling between S&T advisers and the decision-maker can be facilitated by selecting advisers who understand the operations and methods of government, as well as the particular agency served. Depending on the circumstances and nature of the advisory committee, the coupling would be strengthened by having a chairman who is also the full-time S&T adviser to the decision-maker, as in the case of the new President's Council of Science and Technology Advisers. The role of the in-house professional support staff is critical in providing a transducer between the advisers and the decision-maker, in helping to formulate the S&T issues in a decision-making context, and in communicating and following up on the S&T advice received.

> **Guideline:** The decision-maker should have a close and continuing interaction with the science and technology advisers. This relationship should be defined in specific mandates given to advisory committees. Although the advisers should be tasked by the decision-maker for particular advice, advisory bodies should have sufficient flexibility to pro-

pose a reformulation of the question and to initiate studies of emerging problems, with the consent of the decision-maker. S&T support staff of high professional quality and policy sensitivity is all-important.

PRINCIPLE 7.
THERE IS NEED FOR A RELATIONSHIP OF TRUST AND CONFIDENCE BETWEEN THE S&T ADVISER AND THE DECISION-MAKER

There is a privileged relationship between the S&T adviser and the decision-maker. The S&T adviser must respect the confidentiality and trust that should characterize his or her relationship with the decision-maker.

In accepting the invitation to serve, the adviser must also accept certain legitimate limitations, such as respecting the confidentiality of the information provided and not disclosing the substance of the advice rendered without the approval of the requestor as long as the adviser is serving in an advisory capacity. The adviser has the option of severing the advisory connection, and thereafter, taking a public position on the matter involved. The adviser cannot in good faith simultaneously serve the decision-maker and ''go public'' without prior consent.

There are ways in which the American public interest is partially protected from star-chamber advice. The Freedom of Information Act affords public access to unclassified documentation used in or resulting from advisory committee deliberations. The Federal Advisory Committee Act requires that meetings of advisory committees be publicly advertised in advance in the *Federal Register,* with open sessions except for discussions involving national security considerations. Although a gray area, there is some precedent for having informal exchanges in addition to formal public sessions in order to encourage the full and frank exchange of views. A valuable function of the advisers is to serve as a sounding board for the decision-maker.

Unless the privileged relationship between the decision-maker and the science and technology adviser is observed, the use of outside advisers may atrophy. Decision-makers will hesitate to ask for outside S&T advice if they fear that they may confront adversary positions by their advisers on the basis of information provided in confidence.

There are dangers in establishing confidence and trust by appointments to advisory committees based on political inclinations, personal relationships, or patronage pressures. Such appointments may spell smooth relationships between the advisers and decision-makers, but the advice may suffer for lack of credibility and S&T reliability to the detriment of both sides. On the other hand, a personal relationship between the decision-maker and a qualified adviser can be invaluable in assuring access and building mutual confidence.

Guideline: Establishing a relationship of confidence and trust between the science and technology adviser and the decision-maker requires personal interaction and understanding of their mutual obligations. The S&T adviser has the obligation to respect the confidentiality of the privileged relationship and to avoid taking a public position on the issue while serving as adviser. Resignation is an option if these conditions cannot be met in good conscience. The decision-maker should make clear at the outset the conditions attaching to the advisory relationship and, on this basis, assure the full disclosure of information on the issues involved. A relationship of confidence and trust built on political inclinations, personal friendship, or political patronage is unlikely to yield results having public confidence and S&T credibility.

PRINCIPLE 8.
PUBLIC GOOD AND THE INTEGRITY OF THE S&T ADVISORY PROCESS REQUIRE THAT THE S&T ADVISER NOT BE IN A POSITION OF CONFLICT BETWEEN THE ADVISORY FUNCTION AND PERSONAL INTERESTS

Although the problem of conflicts-of-interest involving part-time science and technology advisers may be handled differently in other countries, the principles underlying the policies of the US Government may be applicable.

The first major effort to legislate ethical conduct of US Government employees came with the adoption of the Bribery, Graft and Conflicts of Interest Act in 1962. The covered employees are prohibited from "participating personally and substantially" on behalf of the government in any "particular matter" in which the employee has a "financial interest." The Act sought to distinguish between a full-time federal employee and a consultant who serves intermittently or for a short period of time (with or without compensation for a period not to exceed 130 days a year). In making this distinction, the Congress was mindful of the contributions of temporary advisers and sought to assure that the government could continue to make use of outside advisers.

Although science and technology advisers were not exempted from the criminal provisions, they were accorded the opportunity to have the provisions waived by the agency head under certain conditions where the personal interest was not so substantial as to be deemed likely to affect the integrity of the services rendered. For example, in order to enlist the most qualified advisers, it is likely that the adviser would be professionally active in the S&T field or industrial sector that is broadly the subject of the requested advice. A general waiver might be given in these circumstances. The waiver instrument would not exempt the individual from the obligation of recusal (refusal to participate) in those instances where a specific conflict might arise.

Prospective advisory committee members are subject to some level of financial disclosure. The Administrative Conference of the US has identified three levels of financial information that the adviser should be required to furnished (and update): 1) the identity of the individual's principal employment; 2) a list of positions held and contractual relationships relevant to the purposes of the advisory committee; and 3) the identity, but not the face value, of any other sources of income or any interests exceeding $1,000 in value relevant to the purposes of the advisory committee (ordinarily held confidential).

> **Guideline:** Both the science and technology adviser and the decision-maker must be alert to possible conflicts between the public and private interests involved in rendering S&T advice. Written guidelines should be provided to the potential S&T adviser in advance, including the waiver policy and rules for financial disclosure (with a briefing at the first meeting of the advisory committee). While the responsibility for avoiding conflicts-of-interest lies with the S&T adviser, the decision-maker should instruct the secretariat to be alert to and call to the attention of the S&T adviser any particular matter calling for recusal.

PRINCIPLE 9.
THE COMPOSITION OF S&T ADVISERS NEEDS TO BE CONTINUALLY CHANGED

There should be provision for rotation of S&T advisers serving in individual capacities or as members of advisory groups. Such organizational self-renewal is a difficult process for decision-makers, since it disturbs the status quo. Yet a central rationale for calling on outside advisers would be undermined in the absence of a procedure for rotating and replacing advisers and terminating advisory committees that have outlived their usefulness.

Long-serving advisers on a standing group may become wedded to a singular view, rejecting arguments that do not conform to the established position. They may become "professional" S&T advisers and captives of the decision-maker. They may not be abreast of recent advances in their fields. The character of the issue may no longer match their expertise and experience. Counterproductive interpersonal relationships may develop. Furthermore, maintaining a distribution of age among members of an advisory committee is essential to promote vitality and encourage innovative thinking and courageous positions.

The Federal Advisory Committee Act, mentioned earlier, attempts to deal with the problem of outmoded advisory committees by requiring automatic termination of a committee after a given time unless there is written justification for its continuation. Although this requirement is often observed in a perfunctory way, its message needs to be taken seriously.

> **Guideline:** The decision-maker should provide for the renewal and rotation of science and technology advisers by the use of term appointments, continuity balancing of expertise and age, and the termination of advisory groups no longer needed or justifiable.

PRINCIPLE 10.
BROAD S&T ADVICE NEEDS TO BE SUPPORTED BY
RESEARCH AND ANALYSIS

The decision-maker needs the advice of science and technology advisers selected for their expertise, maturity of judgment, and breadth of view and experience, including understanding of government. As S&T complexity increases, however, the collective advice of individual advisers may not be sufficient per se. It will be increasingly necessary to underpin S&T advisory committees by supporting in-depth analysis. This need is particularly highlighted by issues characterized by interactions within S&T and between S&T and economics and other areas, which have become increasingly dominant aspects of policy advice.

There has been a trend in the direction of increased use of policy research and analysis. This is reflected in the growth of federal contracts with nongovernmental, analytical "think tanks" and government-supported "software" firms to assist policy and program development. The Department of Defense pioneered in the establishment of organizations to provide systems research and analysis for decision-making, such as the Rand and MITRE Corporations and the Institute for Defense Analysis.

On a much smaller scale, there could be similar value in providing analytical support to S&T advisory bodies. The Office of Technology Assessment of the US Congress couples policy analysis by professional staff and consultants with specially constituted S&T advisory panels that weigh the soundness of the in-house analyses and proposed policy options.

The principal outside science and technology advisory mechanism, chartered by the Congress to give S&T advice to the government, is the National Research Council, the operating arm of the National Academies of Sciences and Engineering and the Institute of Medicine (amounting to some $100 million annually). The NRC relies primarily on unpaid members of the S&T communities who serve on advisory committees as a public service. The quality of the experts involved is exceptionally high and uniform. Membership on NRC committees is a mark of prestige and standing in one's peer group. Although the analytical work of the committees is characteristically done by the members themselves, there is increasing use of analytical staff support.

Within the government, policy analysis capabilities are inversely proportional to the level of decision-making. Most of the analytical effort supports middle and lower levels of organization. The number of outside advisers tends to decrease at higher levels of management and policy development, where there are fewer decision-makers and analytical capabilities. Thus, S&T advice to the departments and agencies of government tends to be sub-optimized in relation to particular missions. This underscores the importance of strengthening S&T policy analysis capabilities at higher and broader policy levels, including the use of "horizontal" S&T advisory structures to review and co-ordinate the views and fragmented advice of specialized advisory panels and sub-panels.

At the pinnacle of government, as well as at the level of heads of departments and agencies, there is need for advice that does not conform to jurisdictional lines, and a capability to interrelate S&T considerations with other areas of policy advice: economic, regulatory, legal, international, national security, and political. At this level, integrative experiences and skills become increasingly important and should be complemented by a capability for integrated analyses. The methodologies and data for such analyses are not well developed. The S&T policy-makers, in particular, need to be in the vanguard of those seeking to improve the integration of S&T policy with other considerations. It is unlikely that such leadership will come from the other policy areas.

Guideline: In utilizing science and technology advisory mechanisms, decision-makers should assure that there are sufficient resources for supporting policy research and analysis to underpin the S&T advisory process, particularly at higher levels of government, and that there is a strong coupling between the S&T advisers and the analytical support mechanisms.

PRINCIPLE 11.
THE DECISION-MAKERS' DOORS TO S&T ADVICE SHOULD BE OPEN TO ALL SOURCES OF ADVICE

The principal sources of science and technology advice available to government decision-makers are in-house advisers, outside advisers, consultants and contractors, and not-for-profit S&T organizations. The latter sources are seldom utilized by the decision-maker, yet they constitute a very large potential for S&T advice. They comprise the professional societies, academic and other not-for-profit organizations, and public interest groups in areas ranging from S&T, environment, economics, law, arms control, and national security. Some of these organizations now offer S&T-related advice. Others could be encouraged to do so. Yet it is rare that an unsolicited report from such an organization is placed on the agenda of a decision-maker. They are often regarded with suspicion (as biased and nonauthoritative), lacking inside information and a decision-making perspective.

The gulf between inside needs and the outside-of-government potential for S&T advice is difficult, yet important to bridge. Decision-makers should cast their nets wide for S&T advice. This could be facilitated by having staff responsible for liaison with independent sources of advice, for alerting them to the needs of the decision-makers, and for identifying useful outside reports.

Guideline: Decision-makers should be aware of the potential of not-for-profit, nongovernmental organizations for providing solicited and unsolicited science and technology advice. Staff members should be encouraged to establish linkages with such organizations and to invite their views on S&T-related issues. Significant outside-of-government reports should be placed on the decision-maker's agenda for consideration and possible action.

PRINCIPLE 12.
S&T ADVICE MUST ULTIMATELY BE TESTED BY AN INFORMED AND S&T-LITERATE PUBLIC

Outside science and technology advice can be a powerful political as well as technical tool for policy-makers. As with all political tools, the S&T advisory process can be misused intentionally or unintentionally to the detriment of the public interest. The warning of President Eisenhower is still very much in the wind: beware of the "military-industrial complex." At that time, these words were misinterpreted to imply a warning against the dangers of government domination by scientific and technological elitism—by S&T advisers with special interests, knowledge, and access to the decision-making process. There was perceived lack of public accountability due to the special advantages adhering to those versed in S&T complexities beyond general public understanding. This danger has not materialized. It remains a latent possibility, however, that can be magnified by the public to the detriment of scientific and technological advance, whether it be in the form of anti-nuclear, anti-biotechnology or, more generally, anti-technology attitudes.

Thus there must be room in the S&T advisory process for public participation and challenge, without allowing unreasoned opposition to stifle scientific progress and technological innovation. The S&T advisory process must be—and must be seen to be—credible. This requires transparency and the opportunity for public participation as a normal part of the S&T advisory process.

> **Guideline:** To the extent feasible, decision-makers should foster open meetings of science and technology advisers and should consider public hearings on significant advisory committee reports. Reports by S&T advisers should be widely disseminated.

PRINCIPLE 13.
DECISION-MAKERS SHOULD TREAT THE S&T ADVISORY FUNCTION AS AN INTEGRAL PART OF THE MANAGEMENT-DECISION-MAKING PROCESS

The importance of science and technology advice to decision-making requires that the S&T advisory process be purposefully and carefully managed, taking into consideration the special attributes of S&T advisers and the advisory process.

Proper follow-up of advisory committee reports is often neglected in the absence of an institutionalized follow-up process. A model procedure is the operation of the Defense Science Board in the Office of the Secretary of Defense, where the secretary has directed that there be written response to its conclusions and recommendations. Feedback to the advisory committee can be salutary in terms of its future performance. Significant reports may deserve monitoring and periodic revisiting, even after the advisory group has been terminated, so the decision-maker can know of the actions taken, the reasons for inaction, and whether there are questions requiring further examination.

   Guideline: Heads of government departments and agencies should establish formal policies and procedures for the use of science and technology advisory committees and advisers, taking into consideration the foregoing principles and guidelines. This should include procedures for follow-up of committee reports. The formulation and application of such guidelines requires coordination and monitoring at the highest level of government. The policies and procedures could be incorporated into a reference manual for decision-makers.

Building Up a Common European Science and Technology Policy

Henry Durand

Contrary to the remarkable achievements of Europe in setting up a Common Agricultural Policy or in planning for 1993 a genuine "Single Market," the Europe of science and technology (S&T) is yet to be built. Indeed, some steps have already been taken in this direction, and the pace is being rapidly accelerated with more political power and additional funding being awarded to the European Commission. A definite change of mentality is now taking place in Europe in all fields, and it is likely that such an impetus will also encompass science and technology as a top priority for Europe (at least for those twelve countries which belong to the European Community).

Yet, as of today, the disparities are very large among the European countries in the definition of their S&T policies, in their priorities, and even more so in the amount of human and financial resources allocated to research and development (R&D). There is a strong cleavage between the north of Europe and the south, especially in regard to the "newcomers" in the European Community, such as Greece, Portugal and Spain. All relevant S&T indicators published by OECD, alas, demonstrate the very low scientific level of these countries, as compared with the more industrialized European nations.

Perhaps the most striking illustration of this situation is represented by Table 1, showing the total R&D spending as a percentage of the Gross National Product (the so-called "intensity" of R&D).

Differences can reach seven to one. But the Gross National Product (GNP) per capita between the richest and the poorest countries in Europe varies by a ratio of four, and hence these figures *per capita* may be as different as twenty-eight to one. By taking populations into account (six to one between West Germany and Portugal, for example), the ratio of total R&D spending in absolute terms climbs close to 200 to one. As a matter of fact, the three largest countries in Europe (West Germany, France and the UK) realize 78% of the total R&D of the twelve countries.

It is fair to say, though, that salaries are much lower in the poorer countries,

Henry Durand is Professor of Physics at the University of Paris and former Assistant Secretary General of NATO for Science and Environment (1983–88). In 1989, he served as Executive Vice President of a Review Board assessing the largest European research and development program, the ESPRIT program for information technologies.

Some of the opinions, facts and figures detailed in this essay are summarized in the paper entitled "Science and Technology Policy in France: Evolution of the Decision-Making Processes," co-authored in this volume by Pierre Piganiol and Henry Durand.

Table 1. Intensity of R&D
(As a Percentage of GNP, 1987 or Nearest Year)

	1981	1987
Germany	2.45	2.8
France	2.0	2.36
UK	2.4	2.3*
The Netherlands	2.0	2.3
Belgium	n.a.	1.5
Denmark	1.1	1.3*
Italy	1.0	1.5**
Ireland	0.7	0.9
Spain	0.4	0.7
Portugal	0.35	0.4***
Greece	0.2	0.35**

 *1985
 **1986
 ***1984
 Source: OECD and national data; figures for Luxembourg
  not available.

and hence the disparities in S&T employment are less striking, as shown in Table 2.

The differences in absolute numbers between the highest and the lowest reach a factor of sixty-five to one (instead of 200 to one for total R&D expenses), but only eight to one in relation to total employment (instead of twenty-eight to one in per capita expenses); this demonstrates the effect of lower salaries for R&D personnel in the poorer countries.

One should not, however, look only at the differences in wealth between the

Table 2. R&D Personnel (1987)

	Number (× 1000)	% of Community Total (EURO-12 = 100%)	Number per 1000 Employed (1983)
Germany	398	35	4.8
France	270	24	3.9
UK	174*	15	n.a.
Italy	118	10.5	2.7
The Netherlands	61.5	5.5	3.7
Spain	32	3	1.0
Belgium	32**	3	2.6
Denmark	20	2	2.7
Portugal	9***	1	0.7
Ireland	6***	0.5	2.8 (1984)
Greece	6**	0.5	0.6

 *1986
 **1983
 ***1984
Source: OECD and national data.

European countries; even among the larger and richer countries, there are also *structural* disparities. For instance, defense R&D accounts for 51% in the UK and 34% in France, but only 12.5% in West Germany, the other countries showing figures between 8% and zero.

Likewise, the ratio of public to private funding is 0.67 in West Germany against 1.5 in France (and even three in Greece). In West Germany, 72% of R&D expenditure is spent in industry, while, in most of the other countries, private and public laboratories share equally in expenditure.

These examples of global diversity in the national structure of the budget, the personnel, and the nature of research and development would, of course, be found to be even more striking if broken down according to the various fields of science and technology. In each European country, the traditions, the type of education, the nature of the natural resources, and the requirements of the economy define very different priorities, and there is, today, so little homogeneity between them that it hampers the objectives of a common S&T policy.

In spite of these obstacles, the twelve countries belonging to the European Community, the so-called "EURO-12," do represent, today, an impressive economic and intellectual power, challenging and sometimes overtaking the two other big powers, namely the US and Japan, in the field of science and, to a lesser extent, technology. It is, therefore, worth comparing these three entities, inasmuch as international competition is an important factor in deciding the future priorities of European science and technology policy.

EUROPE VERSUS THE US AND JAPAN

In spite of their excessive globality, the coarse indicators published by OECD can offer some clues about the relative strength of these three "blocs," Europe, the US, and Japan.

Broadly speaking, Europe finds itself in between the US and Japan in terms of total research and development spending, as expressed in Table 3, but "intensity" of R&D expenses places Europe at the third rank: The Europeans make a smaller effort per capita than their two challengers.

The relatively low figure for the intensity of R&D spending in Europe stems

Table 3. Gross Domestic Expenditures on R&D (1985)

	Absolute Values		% of GNP
	Million Current ECUs*	Million US$	
United States	134,645	161,575	2.8
EURO-12	76,250	91,500	1.9
Japan	48,056	57,667	2.6

*As of December 31, 1989, one US dollar was equal to .84 ECU.

Table 4. Published Scientific Papers (%)

	1973	1982
United States	54.4	51.1
Western Europe (including non-EURO-12)	38.5	38.8
Japan	7.1	10.1

Source: Patel & Pavitt, *Research Policy* 16 (1987).

from the low weight of the countries at the bottom of Table 1. Only four European countries (West Germany, France, the UK, and The Netherlands) exceed 2.3% while all the others stand below 1.5%.

These figures should, however, be interpreted with caution. The overwhelming importance of defense R&D in the US budget (up to 67% of the total), as compared with 24% for the EURO-12 and some 2% for Japan, distorts the comparison. Even if some (but in relatively smaller amounts) civil R&D is included in the US defense budget, such as micro-electronics or nuclear reactors, the civil spin-offs of military R&D probably do not compensate for the very strong defense orientation of the US.

The strength of Europe lies mainly in the field of science and especially "Big Science." It is an area in which Europeans have found unity within the past thirty years, having put in common their human and financial resources in such prestigious bodies as CERN (high-energy physics) in Geneva, the European Space Agency, and even in small joint laboratories, such as JET (the Joint European Torus for fusion research) in the UK, the Langevin-Laue Institute (a neutron-producing facility) in France, the European Molecular Biology Organization in West Germany, the Radiation Synchrotron facility under construction in France, etc.

An analysis of published scientific papers is another indicator of the quality of European scientists, ranking below the US, but far ahead of Japan, as shown in Table 4.

By contrast, the situation in Europe is much less favorable for technological fields, and this is *the* major concern in defining European science and technology strategy. This has a very negative impact on the balance of trade, especially for high-tech goods, as shown in Table 5, which lists the export/import ratios in 1981 and 1986 for some selected areas.

The domination of Japan over both Europe and the US in the field of office systems, computers, telecommunications equipment, and scientific instruments is extraordinary (although Europe is not too bad in telecommunications). By contrast, Europe leads in pharmaceuticals, and ranks second to the US in aircraft, a sector which, in Japan, is practically nonexistent. Another worrying feature is that the US lost ground in *all* listed sectors between 1981 and 1986.

The lagging situation of technology in Europe can also be expressed by the

Table 5. Export/Import Ratios in Selected High Technology Goods, 1981 and 1986

	1981					1986				
	Japan	US	FRG	France	UK	Japan	US	FRG	France	UK
Office Equipment and Computers	2.75	3.23	0.93	0.73	0.68	6.63	1.11	0.92	0.70	0.79
Communication Equipment and Electronic Components	6.59	0.70	1.13	1.14	0.96	9.95	0.61	1.14	1.22	0.82
Scientific Instruments	6.59	0.97	1.42	0.76	1.01	6.75	0.61	1.49	0.78	0.88
Drugs	0.28	2.27	1.77	1.99	2.61	0.30	1.42	1.71	1.90	2.21
Electrical Transmission Equipment	4.32	2.30	2.07	1.49	1.44	4.56	0.97	2.00	1.21	1.23
Aircraft and Parts	0.08	3.76	0.78	1.19	1.56	0.09	2.48	0.78	1.56	1.91

Source: OECD, *Main Science and Technology Indicators*, 1981–1987 (Paris: OECD, 1988).

Table 6. Patent Applications

	1980	1987 (* = or nearest year)
Federal Republic of Germany	30,582	32,311
United Kingdom	19,710	20,123
France	11,086	12,895
Other EURO-12 countries	14,078	10,282*
TOTAL EURO-12	75,456	75,611
United States	62,098	68,315
Japan	165,730	310,908

Source: OECD and French Ministry of Research and Technology.

low level of patents applied for in Europe as compared to the US and, even more so, Japan, which accounts for the vast majority of all patent applications in the world.

The most worrying sector is that of office systems and computers, because it represents, as shown in Table 7, a very large volume of imports and also because it can be considered to be a highly strategic and very pervasive sector. These considerations have driven the launching, some five years ago, of the most ambitious R&D program ever conceived by the European Commission, namely ESPRIT (the European Strategic Program in Information Technologies).

The emergence of such huge deficits have induced the Council of Ministers of EURO-12 to recommend a greater emphasis on applied research and tech-

Table 7. European Trade Deficit in Electronics (1986–88)

1986	US$14 billion
1987	US$22 billion
1988	US$33 billion

Source: E.I.C. (Paris, 1989)

Sectoral Breakdown of European Electronic Trade Deficit (1987)

Office Systems	US$2 billion
Industrial Automation (CAM/CIM)	US$3 billion
Active Components and Microelectronics	US$3.5 billion
Computer Systems and Software	US$12 billion

Source: Dataquest

nology in the present and the future research and development programs of the European Community. Nowadays, the majority of Community funding is devoted to industrial research, a much smaller fraction being allocated to the development of scientific excellence and exchanges of researchers. Of course, the European Governments (including the countries of the European Free Exchange Association—EFTA—Austria, Finland, Norway, Sweden and Switzerland) continue and even amplify the funding of the above-mentioned ''Big Science'' organizations, and pursue—outside the Communitarian scheme—their bilateral links and, as well, the newly launched and successful initiative called ''EUREKA.''

DECISION-MAKING MECHANISMS WITHIN THE EUROPEAN COMMUNITIES

One should first recall some institutional facts. Although one speaks usually of *the* European Community, there are, in fact, three European communities, established between 1950 and 1958, originally among six nations (France, Germany, Italy, and the three Benelux countries). These were joined in 1973 by Denmark, Ireland, and the UK, and later on by Greece (1981) and by Portugal and Spain (1987). The three communities were established, respectively, by the first two treaties of technological and industrial natures dealing with Coal and Steel, Nuclear Energy (EURATOM), and then, last, but not least, by the Treaty of Rome which was of economic nature and implemented the so-called ''Common Market.''

These three communities are under the authority of a single body, the Council of Ministers of the Twelve Nations; in fact, there are as many councils of ministers as there are ''specialities'' to be dealt with. While the ''supreme'' council of ministers is that of the Ministries of Foreign Affairs, R&D is dealt with by the Council of Research Ministers and this situation is also true for agriculture, transportation, justice, etc.

The executive power is in the hands of the commission, one single commission for the three communities. The commission has only the initiative of proposals; the council can accept, amend, or reject these proposals, but, at least officially, is not empowered with any initiative rights. In practice, though, the proposals are established by the commission after a close concertation with the presidency of the council. The presidency is represented by the country (rotated every six months in alphabetical order) chairing the council, and is thus entrusted with the establishment of the meeting agendas. The presidency itself consults the other eleven partners, and this system usually works well, except perhaps for budgetary decisions where disagreements and bargaining, followed by compromise, make up the rules of the game.

Until recently (1985), all decisions had to be made unanimously by the twelve members of the council. The ''Single Act'' of 1985, a serious revision amending the previous treaties on many points and establishing the conditions for the

"Single Market" of 1992, has changed this, and has given a bigger role to the European Parliament of Strasbourg in the decision-making process.

The commission retains its exclusive right of initiative, but only *major* decisions, defined by the Single Act, require unanimity. For instance, in the case of research and development programs, the so-called "Framework Program," stating the substance and estimated budget for a five-year plan, is a "major" proposal, and has to be decided upon unanimously. Once this is agreed upon, the detailed contents of the sub-programs (called "specific programs" in EURO-jargon) can be agreed upon by a "qualified majority," namely a vote in which each country is weighted according to its size and economic importance.

The European Parliament has to confirm these decisions. The Single Act has established a rather complex "triangular shuttle" mechanism between the Parliament, the commission, and the council. The Parliament can amend or even refuse a decision, and notifies the commission. The commission can take into account Parliament's opinion or not. In any case, the commission tables, before the council, a possible new proposal. A second round may then start, with a second advice from the Parliament. Should the latter refuse or amend again the council's decision, the same process continues once again through the commission to the council, which has the ultimate right to make the final decision, but *unanimously* this third time. The commission then has the authority to implement the decision and to watch for its proper execution.

Such a decision-making process is obviously rather long and cumbersome. Since the initial draft proposal of the commission is prepared and discussed together with many advisory committees on which the twelve nations are represented, the dialog between European and national civil servants is constant, allowing, in most cases, for an advanced negotiated compromise. If one single country disagrees on a major decision, however, the whole process can last as long as two years (and this happened in 1986, during the discussion of the 1987–1991 "Framework Program," due to a firm budgetary opposition by the UK, which led finally to a down-graded plan). But it is honest to say that the system works fairly well in the vast majority of cases, and that genuine dead-ends do not occur, because, on the whole, all twelve nations finally find their own interests in compromising one decision against another.

THE SIZE OF COMMUNITY R&D PROGRAMS

The emergence of the European Commission as an important actor on the R&D stage is rather recent (1983). Indeed, the Coal-Steel and the EURATOM treaties entrusted the commission to promote R&D in these two specific fields. As early as 1958, a set of in-house laboratories had been implemented under the name of Joint Research Centers (JCR), the larger one being built in Ispra, Italy, dealing with advanced nuclear reactors. The Treaty of Rome was totally (and curiously) silent on R&D except for a vague mention of promoting agri-

cultural progress, as though R&D were not an important economic development feature of modern civilization.

In the early 1970s, however, the commission—of course, with the unani-
mous approval of the council—succeeded in launching modest incentive R&D
programs in favor of European universities and industries, making use of an
obscure article (Number 235) of the Treaty of Rome, which allowed the commission to propose any other measure capable of improving the competitiveness
of the European economic operators.

Following the tradition of the EURATOM nuclear energy policy, the Community started these new R&D activities in 1974, after the first "oil shock,"
with a related field, namely non-nuclear energies, especially renewables, and
energy conservation. Some timid openings toward medical science, marine resources, and materials and standards were eventually made, but, by 1980, over
70% of the commission's R&D efforts were still devoted to the energy sector,
and the total R&D appropriations were well below 1% of the total commission
budget.

Things started to change in 1981, in view of the preparation of the Single
Act. This document explains R&D as a factor of improved economic competition and hence gives competence to the commission to propose more ambitious
R&D goals and to sketch a common European science and technology policy.
The most visible outcome of this new perspective was the acceptance, in 1983,
of the first four-year Framework Program, associated with financial authorizations which doubled the previous R&D budget. This move was, among others,
the occasion for launching a strong technological strategy aimed at developing
the competitiveness of European industry. The best example of this is the information technology program, ESPRIT, which got more than half the total
funding and represented an important step toward establishing a European intellectual and industrial community in information technology.

The first Framework Program was followed by a second, covering five years
(1987–1991) and currently running. Its budget was again increased and now
reaches the level of 5.5 billion ECUs (US$6.6 billion) for five years, namely
1.3 billion per year. Still, such an amount represents less than 2.5% of the
commission's total budget, the overwhelming part being devoted to agricultural
subsidies (50% to 60%) and to the "Structural Funds" (20% aimed at balancing the economic and social disparities between the various regions of Europe).
This budget is also small if compared to national R&D spending in the twelve
countries together, about forty times more.

A further step took place in 1989. Normally, a mid-term review of the five-
year Framework Program was decided upon to suggest modifications of its
content and/or its financial authorizations. But instead of a simple amendment,
the commission proposed an entirely new Framework Program covering the
period 1991–1994, with an overlap of two years (1990 and 1991). After a
remarkably short discussion (only ten months), this solution was adopted by
the Council of Research Ministers on December 15, 1989. Indeed, the amount

of authorization requested by the commission (7.7 billion ECUs = US$9.25 billion for five years) has been substantially reduced, but, because of the superimposition of two Framework Programs for the years 1990–91 and also because of a new revision (or possibly again a new overlapping Framework Program) to be undertaken in 1992, the prospects for the future are quite encouraging.

With the commission's budget now exceeding 3% of the total national R&D expenditures of EURO-12, its impact is becoming substantial, both on the successful contractors and on national science and technology policies. Such a statement may sound odd, as 3% is still a very small figure, but the criteria, the conditions, and the operating methods adopted for the European Community R&D programs are such (or have become so after some years of testing) that each "rule of the game" contributes to augmenting the efficiency of the scheme, thanks to psychological and financial leverage effects.

CRITERIA, CONDITIONS AND METHODOLOGY OF EUROPEAN R&D PROGRAMS

Until 1983, the European R&D programs were generally considered as additional funding to national supports. No condition of "Europeanization" of R&D was imposed, and most of the beneficiaries of the European incentive funds were originating from a single nation. This state of affairs did not please the member-nations, as the commission was just another "funding teller," without any originality of its own and often competing with similar national functions.

In 1983, the rules governing Community R&D programs were completed by new measures aimed at insuring a "European added value" and thus at creating better efficiency in the budgets and a new spirit within the European academic and industrial communities. Hereafter are listed the principal criteria, conditions and methods that are presently enforced for industrial projects supported by the commission (the rules are somewhat less stringent for basic research activities involving universities alone).

As far as the preparation phases of the programs are concerned, a much tighter concertation among governments, industry and academia has been established. The content of the programs is scrutinized by many advisory boards, involving up to a hundred experts. This insures, in general, a consensus within the population of potential contractors (although the influence of big companies is sometimes judged as too important) and allows also for good articulation with national activities.

The selection phase for applicants, after a call for tender which is widely publicized, is also carefully prepared. Here again, many independent experts (several hundred for the largest programs) are mobilized, and advise the commission. While the latter has the sovereign right of decision for the final choice of contractors, the opinions of national representatives, through an *ad hoc* advisory program committee, is carefully weighed.

The seriousness of this selection process, which may involve several feedback loops with the potential contractors on technical or financial issues, is such that the rate of success is rather low, one in six on the average, up to one in twelve for some sub-programs. This insures, of course, the quality of the competition, but may also discourage applicants as the preparation of a full proposal is a costly and cumbersome exercise. Following recommendations made recently by the ESPRIT Review Board, the commission now demands a short "declaration of intent" and, if successful at this stage, a full proposal will be requested.

Each successful project is carefully followed up twice a year by reviewers, a group of independent experts who advise the commission's project officers on the evolution of the research work and the quality of the project management. This method should, in principle, insure the adequacy of the R&D performed with the project objective, correct any deviation and, as the case may be, interrupt or stop projects poor in terms of results and/or management (although, in practice, a great deal of indulgence has been observed).

All Community R&D projects are based on a 50%–50% cost-sharing plan. Universities can, if they so wish, charge 100% of the additional (marginal) cost of the R&D. This condition is readily accepted by most contractors and insures, through their financial contributions, the seriousness of the projects. The normal duration of a project is four to five years, normally split into two phases separated by a mid-term review.

The conditions of eligibility or of preference for participants have been recently revised and consist of the following:

- Contracts can only be awarded to transnational consortia, *i.e.,* a group of at least two enterprises, including—as the case may be—subsidiaries of foreign companies, originating from two different European countries (usually there are many more than two).
- Such a consortium is encouraged to bring in universities or public research laboratories.
- A preference is given to consortia gathering large companies and SMEs.
- Preference is also given to consortia calling on partners from the smaller and/or less industrialized countries of Europe.
- Potential competitors are encouraged to perform joint R&D.

The last condition, defining what is called in EURO-jargon "precompetitive research," is probably the one of the greatest originality and a good reason for the success of the Community's R&D programs. It was, in the beginning, considered with suspicion by the European enterprises, especially the big ones. As a consequence, in the mid-1980s, most of the R&D projects proposed by large companies did not concern their real core business, and consisted usually of non-product-oriented, long-term, or marginal types of research. Precompetitive research was then synonymous with somewhat fundamental or basic research. After several years of work in common, however, companies realized the advantages of sharing, not only the cost, but also the experience and know-how of others, in spite of the potentiality of becoming competitors at the end of the research work. Hence the present empirical definition should probably be turned into a tautology: "Precompetitive research is that type of research that actual or potential competitors agree to perform together."

This type of cooperation within industry is widely used in Japan, but is often criticized in the United States. It is heard sometimes that encouraging competitors to work together precisely in the name of improving competition is self-contradictory (the word "oxymoron" was even used). Indeed, the American tradition may judge such an attitude as unfair to "free" competition. One can find, however, some recent examples of joint research centers established by competitors with the blessing and funding of the US Government; SEMATECH in the sector of micro-electronics is a well-known case.

Indeed, European competitors who decide to do so are totally "free" in their decisions and must, therefore, find some advantages in doing so. Such advantages do, indeed, exist. In spite of the severe industrial property conditions set down by the commission for such cooperations (which are not always welcome), partners in a consortium have to share not only the current results, but also the proprietary "background" information needed by the others in order to perform the common research. If a patent is taken out by one partner, the others automatically get royalty-free licenses.

The acceptance by European companies of such roles can be explained by the relatively limited size of the present national markets, by the desire to challenge the complete opening of European borders in 1993 through reinforced partnership, and also by the strong feeling that the word "competition" should be at least as relevant to the Japanese and American threats as to the intra-European competition.

THE IMPACT OF EUROPEAN R&D PROGRAMS

By looking carefully at the various conditions just described, it can be understood why, in the end and thanks to many amplifying factors, "the 3% Community budget" can have a much more substantial impact on the state of science, technology and industry in Europe.

First, this budget is, in practice, almost totally devoted to *incentives,* contrary to national R&D budgets which always have the burden of financing a very large proportion of institutional R&D, either funded in-house or spent in a more or less compulsory way in universities.

Second, since the commission's programs are nowadays well-focused on a small number of selected topics, chosen in full agreement with the national governments, it so happens that—in these selected areas—the incentive funds coming from the commission exceed, sometimes by a factor of two or three, the national funds freely available for incentives. The phenomenon is ever more striking in the less industrialized countries, which dispose practically of negligible incentive funding.

Third, the quality of the projects carried out by the commission, thanks to the large number of applicants and its severe selection, is, in general, as good or better than that of national programs.

Fourth, the 50%–50% cost-sharing scheme doubles the amount of R&D done with a given amount of funding (it is fair to say that many European countries do carry on similar schemes).

Fifth, the five-year financial authorizations implied in the Framework Programs give definite financial insurance to contractors, contrary to national subsidies which are generally appropriated on a yearly basis.

Sixth, the sharing of "background and foreground" R&D knowledge and results between consortia partners amplifies, by a hardly assessable factor, the efficiency of the funding; obviously, smaller partners can get very high benefits from the knowledge and know-how accumulated in the larger companies.

Seventh, the encouragement to associate the academic world with industry has provided the latter with a considerable—but often hidden—knowledge of the former. The ease of cooperating with foreign universities, often ignored, has been one of the surprising successes of the European program. In fact, these encouragements have been more effective than many measures adopted for years by national governments for promoting university-industry links. Such associations have also allowed for training on topical subjects, usually at the doctoral or post-doctoral level, of many young scientists.

Eighth, the preference given to consortia which include SMEs has given them new R&D opportunities. Highly specialized little companies have thus been able to assess their own quality beside the large R&D teams of the big companies, with the possibility of pursuing their cooperation further.

Ninth, the smaller companies have been given a chance to get acquainted with the R&D of the larger companies. The former perform, generally, very little research activity; their main force lies in their universities and sometimes in some effective SMEs. It has given them an opening to the rest of the world—at least, to the rest of Europe.

INTERESTING SPIN-OFFS

Aside from this list of direct impacts, some interesting spin-offs have been observed, such as the merging of enterprises or commercial partnership agreements. The contacts started with better acquaintances of their R&D teams; then, management became accustomed to meeting its counterparts in other companies; and, finally, through such contacts and often thanks to common developments of new products carried out in the R&D project, the two companies became engaged or even got married. In this respect, the most remarkable success of the commission's R&D programs has been the European opening of industry toward partnership. This was one of the fundamental objectives, and became a real achievement in preparing the future Single Market.

The impact on national policy has also been important, in spite of the sacrifices made by governments in abandoning some of their competence to the commission. The most interesting feature is that the "partnership" notion has also entered the national minds and has influenced the national scientific and technological communities. For instance, ESPRIT has cemented the cohesion of the information technology actors in each country, a phenomenon which would probably not have occurred without the European programs.

The result of this new European spirit can be, for instance, measured by the increasing number of registered mergers or commercial alliances occurring between European companies as opposed to Japanese or American firms. For instance, ten years ago, agreements between European and American companies outnumbered by a factor of six the intra-European alliances. Today, these two numbers are equal.

Another important consequence concerns the academic world in attracting lesser qualified teams. Whereas some of the most qualified laboratories neglected to answer the commission's requests for proposals, others accepted, got associated with excellent partners, and became themselves "centers of excellence." This competition within a given country is, indeed, an unexpected and stimulating spin-off of the European R&D program.

THE CONTENT OF THE EUROPEAN R&D PROGRAMS

At the present time, the current Framework Program (1987–91) is divided into eight chapters. Many of them—and the better funded ones—are designed to match the technological and industrial R&D needs. This trend has been accelerated in recent years, and will become even more dominant in the forthcoming Framework Program (1990–1994). The academic world has not been forgotten, however, and, in spite of the more modest financing, is also given a good opportunity to become "European."

The first chapter deals with the quality of life, and covers health and environment research and development, including radioprotection and remote sensing.

The second chapter is, by far, the largest in size, and gets almost half the total budget. It deals with information technologies (the above-mentioned ESPRIT program) and advanced telecommunications (the RACE—Research on Advanced Communications in Europe—program), mainly aimed at developing ISDN (wide-band networks). Some smaller and more specifically applied programs cover medical data processing (AIM), computer-aided automotive driving (DRIVE), and technologies of education (DELTA).

The third chapter aims at the modernization of more traditional sectors of industry. Under the code name BRITE/EURAM (Basic Research for Industrial Technologies in Europe/European Materials), it covers the development of generic technologies and materials able to offer a wide-range of applications. It is the second largest program after ESPRIT. Some other, smaller initiatives are also included in this chapter, such as programs covering the aeronautical area, metrology, standards, and tests.

The fourth deals with biological resources: biotechnologies, agro-industrial and agro-food R&D, together with a modest program in agricultural research.

The fifth—rather important, as it marks the origin of the commission's R&D activities—deals with energy: research into nuclear safety, fusion (the Joint European Torus project), and non-nuclear energy and energy conservation.

The sixth and seventh lines are much smaller, and deal respectively with the scientific and technological issues in developing countries and with marine resources, a recently launched initiative.

The last chapter is very important, as it deals with "horizontal" scientific activities. Called "SCIENCE," it concerns, on the one hand, the support of young post-doctoral scientists who wish to continue their research in other European countries, and, on the other, the support of "twinning" of scientific laboratories (always in two different European countries) willing to work together. Its five-year budget is about US$200 million.

These R&D programs are completed by two other interesting and very popular initiatives promoted by the Directorate General of Employment, Social Affairs, and Education in the European Commission: One encourages the exchange of students by the mutual recognition of curriculum and credits by their respective universities; the other finances exchanges of people, including students, between the academic and industrial sectors.

It has been felt, however, that eight R&D chapters, themselves subdivided into many specific programs (the number now reaching thirty-five) leads to scattered procedures and to bureaucratic budgetary restraints. The aim of the new (third) Framework Program (1990–94) is, therefore, to reduce somewhat the number of chapters and, even more drastically, the number of specific programs.

Provisionally, this new program is now divided into six big chapters with a limited number of sub-chapters. The big share still goes to information and communication technologies; the second largest will be devoted to manufacturing technologies and materials; and thereafter come energy, environment, and life sciences. The sixth chapter will be concerned with the development of exchanges of researchers and with the education of young scientists and engineers, with a budget more than doubled with respect to the previous one.

The Community programs are open, since 1988, to the member countries of the European Free Exchange Association. Of course, the commission does not pay, in this case, its 50% share, since these countries do not contribute to the European budget. The participants from these countries have to pay, therefore, 100% (often with a contribution of 50% from their national government), but have, otherwise, the same advantages and access to the shared knowledge as Community participants do. Another difference is that the governments of the

EFTA do not participate in the definition of the R&D programs (but they are consulted) and have, therefore, to accept them as they are.

By contrast, the EFTA countries (and also Turkey, which is neither in the Community nor in the EFTA) are full members of the EUREKA scheme, a more recent initiative associating nineteen European countries, plus the commission itself, and a scheme which is much more oriented toward product development and marketing than the commission's R&D activities and which enjoys considerable success.

THE EUREKA PROGRAM

The EUREKA program was launched five years ago at the initiative of the French President. It was wrongly, but persistently said, in those days, that EUREKA was the European answer to SDI in order to give Europe a chance to also benefit from an ambitious technological program. The comparison between the two initiatives is totally erroneous, as EUREKA had, exclusively, a civil objective, namely again improving the technical and commercial competitiveness of Europe. (More recently, in 1989, a EUREKA-type of initiative had been launched for defense R&D by the European partners of NATO under the code name, EUCLID.)

EUREKA has the interesting feature of complementing the commission's initiatives, in that it encourages the development of commercial processes and products. In this sense, it deals with competitive R&D or, better, with ''D'' only (although there is always some feedback from ''D'' to ''R'').

As a matter of fact, EUREKA is not a ''program'' in the usual sense of the word; it is more of a plan, a pure framework. There are no imposed technological contents, no requests for proposals; there is just a tiny secretariat in Brussels which acts more as an information office than a coordinating body. The preparation of the periodic (every six months) meeting of the council of the nineteen research ministers (plus the commission) are organized in turn, by each of the member-nations which act successively as president of the council.

EUREKA is hence the least bureaucratic institution one can think of. Furthermore, applications originate from industry. Contrary to all national and Community programs, which are of ''top-down'' natures, EUREKA is earmarked with a ''bottom-up'' policy. The only condition of eligibility is the partnership between at least two companies from two different member-countries; these companies can be commercial competitors or just complementary, as often occurs.

Of course, the subject of the application should be topical, usually ''high tech,'' and able to draw the attention of the governments involved by the nationalities of the partners. The decision-making process is very simple: those governments involved submit their choices to the full Council of Ministers, which usually confirms the choices and awards the EUREKA label to the project.

This label consists, in practice, of two advantages: first, a degree of quality recognition of the project; and, second, financial incentives. Since EUREKA, as such, does not have a budget of its own, the funding is made available by the governments concerned. Usually, all European governments maintain a budgetary chapter in favor of the modernization of their national industries; the EUREKA label thus provides a priority to those accepted projects. The percentage of funding with respect to the total cost of the development depends, therefore, on the practice of each country, usually between 35% and 50% (the average being about 30%).

Contrary to the European Commission's programs, however, there is no multiannual guarantee for such subsidies. This is perhaps the weak point of the system, although, in practice, the continuation of the funding does not seem, so far, to have been a real problem.

The success of EUREKA is demonstrated by the large number of projects accepted. As of January 1, 1990, the number had reached 297, representing a total amount of R&D close to US$11 billion. The average duration of projects is about four years, and the range of individual costs generally varies from one million to a few hundred million, with a single exception, the JESSI project, which is close to five billion.

The two most spectacular undertakings within EUREKA deal with electronics. First is the High Definition TV project, associating Philips of The Netherlands, Thomson of France, Bosch of Germany, and Nokia of Finland, and second is the five billion dollar JESSI (Joint European Silicon System Initiative), aimed at developing the sub-micron microelectronic technology needed to produce, within six years, 64-megabit memory chips. The definition phase of this project was launched under the auspices of EUREKA in 1988, but recently (as of the end of 1989) the European Commission agreed to join in, and will provide some 20% to 25% of the funds needed for the most advanced phase of the project, namely the R&D indispensable to insuring the basic technologies, including the development of the necessary manufacturing tools. Aside from the three large industries which will lead the project (Philips of The Netherlands, Siemens of Germany, and the Franco-Italian company, SGS-Thomson), some other smaller firms will join in, together with many universities and public laboratories.

TOWARD THE 1993 SINGLE EUROPEAN MARKET

EUREKA obviously cannot solve all the problems that European industry has to face before the opening of the Single Market with the increasing competition from abroad, since it concerns only a limited number of projects. Many more difficult issues of a nontechnical nature remain to be solved, such as psychological attitudes caused by remaining chauvinistic traditions, the insufficient move toward common standards, the nationalistic trend in the public (and even private) procurement procedures, and the lack of information from both manufacturers on their potential European (or even worldwide) customers and from customers on the manufacturers, etc.

Since 1958, the signature date of the Treaty of Rome, a considerable change has occurred in European minds. The mobility of people and goods through the borders has been eased to a degree that would be unbelievable to our parents. Customs barriers have been lifted between the twelve countries and practically between EURO-12 and the EFTA countries. Custom duties are now levied at the external borders of the European Community. Most of the European countries have no more foreign exchange control, and Europeans can choose where and in what currency they prefer to keep their savings or insurance. Intra-European trade has increased faster than international trade.

It still remains to further abolish the institutional discrepancies, probably the most formidable obstacles that still exist and which hamper the full unification (or, at least, the "harmonization," in a first step) of Europe: fiscal disparities, monetary and economic distortions, social differences, etc. This is the ambitious goal of the 1993 Single Market, together with the lifting of all discriminatory employment regulations between European citizens.

In this context, the Single Market should, at the same time, represent a challenging opportunity for industry and a danger for those enterprises that will not adapt themselves to such open competition. It is said, especially in the US, that Europe will thus create a closed market, reserved to European industries—a sort of "European fortress." It is quite clear, on the contrary, that such a large market will also be a remarkable chance for foreign competitors. The Japanese trade and industrial companies have understood this opportunity well, since it will give them a single market of over 300 million citizens, instead of twelve scattered markets, each having its own rules and regulations. They seem much more pleased by the forthcoming events than the Americans.

It is still too early to say whether this market of 300 million will or will not reach six hundred through agreements with the Eastern countries. It appears today that these countries are knocking at the door of the Community (as well as Turkey, with sixty million inhabitants and probably one hundred million in the next generation). The experience gained over the past years with the difficulty of integrating Greece, Spain and Portugal should lead to a prudent attitude. It seems impossible, however, to refuse completely any type of arrangement that will lead to some limited association, especially for such countries as Czechoslovakia or the German Democratic Republic, which have prestigious industrial pasts and relatively sounder economies. In any case, these markets will certainly develop, and will offer new openings to Western European industries as well as to the world's industries, even if, for years to come, these markets may represent economic burdens to the West.

Science and technology in Europe have to meet this multiple challenge, namely preparing, at the same time, European industry to face increased intra-European competition in addition to, possibly, the political and economic turmoil of Eastern Europe. All the initiatives taken in common over the past few years in the area of R&D programs have no other objective than to improve the knowledge, the efficiency, the quality, and the competitiveness of the European economy for the next millennium.

A Blueprint for Science and Technology in the Developing World

Abdus Salam and Azim Kidwai

Science and technology have acquired enormous social power in the present age because of their economic roles as agents of wealth production. High technology, based on science, particularly in recent times, has accelerated the economic and social development of many nations in the North and a few in the East. But most of the southern hemisphere, comprising the developing nations, has been left far behind in the march forward because science and technology, which form the leading edge of development, are very weak in those countries.

The pity is that the immense possibilities for realizing human potential have never been greater than now, and yet almost the entire southern hemisphere—with a few exceptions—is poor and socially backward because the economies of its countries are not knowledge-based and cannot be in step with the change that comes as a corollary to rapid development in science and technology.

An economist or a politician might, perhaps, have somewhat different perceptions and equate other ingredients like lack of political stability, unequal opportunities, and population pressures with low levels of science and technology as the main constraints in the South, dwarfing its socioeconomic development. But few can disagree that, in the ultimate analysis, the crux is the level of science and technology—high or low—that determines the disparities between the rich, advanced nations and the poor underdeveloped countries.

Alfred North Whitehead said

> In the conditions of modern life, the rule is absolute: the race which does not value trained intelligence is doomed. . . . Today we maintain ourselves, tomorrow science will have moved over yet one more step and there will be no appeal from the judgment which will be pronounced . . . on the uneducated.

This is a sort of axiom in the latter half of the present century.

An alarming element in the present situation is that the gap in science and technology between the developed and developing nations is widening. That

Abdus Salam is a Nobel laureate in physics and heads the International Centre for Theoretical Physics in Trieste, Italy. He is also President of the Third World Academy of Sciences and of the Third World Network of Scientific Organizations, based in Trieste.

Azim Kidwai is a science writer and science columnist for the English daily newspaper, Dawn, *in Karachi, Pakistan. He is also editor of* Newsletter *and other publications of the Third World Academy of Sciences.*

has to be, somehow, arrested. There seems no way out except to devise measures internationally, and seek their implementation to make a start in narrowing this gap. Though the widening of the gap seems to be inherent in the present scheme of things, a well-thought-out mechanism can make it reversible. It is a very complex situation that has to be resolved, and concerted efforts—rather, movements—on a global scale have to be mounted to bring corrections to the imbalance and to stem the downward slide that has its own dynamism because of failings in human nature, often loaded with selfish traits. These traits are amply reflected in the policies pursued by many groups and most of the governments.

The imbalance has to be corrected in the interests of the North and of the whole gamut of rich communities that form scarcely one-third of the globe. For, in its present shrunken state, the planet cannot remain divided with the very rich having such a high consumption pattern of the natural resources of the earth and the very poor going to bed without a meal.

In the past, such a pattern was perhaps sustainable as interdependence of one community on another was very small. Now it is a different world, with expectations of the poor rising due to the communications explosion, apart from the overriding factor of interdependability.

If trees are being cut or burned on a large scale in Brazil or forest areas in the tropics are dwindling due to an increase in the use of firewood, the very ecology of the planet is likely to change. If there is a change in the global weather due to such acts, then the granary that the US is today—producing so much more grain than is required—may no longer obtain. Acid rain is already destroying the forests of central Europe: An adverse climatic change factor emerging from the tropics or the Amazon will highly aggravate the situation for the rich communities.

The greenhouse effect is also a common global problem, although the rich nations appear to be higher contributors to the increase of carbon monoxide in the atmosphere than the developing countries.

A NEW SITUATION

This is a new situation in human affairs. On this shrunken globe, the pressures from the South are mounting, and will continue to do so if the present increase in the imbalance is not swiftly arrested.

The interdependence of the different nations which inhabit the earth is now of an entirely different order, and the ideas based on their relations in the past will not work.

For example, the unsustainable lifestyles of the rich 15% of the world population in a world where a billion people go to bed hungry at night is no longer tenable.

At the center of the stage in any remedial action will have to be the upgrading of science and technology in the developing world, without which any correction of the imbalance would be only transitory.

Promotion of science and technology in the Third World is now, therefore, an imperative. To attain such an objective, any blueprint for upgrading science and technology in the Third World must have two distinct components:

- A pattern of development in science and technology in these communities that fits the transition phase they are now in, and
- Strategies and mechanisms that can realize such a dream.

The first component requires a deeper analysis, and one has to start with the historical perspective to understand and resolve the complexities of the present situation.

HISTORICAL BACKGROUND

The first thing to realize about the science and technology gap between the South and the North is that it is of relatively recent origin. In respect to science, George Sarton, in his monumental *History of Science,* chose to divide the story of achievement into ages, each age lasting half a century. With each half-century, he associated one central figure. Thus the years 450–400 B.C. Sarton calls the Age of Plato; this is followed by the half-centuries of Aristotle, Euclid, Archimedes, etc. These were scientists from the Greek Commonwealth, consisting, in addition to the Greeks, of Egyptians, southern Italians, and the ancestors of the modern Syrians and Turks.

From 600 A.D. to 650 A.D., in Sarton's account, is the Chinese age of Hsiian Tsang. From 650 to 700 A.D. is the Age of I-Ching (and of the Indian mathematician, Brahmaguptal), followed by the Ages of Jabir, Khwarizmi, Razi, Masudi, Wafa, Biruni (and Avicenna), and then Omar Khayam—Chinese, Hindus, Arabs, Persians, Turks and Afghans—an unbroken Third World succession for five hundred years. After the year 1100, the first Western names begin to appear—Gerard of Cremona, Roger Bacon, and others, but the honors are still shared for the next 250 years with the Third World men of science like Ibn-Rushd (Averroes), Tusi, and Sultan Ulugh Beg.

The same story repeats itself in technology in China and the Middle East, at least until around 1450 A.D. when the Turks captured Constantinople because of their mastery of superior cannonade. No Sarton has yet chronicled the history of medical and technological creativity in Africa, for example, the early iron-smelting processes in Central Africa 2500 years ago (*Scientific American,* June 1988). Nor has there been a technological history written of the pre-Spanish Mayans and Aztecs, with their independent inventions of the zero and of calendars, of the moon and Venus, and their diverse pharmacological discoveries, including quinine. But one may be sure that it is a story of fair achievement in science and technology.

From around 1450, however, the Third World began to lose out (except for the occasional flash of individual brilliant scientific work), principally because of the lack of tolerant attitudes toward the creation of sciences. And that brings us back to the present century when the cycle begun by Michael the Scot, who went from his native glens in Scotland south to Toledo and then to Sicily (around 1220 A.D.) in order to acquire knowledge of the works of Razi, Avicenna, and even Aristotle, turns full cycle, and it is those in the developing world who must now turn northward for science.

A SHARED HERITAGE

Science and technology are cyclical. They are the shared heritage of all mankind. East and West, North and South have all participated equally in their creation in the past as, it is hoped, they will in the future—the joint endeavor in science becoming one of the unifying forces among the diverse peoples on this globe.

It is not that difficult for the Third World to acquire high-level science and science-based technologies, as is the widespread belief. A man with vision, C. P. Snow in his famous lecture, "The Two Cultures," said that science and technology are the branches of human experience

> that people can learn with predictable results. . . . For a long time, the West misjudged this very badly. After all, a good many Englishmen have been skilled in mechanical crafts for half-a-dozen generations. Somehow, we in the North have made ourselves believe that the whole of technology was a more or less incommunicable art.

In Snow's words,

> There is no evidence that any country or race is better than any other in scientific teachability: There is a good deal of evidence that all are much alike. Tradition and technical background seem to count for surprisingly little. There is no getting away from it. It is . . . possible to carry out the scientific revolution in India, Africa, Southeast Asia, Latin America, the Middle East, within fifty years. There is no excuse for Western man not to know this.

Freeman Dyson in *The Twenty-First Century* also ably stresses the same point:

> Technology is a gift of God. After the gift of life, it is perhaps the greatest of God's gifts. . . . The most revolutionary aspect of technology is its mobility. Anybody can learn it. It jumps easily over barriers of race and language. It took three generations of misery for the older industrial countries to master the technology of coal and iron. The new industrial countries of East Asia, South Korea and Singapore and Taiwan mastered the new technology and made the jump from poverty to wealth in a single generation. . . . If we are to lead the world toward a hopeful future, we must understand that technology is a part of the planetary environment, to be shared like air and water with the rest of mankind. To try to monopolize technology is as stupid as trying to monopolize air. . . . Unlike

our political leaders, we have first-hand knowledge of a business which is not merely multinational, but, in its nature, international. . . . As scientists we work every day in an international community. . . . That is why we are appalled by the narrow-mindedness and ignorance of our political leaders.

Once it is accepted that, given the climate and the opportunity, the under-developed can reach the same levels of science and technology as the nations of the North, an all-out endeavor needs to be mounted that science be given the highest priority in the developing countries, supported by the countries of the North. Such an endeavor should make a beginning with a very crucial element.

SCIENCE EDUCATION

It will have to be education—more particularly, science education—that will form the basis of this endeavor. The base of the pyramid has to have science education on firm ground if the structure is to be viable. With science and high technology based on science at the apex, the pyramid will have to be designed to take care of the whole spectrum of science and technology and their needs.

Figures released by the World Bank reflect the fact that the state of second-ary education in Third World countries is either pathetically low or nil. At times, however, these figures are not indicative of the real state of education. For instance, in the rural areas of Pakistan and India, even though the enroll-ment figures at the primary stage seem respectable, many of the children drop out and never complete the primary level.

There is, therefore, an urgent need to broaden the base of education in the Third World. Also, the component of science in education has to increase since many schools in the developing countries teach hardly any science at the pri-mary level. Special emphasis on teaching arithmetic and science-text reading has to be given in all schools at the primary and secondary levels.

Also, at the secondary level, some sort of laboratory with inexpensive ex-periments and models has to be part of the educational process so as to make it easy for the children to comprehend scientific laws and phenomena.

At the tertiary level, all the four areas—basic sciences, applied sciences, classical technology, and science-based high technology (microelectronics, la-sers, biotechnology, etc.)—have to be presented in real earnest, and education (and research) in these four areas properly organized and promoted from the present low levels.

SECONDARY EDUCATION

After a period of compulsory lower-secondary education, which may be fin-ished at the age of fifteen or sixteen, most modern societies provide for two parallel educational systems. Using the UK terminology of the 1970s, these two systems may be called (1) the system of "professional" education, comprising technical, vocational, agricultural and commercial courses, and (2) the system of "liberal" education, comprising courses which lead to the university level in the sciences, medicine, and the arts.

A major structural failing of Third World educational systems has been that, in general, no creditable professional system has been developed. It is true that a half-hearted system of polytechnic institutions and vocational schools has been built up in recent years in a number of developing countries, but this system has had scant prestige attached to it. (As a general rule, such systems have been run by Ministries of Labor and Employment, rather than Ministries of Education.)

To see how inadequate such a system has been, it should be recalled that, in industrialized countries, the proportion of those enrolled for the two streams is in the order of 50:50. *In the Third World, however, the proportion of the professional versus the liberal enrollment (at the secondary stage) is normally on the order of 10:90.* This preponderance of the technologically illiterate is the major cause of unemployment and of the Third World's technological backwardness.

One of the main educational tasks before the Third World is to change this ratio of 10:90 to 50:50. In the conditions of today, the professional system should be accorded equal status with the better-known liberal system.

A MEASURE OF PRESTIGE

The first concern should be to bring a measure of prestige to the professional system of education. One will need to give serious consideration to the institution of national certificates—or, preferably, decide to identify these with the prevailing awards. Parallel with the present liberal system of education, there should be a second, a professional system of education. Each award—the matriculation or the intermediate or the bachelor's degree—may be obtained either after the present liberal courses in arts and sciences (as now) or after technical, agricultural, or a commercial college. So far as job opportunities in administrative services are concerned, all matriculates or degree holders from general, technical or commercial streams would count as equivalents. Only thus will the exclusive hold on the public mind in the developing countries of the present prestigious liberal system of education be broken.

UNIVERSITY EDUCATION

The proportion of those following science and engineering versus those following the arts at the liberal university level is of the order of 50:50 in most of the industrialized countries. One must aim at a similar 50:50 ratio in the developing countries, where it is certainly not the case. This will require the equipping of laboratories and institutions of higher learning in an adequate manner.

SPECIALIZATION

One proposal which may be considered in this context is that of specialization. Could, for example, a consortium of universities in the US and the UK be helped by their governments and be encouraged to take care of university science in all those developing countries which desire to be helped? Could The Netherlands and Belgium look after the building up of libraries and laboratories? Could Germany and Japan look after technical education at all levels? Could Scandinavia look after the scientific aspects of the ecology? Could Switzerland and Austria (with their well-known pharmaceutical expertise) look after medical education? Could Italy, with its experience in setting up international centers in physics and biology, look after the creation of similar institutions in concert with developing countries? Could the US, Canada, Australia and New Zealand look after education for agriculture and prospecting? Could one envisage the USSR taking care of primary, secondary and vocational education Third Worldwide? Could France, Canada and Spain carry out all these actions for the French- and Spanish-speaking countries if so desired by them?

These are merely illustrations of what the possible divisions of the relevant tasks could be. Eventually, of course, these suggestions would have to be tailored and modified when detailed projects are elaborated.

A pattern of development of science education in the developing world, with strategies and mechanisms as outlined above, could produce a basis on which a sustainable structure of science and technology could be built for the poor communities around the world.

What should be the contours of science and technology development in the Third World?

Each country has its own peculiar problems and any plan for development would have to be modified according to the problems of the particular country. Nevertheless, there is a common denominator for all these countries because of their low socioeconomic levels in the global context and the general contours of the pattern as well as strategies that are likely to be viable and can be indicated.

But, before doing that exercise, a few statistical indicators may be in order to give some perspective on the problems.

The first is the indicator of spending on science in the research and development (R&D) sector. While most of the developed nations spend at least 2% of their much larger Gross National Products (GNPs) on R&D, the developing countries—with a few exceptions—spend less than a half of one percent of their GNPs in that sector.

The second indicator is the number of research workers. The number of research workers in the six top countries of the world is 75% of the world total. These countries are the USSR, the US, Japan, West Germany, the UK, and France. The rest of the world has only 25% of the total research scientists in the world. The developing countries' share is simply dismal.

The example of Pakistan could be a typical case. The 1985 figures show that there were only sixty-five research scientists per million population in the country as against 4,750 in Japan. The figure for South Korea—which has almost graduated to the status of a developed country—is, on the other hand, quite respectable, with 957 research scientists per million in 1985.

A GENERAL PATTERN

With such a perspective in view, the following could be a general pattern for the blueprint for the development of science and technology in the developing countries:

- Promotion of science education as detailed earlier;
- Structuring basic scientific and technological research in the universities with a thrust that can produce a leadership and researchers in its wake, so as to make it a self-reinforcing system. The system should also aim at producing technical cadres to support the researchers. Both should somehow reach a critical size within five years (such an objective can be attained by liberal funding for training and maintaining international contacts);
- Simultaneously, the supportive infrastructure should be strengthened by building up expertise in classical low and medium technologies, with emphasis on craftsmanship and fabrication techniques;
- Drawing up a comprehensive plan for applied sciences, taking into consideration the priorities of the country. For instance, what order of priority should be given to agriculture, livestock, health, energy, minerals, communications, oceans, environment, etc.; what should be developed first and what could wait until last?;
- Focusing on the training of personnel for research and development in the area of science-based high technology which, though difficult, is the quickest way to wealth?

Spending on basic science, applied science, and science-based technology should be 4%, 4% and 8% of the education budget, respectively. Reference is made to the attached schedules, showing, by country, population, Gross National Product, and percentages of expenditures for defense, health, education, and science and technology.

What should be spent on training and development in the "low" technology area? The answer is clearly as much as one can afford.

One minimal figure which has been suggested in this context is that coming from the United Nations Educational, Scientific and Cultural Organization (UNESCO). It is the famous 1% of GNP for *all* (basic and applied) plus *all* technology (classical "low" as well as "high"). On the average basis of 4% of GNP being spent on education in the South, this works out roughly to one-sixth, one-sixth, one-third, one-third of 1% of GNP for basic science versus applied science versus classical ("low") technology versus "high" technology.

Where would one get the necessary initial training? Clearly here one would have to rely on the universities and the institutes in the North (or on South-South collaborative programs) for providing the training facilities in the first place. The reliance on foreign help for the training of one's scientists and technicians should diminish as indigenous personnel becomes available and is utilized for this purpose.

For basic sciences, one may also think of the IAEA- and UNESCO-run International Centre for Theoretical Physics (ICTP) or the UNIDO-run International Centres for Genetic Engineering and Biotechnology (ICGEB) or the International Centre for Science (ICS) with its three projected new components, the International Centre for Earth Sciences and the Environment, the International Centre for Chemistry, Pure and Applied, and the International Centre for High Technology and New Materials.

For applied sciences (for example, agriculture), one would think of centers comprising the CGIAR network, *with the training component of these centers emphasized.* There are three centers devoted to research on tropical agriculture (in Colombia, India and Nigeria), a fourth (in Syria) concentrating on agriculture in arid zones, a fifth (in the Philippines) on the cross-breeding of rice, and three on the genetic improvement of cattle (in Ethiopia, Kenya and the Ivory Coast), plus the International Centre for the Potato (in Peru). In addition, there is the center (in Rome) for the conservation of genetic resources, one (in Holland) for the fostering of rural agricultural cooperation, one (in Washington, DC) for the study of nutrition, and, finally, Norman Borlang's world-famous Wheat Institute (CIMMYT) near Mexico City.

This group of thirteen institutes commands a total of $250 million from The World Bank. There is hope that a similar group of regional institutions may be created (in three to five years) for high technology and for the earth's environment with a similar measure of funding by The World Bank and other donor governments.

Table 1. Comparative Expenditure on Science and Technology versus Proposed Funding for Science and High Technology (16% of the Education Budget) by country. Developed Market Economy Countries

	Country	Population (×1,000)	GNP/Capita (US$)	Defence % of GNP	Health % of GNP	Educ. % of GNP	Science and Technology* Actual Expenditure (Millions US$)	16% of Educ. Budget (Millions US$)
1	Iceland	241	10,720	n.a.	6.80	3.50	20.6	19
2	Luxembourg	366	13,380	0.80	0.80	5.65	n.a.	46
3	New Zealand	3,246	7,310	1.90	4.90	4.40	214	184
4	Ireland	3,560	4,840	1.80	7.05	6.70	155	194
5	Norway	4,144	13,890	2.90	6.40	6.80	921	643
6	Israel	4,296	4,920	27.10	3.50	8.40	528	320
7	Finland	4,919	10,870	1.50	5.30	5.50	802	484
8	Denmark	5,101	11,240	2.40	5.80	6.50	688	614
9	Switzerland	6,421	16,380	2.20	5.60	5.00	2,313	828
10	Austria	7,545	9,150	1.20	4.60	5.80	828	648

11	Sweden	8,330	11,890	3.10	9.10	8.00	2,575	1,329
12	Belgium	9,853	8,450	3.10	5.90	5.90	1,166	810
13	Greece	9,937	3,550	7.20	3.60	2.40	71	161
14	Portugal	10,198	1,970	3.50	3.00	4.80	80	182
15	Netherlands	14,486	9,180	3.20	6.70	7.00	2,660	1,504
16	Australia	15,789	10,840	3.20	5.20	6.00	1,880	1,712
17	Canada	25,414	13,670	2.30	6.40	7.40	4,863	3,954
18	South Africa	32,432	2,010	4.00	0.50	2.70	n.a.	360
19	Spain	38,730	4,360	2.40	4.60	2.50	844	736
20	France	55,133	9,550	4.10	6.70	5.30	9,477	4,721
21	United Kingdom	56,539	8,390	5.40	5.40	5.10	9,962	4,041
22	Italy	56,945	6,520	2.70	5.90	5.60	4,084	3,554
23	Germany Fed. Rep.	61,065	10,940	3.30	8.10	4.60	16,701	4,952
24	Japan	120,579	11,330	1.00	4.60	5.10	35,520	10,168
25	United States	238,780	16,400	6.40	4.30	5.00	101,818	29,203

*Note that for Science and Technology, Ireland, Greece and Portugal—the poorest of the "rich" countries—are spending less than 16% of their Education Expenditures. (Desirable expenditures on classical "Low" Technology are not shown in these tables.)

71

Socialist Countries

	Country	Population (x 1,000)	GNP/Capita (US$)	Defence % of GNP	Health % of GNP	Educ. % of GNP	Science and Technology* Actual Expenditure (Millions US$)	16% of Educ. Budget (Millions US$)
1	Albania	2,943	n.a.	4.40	2.60	3.00	n.a.	23
2	Mongolia	1,909	n.a.	10.50	1.40	5.00	n.a.	15
3	Bulgaria	8,980	n.a.	4.00	4.00	6.20	1,429	448
4	Hungary	10,660	n.a.	2.20	2.80	5.00	1,413	500
5	Czechoslovakia	15,497	n.a.	4.00	5.20	5.20	3,533	809
6	German Dem. Rep.	16,716	n.a.	4.90	2.90	4.50	5,099	964
7	Korea Dem. Rep.	20,357	n.a.	10.20	0.90	3.20	n.a.	115
8	Romania	22,866	n.a.	1.40	2.00	2.00	145	260
9	Poland	37,288	2,120	2.50	3.90	3.90	949	1,054
10	Vietnam	61,640	n.a.	n.a.	n.a.	n.a.	n.a.	n.a.
11	USSR	277,563	n.a.	11.50	3.20	4.70	85,054	14,688
12	China P.R.	1,041,094	310	7.00	1.40	2.80	n.a.	1,395

Developing Countries—Populations up to nearly 3 millions

	Country	Population (x 1,000)	GNP/Capita (US$)	Defence % of GNP	Health % of GNP	Educ. % of GNP	Science and Technology* % GNP	Actual Expenditure (Millions US$)	16% of Educ. Budget (Millions US$)
1	Brunei Darussalam	294	17,580	7.90	0.70	2.00	n.a.	n.a.	12
2	Qatar	320	15,980	5.80	n.a.	4.90	n.a.	n.a.	44
3	Bahrain	423	9,560	3.60	2.20	3.30	n.a.	n.a.	25
4	Cyprus	660	3,790	2.40	1.90	3.80	0.1	2.5	15
5	Fiji	702	1,700	1.20	2.70	6.60	n.a.	n.a.	13
6	Gambia	737	230	2.10	3.00	4.40	n.a.	n.a.	1
7	Swaziland	758	650	1.50	1.80	5.80	n.a.	n.a.	6
8	Guyana	806	570	4.80	3.80	7.40	0.2	1	5
9	Guinea Bissau	886	170	n.a.	n.a.	n.a.	n.a.	n.a.	n.a.
10	Gabon	997	3,340	2.10	1.3	4.20	n.a.	n.a.	24
11	Mauritius	1,036	1,070	0.30	2.20	4.20	0.2	2.2	7
12	Botswana	1,070	840	3.30	2.30	8.40	0.2(1975)	1.8	12
13	Oman	1,181	7,080	27.70	2.30	3.70	n.a.	n.a.	44
14	Trinidad & Tobago	1,187	6,010	1.00	1.80	6.00	0.8	57	72
15	United Arab Em.	1,381	19,120	7.40	1.00	1.80	n.a.	n.a.	73
16	Lesotho	1,515	480	2.90	1.30	3.30	n.a.	n.a.	4
17	Mauritania	1,693	410	6.60	1.31	7.33	n.a.	n.a.	8
18	Kuwait	1,736	14,270	5.30	2.40	4.20	0.9	223	182

(continued)

Developing Countries—Populations up to nearly 3 millions

	Country	Population	GNP/Capita	Defence	Health	Educ.	Science and Technology*		16% of Educ.
		(x 1,000)	(US$)	% of GNP	% of GNP	% of GNP	% GNP	Actual Expenditure (Millions US$)	Budget (Millions US$)
19	Congo	1,872	1,020	2.60	1.40	5.40	n.a.	n.a.	18
20	Yemen PDR	2,086	540	17.00	n.a.	7.00	n.a.	n.a.	12
21	Panama	2,180	2,020	2.10	6.30	5.30	0.2(1975)	8.8	35
22	Liberia	2,196	470	2.60	1.80	4.50	n.a.	n.a.	7
23	Jamaica	2,227	940	1.40	3.50	6.40	0.1(1975)	2.1	31
24	Singapore	2,557	7,420	5.70	1.60	5.30	0.5	94.8	158
25	Central African Rep.	2,583	270	2.00	1.10	5.40	0.2	1.5	6
26	Costa Rica	2,593	1,290	0.00	1.44	6.00	0.1	3.3	33

*These are the desirable figures for Science and (Science-based) High Technology alone.
Expenditure on classical "Low" Technology (which, according to the Third World Academy of Sciences (TWAS) estimates, should minimally amount to another 8% of the educational budgets) are not shown explicitly.

74

Developing Countries—Populations from 3 to 10 millions

	Country	Population (x 1,000)	GNP/Capita (US$)	Defence % of GNP	Health % of GNP	Educ. % of GNP	Science and Technology*		16% of Educ. Budget (Millions US$)
							% GNP	Actual Expenditure (Millions US$)	
27	Uruguay	3,004	1,660	2.90	0.90	2.40	0.2(1975)	10	30
28	Togo	3,038	250	2.50	2.20	6.20	1.4(1975)	10.6	7
29	Nicaragua	3,263	850	12.40	4.60	6.00	0.3	8.3	31
30	Lebanon	3,301	1,833	7.30	1.20	5.80	n.a.	n.a.	55
31	Paraguay	3,388	940	1.20	0.60	1.60	0.2(1975)	6.3	10
32	Papua New Guinea	3,499	710	1.70	3.20	6.90	n.a.	n.a.	27
33	Jordan	3,512	1,560	14.10	1.70	7.80	2(1980)	54.8	49
34	Libyan A. Jamahiriya	3,600	7,500	12.90	1.30	3.70	0.2(1982)	45	169
35	Sierra Leone	3,745	370	0.70	1.10	2.60	n.a.	n.a.	7
36	Benin	4,043	270	2.30	1.40	5.00	n.a.	n.a.	8
37	Honduras	4,396	730	5.30	1.70	4.00	n.a.	n.a.	136
38	Burundi	4,696	240	3.50	0.80	3.40	0.4	4.5	6
39	Chad	4,982	n.a.	10.40	0.70	1.80	0.3(1975)	1.8	1
40	Somalia	5,384	270	10.00	0.60	1.60	n.a.	n.a.	6
41	Haiti	5,451	350	1.60	1.00	1.20	n.a.	n.a.	3
42	El Salvador	5,564	710	5.10	1.50	3.00	0.9	35.5	19
43	Rwanda	6,026	290	1.50	0.60	3.10	0.1	4.9	8
44	Guinea	6,049	320	3.10	1.20	3.30	n.a.	n.a.	10

(continued)

Developing Countries—Populations from 3 to 10 millions (cont.)

	Country	Population (x 1,000)	GNP/Capita (US$)	Defence % of GNP	Health % of GNP	Educ. % of GNP	Science and Technology* % GNP	Science and Technology* Actual Expenditure (Millions US$)	16% of Educ. Budget (Millions US$)
45	Dominican Rep.	6,261	810	1.20	1.40	2.00	n.a.	n.a.	20
46	Bolivia	6,383	470	2.60	1.50	4.90	n.a.	n.a.	20
47	Niger	6,391	200	0.80	1.00	2.90	0.1(1975)	1.5	7
48	Senegal	6,558	370	2.80	1.30	4.90	1(1975)	24	19
49	Zambia	6,640	400	4.10	2.10	5.40	0.5(1975)	13.3	29
50	Malawi	7,044	170	1.70	2.30	2.60	0.2(1975)	2.4	5
51	Tunisia	7,143	1,220	5.60	2.60	5.80	n.a.	n.a.	83
52	Mali	7,511	140	4.90	1.50	3.30	n.a.	n.a.	6
53	Burkina Faso	7,885	140	2.70	0.80	2.70	0.5(1975)	5.5	4
54	Yemen Arab Rep.	7,955	520	17.60	1.70	7.00	0.3(1975)	12.4	46
55	Guatemala	7,966	1,240	2.90	0.90	1.80	0.5	49.4	26
56	Zimbabwe	8,406	650	6.20	2.20	7.50	n.a.	n.a.	79
57	Angola	8,756	n.a.	14.20	1.20	5.20	n.a.	n.a.	58
58	Ecuador	9,367	1,160	1.60	1.10	4.10	0.4(1975)	43.50	87

Developing Countries—Populations from 10 to 20 millions

	Country	Population (x 1,000)	GNP/Capita (US$)	Defence % of GNP	Health % of GNP	Educ. % of GNP	Science and Technology* % GNP	Actual Expenditure (Millions US$)	16% of Educ. Budget (Millions US$)
59	Côte d'Ivoire	10,072	620	1.20	1.30	5.00	0.3(1975)	18.7	52
60	Cuba	10,097	1,852	7.10	3.40	6.30	0.7	130.9	193
61	Cameroon	10,191	810	2.00	1.00	3.50	0.8(1988)	49.5	48
62	Madagascar	10,312	250	2.40	2.20	3.80	0.20(1980)	5.1	17
63	Syrian Arab Rep.	10,483	1,630	16.60	0.40	6.10	n.a.	n.a.	161
64	Saudi Arabia	11,521	8,860	21.70	3.10	7.80	n.a.	n.a.	1,299
65	Chile	11,990	1,440	4.20	2.70	4.80	0.4(1980)	68.50	172
66	Ghana	12,710	390	0.60	0.80	1.50	0.9(1975)	44.6	15
67	Uganda	15,474	n.a.	1.10	0.20	1.30	n.a.	n.a.	13
68	Malaysia	15,611	2,050	5.60	1.20	6.10	n.a.	n.a.	309
69	Iraq	15,654	1,861	50.00	0.80	3.40	0.1(1975)	27	152
70	Sri Lanka	16,143	370	1.70	1.30	2.80	0.2	11.9	29
71	Nepal	16,527	160	1.30	0.80	2.70	n.a.	n.a.	11
72	Venezuela	17,323	3,110	1.60	2.00	6.20	0.4	215	629
73	Mozambique	17,791	n.a.	4.80	0.80	1.90	n.a.	n.a.	17
74	Peru	18,653	960	6.90	1.10	2.90	0.2	35.8	95

Developing Countries—Populations from 20 to 50 millions

	Country	Population (x 1,000)	GNP/Capita (US$)	Defence % of GNP	Health % of GNP	Educ. % of GNP	Science and Technology* % GNP	Science and Technology* Actual Expenditure (Millions US$)	16% of Educ. Budget (Millions US$)
75	Kenya	20,375	290	4.10	2.10	6.00	0.8(1975)	47.2	61
76	Algeria	21,865	2,530	1.80	1.40	4.70	0.3(1975)	165.9	401
77	Morocco	21,924	610	5.60	1.00	7.20	n.a.	n.a.	156
78	Sudan	21,931	330	3.30	0.20	4.70	0.2(1980)	26.7	66
79	United Rep. Tanzania	22,242	270	3.30	1.40	3.30	n.a.	n.a.	37
80	Yugoslavia	23,100	2,070	3.70	4.10	3.50	n.a.	382	381
81	Colombia	28,418	1,320	1.40	0.80	3.10	0.1	37.5	230
82	Argentina	30,531	2,130	2.50	1.40	4.15	0.5(1980)	325	483
83	Zaire	30,557	170	1.20	0.40	3.50	n.a.	n.a.	48
84	Burma	36,831	190	3.60	1.00	2.00	n.a.	n.a.	21
85	Korea Rep.	40,646	2,180	5.40	0.30	4.80	1.1	886	654
86	Ethiopia	42,271	110	9.30	1.40	3.00	n.a.	n.a.	22
87	Iran Islamic Rep.	45,160	1,778	13.30	1.60	7.50	0.5(1975)	401.4	966
88	Egypt Arab Rep.	47,108	710	8.50	1.20	4.30	0.2	67	236
89	Turkey	49,406	1,130	4.80	0.60	3.30	0.6(1980)	335	n.a.

Developing Countries—Populations from 50 to over 100 millions

	Country	Population (x 1,000)	GNP/Capita (US$)	Defence % of GNP	Health % of GNP	Educ. % of GNP	Science and Technology*		16% of Educ. Budget (Millions US$)
							% GNP	Actual Expenditure (Millions US$)	
90	Thailand	50,950	830	4.00	1.10	4.10	0.3	126.80	268
91	Philippines	54,725	600	1.80	0.70	1.80	0.2	65.67	91
92	Mexico	78,820	2,080	0.70	0.40	2.60	0.6	983.6	985
93	Pakistan	94,933	380	6.00	0.40	1.80	0.2(1980)	72.1	109
94	Nigeria	99,669	760	1.80	0.60	2.00	0.3(1980)	227.2	241
95	Bangladesh	100,592	150	1.70	0.40	1.80	0.2(1975)	30.2	43
96	Brazil	135,539	1,640	0.80	1.60	4.00	0.6	1,333.7	1,242
97	Indonesia	162,212	530	3.90	0.60	3.40	0.3	257.9	549
98	India	765,147	250	3.20	0.90	3.10	0.9	1,721	1,004

In the population range of 20 millions upwards, it is to be noted that Argentina, the Republic of Korea, Turkey, Mexico, Brazil and India are the only countries where the actual science expenditures are higher than 16% of their education budgets—the desirable minimum for developing countries recommended by TWAS (Third World Academy of Sciences).

Population and GNP/Capita figures are from "World Bank Atlas 1987" and refer to 1985; Defence, Health and Education figures are from "World Military & Social Expenditures 1987–88" and refer to 1984; Science (% of GNP and Expenditure) are from "UNESCO Statistical Digest 1987" and generally refer to 1984 or 1985—the tables show the year referred to when no figures for 1984 or 1985 are available.

79

Designing a Science-Led Future for Africa: A Suggested Science and Technology Policy Framework

Thomas R. Odhiambo

Africa is tremendously rich in resources—in natural resources, in minerals, in water (84% of which goes to the seas surrounding the continent), and in youth. What Africa is desperately poor in is a coherent policy framework for a long-range effort in fusing its perceived science and technology (S&T) needs with its national development plans within this highly fragmented continent and presently fragile economy. But, basically, it is not a poor continent: It is impoverished in ideas and implementation energies.

The economic and development crisis that gripped Africa during the whole of the 1980s, but which has been discernible since the beginning of the 1970s—barely a decade after the attainment of political independence in most of the continent—has elicited a strong movement toward regional economic and development integration. This can be seen from the Lagos Plan of Action for the Economic Development of Africa 1980-2000, which was adopted by the Assembly of Heads of State and Government of the Organization of Africa Unity (OAU) at a special session held in Lagos, Nigeria, in April 1980.[1]

The Lagos Plan of Action was complemented by the Final Act of Lagos, the principal thrust of which was to overcome the handicaps presented by the post-independence economic fragmentation, deepened by the rise of numerous mini-states on the continent through the encouragement of sub-regional economic cooperation and integration. Nearly ten years later, a similar refrain is still predominant.

In early 1988, the African Development Bank, headquartered in Abidjan, Côte d'Ivoire, appointed a task force, later dubbed "the Committee of Ten," in order to "be primarily responsible for evaluating the results recorded by the Bank and the programmes it projects, and to give an independent opinion on the most suitable policies to be adopted for enhancing and strengthening the impact of the Bank's operations in the future."

The Report of the Committee of Ten, published in March 1989, expressed its conviction that the African economies must move deliberately toward inte-

Thomas R. Odhiambo is Founding Fellow and President of the African Academy of Sciences and Director of the International Centre of Insect Physiology and Ecology in Nairobi. He is also a Founding Fellow and Vice President of the Third World Academy of Sciences. Born in 1931 in Kenya, Dr. Odhiambo has received many awards and has authored many publications during the course of his career.

80

gration not as a "distant dream," but as "an urgent necessity."[2] It said, in part:

> The trading world of the future may be a world of trading blocs. A consolidated Europe in 1992, the US-Canada Free Trade Area, the Australia-New Zealand Free Trade Agreement, and a new economic bloc in Asia and the Far East may seek to dominate the trading scene by the time Uruguay Round Agreement goes into effect. The implication is that, whatever the terms of the Uruguay Round, these trading blocs would be in a stronger position to defend their interests, and to claim advantage and exceptions on the grounds of regional economic integration. The real losers would be those areas (Africa included) where the process of economic integration is yet to be fully consolidated.

Furthermore, in the same year, the United Nations Economic Commission for Africa (ECA), in advancing a major policy framework designed to meet the needs of structural adjustment with a human-centered development ethos, published, in June 1989, an important document which highlights the issue of collective self-reliance (meaning regional economic integration) as a central element in this framework.

> The political balkanisation of the continent into arbitrary nation-states elicits from Africa the understandable impulse to restructure the fragmented region into a more coherent and stronger economic and political entity. The African sense of oneness and solidarity also sparks off natural sentiments for increased socioeconomic cooperation. At the economic level, the numerous obstacles to genuine development that individual African countries confront as a result of their limited and fragmented economic space have provided an objective rationale and galvanized the African resolve to pursue and achieve the goal of collective self-reliance. Overall, Africa sees self-reliance as both the goal and the means through which the region will eventually find its true identity, full dignity, and historic strength. It is also the goal and the means by which the region will find the capacity to master its resources, its development, and its future.

Regional economic integration, human resource development, and institutional capacity-building have become recurring themes as instruments to rehabilitating Africa's shattered dreams which unfolded during the heady days of political independence in the early 1960s, of continental economic vigor and social rehabilitation and development.

FUTURE GOALS

The future-oriented goals stemming from these resurrected development dreams are succinctly highlighted by the ECA report as follows:[3]

> It should be emphasized that the urgency of alleviating mass poverty and of increasing the welfare of the African people is rooted not simply in the humanistic or altruistic aspects of development. It is predicated, above all, on the rational proposition that development has to be engineered and sustained by the people themselves through their full and active partici-

pation. Development should not be undertaken on behalf of a people; rather, it should be the organic outcome of a society's value system, its perceptions, its concerns, and its endeavours. As such, to achieve and sustain development, it is necessary to ensure the education and training, health, well-being, and vitality of the people so that they can participate fully in the development process.

The roots of a regional approach to a science-led development in Africa were laid down by the then metropolitan powers less than a decade before political independence. The rationale and spirit of this movement is captured well by E. B. Worthington in his book, *Science in the Development of Africa,* prepared in 1958 on behalf of the Commission for Technical Cooperation in Africa South of the Sahara (CCTA) and the Scientific Council for Africa South of the Sahara (CSA). He argued that:[4]

> In the competitive world of the 20th century, it is difficult for any small country to be independent of its neighbors and at the same time provide the requirements of modern civilization for its people, unless it is un- usually well endowed with natural and human resources. This principle has special force in Africa where local conditions have led to economic specialization, not merely in one major industry, such as agriculture or mining, but in particular sections of it, such as cotton, cocoa or copper. Any measures for pooling the resources of neighboring countries with different specialties lead to all-around advantage in reducing the eco- nomic risks. As in economics, so in science, considerable specialization has taken place in different territories, so that collaboration, or even a full exchange of information, could give great benefits.

The CCTA, with headquarters in London, UK, was established in 1950 by six colonial governments then operating in Africa: Belgium, the UK, France, Portugal, the Federation of Rhodesia and Nyasaland, and the Union of South Africa. A similar initiative by scientists from these countries led to the creation of the CSA (with headquarters in Bukavu, Zaire) in the same year. Thus, the two organizations sprang from two distinct roots: the CCTA for mutual assis- tance by the metropolitan powers as they related to the economies of their colonial territories, and the CSA for scientific cooperation and consultation as a result of the expressed wishes of the scientists working in those territories. But the two agencies came to work closely and in concert.

The CCTA functioned principally at the managerial policy and resource al- location level and, therefore, concerned itself with all matters affecting techni- cal cooperation between the member governments and their territories. On the other hand, the CSA acted as the principal scientific and technical adviser of the CCTA, since it possessed specialist competence in science policy develop- ment and implementation. The CSA accomplished this major task through the study of what research projects of common interest could be usefully suggested to the member governments concerned and to institutes or agencies for re- search; through the maintenance of close relations with the inter-governmental scientific and technical bureaus which existed or could be created in Africa (such as the Inter-African Bureau of Epizootic Diseases, the Tsetse Fly and Trypanosomiasis Permanent Inter-African Bureau, the Inter-African Labour Institute, and the Inter-African Pedological Service); and to facilitate the exchange and movement of scientific workers between the different territories and countries concerned and, if necessary, to advise on their training.

THE LOSS OF THE COLONIAL IMPETUS

The colonial impetus for regional science policy and implementation did not long survive the demise of the colonial era. The successful regional research and development (R&D) organizations established on the continent, largely for export-oriented commodities such as tea, coffee, cocoa, palm oil, fisheries and cotton, or those for tropical and animal diseases (malaria, bilharzia, and tsetse and trypanosomiasis), or for industrial R&D and consultancy, did not survive for more than a decade or so after independence.

The centrifugal forces became too great, and these vital scientific organizations broke up into small, national units lacking a critical mass of experienced scientists, unable to attract and retain first-class scientists. In a different direction, the CCTA and the CSA became transformed, in 1962, into OAU organs, and they became pan-African in nature—as the OAU is—with the latter consciously asserting that the successor organization to CCTA (the so-called Scientific, Technical and Research Commission—STRC) would become "an instrument of African solidarity" and "a bridge between Europe's science and Africa's needs." Perhaps the latter statement contains the seeds of the special nature of the African crisis: that of the noninvolvement of science and technology (S&T) in an integral manner in national and regional development. Rather S&T has been regarded as a product or service to be purchased or transferred on Africa's behalf by the donor agencies.

The fact is that the STRC is little known outside a small circle of dedicated specialists and governmental planners in Africa: It lacks presence and credibility in its present operational state; its advice only rarely draws attention; and, therefore, it has ceased to be an effective inter-governmental organ for technical cooperation in Africa.

The SCA (the Scientific Council of Africa), the successor science advisory body to the CSA, is even less known: It is moribund, having met only twice in the 1980s; it does not possess a central core of program concerns or S&T policy, nor can it be said to be an advisory and consultative body that can proffer coherent advice to the STRC or any other important development group in Africa. In essence, the STRC and the SCA have operated within OAU almost rudderless, with the principal guiding yardstick being provided by budget and audit processes.

Yet the OAU has demonstrated its efficacy as a unique forum for Africa's geopolitical leadership to work closely in resolving the continent's major development problems, peace and security issues, and economic integration. The

forum has the potential for forging a common front with the continent's R&D
leadership, especially on its development agenda.

POLICY FRAMEWORK FOR
FUTURE-ORIENTED DEVELOPMENT

The scientific community in Africa—small as it is and unsure of itself as it has
grown to be over the years—has more responsibility for the future of Africa
than any other such community in recent history here or anywhere else. At
least three responsibilities face it: the task of promoting R&D as a means of
bringing technology into the mainstream of national development planning; the
responsibility to develop new frontiers of scientific research and technological
development which would directly respond to Africa's singularly difficult problems, particularly in the natural resources field; and the forging of a new partnership between the African scientific community and the African geopolitical
leadership so as to create an enabling environment for the growth of a science-
led development process and for operationalizing the emergent political will for
the latter.

The sense of doom that has descended over Africa during most of the 1980s
is incompatible with the new science/geopolitical partnership that has become
an imperative for Africa's future if it is to pull itself out of the present serious
developmental predicament—even if this gloom can be understood in its historical context:[5]

> The disruption of Africa's cultural autonomy as a result of colonialism,
> and the continued imposition of foreign world-views on the continent
> since then, have had tremendous negative impact on the African psyche.
> First, the neobalkanisation of Africa is continuing to undermine the Pan-
> African ideal and the perception of Africans themselves. Second, the
> continued misrepresentation of African culture and history have ignored
> Africa's quantum achievements: Where are the African heroes? How did
> they see the future? To what extent are they an inspiration to our youth?
> Third, the sociocultural lenses through which Africa views her past and
> her present predicament, including the use and challenges of science and
> technology, must be indigenous and appropriate, not borrowed and in-
> applicable . . . all these, and more, draw down a pall over the future of
> Africa as a continent with a destiny and a hope. This was not always so.

One cannot deny that Africa's diaspora and the colonial interlude have left
deep physical and psychic scars. But Africa must catch up with its future.

What shape should Africa's willed future take? The Special Commission on
Africa, a think-tank within the African Academy of Sciences, believes that the
new paradigm should regard inventive and innovative entrepreneurship, as expressed by African indigenous peoples, as the prime mover of the social and
economic transformation of Africa. Africa should seek to nourish and reward
such entrepreneurship. Such a long-range thrust requires a measure of personal,
group and national self-confidence, just as it will require the recognition of the

vital importance of domestic, multinational and regional markets as the main source of demand stimuli.[5]

In this respect, Africa has been negligent in—and also, in many senses, afraid of—having the accomplished scientist operate at the political-scientific interphase. Yet this ambivalence of ability to operate as a scientist-politician is a quality now in sharp, urgent demand in Africa as never before.

THE SEVEN DESTINATIONS OF SCIENTISTS

Carl Sinderman (1985) distinguished seven destinations of scientists in the industrial world: the research scientist, the scientist-educator, the scientist-administrator, the scientist-bureaucrat, the scientist-politician, the scientist-entrepreneur, and the international scientist.[6] The least-known and the most controversial of these is the scientist-politician. Scientist-politicians "function in the murky territory between politics and the practice of science," and thus attempt to influence politico-economic decisions on behalf of their disciplines, agencies or groups. Even though their roles can lead to some kind of uneasiness, the skillful and concerned scientist-politicians could become a necessity to the promotion of science-led development in Africa. As Sinderman has characterized them:

> (the scientist-politicians) are strategists who plan and analyze any significant activity. They are public relations conscious, examining the effects of their actions on colleagues and on that part of the population which might be interested or affected. They are manipulative, taking full advantage of external opinions and opportunities to shape future activities. They are gregarious, seeking the company and companionship of colleagues and others in positions of power or accomplishment, regardless of their fields of expertise. They are self-assured, acting like professionals and expecting to be treated as such. They have high internal feelings of self-worth and accomplishment, and project these feelings. They have excellent analytical and synthetic abilities, which often transcend their own areas of expertise.

The African Academy of Sciences and the International Centre of Insect Physiology and Ecology (ICIPE), both headquartered in Nairobi, Kenya, have taken the unusual step of working together to create a private, but Africa-wide environment in which three communities can interact and interphase over a sufficiently long time in order to forge a new partnership: the geopolitical leadership, the scientific leadership, and the industrial-financial community.

The two institutions convened a consultative meeting in November 1988 at which the three communities were brought together under a Program on the Management of Science for Development in Africa (MANSCI). The goal of the program is "to consciously create a long-term vision for Africa, in which the social and economic development of Africa will be science-led." It intends to reach its goal through planning, dialogue and advocacy. The success of this consultative meeting can be gauged by the fact that a continuing committee was selected, the so-called Future Actions Committee, led by General Olusegun Obasanjo, former Head of State of Nigeria, and Professor Lydia Makhubu, a professional chemist and Vice Chancellor of the University of Swaziland, with the program's secretariat being based in Nairobi.

The Future Actions Committee has taken up its mandate vigorously, and is planning the assembly of a high-level science summit in September 1990 in Nairobi, intended to commit national leaders to a practical plan for the implementation of a science and technology policy tailored to the rapid rehabilitation and development of Africa. The task before MANSCI and its Future Actions Committee is immense, as can be measured by an introductory address to the November 1988 meeting:[7]

> (since independence in Africa) we have erected stifling barriers and constraints that have all but snuffed out any emerging growth points in science and technology; we have strenuously attempted to build up an African culture from which the vital component of science is divorced; and we have kept our small struggling science enterprise in a separate compartment from all other factors necessary for economic development.

The geopolitical leadership needs to provide the enabling environment to begin to remove the major constraints to science-led development. The policy framework conducive to innovative science and technology and agro-industrial entrepreneurship and a strong sense of political will that transcends the normal state of poverty in most of Africa must be established. The industrial-financial community needs to shed its tunnel view of concentrating almost entirely on the export trade, while neglecting the domestic and intra-African trade potentials, and it should create the necessary instruments for the effective mobilization of venture capital on a regional basis. The science and technology leadership should make apparent the potential benefits of R&D to the people in their neighborhoods, at the national level, and at the multinational regional level.

CAPACITY BUILDING

In the past two years, a recurring theme in designing new mechanisms for Africa's development is the question of capacity building. In an incisive—but wide-ranging—symposium, jointly convened by the ICIPE Foundation, the African Academy of Sciences, and the US National Academy of Sciences in March 1988 at the Rockefeller Foundation Conference Center in Bellagio, Italy, on the theme, "Scientific Institution Building in Africa," the meeting recognized the following distinguishing features of the science capacities prevailing in Africa today:[8]

- The traditional system of S&T education through guilds and apprenticeships was superseded during the colonial period by the formal, white-collar oriented education, which has resulted in most young Africans being "stranded mid-way between traditions to which they cannot wholly return, and a modern, science-based society at which they have not yet arrived."

- The national educational systems are now, in these times of deficit economy, not able to foster excellence, nor to reward innovation and achievement. The teachers are poorly paid, poorly trained, and overworked; learning is often by rote, and science and mathematics are short in quality and of low relevance.
- The national research systems have a narrow focus and "have primarily aimed at short-term solutions to specific problems, rather than at strengthening African capabilities to solve generic problems."

A SPECIAL COMMITMENT

Undoubtedly, Africa must make a special commitment to begin at the beginning—to inculcate a new sense of intellectual space for the African child, and to recreate the social environment which would allow the African mother to build a worthwhile home for future young African adults. Mothers and their children must be freed from the tyranny of a frozen traditional knowledge base by adding new elements to this strong social foundation and thereby updating and bringing this social knowledge to a relevant present. Enlarging and updating this mother-child universe, without cluttering it with the debris of other cultures, is a challenge of the first order for concerned Africans wherever they live.

Even though, in the recent past, the promotion of the idea of capacity building was frowned upon in Africa by the donor community, the Africans and their governments have consistently espoused the cause of institution building and human resource development. It is part of the reason that African educational programs consume 35% or more of the national budgets.

The problem of capacity building can no longer be tackled piecemeal or in a fragmented time-scale. It needs a coherent regional perspective, as well as a long-term commitment to the cause. In its long-term planning for the years 1992-2000, the African Development Bank has boldly suggested that an endowment fund—with an initial sum of US$500 million—should be set up to provide some one hundred professional positions at its headquarters in Abidjan, and at least another 150 professional positions located in carefully selected centers of excellence in Africa in order to provide the intellectual resources to design and advance growth-promoting policies and programs which would assist the process of economic integration in Africa.[2]

Hard on the heels of the bank's proposal has come a similar but larger proposal from the Independent Group on Financial Flows to Developing Countries, reporting in June 1989,[9] which argues that the OECD countries should establish an endowment fund of US $1 billion, to be administered by the African Development Bank. The fund would be used to develop African leadership in policy-making and in professional, technological and managerial sectors, in order to confront on a systematic and informed basis the pressing and over-whelming crisis the continent is facing today.

Finally, The World Bank, in its recent report on Africa, released in October 1989, has drawn particular attention to the creation of regional centers of excellence and the need for forging new cooperative linkages between African R&D institutions and qualified firms and research institutes in the developed countries, as well as the imperative of urgent improvement of Africa's science and technology training, while aiming at the highest standards of achievement.[10]

Other persons and institutions are beginning to talk vaguely of a "Marshall Plan" for Africa. There is no doubt, taking all these various initiatives into careful consideration, that a powerful message is beginning to crystallize, that an indigenous capacity to innovate and to implement a science-led development in Africa, quite separate from the on-going and worthwhile technical assistance effort, is the single most important ingredient of a sustainable development progress in Africa.

The African Academy of Sciences has taken the question of capacity building and the mobilization of scientific talent for the development agenda as its most important task. Thus, its general objective is to identify outstanding scientific talents within the continent, to promote the utilization of these talents in national development, and to encourage a meeting of the minds between the scientific community and the political leadership as partners in the development process.

This mandate has been translated, among other initiatives, into a program on the Mobilization and Strengthening of the African Scientific Community, through networking, internship training projects, development of a data bank on African scientific institutions, etc. The rationale for this intensive beam on the issue of capacity building is dramatically highlighted by Sinderman in these words:[6]

> The scientist . . . is far more than a laboratory-bound stereotype. His or her career destinations are diverse, interesting, and absorbing, but the base remains the same—productive, innovative, relevant research and teaching. Beyond this base . . . are career extensions . . . whether they be managerial, political, or entrepreneurial . . . most readily available to excellent scientists—those who have established credibility and have succeeded in the practice of science.

As we enter the closing decade of the twentieth century, the song of Africa should not be a lament for a lost century; it should be the beginnings of an epic story of how Africa is girding itself to recover its previously lost impetus for growth and development in a scientific area.

NOTES

1. Organization of African Unit, *The Lagos Plan of Action for the Economic Development of Africa 1980-2000* (Addis Ababa: OAU, 1980).

2. African Development Bank (Committee of Ten), *Africa and the African Development Bank: Current and Future Challenges* (Abidjan: African Development Bank, 1989).

3. United Nations Economic Commission for Africa, *African Alternative Framework to Structural Adjustment Programmes for Socio-Economic Recovery and Transformation* (AAF SAP) (Addis Ababa: UN Economic Commission for Africa, 1989).

4. E. B. Worthington, *Science in the Development of Africa* (London: Commission for Technical Cooperation in Africa South of the Sahara, 1958).

5. Thomas R. Odhiambo, *Hope Born Out of Despair: Managing the African Crisis* (Nairobi: Heinemann Kenya Ltd., 1988).

6. C. J. Sinderman, *The Joy of Science: Excellence and Its Rewards* (New York: Plenum Press, 1985).

7. Thomas R. Odhiambo, "Welcoming and Introductory Address" in Thomas R. Odhiambo and T. T. Isoun, eds., *Science for Development in Africa* (Nairobi: ICIPE Science Press and Academy Science Publishers, 1989).

8. International Centre of Insect Physiology and Ecology, *Scientific Institution Building in Africa* (Nairobi: ICIPE Science Press, 1988).

9. H. Schmidt, *Facing One World: Report of an Independent Group on Financial Flows to Developing Countries* (Tokyo: United Nations University, 1989).

10. The World Bank, *Sub-Saharan Africa: From Crisis to Sustainable Growth—A Long-Term Perspective Study* (Washington, DC: The World Bank, 1989).

COUNTRY CHAPTERS

Science and Technology Advice in Australia

G. J. V. Nossal

THE COMMONWEALTH OF AUSTRALIA, *originally a member of the Common-wealth of Nations, became a federal state in 1901 under a democratic parliamentary system of government. Its land area is 2,966,136 square miles, and its estimated population in 1989 was 16,640,000. The official language of the country is English. As of December 31, 1989, the US dollar was equal to 1.27 Australian dollars.*

Science and technology are shaping human affairs to a degree that seems to be still on the increase. For that reason, scientific advice to the highest levels of government is of crucial importance, and Australia has given a great deal of thought and effort to the question of how advice should be structured. The system that has evolved seems to be working reasonably well, and may contain some valuable lessons for other countries.

BACKGROUND

Australia follows the Westminster system of government with a bicameral legislature, the political party with the majority in the lower house, the House of Representatives, forming the government. Executive power, in practice, rests with the ministers, who—unlike the system in the United States—are elected politicians.

Ministers are divided into senior ministers, constituting the Cabinet (effectively, the administration), and junior ministers, each of whom assists a senior minister with his or her portfolio. The idea, which does not always work out in practice, is that the senior minister is chiefly responsible for policy issues and is the chief parliamentary spokesperson, and that the junior minister deals with administrative matters within the department.

The government is backed by a large public service, and a minister normally

Sir Gustav Nossal, M.D., is Director of the Walter and Eliza Hall Institute of Medical Research at the Royal Melbourne Hospital and Professor of medical biology at the University of Melbourne. Born in Bad Ischl, Austria, in 1931, he also holds a Ph.D. and specializes in fundamental immunology on which he has written five books and 350 scientific papers. Sir Gustav is also interested in the interface between science and society, and has been a consultant to the World Health Organization, member of the Australian Science and Technology Council and the council of the Australian Academy of Science. He currently serves as a member of the board of the Commonwealth Scientific and Industrial Research Organization. He has received numerous honors from the United Kingdom, United States, the Federal Republic of Germany, France, India and Israel, including Fellowship in The Royal Society of London and Foreign Associate of the US National Academy of Sciences.

gets the advice of this (theoretically) apolitical and tenured bureaucracy via a permanent head of his or her department.

Australia is a federation of six states and two territories, the states also having Parliaments and ministers of a basically similar pattern. While science and technology policy is chiefly a federal matter, the states have substantial interests as well, and get involved, particularly in the more applied areas. This essay, however, will be confined to the federal arena.

Science and technology are all-pervasive in modern society and, therefore, many portfolios have significant science content. For example, defense and telecommunications are technology-intensive, and Australia's large primary industry sector depends heavily on research. Nevertheless, it would be fair to say that three Departments of State have the greatest direct interest in science and technology policy, namely: Industry, Technology and Commerce, which embraces the former Department of Science; Education, with its responsibility for universities and institutes of technology; and Community Services and Health, which looks after medical research.

THE AUSTRALIAN SCIENCE AND TECHNOLOGY COUNCIL

After the insistent urging of the Australian Academy of Science and a lengthy period of work under interim status, the Fraser Government set up ASTEC, the Australian Science and Technology Council, in 1977, under an Act of Parliament. The key features of ASTEC are essentially threefold: It reports directly to the Prime Minister; it is made up entirely of part-time members independent of the bureaucracy and appointed for their personal qualities rather than for the interests they represent; and it is serviced by a small, elite secretariat of bureaucrats who owe no allegiance to any department of state. Each of these crucial features deserves comment.

Under successive governments, the Department of the Prime Minister and the Cabinet has come to have an extremely powerful policy role. By the very nature of his position, the Prime Minister must become involved in all high matters of state, and, therefore, so must the public servants advising the Prime Minister. Furthermore, the department controls the Cabinet agenda, providing further leverage. Under the ASTEC legislation, all spending proposals or other initiatives deemed to have a significant component of science and technology and of substantial size, *must* be referred to ASTEC for comment.

This involvement of "outsiders" in the Cabinet process caused quite a flutter in the dovecote at first, but—at ASTEC's own insistence—is now rigorously observed, giving ASTEC considerable influence. Its advice comes in the form of briefing notes to the Prime Minister and/or written coordination comments on a Cabinet submission. Of course, this does not mean that ASTEC advice prevails on every occasion, but its record of "wins" is significant. ASTEC members are strongly of the view that this adherence to the Prime Minister (rather than the Minister for Science or any other minister) is critical to its success.

The part-time members of ASTEC usually number about twelve, with a chairman who is expected to spend half his time (or more) on ASTEC business. There have been only three chairmen of ASTEC since it assumed its definitive form, namely: Sir Geoffrey Badger, former Vice Chancellor of the University of Adelaide; Professor Ralph Slatyer, Director of the Research School of Biological Sciences of the Australian National University; and Professor Ray Martin, former Vice Chancellor of Monash University and a distinguished inorganic chemist.

Each person developed a close working relationship with Malcolm Fraser or Robert Hawke. There is no doubt that each became an influential independent adviser to the government of the day. None of these individuals was appointed for political reasons, and this pattern is expected to continue into the future.

The other part-time members of ASTEC include leading academics, industrialists from both primary and other sectors, economists, and trade union leaders. Overall, a high standard in selection has been maintained, with canvassing of names from a wide spectrum and a detailed Prime Ministerial input into the final choices.

Obviously, any committee of part-timers needs the support of an effective secretariat, and here ASTEC has been very fortunate. Under Roy Green and then Bruce Middleton and now Greg Tegart, a first-class, small team of professionals has been assembled, with a sufficient throughput of talent to avoid rigidification. There is a broad perception that, if a bureaucrat does well in ASTEC, promotion to another position in another department will likely follow, and this is a source of great strength. Inevitably, as ASTEC's responsibilities and influence have grown, so, too, has its staff, and there is a conscious effort to ensure that the atmosphere of "just another government department" does not develop.

HOW ASTEC WORKS

Committees—and academics, in particular—are not noted for fast response capacity. Yet, the political process is such that many matters brook little delay. ASTEC has accommodated itself to this constraint by a clever device. Where a fast response is required, the secretariat and the chairman collaborate on a briefing note, not from ASTEC, but from the chairman of ASTEC, embodying what the chairman believes that the ASTEC response would be. At the next meeting, ASTEC then has a chance to review the advice and to endorse it or, if necessary, to modify it, which, fortunately, is virtually never necessary.

It would be a pity to give the impression that ASTEC was purely reactive. Indeed, on many occasions, ASTEC is proactive, identifying areas that it wishes to investigate itself without being asked. The Prime Minister is informed of these initiatives as a matter of courtesy and, with very few exceptions, welcomes ASTEC's involvement. Some of the most forward-looking governmental initiatives in Australian science have started in this way. Substantial ASTEC reports are tabled in the Parliament and are then in the public domain, even though, of course, specific advice on particular Cabinet matters must, of necessity, be confidential. ASTEC goes to great lengths, however, to ensure that its positions are open to public scrutiny and criticism as much as possible.

Obviously, in the real world, it would be counterproductive if ASTEC's advice consistently ran counter to the advice that the ministers receive from their own departments. A strategem to ensure that this does not happen has evolved. Drafts of ASTEC position papers are circulated within the bureaucracy, allowing the departments to know what is in the wind and permitting departmental input either in writing or, frequently, orally directed to ASTEC. On matters that are less urgent, the process can be iterative, with an initiative surfacing on several occasions. This wide consultation materially increases the chances of reaching consensus. Sometimes it also reveals the wide gulf between different departments of state on major policy issues!

Much of ASTEC's work is done by subcommittees that debate and refine issues between the monthly meetings. One of the most important of these is the Technological Change Committee which monitors the impact of technological change on employment, work practices, education, and so forth. Often subcommittees are *ad hoc,* and individuals from outside ASTEC are almost always drafted to help with the work. With rare exceptions, an officer of the secretariat will service the subcommittee ensuring that recommendations are processed in an acceptable form.

ASTEC'S CRITICS

It would be foolish to pretend that ASTEC has no critics. Some department heads obviously see ASTEC as encroaching on their most important and cherished work area, namely policy formulation. Some believe sincerely that a minister responsible for science and technology is weakened because ASTEC does not report to him. Some feel that the chairman must become so involved in political decision-making that ASTEC's independence is thereby compromised. Some consider that ASTEC should be concerned only with long-term strategic issues and should eschew involvement in the budgetary process and detailed priority setting.

No pattern will please everyone. Having had eight years of service successively on the interim ASTEC and the definitive body, however, under both Labor and Liberal/National Party governments, this author has come to have a great regard for the system and its value to the nation.

THE PRIME MINISTER'S SCIENCE COUNCIL

In 1989, a further major step was taken to raise the profile of science in Australia and to involve the most important ministers in science issues in a very direct way. This was the creation of the Prime Minister's Science Council. This body meets only twice or, at the most, thrice per year, for half a day or a day, in the Cabinet room. It is chaired by the Prime Minister personally, and senior ministers involved in science and technology are required to attend as full members.

In fact, the make-up of the council is interesting. Apart from the six ministers, there is the Chief Scientist (currently Ralph Slatyer, a former head of ASTEC); the chairman of ASTEC; the chief executive of the large national scientific and industrial research organization (CSIRO); five managing directors of corporations; a trade union representative; and three academics (a systems engineer, a mathematician, and a medical scientist, namely, myself). In marked contrast to ASTEC, the council is designed to have a high media visibility and to take up individual issues, such as the greenhouse effect, the commercialization of Australian research, or science education in schools, one by one and in a somewhat *ad hoc* manner.

Part of the purpose is to create a climate in Australia in which lay people and the politicians themselves come to take science much more seriously as a vital ingredient of national life. Balancing this highly visible and perhaps, in some senses, superficial exercise is an important bureaucratic structure.

The Chief Scientist is to chair the Coordination Committee on Science and Technology. This group of officials will meet to ensure maximum collaboration and communication between all the many organs of government involved in research. As it will delve into policy issues as well as administrative ones, there is a slight concern that it might venture onto ASTEC's turf, a risk that is not as great for the Science Council itself, with its obvious flag-waving function.

These possible demarcation disputes will simply have to be nipped in the bud by discussions between the Chairman of ASTEC, Ray Martin, and the Chief Scientist, Ralph Slatyer. As both are mature and wise leaders with decades of senior experience on the Australian science scene, no problems are foreseen in this regard.

THE LEARNED ACADEMIES

In the United States, the National Academy of Sciences represents a powerhouse of independent advice on a wide range of subjects. Prior to the establishment of ASTEC and its interim predecessor committee, the Australian Academy of Science played a similar role, although with much less staff support. Given the wider role of the academy in its traditional fields of promotion of international relations in science, science education, and the maintenance of scientific excellence, the academy was, in fact, the main driving force for the establishment of ASTEC, and many ASTEC members have been Fellows of the academy with experience on its council. Now that ASTEC is established, the leverage of the academy as such in the science policy field is less than

before, but its voice is still heard with respect. It can now afford to concentrate
on longer term issues.

One venture of particular value has been the Science and Industry Forum,
where academics and industry leaders meet twice per year for one or one-and-
a-half days to discuss vital policy issues. By the very nature of its democratic
processes, the academy cannot move quickly on issues, but rather must research them to their deep fundamentals, so the demarcation between its functions and ASTEC's is really a fairly natural one.

In the 1970s, a second academy was formed: the Australian Academy of
Technological Sciences and Engineering, roughly equivalent to the US National
Academy of Engineering. It has been very effective in promoting technology-
related issues, being responsible, for example, for helping in the emergence of
tax concessions for investors in research-based, venture capital-dependent companies, and in suggesting an integrated space policy for Australia. Although
the National Research Council (NAS-NAE-IOM) concept does not exist in
Australia, relations between the two academies are good and collaboration is
quite extensive.

CSIRO

Australia has a unique science-based organization called the Commonwealth
Scientific and Industrial Research Organization (CSIRO), which is funded about
75% by the government and about 25% by client groups, the latter component
being on the increase, giving it a total budget of about A$400 million per year.

CSIRO employs 7,000 people, and pursues strategic science aimed, in the
longer term, at improving Australia's industrial competitiveness. The organization traditionally has been best known for its excellence in primary industry
fields, such as agriculture, veterinary medicine, mining, mineral processing,
etc. It is active, however, on a wide front, and is increasing its involvement in
manufacturing technology and innovation-intensive service industries.

CSIRO is a statutory authority answerable to the Minister of Science, but
with its own independent board. The organization, as such, is not charged with
giving policy advice to government, but, because of its size and its public
funding, it is, nevertheless, a considerable information resource for the nation.
For example, parliamentarians and ministers do not hesitate to seek technical
answers from CSIRO in many areas where it is seen as having the greatest
expertise. Australians are very proud of CSIRO, and its power and influence
within Australian science should not be underestimated.

In early 1990, CSIRO is to be headed by a new chief executive, John Stocker.
His appointment marks a departure from tradition, as he is an outsider, with a
background in research and management in the pharmaceutical industry. At the
age of 44, he will inject new dynamism into an organization the energies of
which have been sapped by too many reviews and reorganizations over the past

decade. The appointment also signals the new, serious concern about the establishment of technology-based manufacturing and service industries in Australia.

THE COMMISSION FOR THE FUTURE

The Labor Government created this small, new body—the Commission for the Future—in the mid-1980s with the brief of involving the general community more in the broad processes of harnessing technological change for societal welfare. The commission sees itself more as an educational than a research body. It seeks to lessen community fears about new technology and to promote community debate about sociological issues heavily influenced by science-based innovations.

One of its highly visible and successful activities has been a number of parliamentary briefings, where a leading expert expounds on a major scientific area (medical therapeutics, new agricultural technologies, information science) to a group of parliamentarians, followed by extensive questioning by them. Some of these two-hour sessions have been broadcast nationally and have revealed a surprising thirst in the community for this type of knowledge and interaction.

THE ROLE OF THE BUSINESS COMMUNITY

The most disappointing feature of Australian research and development is the low level of research within the business sector. A heavy reliance on imported technology and a reluctance to accept the view that research and development actually make money for corporations are widespread in the Australian board rooms. The perception is that R&D represents discretionary spending and "comes straight off the bottom line."

To counter this, at ASTEC's instigation, a 150% tax write-off has been introduced for industrial R&D, and this is succeeding in gradually changing the corporate climate. It is still unusual, however, to have science issues debated in official business fora, such as the Business Council of Australia. In just the past few years, while Australia has been struggling economically because of a major current account deficit and high inflation, innovation and technology are being taken more seriously. It is to be hoped that Australia will find suitable niches for technology-based exports, because its fundamental science base is very strong, and has not been adequately exploited for national economic progress.

CONCLUSIONS

Australia shares the belief of the US in the need for checks and balances in the democratic process. Australia's science and technology policy obviously evolves gradually, shaped by many inputs. As technological progress is now high on the national agenda, one can expect Australia's R&D effort to expand substantially over the next decade, probably largely through increased industrial research and development.

Because science is all-pervasive in modern life, it is obvious and desirable that many sectors and agencies within and outside government get in on the science debate. This makes it all the more desirable that the highest level of government receive informed and wise counsel filtered through independent minds as unfettered as possible by vested interests. This is the special value of ASTEC, a group that has seemed to many observers to be working better than some of its counterparts in other countries, and of the Prime Minister's Science Council, with its capacity to galvanize the nation's interest in science.

The Science Advising Organization in Bulgaria

Blagovest Sendov

THE PEOPLE'S REPUBLIC OF BULGARIA *(Narodna Republika Bŭlgariya) is a Communist People's Republic established in 1947; its present constitution has been in effect since 1971. The land area of the country is 42,823 square miles, and its population was estimated at 9,007,000 in 1989. The official language is Bulgarian. As of December 31, 1989, the US dollar was equal to .83 levs at the official rate.*

The system for scientific information and advice to the highest levels of government in a socialist country like Bulgaria has its specifics, which—in the first place—have to do with the character of the political system, the leading role of the Communist Party, and the national traditions.

After World War II, the state formations and governments of the countries of Eastern Europe were based on Marxian theory, further developed by Lenin. This explains, to a great extent, the continuous effort of these governments to have well-grounded scientific approaches to decision-making, which presupposes a well-developed network of institutions for science advice to the highest levels of state government.

In the centrally planned economies, the Parliament and government make many concrete, definite, long-term decisions. In order to prepare these decisions, it is of essential importance to have the advice of many scientists from the fields of economics, the technical sciences, sociology, and so on. A great number of these scientists whose contributions help the process of governmental decision-making work at the Bulgarian Academy of Sciences. That is why it can be said that the Bulgarian Academy is a principal advising organization to the highest levels of the government of Bulgaria.

THE BULGARIAN ACADEMY OF SCIENCES

The Bulgarian Academy of Sciences (BAS) was founded 120 years ago (nine years before the liberation of Bulgaria from the Turks) as a society of patriotic Bulgarians who set the objectives of striving for the general enlightenment of the Bulgarian nation and showing the way to its material enrichment.

After World War II, BAS affirmed itself as the leading complex scientific

Blagovest Sendov is President of the Bulgarian Academy of Sciences and holder of the highest award for science in that country. His main research is in the field of numerical analysis and the theory of approximation, and he is a former Rector of Sofia University. Born in 1932, Dr. Sendov is a member of the Executive Boards of several international organizations.

101

organization of Bulgaria, whose members are the most outstanding Bulgarian scientists. The activities of the academy—fundamental and applied research in all fields of the natural, mathematical, technical, and social sciences, and the humanities—are financed through the state budget. BAS has over 14,000 employees, 4,000 of them scientists who are grouped in approximately eighty institutes.

BAS has agreements for scientific exchange and collaborative research with scientific organizations from over thirty countries around the world. In regard to structure and organization, a substantial difference between the US National Academy of Sciences and the BAS is the fact that the Bulgarian academy has its own research institutes and other scientific units, as well as museums, small production enterprises, and factories and other units.

Post-graduate students undergo training and prepare their Ph.D.s at institutes of the academy. On the other hand, many scientists from BAS are university professors and lecturers. All this speaks for a direct stable link between BAS and the world of learning in Bulgaria.

BAS AS A BASIC ADVISING ORGANIZATION

The academy's activities as an advising agency to the government can be outlined as follows: preparing forecasts, running specific scientific projects, expertise, consultations, and other activities.

Under the guidance of BAS, periodic long-term forecasts for the development of science and technology in Bulgaria are elaborated. These forecasts are prepared so as to advise and orient the planning organs of the country in the process of formulating the five-year plans for the social and economic development of Bulgaria.

A concrete example follows. Before World War II, Bulgaria was basically an agricultural nation with nascent industry. The reason for its backwardness can be found in the five-century Turkish oppression, from which Bulgaria was liberated in 1878. After 1970, a significant volume of business in the electronics industry was developed. Today, Bulgaria is the leading producer of personal computers, direct access storage devices (discs), and parallel computers in Eastern Europe. The decision of the government to make huge investments in electronics has been influenced by a forecast regarding the development of information technologies.

The first Bulgarian computer was constructed in the Institute of Mathematics at BAS in the beginning of the 1960s. This example shows how scientists, working in the fields of information disciplines and technologies, influenced the decision of the Bulgarian Government to invest in and develop the electronics industry.

Several BAS institutes have as their primary tasks the conduct of research in problem areas which relate directly and serve the government in making decisions.

"SCIENCE FOR SCIENCE" SCIENTIFIC CENTER

The Science for Science Scientific Center at BAS conducts research studies on the role of science in societal development. Its research results and findings are of direct importance to decision-making in relation to the organization and management of science, and are of use to the government as information materials in the process of its decision-making. The Science for Science Center investigates the experiences of other countries in the use of science and scientific information systems.

INSTITUTE OF ECONOMICS

The Institute of Economics is another research unit at BAS with the immediate task of assisting the government in its decisions. As is known, the process of restructuring the economies of socialist countries is an extremely complex and difficult task. Even though only these problems came out as dominating, in Bulgaria they have been attentively investigated for many years.

The study of the economic laws and regulations in a well-defined system of economic relations gives objective information for the necessity and characteristics of possible changes, which could lead to improved performance. The Institute of Economics has taken part in many projects and areas of expertise in improving the management of the country's economy. Of course, the axioms of the system of the economy are determined by the politicians and not by the scientists. But, in this activity, the politicians have counted on scientific advice in the framework of the predetermined axioms.

A concrete example in connection with the latest economic reforms follows. In mid-1989, a decision concerning certain basic principles for economic reform relating to the general economic restructuring (*i.e., perestroika*) was undertaken by the senior level of government. One of the recommendations was to create conditions for the general convertibility of the Bulgarian currency, the *lev*.

The nonconvertible Eastern European currencies are one of the reasons for limited external investment and are an obstacle to trade relations with the Western countries. On the other side, the transformation of the currency into a convertible one is a very complex economic and political task. A group of scientists at the Institute of Economics is working intensively on possible scenarios as to how the Bulgarian *lev* could become convertible.

BAS also takes advantage of its international contacts to draw on the expertise of foreign scientists and specialists in addressing the issue of convertibility and in preparing possible scenarios. There is an agreement with the US National Academy of Sciences under the scientific exchange of 1990 for a group of US specialists to visit Bulgaria to investigate some specific aspects of the Bulgarian economy. This will be, in a way, the preparatory stage for the 1991 bilateral seminar between BAS and the US academy on problems of the convertibility of the Bulgarian *lev*.

The above example shows how scientists/economists can be very helpful advisers to their governments. On the other hand, the absence of convertibility between East and West is the most serious economic barrier to cooperation. Nonconvertibility also has an effect on such basic problems as human rights, the idea of a common European home, etc.

THE INSTITUTE OF SOCIOLOGY

The Institute of Sociology at the BAS also has a direct influence on decision-making by the highest levels of government. This institute carries out numerous sociological surveys and, in this way, draws objective pictures of public opinion. Knowing the status of public opinion is indispensable for making popular government decisions.

BAS AS A PRINCIPAL CONSULTANT

There are many other institutes at the BAS that provide direct advice to the government. But it is also important to stress the fact that the BAS and its institutes and scientists are extremely valuable assets to the government in regard to the entire research outcome of the academy.

As a principal scientific consultant to the government, BAS is entrusted with the organization of specific expertise to evaluate significant state projects. In preparing these reports, BAS sets up complex commissions of scientists and specialists.

BAS can also initiate and carry out its own expert studies in order to exercise influence on present and future government decisions and, in some cases, to change their characters.

Today, there is an urgent need for expert studies to evaluate the ecological consequences of large projects in the construction of industrial and power plants. There are concrete examples of such studies, carried out by BAS ten and twenty years ago, that have justified themselves but, unfortunately, have not been borne in mind. Such examples are important components of the authority of the current forecasts and studies that the BAS carries out.

The General Assembly of the BAS, consisting of the academy members and the presidium, plays an important role in advising the government on questions relating to science. This is achieved through the decisions made by these academy bodies on concrete questions dealing with science and the relevant technologies.

INFORMAL MECHANISMS FOR ADVISING

In the Bulgarian government system, an official personal scientific adviser to the highest level of the government does not exist. As already mentioned, such a role is entrusted to various institutions. But informal contacts have always played an important role in suggesting and inspiring ideas and opinions. Of course, it is not possible to formally describe such informal relations.

At the highest levels of the Bulgarian government, there is a significant number of active and highly professional scientists who can be consulted on science matters; such a practice evidently takes place.

For a small country like Bulgaria, it is very important to be abreast of the developments in large and developed countries. Very often, the senior state officials of the country take advantage of the visits of prominent foreign scientists to Bulgaria to meet and discuss various problems with them. This is a widely practiced and very useful informal mechanism for scientific consultation.

Science advice to top-level government officials plays an important role in their immediate activities relating to decision-making in the fields of economics, politics, etc. Science advice to the higher levels of government, however, should also be directed toward issues concerning the development of science in the country. There has been some wrong advice given in the past, coming from unscrupulous advisers, that has left heavy burdens for scientific development. When the effectiveness of scientific advice is discussed, it must not be forgotten that this effectiveness, in the first place, depends upon the capabilities of the person who is advised and, in the second place, on the competence and ethics of the adviser.

The sorry examples in the past had to do with the development of genetic and cybernetic research in the socialist countries following World War II. They are classic cases of negative effectiveness of scientific advice. The lagging behind in biotechnology and information technology in the Eastern European countries is due to the delusion of top-level government officials by scientific advisers of the Lisenko type. Of course, this is a more complex problem and is connected with other phenomena, but it is related to the competence and ethics of the individuals who give advice to the highest levels of government.

CONCLUSION

Finally, the author would like to express an opinion concerning the future development of the mechanisms for scientific advice. These mechanisms could be based either on individual advisers or on institutions. Of course, a mix of these two strategies is also possible. In the case of Bulgaria, the mixed strategy of informal personal and formal institutional mechanisms for scientific advice to top-level government officials has proved to be the most appropriate. But, for a small country like Bulgaria, science advice should not be limited to the framework of the country. This means that the structures engaged in scientific advice to the government should have abundant information regarding developments throughout the world.

In connection with the above, there arises a question concerning the role of the international governmental and nongovernmental organizations in the field of science in support of the national structures which provide science advice to the government. Membership dues for these organizations, to a great extent, should be compensated for by the acquired information and experience of activities related to science advice to the leading governmental officials.

With the warming of East-West political relations and the decreasing threat of nuclear war, ecological problems are beginning to receive primary attention. As a consequence of man's activities on the earth, humankind now faces problems of global environmental changes. It is obvious that only through the most highly developed scientific methods of many disciplines can mankind reach appropriate solutions to these problems. This calls for high scientific professionalism and complex scientific expertise as a basis for governmental decision-making.

Ecological problems are usually international. For this reason, an effective system of international scientific cooperation is needed. In the future, this fact will probably reflect upon the character and structure of scientific advice to the highest levels of government.

The Canadian Situation: Evolution and Revolution in Giving Advice

Larkin Kerwin and Geraldine Kenney-Wallace

CANADA *was granted the status of Dominion under the British North America Act of 1867, became an autonomous state of the Commonwealth of Nations in 1931, and was established with a "patriated" constitution in 1982. Its land area is 3,851,809 square miles, and its estimated population in 1989 was 25,907,000. Its official languages are English and French.*

As the decade of the 1990s opens up for Canada, one witnesses a country poised for a number of major science and technology decisions and science and technology (S&T) machinery that has gone through both evolutionary and revolutionary changes in the past three years. The experiments—both in giving advice and in turning advice into action—are notable for their originality and for their *ad hoc* natures. The success or failure of the plethora of advice-giving activities will depend on whether or not long-yearned-for national goals, political will, and timely and informed S&T advice come to a confluence within the short period of time these S&T issues have high public profile.

Science and technology are key to nation-building for the twenty-first century as, indeed, they have been for the past century. The Canadian situation should be differentiated from the US situation, not so much on current needs and priorities of the respective governments, but rather on the ways these needs and priorities have evolved since the 1950s. The US has a strong industrial infra-

Larkin Kerwin, physicist and Companion of the Order of Canada, was born in 1924, earned his M.Sc. from the Massachusetts Institute of Technology and his Doctor of Science degree from Laval University of which he was Rector from 1972 to 1977. He is President of the International Union of Pure and Applied Physics and, since 1964, a Fellow of The Royal Society of Canada of which he is a past president. He is a recipient of numerous awards and honorary degrees. Dr. Kerwin was President of the National Research Council of Canada from 1980 to 1989 when he became President of the Canadian Space Agency.

Geraldine Kenney-Wallace has been Chairman of the Science Council of Canada since 1987, and was recently appointed President and Vice Chancellor of McMaster University, Hamilton, Ontario, as of July 1990. She is a noted international authority on lasers and optoelectronics, and is Professor of chemistry and physics at the University of Toronto. Through membership on the Prime Minister's National Advisory Board on Science and Technology and as a charter member of The Ontario Premier's Council, Dr. Kenney-Wallace has had extensive experience in the changing machinery and relationships of science advising. Recently, she concluded chairing the Canada-Japan Complementarity Study for enhanced R&D collaborations at the request of the Prime Ministers of Canada and Japan. Dr. Kenney-Wallace is Co-chair of the Foreign Policy Committee of the National Roundtable of the Environment and the Economy, also reporting to the Prime Minister.

structure as well as defense programs based on research and development (R&D), and the federal government in Washington has long recognized the unique requirements of that government for science advice. Canada has a relatively weak industrial infrastructure and defense program, and has chosen to focus on developing exploitation of its resource base as the "new Canada" has reached for a truly independent nationhood.

Until World War II, the patterns of advising governments on science policy were simple. The provinces showed little interest in science and technology insofar as they affected public policy. Federally, the limited advice that trickled in came from the National Research Council (itself established in 1916 under pressure by the UK during World War I), The Royal Society of Canada (1882), and an embryonic group of learned societies.

Following World War II, the importance of technology had been amply demonstrated as an element of industrial might during the conflict, and so the development and use of science and technology burgeoned in Canada as elsewhere. Initially, this growth of activity was concentrated under the pre-war organizations and umbrellas. Traditionally autonomous, these groups strove to operate under conditions and procedures appropriate to the particular needs of research and development, but it was not to last. Presently, as R&D budgets became significant, this quasi-independence of science and technology came to be looked at askance, and a series of committees and task forces, beginning with the Glassco Commission Report (1960) and continuing to this day, inveigled governments to bend research organizations to uniform public service practices. One consequence was the establishment of a number of channels for advising government on science and technology.

A DESIRABLE INDUSTRIAL MIX

The federal government in Ottawa has finally begun to act on the premise that it is science-based innovation, technology-intensive industry, and a value-added resource base that should blend into a desirable industrial mix to meet the demands and international competition of global markets. The Free Trade Agreement signed with the US in 1989, a heightened focus on trade and technology in the current GATT (General Agreements on Tariffs and Trade) negotiations, and a recently completed and expanded bilateral R&D agreement with Japan all reflect movement in this direction. The government, however, has yet to establish a simple process to bring science and technology advice to the senior executive level.

The recently created National Advisory Board on Science and Technology (1987), chaired by the Prime Minister and co-chaired by the Minister of Industry, Science and Technology and the Minister of State for Science, provides an interesting exposé and novel debating forum for its prominent industrial and scientific members, but begs the traditional role of advice-giving from the civil servants in policy roles in the many science-based departments. Sometimes ensuing tensions act as barriers to turning advice into action as a goal-oriented advisory board meets a process-oriented bureaucracy. By signaling his personal interest, the Prime Minister has clearly raised the profile of the role of science and technology in economic renewal, education, environment, and competitiveness issues.

Parliament as a whole is advised by a Parliamentary Committee on Industry, Science and Technology and Regional and Northern Development, a group of fourteen members of Parliament representing all sitting political parties. It holds public hearings on a wide variety of subjects.

The Senate also recently put into place a Standing Committee on Social Affairs, Science and Technology, which calls witnesses on a similar range of issues, and submits reports on government bills.

THE SITUATION TODAY

The situation today (February 1990) is legally as follows. Major decisions for Canada on science and technology are taken by the federal Cabinet. The projects are sponsored by and the Cabinet is advised by the Minister of State for Science and Technology. This minister directs a department that analyses and evaluates projects, as well as carrying out studies on policy and coordinating programs of the various departments. Projects are also advanced by ministers who head mission departments (*e.g.*, Fisheries and Oceans). The government has presented legislation to create a new Ministry of Industry, Science and Technology, which will work with the Ministry of State to involve industry more effectively in the R&D process.

Advice on science policy, as it affects the public and the economy generally, is provided by the Science Council of Canada, a group of thirty experts from industry and academia appointed from every province in the country, people who are assisted by a thirty-person secretariat. Members serve for three-year renewable periods, and carry out both short- and long-term projects on science and technology issues for S&T infrastructure, industrial competitiveness, and environmental impacts of S&T on society. Acting as a arms-length, independent agency under the 1967 Act, the Science Council can set its own agenda, as well as respond to ministerial or Prime Ministerial tasks, as has been its recent pattern of activity. It reports to Parliament through the Ministry of Industry, Science and Technology.

The National Research Council's governing council also provides advice to the government through the Minister of State for Science and Technology. The council consists of twenty-two distinguished scientists and industrial members who serve three-year renewable terms.

The laboratories of the National Research Council (NRC) are provided, in many cases, with boards which channel advice on their sector to the council, which relays it to government. The NRC sponsors a wide spectrum of prestigious associate and advisory committees, all of which proffer advice, through the council, on their respective subjects. Mission-oriented departments act similarly. There are also two granting councils: MRC, the Medical Research Council, and NSERC, the Natural Sciences and Engineering Research Council, which subsidize research in the universities and which provide advice on their areas to the Cabinet and Parliament.

At the provincial level, each government has a minister in charge of science and technology, usually associated with another portfolio. In most provinces, there is an echo of the national situation, with science councils advising on policy and provincial laboratories and granting councils active in their various spheres.

THE NONGOVERNMENTAL SECTOR

In the nongovernmental sector, there are also many sources of advice. The Royal Society of Canada continues to offer advice on very long-range subjects. The success of the Association Canadienne Française pour l'Avancement de la Science has been effective in influencing science policy in Quebec and in popularizing the subject as well. The numerous learned societies and professional associations make sporadic gestures to influence policy in particular fields, but have not been coordinated.

Paradoxically, the Canadian Association of Universities and Colleges (education is generally admitted to be a provincial responsibility) has had rather more influence on federal policy than most other groups. The fledgling Canada Association for the Advancement of Science has not generated much support in the community.

Currently, it would be difficult to devise an orderly organigram of these numerous and overlapping sources of advice to governments in Canada on science and technology. In practice, various influences have waxed and waned according to the public interest in the topic under consideration.

The science policy advisory channels in Canada clearly have evolved in a patchwork manner. At the present time, a more orderly routing of the various inputs, under the stimulus of the Minister of State for Science and Technology, is developing, with particular emphasis on industrial problems and cooperation among the federal and provincial governments.

The Role of the State and Government in Chile's Scientific and Technological Development

Jaime Lavados

THE REPUBLIC OF CHILE *has been an independent state since 1818. Approved in 1980 and taking effect in 1981, its present "transitional" constitution partially superseded the military government that had been in power since 1973. The country's land area is 292,256 square miles, and its estimated 1989 population was 12,828,000. The official language is Spanish.*

Prior to 1920, scientific and technical activities in Chile were considered to be almost purely instrumental, that is to say, in regard to their immediate practical applications. Government naturally shared this extended concept. The point was to know reality through natural history (zoology, botany, physical geography, mineralogy). Professional expertise was to be gained through the scarce scholarships available, generally in Europe, or in solving specific problems (yellow fever, specific farming and animal husbandry problems, etc.).

No scientific community existed as such nor any academic community in its wider sense. Professors at universities were successful professionals or foreigners expressly hired abroad; there were no scientific nor technological experts wholly dedicated to research and teaching; basic science had no prestige nor did it make any social sense from the point of view of the government or the ordinary citizen. In social areas, political philosophy or social essays were given preference over social sciences with an empirical foundation as exists today. The government had no specific structure oriented toward science and technology.

Since then and to date, several periods can be observed with regard to the role of government in Chilean scientific and technological development, as follows:

- A first stage, from 1920 until the end of World War II (in Chile, this period lasted until 1946–50);

Jaime Lavados is former Executive Director of CONYCIT, the Chilean Council for Science and Technology, and has served as OAS and UN consultant for science and technology development programs in other Latin American countries. He is President of the Corporation for University Development, a Chilean "think-tank" concerned with science and technology development and higher education; Head of the Science and Technology Research Group, and Professor of Neurology at the University of Chile Medical School. Dr. Lavados is former Director of the Office for Science and Technology at the university and President of the Committee on Science and Technology, and Council of Rectors of Chilean Universities.

111

- A second stage from 1950 (or from World War II) until the beginning of the 1970s);
- A third stage, which started after 1970 and continued through the beginning of the 1980s; and
- The most recent stage, from the beginning of the 1980s until the present.

THE BEGINNING YEARS (1920–1950)

In general, this was the period when the establishment of a scientific community in the country began. During these years, biologists and physicians started to imagine a task which was a different profession, that of research. They went abroad, not only to improve their professional qualifications, but also to train as researchers. They were generally financed by foreign foundations, particularly from North America. These foundations not only sent Chileans to the United States, but assisted them in the installation of research laboratories on their return to Chile.

A certain number of these first scientists achieved some status, mainly at the universities, and turned into leaders who headed the development of basically experimental work laboratories; they encouraged young people to dedicate themselves fully to the academic life of research and teaching and to try to convince the authorities that their work was important. These authorities—universities and the government—provided help to the researchers, but did not carry out explicit and consistent policies to further promote research.

THE DEVELOPMENT OF DISCIPLINES

Soon scientific disciplines started to develop around the specialities of the leaders. Thus the uneven development of sciences in Chile can be explained, since it is not necessarily related to priority or importance. This has to do—partially, not totally—with leaders who were capable of "pushing" within their own fields, particularly in development.

On the other hand, it is clear that developments were quicker and specifically more important in disciplines relating to health and medicine and slightly less important in farming and animal husbandry. This can possibly be explained by the slight industrialization of the country at that time. There was no demand for knowledge or encouragement of research from areas related to industry with the exception of initial infrastructure projects (roads, ports, etc.). Also, the most important production entities of the country (saltpeter and copper) were owned by foreigners who complied with the research requirements in their own native countries.

Toward the end of this period, practical laboratory work was undertaken for the first time by university students, first in medicine and, shortly thereafter, by professions relating to the exact and natural sciences.

The period between 1920 and the end of World War II was of growth and development, of the search for and learning of research methods and modalities of managing laboratories, personnel, etc. It was a rather chaotic and unstructured period, wherein research and knowledge activities nonetheless transcended the worlds of the scientists themselves.

The underlying concept—within state power—during this period was that science and technology were activities belonging to the universities. It was believed that the universities were the ones to foster the growth of knowledge, shelter the professors (scientists and technologists), and diffuse science and technology specialization. The scientific and technological policies implicit in the actions of the government and the country's leaders emphasized the cultural and educational roles of scientific achievements and gave almost no importance to an eventually productive use of the knowledge obtained through local research.

This affirmation, in global terms, has some exceptions, as shown by the early founding (at the beginning of the 1940s) of the Instituto Bacteriológico Nacional,[1] in charge of microbiology research and the manufacture of vaccines and, sometimes later, the Instituto Nacional de Investigación Technológica y Normalización (Inditecnor),[2] which started with relative success in working on norms and quality controls.

DEVELOPMENT AND GROWTH

After World War II, the burgeoning ideas were further developed. The war itself gave a practical demonstration of the effects which scientific knowledge could have, such as radar, the V-2 bomb, and a large number of similar innovations. But this alone would probably have been insignificant, since World War I also produced such inventions as the tank and the airplane.

Perhaps the most decisive factor was that, during that period, the United States placed much power and prestige and many resources at the disposal of scientific development. There was doubtless a change also as the European influence diminished and that of the United States increased significantly.

Another fact, of an international character and special significance in the case of Chile, was the founding of UNESCO and its scientific department. The latter developed a model of scientific and technological policy, wherein interest was focused on the feasibility of doing the highest quality scientific research possible. It was considered that the knowledge and experience achieved through research would translate itself almost automatically into socio-economic development.

If good quality science—good physics, good chemistry—was available, the use of knowledge toward productive ends would be demonstrated immediately. Throughout the years, this idea has been found to be not exactly true in Chile, as this country lacked the productive and organizational foundation which makes possible the utilization of knowledge originating in the specific demands of end users.

THE CONCEPT OF DEVELOPMENT

At that time, the concept of development appeared in Chile, including—although not very significantly at first—science and technology as parts of the same. The industrialization effort headed by the Corporación de Fomento de la Producción (CORFO)[3] meant facing a number of requirements for knowledge and technical experience due to the production activities or the installation of a basis for industrialization (such as energy, communications, etc.), which CORFO and its subsidiaries began to develop. The underlying concept of the work of these institutions was *development planning.*

In the meantime, the scientific community had continued to increase, not only in number and quality, but also in self-respect and organization, and started to exert pressure upon the university authorities and the government to institutionalize its work. This implied the possibility of obtaining support, resources, and consideration of its work in a permanent and coherent manner. These factors—industrialization, development, planning, organization, self-identification of the scientific community—together with the international situation and pressure generated results which became apparent in the following years.

At the universities, the impulse to encourage scientific and technological development grew and became a common objective among different areas, faculties, and even the units which originated the process. Full-time dedication increased. Publications and libraries improved and stabilized. Only during the 1950s did the government take a more active role. In 1954, Law 11.575 was approved which acknowledged that universities should provide stable resources to develop scientific activities; a specific percentage of the taxes to be applied to certain exports was granted to them.

Some technology institutes started to appear, sometimes in the form of committees within CORFO or some other ministries. These grew, during the decade that followed, into more formal organizations as an answer to the requirements of sectors and subsectors and, in general, due to government department initiatives, but independent of each other. All of these sectoral and partial efforts were not translated into broader concepts of scientific and technological policies or in organizations or mechanisms with a common objective at the highest levels of government.

Several events of importance took place toward the end of this period. The first was the founding of CONYCIT (the National Council for Science and Technology). The effort undertaken by the scientific community, beginning in the 1950s, resulted in the government's acceptance, in 1965, of the naming of a commission by Supreme Decree. This commission represented the institutionalization of science for local scientists.

The model used was the one popular at the time in several countries throughout Latin America, one which followed closely the UNESCO ideas. It was planned more to develop science and that which is considered scientific in technological research than to encourage the practical application of technology itself. Its primary focus was to increase the quality and scope of scientific activity. Only in certain areas—food technology, fruit growing, mining, etc.— were "development programs" designed and put into operation. Their purpose was only to improve local scientific and technological capabilities in those selected priority areas. No actions or instruments were considered for encouraging specific production applications of the knowledge that was eventually developed.

CONYCIT

The Chilean CONYCIT was formed by high-quality active scientists and technology experts, including some representatives of the President, who named scientists to represent him. Structurally, CONYCIT was linked to the President of Chile, and, as to ceremonial activities and financing, to the Ministry of Education. It was not related to any production ministry or organization in the country.

During 1969, an effort was made to establish a Coordination Committee through which the development of scientific and technological research would be connected to the requirements of the production sector. This initiative produced no result. On the other hand, the budgets approved for CONYCIT up to 1970 were relatively small for carrying out experimental development or true technological innovation.

Nevertheless (at the same time as the founding of CONYCIT in the late 1960s) more than a dozen state research institutions had started to operate, sometimes with budgets larger than that of CONYCIT and with significant investments in equipment and the initiation of activities. These institutions were born out of initiatives in specific sectors (agriculture, forestry, mining, fishing, industrial technology, etc.), some dependent upon CORFO and others upon the relevant ministry.

It is quite clear then, that also throughout this period the Chilean government did not consider as a whole the activities, mechanisms and instruments which produce or generate knowledge, transfer it, or are capable of encouraging its further applications. It strengthened some of these mechanisms and instruments, but, as these were isolated efforts, they were not considered as parts of more coherent or interconnected processes.

THE EFFORTS OF UNIVERSITIES

At the universities, both the prestige of and the efforts to organize scientific activities were heightened. At the beginning of the 1970s, the four or five most important local universities created some type of unit (service, vice-rectory, commission, etc.) for scientific and technical development which was connected to the highest level of the corporation and had resources of its own oriented specifically to the financing of research projects.

The institutional crystallization of this long process of development and the contradictions (or, rather, the lack of coordination) present did not reach a stabilization point by the end of the 1960s. There is some natural balance between various and even opposing points of view which can only be limited and brought into harmony through practice and experience.

The idea itself of a scientific and technological policy appeared as such in Chile in the 1960s and developed rapidly, but without reaching the necessary levels of complexity, articulation and definition. It did not materialize among the country's governmental authorities.

At the end of the 1960s and beginning of the 1970s, it was evident that several of the simple and rather naive solutions applied during the previous ten or fifteen years were not working as automatically as had been expected. The increase in the numbers of researchers and research projects and the improvements in libraries and equipment did not directly result in an increase in the production capacity of the country.

The different groups which, in some way or another, participated in the generation, diffusion and use of knowledge, even through participants in the same process, had different objectives. In some, it was of understanding; in others, it was in improving production; in still others, it was in improving employment or the capacity for export, etc. Also, because of structure, organization, and working modality, each of the several actors (scientists, teachers, businessmen and administrators) responded to ways of management, incentives, and even restrictions of diverse characters in different ways.

It can also be appreciated that the spontaneous founding of a scientific community and its fight to institutionalize science, the founding of state technological research institutes, or the improvement of university research were not capable of defining, within the country, technological and scientific policies that were both conceptually adequate and operatively efficient. The lack of identification of mechanisms and instruments which encourage the effective utilization of the increasing scientific and technological capacity was evident.

WEAKENING OF INTEREST ON THE PART OF GOVERNMENT (1970–1980)

At the end of the 1960s and the beginning of the 1970s, the Chilean government, through its agencies, was searching for ways to solve conceptual and operating problems of scientific and technological development. This search was encouraged by the increase in these activities. Nevertheless, throughout the decade of the 1970s, this search at the government level was at a standstill.

It is difficult to know why this happened. Probably the various political, social and economic crises that the country experienced during that decade are partly responsible. Perhaps, with the increasing concept of technological and scientific policy, which was never put into practice, it was considered that levels of globality and complexity could be achieved that would be impossible by any other means.

The Chilean example, in fact, shows that it is possible for scientific policies to be somewhat independent from the general state economic policy. But this does not happen as easily with the productive applications of technology. The specific behavior of enterprises (even those which are state-dependent) is intimately related to the "rules of the game" implied in macroeconomics, financing, duty taxes, employment, and other matters. Evidently, mechanisms and instruments can be designed in regard to any economic policy to be consistent with that policy as well as being explicitly oriented toward technologies and their applications. This was not done in Chile.

A significant factor, also, was the change of orientation of the government. Many of the assumptions which gave birth to the organization of programs in science and technology by state authorities were not respected by the Chilean authorities during the past sixteen years. Planning for S&T, the country's scientific development, the social value of science, the search for local technological capability, etc., were neglected. The economic policy that was put into practice did not foster the idea of developing some level of independence or efficient utilization of local scientific capacity. It was thought that the state was not responsible for improving the interrelationships between the elements of the scientific and technological system or for encouraging those in need of encouragement or for orienting S&T activities.

MARKET DEMAND AND COMPETITION

The system of market demand and competitiveness (not only at a local, but at an international level) was preferred as a more important and decisive factor in fostering and orienting technology.

Some facts are worth mentioning. From 1971 through 1982, CONYCIT reduced and then almost totally put an end to financing programs for research projects and programs oriented toward the strengthening of scientific and technological capacity (both in personnel and in infrastructure). At the same time, the state contribution to the university system was cut almost by half. The situation was partially corrected through an increase in the cost of tuition fees paid by the students.

The state's aggressive policy of obtaining international technical assistance (professional and scientific education abroad, international expertise, infrastructure, and equipment), which was characteristic of the 1960s, also deteriorated.

Although the state diminished its interest in supporting the development of scientific capacity, the number of research and development activities which the country undertook during this decade did not decrease. In some areas, it even increased. The education of new scientists, now primarily within the country, covered—although not to the same extent in all areas—the resulting shortage of personnel.

The creation of science and technology units within the universities maintained the continuity of tasks undertaken in various fields. In purely financial terms, in some places the costs of scientific research projects increased, although investments in the infrastructure stopped. Thus small projects continued to develop, keeping researchers active, but no new lines were opened up nor were installations and equipment replaced.

Scientific research did not deteriorate too much in spite of the lack of explicit policies designed and applied by the government. The situation was different in regard to technology and its application in productive areas of goods and facilities. The direct dependence on government agencies by the technology institutes made them more sensitive to the government's lack of interest and change of objectives. Personnel and budget reductions, obsolescence of infrastructure and equipment, and the transformation from technical research units to routine technical service units occurred frequently. Instruments or mechanisms that encouraged the demand for true technological research were nonexistent throughout this period. Problems such as the transfer of technology, the purchasing power of the state, taxes, and financial mechanisms to encourage the use of local technology were not state concerns during those years.

In the latter part of this period, emphasis was placed upon the immediate application of knowledge. This was encouraged over creativity. At the same time, some lines of action which agreed with the general orientation of the state were granted support. Therefore, for example, investments in the Chilean Commission for Nuclear Energy significantly increased, and the Fundación Chile was formed under an agreement with ITT. The assets of this foundation were nationalized in 1975. Its work is basically oriented toward the transfer of technology in the areas of food, fishing and telecommunications.

THE PRESENT

In the early 1980s, an overall disposition toward promoting the use of local talent with incentives for the productive application of knowledge was observed. The underlying theory (known as the "pull" theory) is that technological and scientific development must be undertaken within the outlines of the requirements of the end beneficiaries which are represented by the production sector. The link between the demands of this area and the suitability of the research happens automatically, the model states. Theoretically, this would produce a scientific and technological development process that would prove to be efficient, harmonic, and in accord with the real needs of the country.

The materialization of these ideas into policy instruments has been oriented primarily toward the modification of the system of assigning resources which, in turn, has meant a reduction in the institutional type of support awarded (a fact that was evident during the preceding period) and the creation and support of various funds to be granted through competitions. The basic concept is the "research project" and the concept of "infrastructure" has disappeared.

Some of the most significant actions which have been taken during this period are:

- The creation, in 1980, of a fund at the Ministry of Agriculture for research and development in forestry, agriculture and animal husbandry to be awarded by solicitation.
- The founding of FONDECYT (Fondo Nacional de Desarrollo Científico y Tecnológico). The resources awarded by the state through this entity were very restricted initially (less than US$1 million), affecting negatively the projects approved. Nonetheless, a very significant increase in the volume of such funds has been seen since 1987, obtained for the most part from the transfer of state funds originally assigned to the universities (approximately US$10 million in 1988). Thus, although this mechanism has increased the relative importance of the entity within the local technological and scientific system, the general activity level of the system remains intact.
- The founding, in 1984, of CORFO's Fondo de Desarrollo Productivo, which finances a direct percentage (up to 50%) of activities in research, development and the adaptation of technologies, and the prospecting of natural resources undertaken by the production sector. This mechanism is restrictive in that patrons of different projects cannot obtain the exclusive use of the results of their efforts, thus making it difficult for really innovative projects to participate in the competitions. The resources presently channeled through this mechanism total US$1 million.
- The founding, in 1987, of a Fondo Capital des Riesgo, amounting to US$5 million, under the auspices of the Servicio de Cooperación Tecnica, with resources for financing investments up to US$200,000.[4] Because of its recent creation, no results are known yet.
- Since 1988, an article in the Fiscal Budget Law through which business is allowed to deduct up to 50% from taxes for donations to universities of cultural, technological or scientific research nature. Regrettably, this disposition does not apply to research institutes, making competition difficult in this area.

It has been suggested within the Plan for Technological and Scientific Development, under study in CONYCIT since 1987, that, in addition to other activities, a proposition for doubling the local budget for science and technology be included. The decision of the government's economic agents is as yet unknown.

THE RESULTS

The results obtained so far—of the actions undertaken within the present decade—show a relative increase in the relationship between the available scientific capacity and some production sectors.

Figure 1. Institutional Mechanisms of Coordination of the System of Scientific and Technological Development with National Objectives

I. Plan effective in 1970

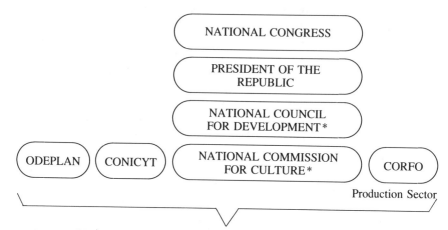

NATIONAL SYSTEM OF SCIENCE AND TECHNOLOGY

*These laws were requested in the general plan, but have not yet been effectively implemented.

II. Plan effective in 1983

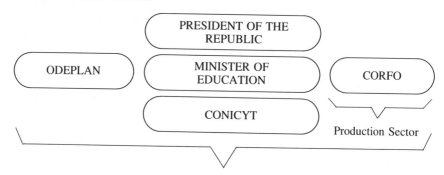

NATIONAL SYSTEM OF SCIENCE AND TECHNOLOGY

The universities and research institutes have seen their resources that are not related to research badly depleted. As in the earlier period, the lack of investment has negatively affected the opening up of new research areas of immediate applicability.

On the other hand, the reaction of the principal agents involved on either side—scientific and technological, for one, and consumers, for the other—has been more unsatisfactory than expected. The appearance of a series of ways for directing resources toward research and development implies an in-depth transformation of these agents and signals a change in the attitude of the government with respect to science and technology.

The institutions which traditionally have undertaken research and development evidence a number of difficulties in adapting their internal structures (working modalities, internal organizations, etc.) to these new conditions. In the same manner, the production system has not reacted as expected. A major inadequacy on the part of business enterprises to define technology requirements has been noticed, along with a lack of disposition of investments toward long-term objectives.

Distrust is evident on the parts of businessmen in regard to the capacity of the institutions which traditionally have been the centers of scientific and technological development in the country. This, added to the weakness of the Chilean industrial sector and the lack of mechanisms explicitly oriented toward promoting the incorporation of local technology (capital assets, engineering services, etc.) in important investment projects, both public and private, has contributed to the weakening of the technological capacity of the actors in the production system, who have turned their efforts mainly toward the importing of the elements necessary for competitive short-term success.

CONCLUSION

It is obvious throughout this summary that the actions of the Chilean government in science and technology have been carried out in sectors and institutions and through more or less independent actions without much coherency. Only toward the end of the 1960s were the President and his counselors specifically concerned with science and technology. Before and after that time, sectoral economic policies prevailed and their effect on technological development (through CORFO and Odeplan,[5] for example) has been noted through cultural-scientific and educational policies in the Ministry of Education, the universities, and CONYCIT. The last has been the only Chilean institution which (1969–70) started to conceptualize in a more or less integrated manner the several objectives, actors, mechanisms and instruments of a coherent technological and scientific policy, designed by and with the encouragement of the highest levels of government.

The government in power in 1970 and, later, the governing system established in 1973 did not continue these efforts. The Plan for Scientific and Technological Development, prepared in 1987, concerns itself only with financing mechanisms for encouragement and promotion.

Notwithstanding the above and without specific mechanisms at the highest level of government, an evolution can be observed in the state's ideas on the roles of science and technology in local development. Consistent with these perceptions and concepts, institutions, mechanisms and action instruments are born.

The first stage of this policy development was when the government had no concern for science and technology other than that which originated from its interest in being aware of its country's territory and resources. This was followed in the 1950s and 1960s by a more intense effort to establish research capabilities in Chile. Universities were provided with resources, CONYCIT was created, and technology institutes were founded (twelve in all). The "push" theory predominated as the authorities considered that the mere existence of science and technology capability would be enough to automatically achieve production results. On the other hand, the cultural and educational effects of science policy seemed to be, initially, the main objectives.

During the following period (from 1973 to the early 1980s), a vacuum existed, during which the government had no interest in science and technology. It is only from the start of the present decade that the predominance of the "pull" theory has stabilized. This means that the consumer (production enterprise, public service agency, etc.), who requires the knowledge, encourages, maintains and orients research capability through specific demands and purchases of services. But this concept has shown itself to be a halfway measure of limited effect, both in increasing and improving the research capability of key areas of the country and in efficiently associating it with real production requirements.

State orientations, though unstructured, did achieve some results. In the first case ("push"), a scientific and technological infrastructure was founded (personnel, laboratories, experience, tradition, etc.), which—to date and in spite of its defects—still remains and which has shown itself to be an indispensable basis for later development. The "pull" theory pointed out the necessity of the participation of production enterprises in technological development. Financing operations and other instruments to motivate the smooth participation of the knowledge consumers were recognized.

It seems evident that, in the near future, as well as strengthening and improving what has been achieved so far, the state should concern itself primarily with mechanisms for a relationship between the scientific and technological capabilities available and the requirements of the production sector. Mechanisms which will emphasize these interactions and instruments that will encourage exchange will have to be designed. Various means of financing (cooperative exchanges, credit-oriented plans, venture capital, incentives to local engineering organizations, support for local consultants) need to be encouraged. There are also multiple modes of interrelationships which different countries have developed and from which Chile can borrow experience.

This is a very significant challenge for the scientific and technological development of the country. It is impossible to say at the present time which new organizational structures will be adopted by the government. It will doubtless be necessary to establish mechanisms at the highest level of government which will permit coherent action on this complex problem.

NOTES

1. For information about the place of this organization in the government hierarchy, as well as that of others mentioned in the text, please see Figure 1.
2. See note 1.
3. CORFO was founded in 1940.
4. This service was established in 1958 as part of CORFO to provide technical assistance to small- and medium-sized production enterprises. It does not carry out research.
5. Oficina de Planificación Nacional, dedicated to the social and economic aspects of Chilean development, focuses on the technological components of some production problems.

Science and Technology Advice to the Chinese Highest Authority

Zhang Dengyi, Duan Ruichun, Kong Deyong, and Yang Lincun

THE PEOPLE'S REPUBLIC OF CHINA *(Zhonghua Renmin Gongheguo) has oper-*
ated under a Communist government since 1949, and controls mainland China. Its land
area is 691,795 square miles, and its population in 1989 was estimated at 1,122,901,000.
Mandarin Chinese is the official language.

For the nearly forty years since the founding of the People's Republic of China, science and technology advice has many times made positive impacts on major national policy-making, and, thereby, has contributed to the social and economic development of China. The development of Chinese science and technology advising has, however, also experienced a long, tortuous and arduous history. The actual development of Chinese science and technology advising did not occur until after the third session of the Eleventh National Congress of the Central Committee of the Chinese Communist Party, which was held in December 1978. Today, science research, with the objective of giving advice to policy-makers, is in place, and a scientific and democratic system of advice on policy-making is being set up.

Early in the 1950s, with the goal of leading the Chinese people to construct a new China on the poor, undeveloped ruins of the old, the Chinese govern-

Zhang Dengyi is Director General of the Department of Policy and Legislation of the State Science and Technology Commission, PRC, and Vice Chairman of China's Research As-sociation on Science and S&T policy. Born in 1939, he has prepared a series of important policies in Chinese science and technology over the past ten years, and supervised the preparation of an annual white paper, "Guide to China's S&T Policy."

Duan Ruichun is Vice Chairman of China's Association for Science and Technology Law and Deputy Director of the Department of Policy and Legislation, State Science and Tech-nology Commission. Born in 1943, he has been in charge of the preparation of China's Technology Contract Law and Atomic Energy Law, among others.

Kong Deyong is Director General of the Department of Policy and Legislation, State Sci-ence and Technology Commission, and Secretary General of China's Research Association in Socioeconomic Analysis. Born in 1936, he is a Professor of science and technology policy and systems science, and has formulated many national science and technology plans and policies.

Yang Lincun is Director of the Science and Technology Policy Division of the State Science and Technology Commission. He has participated in the research and formulation of Chi-na's technology policy for fourteen industries. He was born in 1952.

124

ment attached great importance to suggestions and propositions from intellectuals, especially science and engineering experts. This input made it possible for the government to formulate some important science and technology policies of high efficiency and limited failure.

For example, science and engineering experts have given helpful advice and suggestions about the 156 key projects of the First Five-Year Plan and many other construction projects. It is important to mention that the highest authority at that time could (wisely) accept and take into account these predictive suggestions by scientists and make decisions, in spite of certain risks.

In 1956, more than 600 scientists and technical experts organized by the State Council worked out a "Long-Range Plan for National S&T Development for 1956–1967," in which six major newly emerging technologies (including computer technology, semiconductor technology, automation technology, radio technology, nuclear technology, and jet technology), which were then regarded as frontier technologies throughout the world, were listed as major areas for development. This plan later made a profound impact on science and technology development in China.

For another example, the Chinese authorities accepted the "Theory of Petroleum Formation on Continental Sediment," developed by an outstanding geologist, Li Siguang. With the application of this theory as the guideline in Chinese oil exploration, the country—which had long been regarded as poor in oil resources—became a major oil producer.

Certainly, science and technology advising in the 1950s was in its initial stages, and the procedures of policy-making and advising were still far from reaching standardization, systematization and legalization.

UNDERDEVELOPMENT AND DAMAGE

From the Anti-Rightist Movement in the late 1950s until the termination of the Cultural Revolution in 1976, science and technology advising, as well as other cultural, scientific and technological causes, not only suffered from underdevelopment, but sustained heavy damage. A typical example is the criticism of the proposal by Professor Ma Yinchu on control of the overexpansion of the Chinese population. Under the erroneous population policy, the Chinese population expanded excessively and finally became a heavy burden on the development of the economy, the culture, and science and technology.

Another example can be mentioned in regard to the Extensive Iron and Steel-Smelting Movement in 1956, which used old-style workshops and small furnaces. This led to an enormous waste of natural resources and serious damage to the ecological balance. Also, for a long time, the policy of accepting grain production as a key link was pursued, and the coordinated development of a diversified agriculture based on local conditions was restrained. As a result, this policy led agricultural production backward, and the standard of living consequently fell.

Only in 1978, when the third session of the Eleventh National Congress was held, did Chinese science and technology advising really begin, leading to a prosperous period of development. At this session, the focus was shifted to modernization and a reform policy of "opening up to the outside world" was adopted.

Fully realizing the bitter lessons it had been taught by the history of heavy losses brought on by mistakes in policy-making, the Chinese government began to attach greater importance to suggestions and advice from experts in various fields. Whenever major economic, social, scientific or technological development strategy needs to be formulated or large construction projects need to be planned, scientists and technical experts are now called upon to offer their suggestions and advice in discussion and examination so as to assure that the ultimate decisions are as scientific and rational as possible.

In July 1986, at the First National Conference on Soft Science Research, former Vice President Wan Li gave a speech entitled "Scientific and Democratic Policy-Making Is an Important Topic of Political Reform." This speech comprehensively summarized the historical lessons in Chinese policy-making and fully affirmed the role of science and technology advice, as well as the necessity for soft science research for S&T advising. He also pointed out that democratic and scientific methods in policy-making should be standardized and legalized.

This speech was a milestone in the development of the Chinese science and technology advisory mechanism. Since then, science and technology advising has developed very rapidly and has become increasingly influential in policy-making at different levels of the Chinese government.

DEVELOPMENT OF S&T ADVICE TO THE HIGHEST LEVELS

Since 1978, the highest levels of the Chinese government have attached more importance to scientific policy-making and advice, and have developed a decision-making responsibility system and methodology. The Chinese Communist Party Central Committee is responsible for formulating and examining the national science and technology development general guidelines, strategies and policies, as well as the orientation of science and technology system reform.

For example, "Decision on Reform of the S&T Management System by the Central Committee of the Chinese Communist Party," published in 1985, is one of the important long-term policies set by the committee. The Standing Committee of the National People's Congress (NPC), the Chinese "Parliament," is responsible for the examination and approval of science and technology-related laws. One of these is the Law on Technological Contract of the People's Republic of China, passed in 1978.

The State Council is responsible for the examination and approval of medium-long-term plans and the five-year-plan for science and technology development, other major development plans and projects, and the announcement and implementation of relevant administrative rules and regulations.

In the process of science and technology policy formulation, the highest level of the Chinese government generally holds extensive consultations and assimilates helpful suggestions. These consultations are conducted in diversified forms through various channels.

Senior Chinese leaders constantly heed opinions obtained from their frequent meetings with famous domestic and foreign scientists and engineers. These advisors also, on occasion, present their suggestions to the Chinese government or the Chinese Communist Party (CPC) by correspondence, private interviews, and participation in conferences. The comparatively more formal channel of communication is to present advisory proposals through the NPC or the CPPCC[1] deputies via their respective motion offices. These proposals must be answered by the governmental departments involved within certain periods of time.

Since policy-making is, indeed, very complicated, mistakes could possibly be made due to partiality if suggestions by only several individual scientists are considered. In recent years, therefore, a number of research organizations and specialized consulting organizations have been involved in systematic research, analysis and studies of a number of major national or local economic, social, scientific and technological issues. Important research results are submitted to the highest level of government. Most advisory suggestions are created by concentrating intelligence from scientists and expert groups, and are comparatively comprehensive, systematic, and less likely to fail. Therefore, they are highly appreciated by the different levels of the government. Thus far, typical research results that have been acquired are as follows:

- According to the strategic deployment of the State Council, technical policies have been formulated in fourteen major areas: energy, transportation, communications, agriculture, consumer goods, the machinery industry, the material industry, the building materials industry, urban construction, village and township construction, housing construction, environmental protection, information technology, and biotechnology. These policies have been developed by more than 2,000 scientists and technical experts under the organization of the SSTC[2] and the SPC.[3] After approval by the State Council, these policies have already been announced for implementation throughout China.
- "China in the Year 2000," a report developed by nearly 400 experts organized mainly by the Research Center for Advice on Economic, Technological and Social Development under the State Council, has been listed as one of the most important bases for the formulation of Chinese medium- and long-term development plans.
- "Control of Chinese Population," a study worked out under the leadership of Song Jian, State Councillor and Chairman of SSTC, has provided a complete set of scientific theories and methods for Chinese population

prediction and control, and has heavily influenced China's population policy.

The above-mentioned research achievements have all won the first-class prize, the National Award for Science and Technology Advancement, and dozens of other achievements have been awarded second and third prizes for such work.

THE DEVELOPMENT OF RESEARCH INSTITUTIONS

With the increasing influence of advisory research, science and technology research institutions have developed rapidly. According to statistics from a survey done in 1988, there are, altogether, about 1,000 professional and non-professional institutions offering science and technology advisory services with staffs totaling 50,000 individuals. Nearly 3,000 fairly large projects have been completed by these institutions in recent years.

Some representative organizations of science and technology advisory management and research are:

- The Department of Science and Technology Policy of the State Science and Technology Council. This department is in charge of organizing and supporting national science and technology advisory research and submitting research achievements which demonstrate excellence to the highest levels of government. In the past few years, the department has organized about eighty projects each year.
- The Research Center for Advice on Economic, Technological and Social Development (under the State Council). This center primarily undertakes research on comprehensive topics of development. Some important technological and economic topics are used as important components in the research work of this center.
- The National Research Center for Science and Technology for Development, SSTC. Major undertakings of this center are assessment of science and technology development strategy and planning, science and technology management system reform, technical policy, science and technology management, and major technologies.

With the progress of reform, departments in various localities and government at all levels are successively setting up their own respective science and technology advisory research organizations. In recent years, even private science and technology research institutions have begun to appear.

While developing Chinese domestic science and technology advisory research, China is also actively concentrating on international cooperation in this field. Taking only those international cooperation projects conducted by the SSTC into account, such projects include:

- Joint research with the Stanford International Research Institute (SRI) on the computerization of the Chinese banking system;

- Joint research with the Institute of International Applied Systems Analysis (IIASA) on the basis of the comprehensive utilization of energy resources in Shanxi Province, China, to develop a computerized decision support system; and
- Joint research with the East-West Center on several topics, such as water resources in the Beijing and Tianjin areas, the way of urbanization in China, and the Chinese population problem, etc.

Some of these research projects have already achieved success.

FURTHER DEVELOPMENT

Chinese science and technology advising is now already on its way to success, but further efforts are going to be required.

First, the country plans to make an even greater effort to create a democratic and equal-in-consultation political environment so that scientists and technical experts can freely give their opinions. Government will also carefully study suggestions from experts, and select and accept prudently the most helpful ideas in order to improve the accuracy of their decision-making.

Second, relevant laws and legislation must be formulated and consummated so that science and technology advice can be standardized, systematized and legalized, thus becoming an indispensable part of the policy-making process.

Finally, the Chinese government is planning to further strengthen international cooperation in the area of science and technology advice to draw valuable suggestions from foreign scientists and technical experts in various fields.

NOTES

1. The Chinese People's Political Consultative Conference.
2. The State Science and Technology Commission of the People's Republic of China.
3. The State Planning Commission of China.

An Example of Science Policy-Making in the People's Republic of China

Zhou Guangzhao

Many factors contribute to the development of science and technology in a country, including efforts by the science and technology community, the level of economic and industrial development, international exchange and cooperation, and government policy. Only when the science and technology community, the industrial enterprises, and the government—under the circumstances of opening up to the outside world—coordinate their endeavors and make concerted efforts can science and technology be ensured a steady and continuous development.

In the People's Republic of China, the planned economic system has long been in practice, and the science and technology policies formulated by the government to meet society's immediate and long-term needs have played a key role. Such needs are reflected in the following:

- For national defense, to preserve national independence and prevent aggression;
- Economically, to raise the standard of living of the people and improve their quality of life; and
- Culturally, to achieve world-level results in scientific research so as to enrich mankind's treasury of knowledge and raise the national self-esteem.

The Chinese government has now focused its work on economic construction, and is reforming the relevant structure, shifting from a planned economy to a planned market economy. Economic development has, therefore, become the overwhelming national task. Thus the general policy of "economic development must rely on science and technology, while science and technology should be oriented toward economic development" has come into being.

Chinese scientists are enthusiastic in their pursuits toward understanding natural phenomena and the laws of motion. Many of them are accustomed to doing laboratory work, publishing their research results in the form of papers, and paying little attention to the practical applications of their work. They hope

Zhou Guangzhao is President of the Chinese Academy of Sciences and Director of its Institute of Theoretical Physics. He is a Foreign Associate of the National Academy of Sciences of the United States and a Foreign Member of the Academy of Sciences of the USSR. He was born in 1929 in Hunan Province, China.

for stable sources of funding and support from other sectors, but they are not fully aware that—to obtain that support—they must make constant contributions to social and economic development. They are afraid that stressing science and technology in the service of the national economy would affect basic research and hinder the development of science itself.

There are 325 members of the Chinese Academy of Sciences and many other excellent scientists in China. Working in major research institutes and schools of higher learning all over the country, they are specialists who have made outstanding contributions to China's science and technology. They often provide consultations and give advice to the government concerning its process of formulating plans for economic development and science policies.

DIFFERENCES OF OPINION

The government and the science community often differ in their opinions of issues, such as priority projects, the selection of research targets, the evaluation of research results, etc. Sometimes these conflicting ideas cause internal friction. A good policy proposal should be acceptable to the science community as well as being in accord with national and societal requirements.

On one hand, it should bring into full play the initiatives of more scientists to serve the national economic development, with due respect to the law of the development of science itself. On the other hand, in the course of serving national economic development, it must gain the understanding and support of society for scientific and technological work, which will, in turn, promote the progress of science and technology.

In the past few years, the Chinese Academy of Sciences has been confronted with the difficulties of policy selection and decision-making. Under the jurisdiction of the academy, there are 123 independent research institutes with staff totaling more than 80,000 people. In this new period of the reform of the economic structure and economic development, what are their tasks? What contributions should or could be made to the country and to society as a whole? Where will the research funding come from? These questions have evoked different and even contradictory answers from the government and from the science community.

THE REFORM PLAN

In recent years, meticulous and painstaking efforts have been made by the leadership of the academy in its reform drive by organizing various panels or public discussions, lobbying government departments, collecting reasonable advice, etc. After linking together the ideas of the science and technology community with those of the government, the academy has succeeded in formulating a reform plan, which has been accepted by the scientists and approved by the government.

The basic points of the plan are as follows:

- The maintenance of a small crack force to conduct basic research and establish key laboratories, following the principles of opening up to the outside world, collaborating with the universities and economic sectors, and providing for the mobility of researchers.
- The establishment of comprehensive research centers by strengthening work on the accumulation of data in regard to natural resources, the environment, ecology, oceanography, and atmospheric sciences, and enhancing the ability of comprehensive analysis so as to provide scientific bases for macroscopic policy-making on national economic development; and
- The promotion of applied and developmental technological research work, and—aiming at the market—the formulation of associations with industrial enterprises for scientific research, development, production, sales and service in order to provide technology and products directly to the market.

Many difficulties may arise in carrying out this plan, but China is confident that—based on the common understanding and efforts of the scientific community with the support of the government—good results will be achieved.

The Role of Foreign Science Advisers in the Republic of China (Taiwan)

K. T. Li

THE REPUBLIC OF CHINA *is headquartered in Taiwan and also encompasses the Pescadores and certain offshore islands, including Quemoy and Matsu. The land area of the country is 13,592 square miles, and its population in 1989 was estimated at 20,265,000. The official language of the country is mandarin Chinese. As of December 31, 1989, one US dollar was equal to $26.17 Taiwan dollars (at the official rate).*

It is important to offer a brief account of the background of the development of science and technology in the Republic of China before becoming involved in the appointment of foreign science advisers. It will also be important to describe the roles played by such advisers and the major impact that their advice has had on the formation of science policy in the Chinese government.

The mid-1960s—the period in which the foundation for science, education and research was laid—marked the time in which economic assistance to Taiwan from the United States was terminated, and the country entered a time of self-reliance which required attention to industrialization. A concurrent step undertaken at that time was the strengthening of science education.

Through the support of the National Council for Economic Cooperation and Development, five science centers were established: the Mathematics and Chemistry Centers at the National Taiwan University, the Physics Center at the National Hsing Hwa University, the Biology Center at the Academia Sinica, and the Engineering Science Center at the National Cheng Kung University.

In the meantime, the various universities were encouraged to set up research institutes that would offer studies for the master's degree in the initial stages.

A relationship between the US National Academy of Sciences and the Chinese Academia Sinica was established by President Frederick Seitz of the US academy and President Wang Shi-Chih of the Chinese academy. Cooperative workshops on appropriate subjects were set up annually to exchange information concerning current developments and to help solve problems. In general, each side mobilized appropriate experts in each country to participate in this cooperative work.

In 1967, the then US President Lyndon Johnson invited the former Chinese Vice President and Premier, C. K. Yen, to the United States for an official

K. T. Li is Senior Adviser to the President of the Republic of China. He is a physicist with extensive experience in industrial planning on Taiwan and in the government. Dr. Li has been Minister of Economic Affairs, Minister of Finance, and Minister without Portfolio.

visit. An agreement was reached that the US would send a team of top scientists to the Republic of China to study ways and means of strengthening science cooperation between the two countries.

A US Science Mission, headed by Donald Hornig, who was then Science Advisor to the US President, visited China to examine the progress of science development and the possibilities for providing additional Chinese-American cooperation in the various fields of science. James Fisk, who was then President of Bell Laboratories in the US, was a member of the mission. One of the observations made by the mission during its visit was that the electronics industry could, in principle, have a high potential for growth in Taiwan as the country proceeded with industrialization. Along with the recommendation that such a course be pursued, the mission also recommended that an agreement on cooperation in science and technology be signed and that the National Science Council should provide the counterpart role on the Chinese side. Moreover, the American Embassy should select a top-notch scientist to serve as adviser or counselor.

THE NATIONAL SECURITY COUNCIL

Dr. Hornig and his mission were personally received by the late President of the Republic, Chiang Kai-Shek. Just a year earlier, after his re-election, President Chiang had ordered the establishment of a National Security Council (NSC) under the President's Office with the responsibility for establishing policies in relation to national development as one of its principal functions.

The National Security Council incorporates the Guidance Committee for Science Development and the Committee for National Reconstruction. It is, in effect, the President's advisory board. As a result of the recommendations made by Dr. Hornig and his team, President Chiang instructed the Premier to set aside a proper percentage of funds in the national budget each year to be used for science development. He also ordered the Ministry of National Defense to take steps to set up the Chung Shan Institute of Science and Technology for the research and development of defensive weapons. In the early 1970s, the Industrial Technology Research Institute was established by the Ministry of Economic Affairs through legislation to assume responsibility for coordinating the promotion of applied science and technology within the private sector as a non-profit corporate body avoiding government restrictions on pay-scale. Among other things, it combined the former Union Chemical Laboratories, the Metal Research Institute, and the Mining Research and Service Organization.

In response to the President's call that more money should be spent for research, two government enterprises—the Taiwan Sugar Company under the Ministry of Economic Affairs and the Telecommunications Laboratory under the Taiwan Telecommunications Administration of the Ministry of Communications—both committed to spending 2% of their sales for research and development because both of them have some facilities to do research for their organizations.

The establishment of the Chung Shan Institute of Science and Technology and the Industrial Technology Research Institute solidified, respectively, the base for the development of the country's defense technology and the applied industrial research to serve the needs of industry. By the mid-1970s with more than ten years of hard work behind it, the country had accomplished concrete achievements in industrial modernization in what is now regarded as its first wave of science and technology development.

AN ACCELERATED PACE IN DEVELOPMENT

Following the first energy crisis in the early 1970s, there was much more earnest recognition on the part of the Taiwan government than previously of the importance of promoting applied research. As a result, the Committee for Research and Development on Applied Technology was set up in 1976 under the Executive Yuan (Cabinet) to oversee the coordinated promotion of applied science and technology by the relevant departments of the government. This author, then holding the position of Minister without Portfolio, was appointed convener of that committee.

As a major step, the first National Conference on Science and Technology was called in 1978. Out of this, the decision was reached to accelerate nationwide development of science and technology. In the following year, a Science and Technology Development Program was approved by the Cabinet. That all-important program outlined for the first time the objectives, strategies, and major tactics that would be followed in order to carry out across-the-board development of science and technology.

This was a particularly timely move because it came just before the second energy crisis. It became necessary to pay much more attention to technology-intensive industries in looking toward the future.

The new all-important Development Program set forth the overall approach to science and technology development that was to be undertaken by the various departments of the government in a comprehensive manner. Establishment of the Hsin Chu Science-Based Industrial Park that was proposed by the National Science Council was part of the program to accommodate the initiation of high-tech industries.

In view of the breadth of this program, detailed projects were worked out, in the meantime, by different governmental institutions. The Science and Technology Development Program provides for the inauguration of a board of foreign science advisers, composed of some of the world's leading scientists, who would offer advice to the Premier on science policies and review the performance of projects in line with international practices.

From 1979 onward, prominent foreign scientists have been engaged to serve as advisers in different disciplines. At the beginning, there were six American

Figure 1. Major R&D Institutes Established During 1979-87

Basic Research

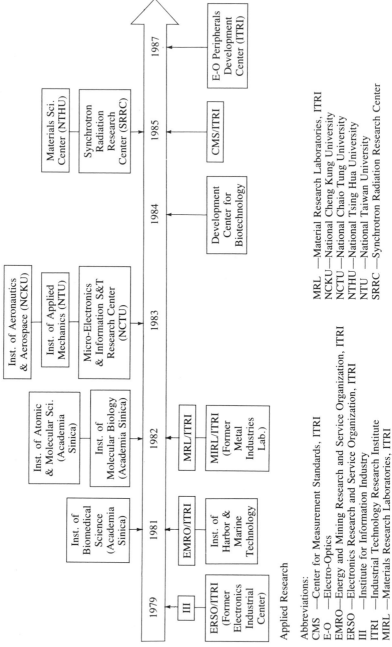

Applied Research

Abbreviations:

CMS —Center for Measurement Standards, ITRI
E-O —Electro-Optics
EMRO—Energy and Mining Research and Service Organization, ITRI
ERSO —Electronics Research and Service Organization, ITRI
III —Institute for Information Industry
ITRI —Industrial Technology Research Institute
MIRL —Materials Research Laboratories, ITRI

MRL —Material Research Laboratories, ITRI
NCKU—National Cheng Kung University
NCTU—National Chaio Tung University
NTHU—National Tsing Hua University
NTU —National Taiwan University
SRRC —Synchrotron Radiation Research Center

136

advisers. The number has now been increased to eleven, with the addition of three from France, Germany and Italy, and two from Japan to provide an international orientation.

The announcement by the Chinese government of the Science and Technology Development Program in 1979 and the appointment, the same year, of the foreign science advisers can be regarded as the start of the second wave of the country's efforts to accelerate the development of science and technology in anticipation of the problems and opportunities which would inevitably arise during the decade of the 1980s.

SETTING UP THE MINISTERIAL ADVISERS' OFFICES

At about the same time that the foreign advisers were engaged, a special organization known as the Science and Technology Advisory Group (STAG) was established directly under the Cabinet to coordinate essential matters related to their activities. STAG functions as a secretariat to the board of foreign science advisors.

In the meantime, as the result of the enactment of the Science and Technology Development Program and the growing need to strengthen inter-ministerial cooperation in the formulation and implementation of interrelated science and technology projects which had been increasing in number with the passing years, new ministerial science and technology advisers' offices—consisting primarily of domestic talent—were established in individual government departments, such as the Ministry of Education, the Ministry of Economic Affairs, the Ministry of Communications, and the Ministry of National Defense. Both the Council of Agriculture and the Department of Health assigned such responsibility to groups which already existed under their jurisdiction. These advisory offices now coordinate activities in their individual ministries in exactly the same way that STAG does under the Cabinet.

These modifications of the governmental administrative structure, carried out in order to meet the need to use additional science and technology manpower for national development, represented a significant step in the process of making certain that the nation would be prepared for the advent of the 1980s.

THE OPERATION AND ROLES OF SCIENCE ADVISERS

Annual Board Meetings and Mid-Term Consultative Meetings

Since 1980, a full meeting of the STAG board has been held once every year. The principal part of the meeting, which lasts for about a week, takes place in the form of group and individual sector discussions among the science advisers, the relevant government officials, Chinese experts, and representatives of private industry.

Such group discussions, in addition to covering the areas of specialization of

Figure 2. Three Stages of Science and Technology Development in the Republic of China

Period / Item	1st Period BASIC 1966–76	2nd Period DEVELOPMENT 1976–86	3rd Period CRUCIAL TIME 1986–2000
Economic Situation	• Improve environment for investment • Develop labor-intensive & export-oriented industries	• Readjust industrial structure • Encourage industrial research and development • Develop technology-intensive industries	• Join the group of developed countries
Emphasis on S&T Development	• Improve S&T education • Promote basic research	• Promote major thrust programs and basic science • Training of S&T personnel	• Continue development in high technology
Major Measures	• Set up more departments and graduate schools at universities and improve quality of facilities • Establish five basic science research and engineering centers (1964–65) • Scientific Development Steering Committee (1967) • National Science Council (1967) • Chung-Shan Institute of Science & Technology (1969) • Telecommunication Research Institute (1968) • Industrial Technology Research Institute (1973)	• Committee for Scientific Development of the Executive Yuan established (1976) • 1st and 2nd National Conf. on S&T held (1978, 1982) • S&T Development Program promulgated (1979, 1982) • Science and Technology Advisory Group set up (1979) • Establishment of Hsinchu Science Industrial Park (1980) • Academia Sinica formulated two five-year plans (1st: 1981–1986; 2nd: 1986–1991) • Training and recruiting of S&T Personnel Program promulgated (1983) • SRCC established (1984)	• 3rd National Conf. on S&T held (1986) • Ten-year S&T Development Program (1986–1995) • Promotion of large-scale research projects • Encouragement of R&D in private industry
Economic Development GNP	US$2,361,132	US$1,132,841	GNP Target 2000 US$13,400

the respective science advisers, include sessions involving interdisciplinary matters. For example, sessions dealing with water resources, satellite development, and ocean science and technology were discussed in 1989. More recently, issues related to environmental protection and manufacturing technology were included in the areas for discussion.

A mid-term consultative meeting of the STAG board is held once every year outside of Taiwan. On this occasion, progress reports are made concerning the implementation of recommendations that were developed during the annual meetings. Through this means and by follow-up visits to the Republic of China just prior to the annual meetings, the advisers are kept well informed of developments, and they are in good positions to hold in-depth discussions with their Chinese colleagues during the major annual meetings.

Following each meeting of the STAG board, the conclusions that have been reached as a result of the group discussions and the recommendations made by the advisers are presented to the Premier by the advisers in a special session. Subsequently, the recommendations are transmitted to the relevant government departments for further study and implementation as circumstances permit. Through this pattern of continuous review and evaluation, the recommendations advanced by the science advisers have provided an important source of information for the formulation of national policy in areas related to science and technology on a continuous basis.

Technical Review Boards

Depending upon their fields of specialization, some science advisers have also contributed—when the need has arisen—to the formulation of policy on specific technical issues dealing with new projects in the fields of science and industrial development. Such work is usually carried out through a special board, consisting of distinguished experts, of which a large proportion are Chinese professionals who have acquired extensive experience while working abroad. The boards also include experts and project managers from local industries and institutions. Two such boards, one of which covers industrial electronics and computer technology, have been working harmoniously within the country to help it acquire state-of-the-art expertise in their fields.

It must be emphasized that the engagement of foreign science advisers to assist the government in the formulation of long-range policies for the development of science, as well as in the evaluation of the results of implementing existing policies, represents but one aspect of the various endeavors of the government to promote the development of science and technology. The convocation of the first National Science and Technology Conference in 1978 marked one of the first important steps undertaken by the government to solicit a concerted effort in the promotion of these areas at a national level. Scientists, intellectuals from academic institutions, and other experts, as well as representatives of government and private enterprise and officials concerned with planning and implementation, have all contributed opinions regarding policies for improving science education and other activities that could accelerate the development of science and technology.

Moreover, the convocation of special seminars, such as the Modern Engineering and Technology Seminar, sponsored by the Chinese Institute of Engineers on a bi-annual basis, have been very important. Still further, the activities associated with the various research institutes of the universities and the Industrial Technology Research Institute have contributed to the development of individual fields of science and technology in a concerted way. Nevertheless, the formation of the STAG board has brought an added international dimension to the entire process of evaluating strategic goals for the country.

THE ADVISER'S CONTRIBUTIONS TO POLICY

The following provide some examples of the way in which the new advisory structure has functioned to help the Chinese government.

Collecting Data for Policy Formation

As early as 1980, the science advisers proposed that the country conduct a national survey of existing science and technology activities in order to provide the government with comprehensive information about manpower and the expenditures associated with the work of professional scientists and engineers. Such information could clearly form a basis for the continuous evaluation of the country's technical strength and the resources devoted to sustaining it. Such surveys have been carried out through the intervening years by the National Science Council, and have been published by that agency in the form of special annual reports.

Strengthening the Cultivation of Young Talent

Following the suggestion of the science advisers that China adopt a more flexible approach toward the cultivation of young scientists, the Cabinet generated, in 1983, the policy document, "Measures for Strengthening the Cultivation and Engagement of High-Level Scientific Personnel." This document marked a breakthrough since it provided a new approach to the process of refining the system of science education in the country. The new provisions have injected flexibility into the educational system and have helped it keep pace with the advancement of science and technology. The improvements have been continuous in the course of recent years.

Emphasis on Fields of Specialization in Universities

The members of the advisory board have helped the universities define and promote their respective long-term development programs. In particular, they have encouraged various institutions to select and develop individual fields of specialization.

Hepatitis B Control and New Medical Systems

Intensive research on the prevention and control of hepatitis B was started in 1981. The results of such research led the government to decide on the use of injected vaccine for high-risk groups, starting on July 1, 1984. By July 1, 1986, all newborn babies in the country had been given hepatitis B vaccine immunization. In addition, a guidance committee on hepatitis B control, consisting of American experts, was established. The director of the New York Blood Center, who serves as a member of the committee, has been invited to Taiwan each year, together with two or three other experts. The experts review the progress of the control program and evaluate its achievements. They have also offered advice on experimentation with locally produced hepatitis B vaccine plasmas.

In addition and to support the effective distribution of health care facilities, the Department of Health initiated a program for setting up group practice centers in remote areas where doctors are scarce. Along with this, support was given to grade A and B hospitals. As the years have passed, such innovative programs as a medicare network and three-level medicare systems have been adopted in sequence by the Department of Health. The results have been quite successful.

Emphasis on Environmental Protection

The science advisers have shown concern about the pollution of the country's environment for many years. Apart from urging the government quite early to take active steps to strengthen the protection of the environment, they presented to the government, in May 1986, the suggestion that a special government agency be established to undertake overall responsibility for enforcing environmental protection.

As a first step, the Committee for Environmental Protection was established, under the Cabinet, in July of the same year. During the following year, it was elevated to the Department of Environmental Protection under the Cabinet. Moreover, "environmental science and technology" has been included among the twelve strategic areas of science and technology for special development.

Initiation of Venture Capital Investments

With a view to improving the country's investment climate in such a way as to accommodate high-tech industries, the advisers recommended, in a 1983 meeting, that an appropriate venture capital system be studied and introduced. The government initiated work on this matter with the help of the advisers and, in

1985, proclaimed new measures for the encouragement of venture capital investment in the country, initially from sources in the United States.

Up to 1989, eleven cases of venture capital investment by foreign and domestic investors had been realized. These have exerted a stimulus on additional investment in high technology in the country.

Overall Improvement of Product Quality

Another concern shared by the relevant government authorities and the science advisers relates to the adoption of effective measures for encouraging domestic industry to improve the quality of its products. At present, the China Productivity Center has been given overall responsibility for carrying out such improvements on a nationwide basis.

Modification of Government Regulations

Another significant contribution of the advisers is their advocacy of flexibility in attitude toward the modification of governmental systems and regulations to enable the country to create a climate more conducive to rapid science and technology development. The barrier to innovations and systems must be removed in order to attract talented people and meet the needs of a modern scientific society. Many actions have been taken to meet this need in the science and technology development program.

TOWARD THE THIRD WAVE

The decade from 1990 to 2000 will mark the third wave of science and technology development in China—a period in which the country expects to join the ranks of advanced countries. To meet the challenges of this new era, the development effort in China will be committed to the following:

- Accelerating the growth of domestic high-tech industries and participating in investment in such industries abroad;
- Introducing new technologies for the upgrading of traditional industries in order to enable them to produce high value-added products;
- Encouraging private industry to increase its research and development expenditure and manpower so that it can be ready to meet new competition and new challenges. When launching the third wave of effort for the extended development of science and technology, it is clear that there is a continued need for China to make judgments and decisions within an extended international perspective. It must narrow the technological gap that exists between the Republic of China and the advanced coun-

tries, and it must strengthen international cooperation in science and technology in order to enable the country to reach higher levels of accomplishment. In these circumstances, the science advisers will, of necessity, assume even more important roles than before in the formulation of policies.

Science and Technology: Their Roles in the Development of Cuba

Rosa Elena Simeón Negrín

THE REPUBLIC OF CUBA *was founded in 1902 as an independent state, and came under a Marxist-dominated regime in 1959. It was established as a Communist country in 1961, and the constitution in effect at present was adopted in 1976. Its land area is 110,860 square kilometers, and its population is 10,199,276. Spanish is the official language. As of December 31, 1989, the US dollar was equal to .79 pesos at the official rate.*

The island of Cuba measures 110,860 square kilometers. It is the largest in the archipelago of the Antilles. Its population is 10,199,276. Havana City, with approximately 2.2 million inhabitants, is the capitol of the Republic of Cuba. The mean annual temperature is 25.5 Celsius, and the mean rainfall per year is 1,375 millimeters.

Cuba is a socialist state. The National Assembly of People's Power is the supreme state body and the only one with constitutional and legislative powers. It is composed of deputies elected by Municipal Assemblies. The Council of State is the body that represents the assembly between seasons.

The highest executive and administrative body is the Council of Ministers, which is responsible to the National Assembly. The president and vice presidents are members of its Executive Committee; they control and coordinate the Central Agencies by sectors. These agencies of the state's Administration are subordinate to the Council of Ministers, and are classified into three entities: the state committee, the ministry, and the institute. The administration of justice is the function of the Supreme People's Court and other courts.

The political, economic and cultural conditions imposed on Cuba, first by the colonial regime and later by the neocolonial one, determined an extremely unfavorable framework for any national development of science and technology. Even so, the country had some figures of relevance in scientific fields, such as Carlos J. Finlay, Felipe Poey, Alvaro Reynoso, Enrique José Varona, and other distinguished Cuban naturalists and scientists who, on many occasions—thanks to their personal efforts and exceptional perseverance—sur-

Rosa Elena Simeón Negrín, M.D., has been President of the Cuban Academy of Sciences since 1985. Born in 1943, she is an Adjunct Professor at the University of Havana from which she received her medical degree in 1966. She is a member of a number of scientific societies and has been widely published.

mounted the official disinterest of the time. At some times, even in spite of persecution and harrassment, they were able to create enduring work.

The situation was compounded by a high rate of illiteracy and poor development in the training of middle-level and higher technicians and specialists. The implementation of the project presented by Fidel Castro during his defense at the trial for the attack on the Moncada Barracks (known as the "Moncada Program") began in 1959, the year of the Cuban Revolution.

The thrust of the program was to change nature, revolutionize education, and place the world's scientific progress at the service of the Cuban people. In 1960, the Chief of the Revolution asserted: ". . . we are planning opportunities for intelligence . . . so that our future is that of men of science."

In the early 1960s, concrete steps were taken, under his guidance, to promote and generalize the research activities at the universities.

The commission in charge of organizing the Academy of Sciences of Cuba was created in 1962, and the structuring of its institutes began. It was then that the Centro Nacional de Investigaciónes Cientificas (the National Research Center), the Instituto de Ciencia Animal (the Animal Science Institute), the Centro de Investigación Digital (the Digital Research Institute), and the Instituto de Fisica Nuclear (the Nuclear Physics Institute) were created.

THE FIRST RESEARCH CENTERS

The organization of the first technological research centers in the country was closely linked to the foresight and encouragement of Commander Ernesto "Che" Guevara, Minister of Industry. At his initiative, the Cuban Institutes of Sugar Cane Derivatives, Mineral Resources, and Mining and Metallurgical Research were started.

It was also during the mid-1960s that the first medical research institutions of the country were established. They were to serve as the scientific backing of an intense transfer and assimilation of know-how and specialized technology to implement the extraordinary programs of the revolution aimed at promoting and preserving the health of the population.

All this potential contributed to providing the necessary impetus to develop the national economy, to undertake the complex tasks related to the diversification of production, and to confront—in the scientific and technological fields— the economic blockade and all sorts of aggressions to which the country has been—and is—subjected.

The strategy charted for science, from the early years of the revolution to date, has allowed the most valuable result of the creative efforts of the revolution in this area: the formation of a large contingent of specialists highly trained for creative work in science and technology. This has enabled the country to attain undeniable scientific and technical achievements and to have a vast and well prepared contingent of professionals and technicians that, from the factories to the service units, has the capability to meet the complex problems in their daily activities and to obtain higher quality and productive efficiency with important social results.

In the past decade, in line with the newest international scientific objectives designed to revolutionize different areas of human knowledge and put them at the service of production and society, Cuban science has advanced in four directions: genetic engineering, biotechnology, computer science, and nuclear energy development.

This has given rise to new research centers, such as the Centro de Ingeniería Genetica y Biotécnologia (Genetic Engineering and Biotechnology Center), the Centro de Immunoensayo (Immunoassay Investigation Center), the Centro de Estudios Aplicados al Desarrollo de la Energia Nuclear (Center for Research Applied to Nuclear Energy Development), the Centro Nacional de Biopreparados (National Biopreparations Center), the Centro de Robotica y Software (the Robotics and Software Center), and the Centro de Investigaciónes Nucleares (Nuclear Research Center).

All of these now make significant contributions to production and health care in the country. Their work allows the use of the knowledge and technology that distinguish the contemporary scientific and technological revolution and are expressed in accomplishments such as the construction of the first nuclear power plant and different applications of atomic energy; the introduction and expansion of electronics, cybernetics and computers in social and economic activities; and the applications of achievements in biotechnology and modern biology, among others. The first scientific research ship, the "Ulises," has carried out several expeditions on our seas with encouraging results.

STATE ORGANIZATION FOR THE DEVELOPMENT OF SCIENTIFIC AND TECHNOLOGICAL POLICIES

National scientific and technological policy is laid down in documents of the Cuban Communist Party, both in the Programmatic Platform and the Party Platform, consisting essentially of turning science into a direct asset for production, economic activity, and social development. The fundamental principles for the implementation of this policy are:

- Planned development of science and technology to serve the development of the productive forces of society and the improvement of life as a whole;
- Adequate combination of basic and applied research with emphasis on the latter, so that science responds to the major tasks stemming from the industrialization process of the country, the intensification of agricultural production, and the fulfillment of long-term economic strategy;
- Accelerated assimilation and use of technologies and achievements of other countries and the strengthening of national capabilities for technological generation in line with national possibilities;

- Strengthening adequate branch distribution of scientific and technical potential by organized development of materials and human resources; and
- Constant upgrading of the scientific and technical information network.

ORGANIZATIONS IN THE NATIONAL S&T SYSTEM

The Academy of Sciences of Cuba is the national organization charged with controlling the application of government policies to the development of science and technology. To this end, it directs, coordinates and executes the scientific and technical research activities of the country. Among its functions are the following:

- To draw up the National Science and Technology Plan, both the five-year and the annual plans, taking into account its impact on the economic and social development strategy of the country, controlling its implementation, and recommending draft budgets for scientific research and the different scientific-technical services;
- To propose to the government the creation, modification and deactivation of research and scientific-technical entities;
- To direct and conduct scientific research related to natural resources, environmental conservation, cultural and social development of the country, and research associated with modern methods in mathematics, physics and high technology development;
- To propose and control, once approved, the plan for the practical application of scientific-technical findings;
- To determine the norms and procedures related to the planning, organization and control of scientific-technical activity in coordination with the rest of the state administration entities;
- To coordinate and control the national environmental protection network and the rational use of natural resources;
- To determine, direct and control the development and upgrading of the different national scientific-technical service systems, such as scientific-technical information; meteorological services; registry of patent applications for innovations, industrial models, and new trademarks and other forms of industrial property; and the National Archives;
- To direct, supervise and control the application of the scientific categories system, and participate in the design and execution of the scientific cadre training policy and the granting of scientific degrees; and
- To promote, supervise and control the development of scientific and technical organizations and societies in coordination with the rest of the state administration entities.

The Academy of Sciences organizes the necessary consultancy through a system of scientific councils to direct, execute and control the implementation of state and government policy in science and technology; formulate and apply scientific policy, analyses of plans and tasks, and recommendations stemming from research; and evaluate the scientific findings and their practical applications, among others.

The Scientific Councils are organized to advise the academy and all research centers which adopt conveniently flexible structures and compositions. The council draws upon the most qualified individuals in institutions and agencies, be they related to research, production, or public service activities.

Other organizations that participate in the formulation and realization of scientific policy by directing and controlling the application of state policy in their areas of competence are:

- The State Committee for Norms (in the applications of norms, measures and quality control);
- The State Committee on Economic Cooperation (in the development of economic and scientific-technical cooperation activities in coordination with the Academy of Sciences);
- The State Committee for Finance (in the application of state and government financial policy);
- The Ministry of Education (in the direction and realization of state educational policy for elementary, middle and secondary education);
- The Ministry of Higher Education (in the direction and application of state and government policy on university education); and
- The National Institute for Automated Systems and Computer Techniques (in activities related to automated management and computer techniques).

SPECIALIZATION OF THE R&D INSTITUTIONS

In 1987, the country had 143 institutions, research centers, and areas for research and development (R&D) to carry out scientific investigations. Their structures were organized according to their research themes and grouped in five main branches.

R&D institutes totaled 110, with twenty-six for agriculture, forty for technical research, nineteen for medical, twenty for social, and five for the exact sciences. R&D areas consisted of thirty-three including one for agricultural research, seventeen for technical, three for medical, eleven for social, and one for the natural and exact sciences. This meant that, of the total of 143 institutions, twenty-seven were for agricultural research, fifty-seven for technical research, twenty-two for medical, thirty-one for social, and six for the natural and exact sciences.

THE NATIONAL SCIENCE AND DEVELOPMENT BUDGET

The country earmarked 228.7 million pesos for scientific activities in 1987. This amount represented a tripling of that figure during the present decade.

Table 1. Research Institutions by Organizations, 1987

	Number of R&D Institutions	Current Expenditures (Millions of Pesos)
Ministry of Public Health	16	25.3
Ministry of Agriculture	17	23.7
Ministry of the Sugar Industry	4	22.6
Ministry of Higher Education	24	19.2
Academy of Sciences	17	8.9
Ministry of Steel & Engineering Industry	10	7.4
Ministry of Basic Industry	9	7.4
Council of State	2	3.2
Ministry of the Food Industry	2	3.2
Ministry of the Fishing Industry	5	3.1
National Institute for Automated Systems and Computer Techniques	2	3.0
Ministry of Transport	1	1.9
Ministry of Communications	1	1.8
Ministry of the Building Materials Industry	1	1.6
Ministry of Construction	2	1.4
State Committee for Technical and Material Supplies	2	1.0
Nuclear Matters Secretariat	2	1.0
National Institute for Sport, Physical Education, and Recreation	2	0.8
Ministry of Light Industry	1	0.7
Ministry of Culture	10	0.6
State Committee for Labor and Social Security	2	0.5
Central Planning Board	2	0.5
Ministry for Education	1	0.4
Cuban Hydroeconomics Institute	1	0.3
State Committee for Statistics	1	0.3
Ministry of Foreign Trade	1	0.3
People's Power	3	0.2
State Committee for Finance	1	0.1
National Bank of Cuba	1	0.1
Total	143	140.5

One-third of these expenses went toward new investments in science and technology. Of the remaining amount, 92% went to scientific research, 7% to scientific-technical services, and 1% to scientific-technical information.

In Cuba, twenty-nine organizations of the State Central Administration have research and development institutions. According to their financing, the distribution by organization is shown in Table 1.

HUMAN RESOURCES DEDICATED
TO SCIENTIFIC R&D

In 1987, the research center network of the country had 28,089 Cuban workers of which 47% were women and 8,468 were university graduates. Of the latter, 63% (5,338) met the requirements for undertaking scientific research, and the rest were mid-level technicians. High scientific categories had been attained by 1,383 university graduates who were joined by 12,302 highly qualified professionals in higher education whose functions included scientific research. At that time, the country had 2,524 Ph.D. candidates and 177 Ph.D.s in different areas of science.

Of those individuals engaged in R&D activities, 34% were in the agricultural sciences, 33% in the technical sciences, 24% in biomedical, 5% in social, and 4% in the natural and exact sciences.

In 1987, Cuba had 846 R&D scientists and engineers per million population, wholly devoted to scientific research.

THE PLAN FOR 1986–90

The third Cuban five-year plan for science and technology, directed by the Academy of Sciences, is based on applying scientific findings as the objects of planning and control. These are presently designed and executed from the research phase to their applications in social practice. The main expression of the plan—the twenty-two scientific-technical programs—are associated with the most important national economic programs and their scientific findings promote the increase of export products, import substitution, energy savings, the optimal use of natural resources, the development of new materials, and other national interests.

To guarantee adequate relationships among the different organizations participating in the planning, execution and control of the different categories of the National Science and Technology Plan, each program or research problem is systematically submitted to a group of experts. These individuals are highly qualified and prominent specialists who direct the branches of research as well as technicians in the relevant production areas.

Expenditures in 1987 under the National Science and Technology Plan were divided into categories as follows: 31% into scientific-technical programs, 39% into branch research problems, 20% into biomedical research problems, 2% into social science research problems, 7% into fundamental research problems, and 1% into scientific works.

Another category of the National Research Plan is being developed for the future: "Territorial, Entrepreneurial, and Other Interests."

SCIENTIFIC-TECHNICAL SERVICES

The country has deployed significant efforts to develop scientific-technical services that were not in existence or were extremely weak in 1959 at the time of the triumph of the revolution.

At present, the main scientific-technical services provided in the country (scientific information; meteorological and seismological data; brands, trademarks and inventions, among others) are subordinate to the Academy of Sciences of Cuba. These services are provided by especially created institutions that have networks and branches throughout the country.

The national scientific-technical information network is composed of 886 information units that, in 1987, provided 4.7 million information services and had holdings of 2.2 million volumes.

The National Library of Science and Technology—with modern techniques to capture, process, store, transfer, and use information—offers specialized services. It includes an established, automated information and remote access network with services like the creation of data bases, access to foreign data banks, and telematic and telecommunication services. From 1981 to 1987, the number of users has increased thirty-one times, the number of documents disseminated has trebled, and the information sources have grown by a factor of thirty-four.

A total of 197 scientific and technical journals are published in Cuba.

The Meteorological Institute devotes its activities to the execution of eight scientific-technical services and the scientific and technological research that supports these activities. These include weather forecasting, marine meteorology, climatic advisory and information, agrometeorology, monitoring atmospheric pollution, actinometrics, specialized instruments, and artificial rain. The institute possesses a network of over seventy meteorological stations of diverse types, located throughout the country.

Legal protection to create activity that results from R&D, as well as production and service findings, is attained by submitting applications to the National Office for Inventions, Technical Information, and Trademarks. The main objectives of this office are to offer national methodological guidance related to industrial property, technical information service, and assessment to Cuban and foreign enterprises and entities, and to grant the rights which the law confers in order to protect inventions, scientific discoveries, models, and trademarks. It has holdings of thirteen million titles, which are increased annually by more than 700,000 new documents.

The National Archive is the depository of important national historical papers and other documentary holdings. Allied closely with the production sphere, other types of scientific services are offered, including normalization, measures, and quality control. The national seismological service runs six specialized stations located at risk spots and devoted to detecting seismic activity.

ENVIRONMENTAL PROTECTION

The National Commission for the Protection of the Environment and Natural Resources, an adjunct of the Presidency of the Academy of Sciences and under the direction of the Local Organizations of People's Power, has the objectives of coordinating and controlling the environmental protection tasks that are the responsibility of the different organizations of the Cuban State. The problems that have received the most attention and hold the top priorities are related to the protection of water resources, soil, beach preservation, forests and animal life, and the atmosphere.

Special attention has been given to the pollution of Cuba's bays and the environmental situation in tourist areas, as well as the National System of Protected Areas and Reforestation. The country does not, in general, face grave pollution problems, although work is being carried out to solve some local problems caused by industry and automotive transport. Active work is being conducted also in the economic reutilization of waste, particularly in the sugar industry.

INTERNATIONAL COOPERATION

In the development of the scientific institutions of the country and the training and upgrading of the human potential, invaluable contributions have come in the form of international cooperation, especially from the Academies of Sciences in Socialist countries and particularly that of the Soviet Union. No less important are the contributions that Cuba has received from institutions and individuals in the countries of the world which cooperated disinterestedly in the Cuban Revolution.

Science and Technology Advice to the Federal Government and Parliament in Czechoslovakia

Anton Blažej

THE CZECHOSLOVAK SOCIALIST REPUBLIC *(Československá Socialistická Republika) is an independent republic which was established in 1918. In 1948, a Communist People's Republic was formed, followed by the establishment of a Socialist republic in 1960. In late 1989, a nonCommunist leadership took over the country. The land area of the country is 49,370 square miles, and the population was estimated at 15,606,000 in 1989. The official languages of the country are Czech and Slovak.*

The Czechoslovak Socialist Republic (CSR) is a highly industrialized nation with a plan-based economy. In this sense, the Czechoslovak experience and a comparison of the present state and future trends in governmental science and technology policy can be fruitful, interesting and instructive.

The scientific and technological revolution currently taking place in industrially developed countries has a significant influence also in the developing countries where it affects the process of industrialization. It is, therefore, of a global character. As a social phenomenon, this revolution is reflected in qualitative changes in production forces and affects mainly the material and technological bases of industrial and agricultural production. Similarly, it is reflected in the service industries and, indeed, it influences all aspects of life, both in society in general and individually.

Technical advancement typical of the period of industrialization is transformed into scientific-technological advancement. Science becomes the driving force, the chief factor of the economic and social growth of the national economy. Scientific and technological development becomes a new type of development: the integration of new scientific knowledge, its acquisition, and its utilization and implementation in practice. That is why it becomes the main source of productivity of labor, the key factor in the growth of the Gross National Product (GNP), and a basic source of improvements in the standard of living and changes in lifestyles. It introduces a new dimension into the economic, social and cultural development of society.

Anton Blažej is President of the Slovak Technical University in Bratislava, Czechoslovakia, and a member of the Slovak and Czechoslovak Academies of Science. He is a member of the country's Parliament and its presidium and serves on committees for the human environment and science and technology. Dr. Blažej's fields are macromolecular chemistry and biochemistry, and he is author or co-author of twenty-three books and 356 scientific papers. He also serves on many international committees.

The need is to develop a new economic and ecological thinking among all citizens in all nations. This will require new national school systems in all countries.

The successful development of the Czechoslovak national economy will be conditioned by the effective use of science and the rational exploitation of creative invention and the creative activities of people. This is why Czechoslovakia has prioritized education as a decisive factor in the intensification of the national economy.

The educational system is strategic, and the Czechoslovak philosophy is that not science or technology or manufacture, but the education of people along with their creative initiatives and activities will influence basic research, the levels of technology, industry, agriculture and services, and productivity.

Economic competition in international trade is technological competition, and technological competition has its roots in the school system of a nation.

THE CONCEPT OF CZECHOSLOVAK SCIENCE AND TECHNOLOGY POLICY

The Czechoslovak Government's science and technology policy is based on the following concepts:

- Strengthening the scientific and technological potential and increasing the ability to effectively use this potential in the national economy. (The scientific and technological potential involves the use of human resources—such as scientists and engineers, material and equipment, sophisticated devices, machine and pilot-scale manufacturing, a system of information resources, and the scientific management of research and development.);
- Strengthening the link between government and research and development institutions with the cooperation of industry;
- Choosing national priorities and approving long-term, large-scale projects in the national research and development program;
- Promoting technological development in the industrial, agricultural and service sectors;
- Supporting international cooperation in research and development;
- Strengthening human resources for science and technology through a new system of science education;
- Increasing the governmental budget from 4.5% of the national income to 5.5% for 1990. (Annual growth depends upon economic growth.); and
- Improving the efficiency of research and development and the promotion of the transfer of scientific and technological knowledge in industry, agriculture and services.

THE ORGANIZATION STRUCTURE OF SCIENCE AND TECHNOLOGY

The responsible organization for basic science policy for government is the Czechoslovak Academy of Sciences, which is an administrative and executive institution. University research in basic science also falls under the auspices of this academy.

Basic science research represents 12% of the research and development potential in the country. The President of the Academy of Sciences is an "invited member" of the federal government, and as such is the chief adviser to the Prime Minister for Science.

For industrial science, technological research, and development, the Federal Committee for Scientific Technological Development and Investment has been set up. The chairman of this committee is a vice prime minister and is responsible to the Prime Minister for Industrial Science and Technology.

The roles of the Federal Committee are as follows:

- To serve as an advisory body to government in the field of industrial research and development;
- To prepare long-term forecasts for research and development;
- To approve research and development projects and the national research and development program;
- To distribute government budget for research and development projects;
- To create and develop a new potential for research and development;
- To manage the federal research institutions and governmental agencies, such as the National Office for Metrology, the National Office for Patents, and the National Office for Scientific Technological Information;
- To coordinate industrial research and development in the respective branches of the national economy;
- To develop legislation in the framework of science, technology, and the human environment;
- To strengthen systematic collaboration between government, research and development institutions, universities, and industry;
- To improve efficiency in capital investment;
- To assess research and development projects and the levels of results and their conformity with social needs, the economic value of their results, their potential utilization in the national economy, and their practicality, etc.; and
- To make policy in regard to the human environment.

THE COMMITTEE FOR DEVELOPMENT AND INVESTMENT

The vice prime minister heads the Council of Committees which includes forty-five members. The composition of the council is made up of leading scientists and engineers, directors of selected research institutions, leading managers from industry and agriculture, professional scientific-technological association members, the President of the Academy of Sciences, members of government agencies, and representatives of industrial branches.

Members of the council are chairmen of twelve different sections, each of which consists of twenty-five to thirty members, for industrial branches, and general research and development affairs (planning, information technology, cybernetics, etc.). The whole advisory potential represents about 350 professionals, and its headquarters contain more than 300 staff members and executives. Thus the federal government has a highly intellectual advisory potential for policy-making in science, technology, and research and development.

In the Czechoslovak political system, the President does not have power equivalent to that of the President of the United States. Therefore, it is not necessary to have a President's Science Advisory Committee.

The same situation exists in the Federal Assembly (Parliament), which does not have a body representing science and technology. Policy-making has until now been concentrated in the Czechoslovak Communist Party, which has a standing committee on science and technology. This committee has forty-five members who are leading professionals from many sectors of the national economy.

PRACTICAL EXPERIENCE WITH COMMITTEES

Czechoslovakia has a high level of research and development. Its reputation in science and technology, capability of research workers, educational system, and the level of university education in science holds a leading position in Europe. A very topical issue is the question arising as to the Czechoslovak share in the development of new high technologies. It is a great pity that, from administrative and directive central planning and management, the country has not been able to better utilize and effectively commercialize this potential to the benefit of the national economy.

Another reason for this is the low level of stimulation and motivation of gifted research workers and professionals. There has not been an adequate climate of stimulation for entrepreneurs.

Also, the overcentralized economy and rigid system of economic management that had contributed to the rate of economic growth during the past twenty years has dropped in production efficiency, quality of output, productivity, and science-based technology as compared with most industrialized countries.

International cooperation in science and technology has been oriented only within the Council of Mutual Economic Assistance (CMEA) in the socialist countries. This group, for a long time, believed in the fact that the socialist community had the world's leading edge in basic science and in high technology. This illusion was removed during the Gorbachev era, and opened the door to cooperation with developed countries in the West. The monopolistic and bureaucratic structure and the directive central planning of science and technology have been overcome. Conditions have been created for a new kind of science. Scientific and technological development has become a driving force in the new strategies toward economic and social progress. The wide application of science and technology has appeared in all spheres of human life and society.

THE 1990S AND BEYOND

Science and scientific-technological knowledge are the most important sources of socioeconomic growth and a better quality of life. The coming century will be:

- The age of science;
- The age of high technology; and
- The age of science-based industry, agriculture and services.

Science will shape both our professional and our private lives. The scientific literacy of every private individual will be needed. Policy decision-makers will have to be capable of accepting science-based policies. High-level politicians will need to understand the following:

- Scientific thinking;
- Scientific language;
- Know-how of science;
- How to support native pioneer research projects and technological development based on original scientific discoveries and technological breakthroughs;
- How to support freedom of individual creative scientific activity and innovation;
- Rejection of stereotypical, ideological dogmas in scientific activity;
- Assessment of a new quality of national economic development; and
- Removal of complacency and the necessity to rely on what is developed "in-house" in the socialist world and go beyond the borders of the socialist community.

CONCLUSION

The conclusions are:

- Science and technology and creative skilled manpower are the main factors in intensification of the national economy through scientific and technological innovation;
- It is necessary to create new high technologies and new original manufacturing processes through creatively applying scientific knowledge to all spheres of practice;

- New technology creates new economic potential; and
- New economic potential brings new qualitative socioeconomic and cultural growth.

None of these goals can be reached without the understanding and support of science and technology in the highest levels of government. The country's leaders need to create an advisory committee for science and technology or a Department of Science and Technology for the future. Czechoslovakia is already on the right track with its Committees on Science and Technology.

The Central Science and Technology Organization in Egypt

Aboui-Fotouh Abdel-Latif

THE ARAB REPUBLIC OF EGYPT *(Jumhuriyat Misr al-'Arabiyah) was established as a republic in 1953, and joined with Syria as the United Arab Republic in 1958, retaining the name after Syria withdrew in 1961. The present name has been in effect since 1971, and the limited multiparty system of government since 1980. Its land area is 386,659 square miles, and its estimated 1989 population was 53,573,000. The country's official language is Arabic.*

Though science and technology have deep roots in Egypt, the need for scientific research—in the contemporary sense of the phrase—began to be recognized only during the 19th century. High schools for engineering, medicine and agricultural science were established in the years 1820, 1827 and 1829, respectively. The introduction of cotton farming, which was to become the backbone of the Egyptian economy, and the subsequent development of irrigation systems to assure its production; the expansion of the mining industry, particularly in regard to phosphate and manganese for export; and the ever-increasing interest in the medical aspects of endemic diseases all acted as spurs to modern technological development.

Basic research was started with the establishment of the first national university in Cairo in 1925. Aside from serving general educational purposes, the university created recognized schools of research into the fundamental sciences. The emphasis on basic research also dominated most of the activities carried out in the many research centers that were established during the years that followed. These research entities were encouraged by the Egyptian Government to gradually include applied research, especially in the fields of agriculture, medicine, and civil engineering.

At the present time, Egypt has twelve universities and over one hundred research institutes or centers that are affiliated with ministries of the government. The year 1952 witnessed a radical change with the establishment of research bodies to carry out applied research in fields having direct impacts on the national economy. Examples of these organizations are the National Research Center, the Atomic Energy Organization, and the Desert Research Insti-

Aboui-Fotouh Abdel-Latif is President of the Academy of Scientific Research and Technology, of which he previously served as Vice President and Secretary General. He was Director of the Lake Nasser Development Project (1967–1974); the Institute of Oceanography and Fisheries, Red Sea (1974–75); and the Institute of Oceanography and Fisheries, Egypt, 1975–77. Born in 1930, Dr. Abdel-Latif holds a Ph.D. in zoology and marine biology and is an ichthyologist.

tute. This development also stimulated the establishment of scientific societies and other nongovernmental bodies. Egypt thus became a member of the International (nongovernmental) Scientific Unions, Associations and Committees.

SCIENCE AND TECHNOLOGY MANPOWER AND INSTITUTIONS

The results of a national survey conducted in 1982–83 revealed the presence of 297 agencies involved in different aspects of science and technology, carrying out research and development or serving in the education and training of specialists and technicians to participate in scientific and technical activities.

Of these 297 entities, 189 or 63.6% are engaged in higher education, sixty-six or 22.3% in the production sector, and forty-two or 14.1% in the services sector.

Statistics on science and technology manpower reveal that there are over 30,000 holders of M.Sc., Ph.D. and D.Sc. degrees in all fields of science and technology in the country. Sixty-four percent of active scientists at Egyptian universities and research institutes are involved in the applied sciences, 18% in the social sciences, and 18% in the basic sciences.

Examples of institutions with well-recognized research activities in the country are the National Research Center, the Agricultural Research Center (under the Ministry of Agriculture and Food Security), the Water Research Center (Ministry of Irrigation), the Tibbin Institute for Metallurgical Studies (Ministry of Industry), the Atomic Energy Authority (Ministry of Electricity and Energy), and the Building Research Institute (Ministry of Housing and New Communities).

THE CENTRAL ORGANIZATION: ITS HISTORY

The increased awareness of and high regard for the roles of science and technology in promoting the national economic development, especially in agriculture and industry; the very sizeable and well-trained science community; and the existence of large numbers of research institutes necessitated the establishment of a central body to organize and coordinate these valuable resources and to direct them to problems in the national interest. Through the years, the central organization went through various stages, which included the Supreme Science Council (1956–61), the Ministry of Scientific Research (1961–65), the Supreme Council of Scientific Research (1965–68), the Ministry of Scientific Research (1968) and, lastly, in 1971, the Academy of Scientific Research and Technology (ASRT), affiliated with the Prime Minister.

Since 1974, the academy has been successively attached to ministers of scientific research and atomic energy or ministers of higher education and scientific research. The ministers represent the central policy-making body for scientific research in the Ministerial Cabinet.

The establishment of the academy coincided with the setting up of the National Council for Education and Scientific Research and Technology in 1974 as one of six specialized national councils linked directly to the President of the Republic. These councils are concerned with setting long-term policies to meet national objectives.

In 1972, the Supreme Council for Universities was established to elaborate on, orient and coordinate the general university policy of education and scientific research to meet the needs of the country and to attain the national, social, economic and scientific objectives of the state.

THE ACADEMY OF SCIENTIFIC RESEARCH AND TECHNOLOGY

The Academy of Scientific Research and Technology (ASRT) is the national governmental organization responsible for science and technology. The President of ASRT is appointed by a Presidential Decree, has the rank and power of a minister, and is chairman of the Academy Council. He is assisted by three vice presidents and a number of undersecretaries.

The main task of the academy is to support scientific research and to apply modern technology in socioeconomic development programs. The academy formulates and implements policies that mobilize the resources of science and technology institutes and centers and direct them to meet the needs of the national development plan. Within this context, ASRT encourages basic and applied research and organizes material and moral incentives, grants state awards in all branches of science, supports scientific societies, and works toward the popularization of science.

INSTRUMENTS OF ASRT

The instruments through which ASRT works include committees and councils, regional research centers, conferences and symposia, research institutions, and science and technology support services.

Committees and Councils

The Academy Council's membership clearly reflects its national responsibilities. The forty-two members are top policy-makers in national planning, production, services, and the executive level. Resolutions of the council are generally based on recommendations submitted by the various technical and planning councils.

Specialized Research Councils, Divisions and Committees have been established to carry out the ASRT functions of planning and coordinating scientific research at the national level, and number thirteen in all. Sixty divisions and committees support the functions of the specialized councils. Intercouncil committees are established to manage multidisciplinary programs involving several councils. *Ad hoc* committees are formed for certain necessary studies.

Over 2,000 specialists, experts and scientists affiliated with ministries, universities and research institutions are involved in the specialized councils and their affiliated divisions and committees.

Regional Research Centers

The ASRT is establishing a number of regional research centers that will identify, design and follow up on research programs that reflect the real needs of particular regions and serve regional development plans. The plans are prepared and implemented mainly by scientists and specialists from provincial universities, research stations, local government units, and, when required, national research centers and institutions.

Conferences and Symposia

The ASRT organizes conferences and symposia on technical and policy matters. It also gives financial and technical support to national institutes in this regard. The Academy Conference and the Specialized Research Councils Conferences are held annually to review policies and develop plans of action.

Research Institutions

The academy has established and supported a number of research and development institutes and centers, including the National Research Center, the National Institute for Standards, the Egyptian Petroleum Research Institute, the National Institute for Astronomy and Geophysics Research, the Central Metallurgical Research and Development Institute, the Theodore Bilharz Institute, and the National Institute of Oceanography and Fisheries. These institutes were formerly affiliated with the President of the ASRT and now come under the Minister of State for Scientific Research.

Science and Technology Support Services

The National Information and Documentation Center (NIDOC), the Patent Office, and the Statistical Information Division are affiliated with the ASRT. A National Science and Technology Information Network (ENSTINET) has been established in collaboration with USAID. Five components, covering the areas of agriculture, industry, health and medicine, science and technology, and energy are responsible for serving corresponding user sectors nationwide.

Instrumentation, Repair and Maintenance are carried out by the Scientific Instrumentation Center which is affiliated with ASRT and is considered a national multifunction center. Repair and maintenance workshops have been established at the National Research Center and at six universities.

The Egyptian Patent Office has more than 15,000 Egyptian patents in addition to over six million foreign patents. *The Innovation Office* is responsible for supporting innovation at the national level.

NATIONAL SCIENCE POLICIES AND PLANNING

The national science policy and the mechanisms for its implementation are based mainly on individual policies which have been adopted by the country in the fields of industry, agriculture, education, health, the economy, etc.

Generally speaking, science policy is intended to strengthen and mobilize the country's potential in science and technology for the implementation of national development plans. It embraces support for basic and applied sciences, provision of qualified scientific manpower, the proper utilization of natural resources, and the use of appropriate technologies. A science policy must address three major elements:

- Setting scientific and technological objectives consistent with national development plans;
- Optimizing the utilization of human and natural resources; and
- Setting criteria for the evaluation of the impact of the developed policy.

Program Planning and Project Support

In 1974, the academy started a system of contracted research. Over three hundred research projects were contracted for and implemented by national institutes and centers.

The 1980s have witnessed progress in the implementation of academy functions. This came about as a result of national recognition of the role of research and development, as well as increased financing, manpower training in research and development management, and infrastructure development.

The first five-year plan (July 1982–June 1987), which was followed by a second five-year plan, was an important milestone in the process of developing the functions of ASRT.

The First Five-Year Plan

The Specialized Councils of the academy played a major role in the development of the first five-year science and technology plan. This plan was based on extensive examination of the development objectives of the National Five-Year Development Plan. The science and technology plan is made up of research and development projects that have direct impacts on the National Development

Plan. All concerned ministries reviewed and approved the science and technology plan before it was carried out.

The academy produced a manual which included the procedures and by-laws for the preparation and implementation of contracted research. The sequential steps in the process are as follows:

- Advertisement,
- Submission of research proposals,
- Selection of a suitable candidate and institution,
- Contracting,
- Follow-up, and
- Evaluation.

Sometimes two or more institutions may be contracted with to be implementing agencies for one project.

The Second Five-Year Plan

The experience gained in the implementation of the first plan served in setting up the second plan. As major targets, the Second Five-Year Plan considered the following:

- More concentration on national development problems of multidisciplinary natures;
- Maximum benefits from foreign resources;
- Strengthening the links between the production sector and the research sector;
- Giving special emphasis to manpower development, particularly in the areas of research and development management, marketing, and design engineering; and
- Strengthening the role of local universities for effectively participating in local and regional development problems.

The Second Five-Year Science and Technology Plan includes the following programs:

- Sectoral research projects,
- Technology development,
- Development of local and regional programs,
- Multidisciplinary national programs,
- Science and technology infrastructure,
- Scientific and technological services,
- Scientific information and popularization of science, and
- Scientific relations (bilateral, regional, and international).

ACHIEVEMENTS AND EFFECTIVENESS OF ASRT

National science and technology policies have the primary objective of building indigenous capabilities to deal with national development problems. Therefore, science and technology policy has to include all the elements needed for the effective participation of science and technology in the country's development. This necessitates the following:

- Support from the highest governmental levels;
- The effective participation of all parties concerned with science and technology and its role in development, which must be in harmony with national development programs; and
- Continuity, consistence, commitment, and determination to carry it through.

The Five-Year Science and Technology Plan considered the foregoing elements of science policy, and all implementing agencies were involved in the preparation and follow-up of the plan.

The preparation and implementation of the ASRT five-year plan furnished the following general results.

The Role of ASRT as a National Body

The Egyptian Government and, in particular, the highest level of decision-makers and political leadership in the country have a very high regard for the role of ASRT in scientific and technical planning and management. ASRT is charged with formulating better definitions of national problems and appropriate subprojects with deliverables that meet user needs. Five intercouncil committees have been established to follow up on multidisciplinary, multi-institutional programs (the development of Sinai, integrated rural development, potable water and sewage, feed and food industries, and urbanization and megalopolis. The efforts of the members of the Specialized Councils, their commissions, and their committees are rationalized as top-level expertise.

ASRT is also responsible for establishing a sound basis for research and development management, upgrading the contracting system to suit client-oriented research and setting procedures and by-laws, and the rationalization of funds and other resources allocated for research and development.

In regard to research institutions, ASRT is responsible for collecting and disseminating information on the capabilities and potentials of the various research institutions, and effecting a competitive atmosphere among scientific institutions in regard to collaborating on projects.

Technical results for which ASRT is responsible include nationally recognized achievements in the areas of food and agriculture, industry, energy, the environment, and others.

About 13,000 persons participated in the implementation of the first five-

year plan. Among these were about 2,850 Ph.D's and about 1,100 experts.
The plan had thus succeeded in the mobilization of a broad base of science and
technology and in directing it toward national development priorities.

STRENGTHENING THE SCIENCE AND TECHNOLOGY
COMMUNITY

The ASRT supports scientific societies and faculties in the organization of conferences, symposia and workshops on crucial areas of science and technology.
The budgets allocated to scientific services are constantly being expanded, and
the ASRT is the national body that is responsible for this type of activity.

ASRT has established several research institutes (petroleum, metallurgy,
ophthalmology, Bilharziasis, beach erosion, remote-sensing, and electronics)
that operate side by side with older institutions, such as the National Research
Center and institutions concerned with oceanography and fisheries, metrology
and standards, and astronomy and geophysics.

The Five-Year Science and Technology Plan acted as a vehicle for communication and collaboration of the ASRT with national agencies in the production, services, and research and development sectors. The ASRT is looked
upon as the "House of the Scientific Community."

At the international level, a number of agreements of bilateral nature have
been in effect. These normally involve fact-finding missions by scientists, the
training of junior staff, and projects of mutual interest.

France helped in the establishment of the Petroleum Research Institute. The
Federal Republic of Germany assisted in forming the Theodore Bilharz Institution for Endemic Diseases.

The United Nations Development Plan assisted with the Scientific Instruments Center, the National Institute for Standards, the Shore Protection Institute, and the Oceanographic Data Center. The United States has supported a
number of research projects in different fields. Cooperation in the Remote Sensing
and Solar Energy projects with the National Science Foundation and Nile and
Lake Nasser project with the Environmental Protection Agency are three examples.

The Applied Science and Technology Program with the US included several
projects that served the production and services sectors, and gave special consideration to research and development management, instrumentation, and the
maintenance and repair of equipment.

A new agreement with USAID, signed in 1988, addresses three major levels
of action: national problems, regional problems, and new technologies. Also
the ASRT acts as the focal point for a number of international bodies and
unions, and it has formulated about thirty national committees affiliated with
the unions.

The science and technology community has become more aware of the real needs of the production and services sectors, which, in turn, have developed awareness among the community of users of science and technology results.

ASRT'S ADVISORY ROLE

The advisory role of ASRT has been expanding. The Specialized Councils have achieved results which are of great significance to national policies, plans and programs. Examples are the national campaigns for major crops which were initiated by the academy and now are exclusively implemented by the Ministry of Agriculture in collaboration with research institutes and universities. ASRT also sponsors national conferences directed at major problems in cooperation with concerned organizations, such as the Conference on Animal Development with the Ministry of Agriculture, water and sewage problems, the role of science in the development of desert provinces with local governorates, etc. The ASRT receives assignments from national political authorities, *e.g.*, the Prime Minister's request that ASRT study the energy conservation system, the problem of Alexandria's sewage, etc.

ASRT has provided stability and continuity to the science and technology system in Egypt. This has facilitated the growth and development of plans and programs. The academy directs, coordinates and integrates its activities with other systems of education, the economy, agriculture, health, construction, and so forth, which created a national awareness of local capabilities that can satisfy the national needs.

CONSTRAINTS AND NEEDS

In Egypt, as in many developing countries, a good part of the scientific effort is directed at fundamental research. Work on multidisciplinary applied research, however, still needs to be strengthened.

The emigration of scientists and skilled technicians to foreign countries, especially to the Arab countries, is another problem. The present regulations for recruitment, promotion, and financial incentives for scientific researchers need to be assessed. The centers of research and technology should not become institutions of academic study and theoretical research; they should cope with national development problems through applied research. Links between research and development institutions and the production and services sectors should be further strengthened.

A major constraint in the process of research and development is the proper maintenance of scientific and technical equipment. The need for workshops in research institutes to maintain and repair equipment is crucial. The presence of suitable stocks of spare parts is also vital.

At present, the budget allocated by the government is the major source of funding for science and technology activities. The participation of the production and services agencies and the private sector is limited.

CONCLUSION

As the policy-making body, the ASRT should adopt strategies that strengthen its role in applying science and technology to development. This will necessitate the following steps:

- The definition of long-term indicators of development strategy and its implementation plans, as well as the elucidation of the role of science and technology in these plans.
- The definition of future needs of scientists and technicians and the setting up of appropriate training for manpower development.
- The development of research and development marketing skills and the encouragement of end-user oriented research.
- The development of a strong system of science and technology information.
- The development of a national plan for the utilization of foreign financial resources. The steps taken by ASRT to establish research institutes for new technologies, such as biotechnology and genetic engineering, need foreign support.

Science and Technology Policy Advice in Finland

Esko-Olavi Seppälä

THE REPUBLIC OF FINLAND *(Suomen Tasavalta) has enjoyed an independent status since 1917, and has been a republic under the presidential-parliamentary system since 1919. Its land area is 130,119 square miles, and its population was estimated to be 4,960,000 in 1989. The official languages are Finnish and Swedish.*

In Finland, an advisory Science Policy Council was established in 1963. It was set up under a decree passed by the Council of State (the government).[1] The council was thus instituted by and for the government, but at the request of the scientific community. Representatives of the research community had wanted to create, within the government, a special ministerial committee that would also have included experts. Ultimately, the Science Policy Council was instituted outside the system of Cabinet committees, but its membership did include several Cabinet members and its chairman was the Prime Minister.[2]

At the time that the Science Policy Council was being considered, reference was made to two shortcomings that such a council would help put right. They were:

- Cabinet members' access to advice in scientific matters was seen to be inadequate unless representatives of the research committee had direct institutionalized contacts with ministers; and
- Without a council of this type, the government had no permanent system for examining plans for the promotion of research, which was seen as an obstacle to purposeful science policy.[3]

These two considerations explain why the work of the Science Policy Council was built on cooperation between Cabinet ministers and representatives of the research community.

ACTIVITIES OF THE SCIENCE POLICY COUNCIL

In its early years, the council handled primarily matters under the competence of the Ministry of Education. It was not until the late 1960s that there emerged any debate about the need to devise a comprehensive national science policy

Esko-Olavi Seppälä is Chief Planning Officer of the Science and Technology Policy Council of Finland. He is on leave from the Academy of Finland, where he serves as Head of the Planning Office. He is a member of the Finnish Society for Science Studies and the Editorial Board of the society's Scandinavian journal, Science Studies. *He previously served as Secretary to the Science Research Council of the academy.*

169

program and a scheme for increasing research resources.[4] The first Finnish science policy program was prepared by the Science Policy Council in 1973.[5]

The goals set for the preparation of the national science policy program were very ambitious. During the late 1960s, planning work was generally character-ized by a belief in comprehensive planning and in systems which were con-sidered stable and predictable and which were governed by the demands of efficiency. In accordance with this prevailing concept, the Science Policy Council aimed at creating a management system by means of which the use of the whole national R&D capacity could be efficiently planned, coordinated and directed.[6]

The program mentioned five priority areas of goal-oriented research arising from social needs. The idea of priority areas had been introduced into the Fin-nish science policy debate by the Central Board of Research Councils of the Academy of Finland (see Figure 1).

For the priority areas, the program implied a "top-down" planning process in order to specify the areas in scientific terms. This urgent task was assigned to the Academy of Finland. The academy, however, which was structured into disciplinary research councils, was not able to resolve the question of organiz-ing the planning of interdisciplinary research; further planning thus encountered great difficulties.[7] Further, since the funding of priority research could not be taken from a real increase in public research finance, as planned, the scientific community became worried about the future of other research.[8]

The recommendations of an advisory policy organ, *i.e.,* the Science Policy Council, had thus taken root in neither the administrative machinery nor the traditional scientific communities. In addition, a manifestly social policy ap-proach to industrial research also gave rise to objections. Furthermore, the funding scheme presented in the program was not implemented. Had this scheme been realized, it would have meant that Finnish R&D input would have risen from the 1971 level of 0.9% to 1.7% of the GNP by 1980. Because the scheme was never carried out, R&D financing was only 1.1% of the GNP in 1979. All in all, it was easy to agree with the OECD examiners, who said of this first round of Finland's national science policy planning:

> As a first comprehensive move in policy planning it was impressive. How far has the promise been realized? That is the question to which we have to devote attention.

> Unfortunately, the policy was permitted no time to prove itself. Finan-cially, things began to go wrong immediately. . . . As all experience shows, innovation is not difficult to introduce when extra funds are avail-able to finance it: When it has to be at the expense of some on-going project, resistance is apt to be strong from the interests which are threat-ened. The broad political support needed to overcome conservative forces also proved elusive.[9]

This evaluation does not, however, exclude the fact that many of the ideas and lines of thinking adopted for the 1973 program have subsequently received wide support and have been put into practice, both in administration and in the scientific community.

THE GROWING IMPORTANCE OF TECHNOLOGY AND TECHNOLOGY POLICY

The science policy issues examined above had primarily to do with basic research and other university research. Questions concerning applied research and development became objects of national interest in the course of the 1970s.

In the mid-1970s, after the first oil crisis, increasing attention began to be paid to the possibilities offered by technological research and development. This interest was particularly keen in business and industry. Traditional industrial policy thinking began to give way to an approach that stressed the primacy of technological development and exploitation of technology. One of the major factors here was the growing importance of information technology.

The increase in public technology financing effected a new growth in the appropriations for universities and the Academy of Finland in the late 1970s. This coincided with the general economic recovery. The Science Policy Council began gradually—after a long pause—to issue public statements and recommendations concerning future lines of development. It did not venture to offer new recommendations for research funding before the 1980s, but there was general agreement that Finnish research financing was not up to international standards. Attention began to be paid to the precept that it is essential to ensure a balanced development of financing.

The early 1980s were clearly marked by a science policy with an emphasis on technology. A Technology Development Centre was established in 1983 (see Figure 1). It is true that the relative GNP proportion of national research investment grew only from 1.1% to 1.3% between 1979 and 1983, but considering that the GNP grew by 14.5% in real terms, the aggregate real growth in research financing was 35% during this four-year period.

Such rapid growth naturally also revived research planning. Between 1979 and 1983, about fifteen "national development programs" were drawn up for different sectors, such as basic research, technological research in general, R&D promoting domestic production, and energy research. Each program was devised independently by the sector in question.

The Science Policy Council was left with the task of reconciling these sectoral development plans. It was considered that success in this—if the known or foreseeable total increase in research financing could accommodate the needs expressed by the various sectors—would be all one should expect from national science policy. This is also what the science Policy Council stated in its reports of 1981 [10] and 1984, [11] in which the main link between the individual sectoral plans was the council's recommendation for the growth of research funds over the next few years. One of the major aims was to restore the credibility of science policy planning, and this succeeded.

Figure 1. Organization of R&D in Finland

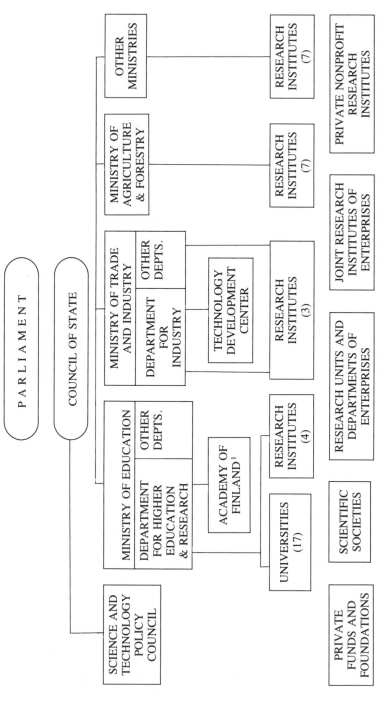

[1] The Academy of Finland is a central body for science administration, consisting of the Central Board of Research Councils and seven research councils.

THE ERA OF THE SCIENCE AND TECHNOLOGY POLICY COUNCIL

Research and development have continued to fare well all through the 1980s. In 1987, the national research input was 1.7% of the GNP. The GNP grew by 13% from 1983 to 1987, which raised the real growth in research financing as high as 50% over the four-year period 1983–1987. The relative share of industry in research financing grew during that time. Thus, the emphasis in recent years has also been on technology; yet, just as before, it has been possible to retain a balance between the various parts of the research system.

In the autumn of 1985, the government submitted two reports on science policy and on technology policy to Parliament.[12] Although the reports were submitted at the same time, they had been prepared through different channels. The science policy report was prepared in the traditional manner with the leading roles played by the Ministry of Education as the preparing agency and the Science Policy Council as the conservative expert body. The sporadic nature and short tradition of the technology policy machinery were shown by the fact that the technology policy report was prepared by an *ad hoc* committee set up by the Prime Minister's Office.

As to the content, the reports were in no way conflicting and, in the technology policy report, it was proposed that the Science Policy Council should be developed to enable it to act as a cooperative body in the field of technology policy as well. The national questions relating to technology policy had gained such great importance that measures had to be taken to organize national advice. For this, the Science Policy Council offered a ready-made forum.

The Science Policy Council was abolished and a Science and Technology Policy Council was set up in March 1987.[13] The change was by no means dramatic, as the following list of its functions shows.

The council assists the Council of State and its ministries in issues relating to science and technology and, in particular, the following:

- It directs and coordinates S&T policy and prepares relevant plans and proposals for the government;
- It takes care of the overall development of scientific research and education, prepares relevant plans and reviews for the government, and follows the development of and the need for research in the various fields;
- It deals with, follows and assesses measures taken to develop and implement technology, and prevents or solves possible problems;
- It deals with central issues relating to Finland's participation in international cooperation on science and technology;
- It gives statements on the allocation of science and technology funds to the ministries and their further distribution between the various research fields;

- It handles the most important legislative matters pertaining to the organization and prerequisites of research and to the promotion and implementation of technology; and
- It takes initiatives in matters under its competence and makes relevant proposals to the Council of State and its ministries.

It was not considered necessary to change the principles underlying the council's composition. The Science and Technology Policy Council is also chaired by the Prime Minister. The membership of the council consists of the Prime Minister, the minister in charge of higher education and research, the Minister of Trade and Industry, the Minister of Finance, and two other ministers, as well as ten experts from the fields of science and technology. The membership must include representatives of the Academy of Finland, the Technology Development Centre, the Council for Higher Education; industry; and employers' and employees' organizations. The government appoints the members for three-year terms.

The Science and Technology Policy Council has an executive committee and two subcommittees that prepare the decisions and recommendations: one for science policy and the other for technology policy. These are chaired by the minister in charge of higher education and research and by the Minister of Trade and Industry. In 1988, the council convened twice, and its committees met twenty times in all.

The Science and Technology Policy Council's secretariat consists of a secretary general and two full-time secretaries (chief planning officers). The secretary general is appointed by the government on the proposal of the council and the secretaries by the council itself for terms of three years.

WHAT THE NEW COUNCIL DOES

The first major undertaking of the new Council was to draw up a public science and technology policy review.[14] In its review, the council notes that the Finnish research system has developed rapidly throughout the 1980s. The main lines of future development, which are the basic elements of the present national policy, are defined as the growth of research, continued balanced development, the organization of postgraduate education, and internationalization.

These development trends show that Finnish national science and technology policy is entering a more active phase. This is manifested, for instance, by the goal of internationalization as such and by a more purposeful participation in costly cooperative and international projects. The long period of continued growth of research activities has accentuated the bottlenecks of the research system. The most important of these is postgraduate education, which is only now being developed systematically in Finland. This drawback was also mentioned by the OECD examiners who scrutinized Finnish science and technology policy in

1986.[15] The present need to develop and intensify postgraduate education also demonstrates how important it is, in a phase of rapid internationalization, to ensure that international cooperation and domestic research activities support and strengthen each other.

In the long term, the Science and Technology Policy Council has set an ambitious goal of raising the national research input to 2.7% of the GNP by the year 2000. This would raise the Finnish input close to the present level of the leading industrialized countries. How realistic this goal is, in view of the failed resource planning in the 1970s, remains to be seen. In any case, the context in which the present Science and Technology Policy Council issued this recommendation is essentially different from that of the 1970s.

The Science and Technology Policy Council has got off to an active start. National technology policy issues have found in the council a permanent forum. The council has good contacts with the major public agencies that plan and finance science and technology, the Academy of Finland and the Technology Development Centre. The fact that the council's membership includes representatives of industry, employers and employees, has improved interaction between the public and private sectors in science and technology policy issues. The advice provided by the Science and Technology Policy Council covers technology much more extensively and is based on a broader expertise than that of the earlier council.

NOTES

1. Decree 97/1963.
2. Lemola, T., Räty, T. and Vesikansa, E., *Valtion tiedepolitiikka* (government science policy) (Helsinki: Academy of Finland, 1975).
3. Aho, L., *Valtion tiedeneuvoston asemasta ja tehtävistä.* (Valtion tiedeneuvoston ensimmäisen kokouksen pöytäkirjan liitemuistio: On the status and tasks of the Science Policy Council.) Memorandum annexed to the minutes of the first session of the Science Policy Council, Helsinki, Finland, April 6, 1963.
4. See note 2.
5. *The Outlines of Finnish Science Policy in the 1970s* (Helsinki: Science Policy Council of Finland, 1975).
6. *Science, Growth and Society: A New Perspective* (Paris: OECD, 1971).
7. Seppälä, E-O., "Planning Science Policy in Finland," *Science Policy in Finland—Studies and Documents,* no. 2 (Helsinki: Academy of Finland, 1986).
8. *Tieteen keskustoimikunnan arvio painoaluetutkimuksen kehittämisestä.* (Tieteen keskustoimikunnan pöytäkirja 10/1976, liite 2: Developing priority research, an evaluation by the Central Board of Research Councils.) The minutes of the Central Board of Research Councils 10/1976, appendix 2.
9. *Social Science Policy: Finland* (Paris: OECD, 1981).
10. *Research and Development Work in Finland in the 1980s* (Helsinki: Science Policy Council of Finland, 1981).
11. *A Review of and Recommendations for the Development of Scientific Research* (Helsinki: Science Policy Council of Finland, 1984).

12. *Reports by the Council of State to Parliament on Finland's Science and Technoligy Policy on 12 September 1985* (Helsinki: Council of State, 1985).
13. Decree 934/1986.
14. *Science and Technology Policy Review* (Helsinki: Science and Technology Policy Council of Finland, 1987).
15. *Reviews of National Science and Technology Policy: Finland* (Paris: OECD, 1987).

Science and Technology Policy in France: Evolution of the Decision-Making Processes

Pierre Piganiol and Henry Durand

THE FRENCH REPUBLIC *(République Française) is a republic under a parliamentary system of government with a presidential regime created in 1958–59. Its land area is 211,207 square miles, and its population in 1989 was estimated at 56,115,000. The official language of the country is French.*

It is now commonplace to say that scientific and technical research and development constitute one of the basic elements of overall national policy. Nowadays, in all modern countries, the initials S&T (science and technology) and R&D (research and development) correspond to specific institutions aimed at promoting and coordinating research activities and more efficiently exploiting their results. R&D is pivotal to reaching most of the economic and social objectives of national policies. Its quality has become a strong element of prestige for nations, as well as an important trump card in international competition and negotiation. Research feeds the ''intelligence'' of a country and enriches its culture in the broadest sense of the word.

Identifying scientific and technological priorities and managing research and development are critical political tasks, but remain dangerous and difficult exercises. In this respect, the evolution of the French science concept is rich in useful lessons.

THE BIRTH OF FRENCH SCIENCE POLICY

Before World War II, support for research in France was weak and timid. Some technical ministries financed research funds, and basic research was sup-

Pierre Piganiol, chemist, is a former (1958–62) head of the French Agency for Scientific and Technological Research (Délégation Générale à la Recherche Scientifique et Technique) under the supervision of the Prime Minister.

Henry Durand is Professor of physics at the University of Paris and former Assistant Secretary General (Science and Environment) of the North Atlantic Treaty Organization in Brussels. He has contributed to the final sections of this essay, on international cooperation and European science and technology policy.

ported by the Ministry of Education. In 1935, the various funding mechanisms were merged into a single National Scientific Research Fund (Caisse Nationale de la Recherche Scientifique) under the chairmanship of the well-known physicist, Jean Perrin. The socialist government of 1936 went a step further in promoting research through the appointment of an Undersecretary for Scientific Research. Irene Joliot, the daughter of Pierre and Marie Curie, and, later, Jean Perrin were the first appointees.

This was the first real move toward the institutionalization of scientific research policy in France. Personnel was recruited from the many "unemployed intellectuals" that existed in those days and, in 1936, a body for applied research (Centre National de la Recherche Scientifique Appliquée—CNRSA) was created, aimed at promoting and coordinating the national effort. A year later, a merger of the CNRSA and the many scattered institutes and university laboratories gave birth to the Centre National de la Recherche Scientifique (CNRS), which still exists fifty years later and represents the largest single European research organization at the present time.

World War II interrupted this move, but, afterward, the reconstruction of the country's economy became the first priority, and national research policy was of somewhat secondary importance. Nevertheless, the "technical" ministries were conscious of the importance of scientific challenge and resumed their policies of launching or supporting their specialized research centers. (A National Institute of Hygiene was even started during the war.)

The establishment of the French Atomic Energy Commission (Commissariat à l'Energie Atomique—CEA) was, indeed, the first political decision that recognized the paramount importance of research, as had been done in the United States some years before. In parallel, the larger French companies became aware of such a necessity, and started creating—as early as 1947—structured corporate research centers. Among them were Saint-Gobain, Rhône-Poulenc, CSF, etc.

In spite of these positive moves, the overall situation in the public sector was dramatic in terms of the scarcity of human and financial resources. In 1953, CNRS, the largest public scientific establishment, employed few more than 2,500 persons, ten times fewer than today. But, even worse, there was no coordination, a lack of coherence in policy issues, and a tremendous gap in key areas, such as computer science, biology and chemistry.

Vast movements arose in public opinion, supported by academics and researchers, who organized many public meetings aimed at revealing the poverty of French R&D. Indeed, some limited efforts in favor of global reflection on sound government science policy were made during the preparation of the second Five-Year Plan. But, not until 1952, when Pierre Mendés-France was Prime Minister (he was called President of the Council), was the necessity of integrating science into the overall national policy efficiently considered. Among the measures that were decided upon were:

- The establishment of a Secretary for Research and Technical Development directly under the president of the council;
- The institution of a Higher Council for Research in charge of preparing a cohesive national science and technology policy; and
- The creation (somewhat later, in 1954) of a research-oriented ''postgraduate'' cycle in the universities.

These positive measures were not as fruitful as had been expected, however. On the one hand, the financial effort remained well below the needed funding. On the other hand, the Higher Council became a real ''parliament for research,'' and had a hard time defining its doctrine. The impetus was launched, however, and many bodies—such as the Association for the Study and Development of Scientific Research—helped to entertain the movement. In 1956, the consciousness of those in political circles and the support of public opinion was such that a consensus was reached in favor of implementing a sound concept for science and technology policy. It remained only to define the proper mechanism for such an implementation. This would be the achievement of the DeGaulle government in 1958.

THE EXPANSION OF S&T POLICY IN FRANCE

The basic idea put forward in November 1958 was the recognition that such a policy jointly involves all ministries. Indeed, each ministry could pursue its own research activities, but the overall coordination and coherence of all efforts—the synergy of all the actors—were to be the responsibility of an Inter-Ministerial Committee. Aside from the ministers who were sitting on this committee, twelve scientists—with advisory roles—were appointed to insure communication between the scientific and the political worlds.

These ''twelve wise men'' constituted an advisory board in charge of reflecting upon all scientific and technological problems. A Secretariat, headed by a ''Délégue Général à la Recherche Scientifique et Technique,'' representing and reporting to the Prime Minister, was the supporting administration for these activities. (Pierre Piganiol was the first Délégue Général appointed by General de Gaulle.)

The overall framework was thus set; it remained to define its content. It rapidly appeared that the sole task of the secretariat of the advisory board was clearly not adapted to carrying out the urgent tasks that faced French research and development policy. No matter how bright it may be, an advisory board cannot be an executive body. Indeed, its reflections were often adopted by the Inter-Ministerial Committee and eventually became part of legislation. But, beyond the important mission of the advisory board, it was felt that it was necessary to take concrete actions, to prepare and draft legislation and budgetary discussions, to create new management processes, to reshuffle the research mechanisms and institutions, and to prepare new statutes for the public research organizations and their personnel. Initially, a single head of the secretariat, the Délégue, became the chief of the government science and technology agency, called the Délégation Générale à la Recherche Scientifique et Technique (DGRST), a body which kept its mission and objectives until 1981.

Thanks to the recommendations of the advisory board and to the operational work performed by the DGRST, French science policy received an efficient doctrine in 1959. It was strongly supported by the political will of General de Gaulle and, later, by Prime Minister Michel Debré when De Gaulle became President of the Republic. Through their decisions, the necessary finances were rapidly appropriated.

The issue was to build a coherent infrastructure for executing good research, as well as to optimize the science and technology programs in view of gaining more knowledge—policy *for* science—and of achieving better exploitation of the results—policy *through* science. The request for satisfying the concrete needs was immense—for instance, in the sectors of health and energy, but it was no less important to insure the presence of France on the international scene, entering the space or oceanography fields or helping with the development of the Third World.

From all the answers given by the advisory board and the DGRST to these problems, two types of initiatives should be retained, because they still constitute the backbone of French science and technology policy today.

The first type of decision aims at raising the general level of research operations and adapting them to their objectives and their future evolution. It concerns the budgets, the structure of the public research organizations, and the programs of these organizations. Within the overall budget as defined by the Inter-Ministerial Committee, the DGRST discusses the individual budget of each organization with its director and its corresponding tutoring ministry. This process insures the coherence of the programs and activities of each institution with the global national policy in research and development.

CONCERTED ACTIONS

The second group of measures was entirely original. The traditional and unavoidable splitting of research activities into scientific disciplines and technological fields calls for corrective actions aimed at gathering different actors toward a common objective that cannot be reached by a single organization. This observation gave birth, in 1959, to the so-called "Concerted Actions" (Actions Concertées) managed and funded by DGRST. The qualification of concerted actions stems from the fact that they consisted of incentive operations co-decided upon and co-financed by the government and the recipients of the grants. Such schemes are now commonplace, but there were few of them thirty years ago.

Some of these actions were quite normally discontinued at the end of their programmed life and often induced a thematic modification of the participating organizations (as happened, for example, in the field of molecular biology). Others were of a more permanent nature and suggested the creation of new institutions or the transformation of existing ones. For example, two concerted actions in the fields of oceanology and of space led to the implementation of the National Centre for the Exploitation of the Oceans (Centre National d'Exploitation des Océans—CNEXO) and of the National Space Center (Centre National d'Etudes Spatiales—CNES). The initial concerted actions helped to define the scope of future research programs and the areas that needed further implementation.

It should be underscored that this initiative had yet another goal: the breaking of traditional barriers and the teaching of the various teams to work together. It helped greatly in initiating the necessary bridge between basic and applied research, as well as between the public and the private sectors.

A last point of doctrine should be mentioned. DGRST was instrumental in introducing a better definition of the relationship between the academic research traditionally linked to higher education and the many institutions dealing with basic research and employing full-time researchers. It introduced new sets of links between the universities and the CNRS, and helped CNRS itself, which had become a huge organization in the 1960s, to adapt its program management procedures to internal concerted actions, associated with the academic world.

Broadly speaking, the new mechanisms introduced in 1958 demonstrated their success and are still in use today. One can, however, observe some weaknesses—which occur also in other modern countries—which result from the evolution of the science policy itself. For instance, France has committed an error in substituting a light inter-ministerial body attached to the Prime Minister for a full-fledged Ministry of Research and Technology, which acts at the same level as the other ministries.

While the principle of such a decision contradicts the very nature of the research activities, no serious consequences have arisen, thanks to the personality of the minister (Professor Hubert Curien, minister since 1984 with a short interruption in 1986–88). He is sufficiently competent and respected so that he can make his voice heard among his colleagues in the Cabinet.

Many of the difficulties that arise today do not result from the new administrative structure, but from the very nature of present-day research and development. While research is now pervasive in most human activity, politicians are somewhat unable to grasp the reality of mutually interacting elements which interfere with a great variety of economic, industrial and even social and cultural issues.

A NEW WORLD

The technological explosion which followed the end of World War II was due to the size of the reconstruction problems that Europe had to face, as well as to the enormous amount of knowledge that had been accumulated since the beginning of the twentieth century. This knowledge bore all the necessary ingredients needed for the birth of new industries, such as those in plastics, synthetic fibers, and high-performance alloys, not to mention nuclear energy which was at that time only ten years old. Knowledge and know-how now appear as being clearly and intimately linked. It is no longer necessary to question whether basic research can have practical spin-offs; it is a certainty.

Hence the distinction collapses between a policy *for* science and a policy *through* science: The scientific content of any technological activity has become so dense that the difference between basic and applied research is now fuzzy, except perhaps for their very names or sometimes for the motivations of participants.

Another characteristic feature of the present evolution is the disappearance of borderlines between disciplines. Starting from well-defined poles, knowledge has developed throughout the frontiers, and each field has grown in such a way as to overlap the others. New problems arise precisely at the borderline. No specialist—and specialization is vital for progress—can be fully efficient without having a broad view of the "system" of science.

A third characteristic is that most modern technologies aimed at satisfying human needs are complex and call for diversified knowledge. Machine tools are, indeed, mechanical devices, but cannot be operated without computers. Civil engineering depends as much on radar as on electrochemistry or radioisotopes.

No one can master all science nor be knowledgeable in all technologies. Teamwork and effort coordination become the rule for science policy-makers.

THE ANSWERS TO SCIENCE POLICY

Such a new situation can be coped with by two types of answers: one at the level of the research organizations and the other at the government-action level.

Research organizations cannot constantly change their structures or modify their programs. This has led them to interlace two types of operating modes. The first is classical and consists of a stable disciplinary approach; the second departs from the traditional frame and creates provisional structures aimed at cooperating toward goal-oriented programs. Such cooperative gatherings perturb the classical hierarchy, notably through the necessity of appointing a responsible program officer who is effective. Contrary to common thinking, such superimposition of "horizontal" and "vertical" management structures is, in most cases, quite efficient.

It thus appears that a new flexibility allows the research organizations to adapt to fast-moving research and development approaches. In most cases, however, this flexibility is limited to the borders of the said organization, although spontaneous cooperation agreements occasionally develop harmoniously.

At the government level, it appeared rapidly that it was going to be necessary to overshadow the individualism in large research organizations through intensive cooperation toward common solutions to complex problems. This kind of incentive process, stemming from the concerted actions concept, has thus been generalized, not only within the Ministry of Research and Technology, but also in the more traditional ministries which have some technical activities, such as Agriculture, Telecommunications and Public Works.

In parallel, the administration has seen the development of a new "intermediate layer" of high-quality civil servants, insuring a proper liaison between the research structure and political power.

But the very quality and success of this intermediate level have had unexpected, perverse consequences: These concerted actions—whether they are called "priority programs" or "incentive activities"—have grown in number, and each one has been given a "committee" (scientific committee or coordinating committee). This has grown to such an extent that France has now exceeded the reasonable balance between the time spent on research and the time spent on reflecting on research. The procedures have become more cumbersome.

Indeed, this system has advantages: There is a closer relationship between scientists and those who will make use of the results of their research, and applied research has taken advantage of such a communality of thinking. The time spent seems excessive, however, and this goes together with a decreased effort on the part of the responsible authorities to take direct action on the programs of the research organizations. To caricature the situation, one could say that the responsible officers have more confidence in the programs that they, themselves, coordinate, rather than in the competence and abilities of the organizations that they are supposed to supervise. This is not a purely French phenomenon: One hears that foreign governments have the same complaint about the "excessive" power and independence of the big research institutions.

Looking at the other side of the coin, one may wonder why these research institutions react so mildly to such criticism. The answer is obvious: All these specific research "actions" or "programs," decided upon at a higher level, bring them additional budget funds. Their silence hides the necessity for finding a proper equilibrium between the responsibilities of the research organizations and the top-level body which is coordinating these complex programs (which, indeed, are justified in only a few cases).

It has been said earlier that modern research overlaps—almost always—traditional framework, but that even the larger organizations do not have all the in-house competence required to tackle complex issues. How can one solve this "catch-22?"

TOWARD A NEW SCIENCE POLICY

It is obvious that any research organization or even any research unit should be welcome to call, when necessary, upon outside competent teams, either through a simple joint agreement or through a contracting procedure. In theory, there is nothing to oppose such cooperation, which has become a necessity in modern research and development. In practice, one obstacle often appears, namely, the financing, since it is always difficult to subtract from one's budget—by definition, always insufficient to one's ambitions—a share to be allocated to outsiders.

It is possible to think of a simple solution consisting of transferring to each research unit the financial responsibility for such cooperation, instead of relying on the good will of centrally decided programs. Of course, an upper limit should be set to such "blank checks" offered by the administration to the research organizations; for example, putting at their disposal a maximum amount of 10% of their "normal" budgets would represent a reasonable incentive for cooperative research. Above this percentage, specific procedures would be required.

Finding this extra 10% in the French Government's research and development budget should not be too difficult, since there is a clear political will to substantially increase R&D efforts in the next few years. A top priority for research and development has already been observed during the past two years, but there is still some way to go in order to meet the objectives of the government, namely bringing the "intensity" of research and development close to 3%. (The intensity of research and development is defined as the percentage of total—public and private—R&D expenditure to the Gross Domestic Product (GDP). The figure for France in 1987 was 2.35% against 2.8% for West Germany and the United States.)

This percentage of 10% is, of course, purely indicative. A too large figure, however, would mean that the present research structure is not adapted to the present concept of cooperative research, and a too small one would probably be ineffective.

Such a transfer of responsibility would relieve the government authorities of the burden of deciding and then of monitoring the details of the cooperative actions taken by the various research operators, and give them more time to concentrate on a handful of exceptionally large cooperative projects. It would also allow them to watch the "spontaneous" cooperation this implemented and, as the case may be, to advise the researchers rather than decide on their behalf.

It would mean changing the present "mosaic-type" spreading of government funding into a freely chosen "network type" of cooperative research and development.

Such a scheme would also improve the necessary mobility of scientists. Most of the researchers hired by the large public research organizations in France are civil servants with lifetime guarantees of employment. This leads to a deplorable rigidity, in spite of measures taken to avoid its perverse effects. Indeed, such a guarantee assures a great freedom and an absence of concern about the careers of professional scientists. But it restricts the mobility of the researchers inasmuch as each research organization may offer somewhat different personnel status. This rigidity of the French system is a major problem, and the suggested scheme would allow for greater mobility of researchers through temporary exchanges of personnel without hampering too much the sacrosanct idea of personnel status.

RESEARCH ASSESSMENT

In recent years, science policy management has had a tendency to multiply assessment studies, in France and elsewhere. This notion needs to be further clarified, because it covers two distinct types of objectives.

A first concern deals with the worries or possible criticisms expressed by the funding agent—often, for instance, the Ministry of Finance. The purpose of the exercise here is to set up a critical analysis of future research work aimed at checking its proper orientation and its expected effectiveness. This analysis should be indisputable and hence totally independent from both the requesting body and the executing organization.

A second goal may lie in improving the way in which the objectives of research, the content of the programs, and the management procedures can be set through the examination of terminated actions. Here the main concern is to make good use of past experience, indeed a logical move for those who have the responsibility for science policy.

Both these approaches are legitimate. One should, however, restrict the first type to a limited number of cases, such as the "big programs." The second type does not need heavy mechanisms, since those people dealing with science policy should be competent enough (and they usually are) to draw their own lessons from the research operations for which they are responsible.

But the present tendency is to extend such assessment procedures to all programs, even the smaller ones. This phenomenon multiplies the committees: A first one will be set up in order to define the details of the activities to be undertaken. Then, a second and, possibly, a third committee will be created, one to act as a scientific advisory board aimed at helping, advising and orienting the project manager, the other to control the work and check its adequacy against future utilization of the results. Such committees would be welcome if they are peripheral and helpful, but they may become heavy, cumbersome, and inefficient, and remove the responsibility from the project manager. They are set up just to make the project credible in the face of possible criticism or misinformation.

If a mid-term or final review board is added to these existing committees, one may wonder if something isn't going wrong with the system. Either the program has suffered from misconceptions or from a lack of proper execution, or the work and reports of the preceding committees have been ignored or read improperly. This is a consequence of an overload of the "intermediate level" of policy decision-makers, who are encumbered by their own inability to control their workloads and cannot find enough time to make their own judgments.

There is, therefore, a great risk of seeing the assessment procedures substituting for the necessary dialogue between the decision-makers and the executing managers.

Furthermore, both in France and elsewhere, there is a tendency to consider the evaluation of the quality of research organizations themselves. Yet, these bodies also have their own councils, they publish annual reports, and, in principle, they cannot receive their budgets without a thorough discussion of their objectives and their means with the governmental authorities who, therefore, have all the information necessary for assessing properly the quality, the content, and the orientations of the forthcoming activities.

Does all this mean that the concept of assessment is meaningless? On the contrary, no efficient management of a project, a program, or an organization can exist without a permanent assessment, which remains an essential factor for a judgment of quality. The questions raised here are different. The answer is simple: Only in those cases where, for whatever reason, there is a doubt about the effectiveness of the local management should these assessments apply.

A PROPOSAL FOR A NEW MANAGEMENT OF SCIENCE POLICY

Facing these risks leading to an increased bureaucracy in science policy and making the players less and less responsible, steps should be taken and new principles laid down.

The basis of a sound science policy in France should rely on an inter-ministerial body acting either directly with the researchers or indirectly through the competent services of other ministries. This body need not be a unwieldly mechanism; on the contrary, it should be composed of a relatively small number of highly qualified persons, appointed for terms of limited duration (three to five years), thus preventing them from considering that their responsibility represents an end in itself.

Their main concern should be insuring a self-adaptation of the research and development systems to the evolution of science and technology and to the national priorities, as well as guaranteeing the "transparency" of research activities.

The use of direct interference with the researchers should remain exceptional: Such intervention should only occur when it is clear that the research structures cannot adapt themselves to changing circumstances. One must then—and only then—modify, suppress, merge or create adequate organizations.

Otherwise, this "lightweight" body should remain well informed through close contacts with the researchers and with the end users. Its essential task is to supervise the interactions between the actors and to monitor the feedback from the outside world. Permanently watching the spontaneous cooperative ventures mentioned earlier is a very precious indicator for management of the whole system, and is a good alarm system to insure that "ivory towers" do not appear.

In short, instead of maintaining the present plan, consisting of managing a mosaic of programs and organizations, it would be preferable to adopt a more efficient plan based on the principle of involving the actors rather than intervening with them. But isn't this conclusion applicable to most government activities?

THE NECESSARY INTERNATIONALIZATION OF SCIENCE POLICY

The conclusion drawn so far concerns mostly the case of France. But a country of 55 million people cannot dream of covering the whole realm of modern research and development. The need for cooperation has been emphasized for national activities, but it is now even more urgent on the international scene.

With a research and development intensity of 2.35%, France stands below the US and Germany or Japan (2.6%), but slightly above the UK. This indicator increases rapidly, however, and, as mentioned earlier, the ambition of the French government is to meet the US and Japan at the 3% level within the next few years. Indeed, a thorough examination of the real situation should take into account the difference between civil and military expenditures which may vary enormously from one country to another. (The ratios of defense to total research and development expenditures are: US, 67%; UK, 51%; France, 25%; and Germany, 13%.)

France, Germany and England together accomplish 78% of the total research and development activities performed in the European Community countries (the so-called "EURO-12") and, in absolute terms, overtake Japan by a small margin while remaining well below the US. These figures demonstrate quite obviously that none of the major European countries can expect to become a leader on the international scene unless real and sincere cooperation is established among them.

The recently published "Science Indicators 1981–87" (OECD) gives, however, a contrasting picture of the competitivity of some "high-tech" industrial branches in Europe as compared to those of Japan or the US. For instance, the export/import ratio (1986) for computers and business equipment reaches 6.6 for Japan, compared to 1.1. for the US and 0.7–0.9 for France, Germany, and the UK. This ratio is somewhat better for exports of these countries in telecommunication and electronic equipment (slightly higher than one), but Japan reaches a ratio of nine (and, vice versa, the US is a net importer with a ratio of 0.6). The same situation is true of scientific instruments.

Such figures, especially as regards computers, have alarmed the European countries, and have inspired the launching of the vigorous "ESPRIT" (European Strategic Programme for Information Technology) Program, managed by the European Commission.

Yet, if the situation in Europe in some fields of advanced technology is worrying, the situation is much better for science and, especially, for "big science."

EUROPE AND "BIG SCIENCE"

Thanks to successful cooperative efforts, many sectors of science are extremely lively in Europe. The best example of an outstanding success is that of CERN (Centre Européen de Recherche Nucleaires), the high-energy physics laboratory established in Geneva in the mid-1950s. But many others can be mentioned: the European Space Agency in Paris; the European Molecular Biology Organization in Heidelberg, Germany; the European Southern Hemisphere Observatory in Chile; the Joint European Torus (JET) in Culham, UK, not to mention the more recent European decisions concerning the establishment of a radiation synchrotron in France and a cryogenic wind tunnel in Germany.

All these *ad hoc* organizations have some specific features in common:

- They all concern large equipment that is obviously out of the reach of any single European country;
- They were genuinely proposed by European scientists (although it is fair to say that the late American scientist, I. I. Rabi, was a remarkable advocate for the establishment of CERN); and
- They are open to collaboration with nonEuropean scientists.

The geographical composition of these European organizations varies from one to the other. France (as well as Germany, Italy, The Netherlands, and the UK) represents the "hard core" of the founding members. But the usual number of partners in such enterprises can reach twelve to eighteen European members, including, therefore (aside from the EURO-12 nations), the countries of the European Free Exchange Association (Austria, Finland, Iceland, Norway, Sweden and Switzerland).

These permanent organizations were generally accepted quite readily by the member governments, in spite of some traditional bargaining about the site locations. These nations should be congratulated for their interest in science and for their willingness to pay for it.

The decision-making process for current programs and budgets is usually one of consensus, which, in diplomatic terms, is a "unanimity on nonopposition." But, in practice, the leading countries—who are also the largest financial contributors—carry more weight than the smaller partners. This consensus is obviously prepared by thorough studies and discussions which take place among the scientists concerned, and which are then ratified by the political authorities insofar as the financial terms are reasonable.

One exception to the rule of consensus is the European Space Agency; part of its programs dealing with scientific issues are "compulsory" and cofinanced by all member states under the consensus rule. Others, mainly of technological or commercial natures, are open to volunteers willing to contribute, but are, quite logically, also getting the benefits of the programs. The European Space Agency has adopted a policy of "just return," *i.e.,* the percentage of financial return to national industries or laboratories should be, as much as possible, equal to the percentage of the contribution of each nation.

The existence of these large European institutions started, some thirty years ago, to modify the mentalities of national science policy-makers, in that there has been, to a large degree, a "transfer of sovereignty" from the national authorities to these international bodies. On the whole, it has worked well, although here or there political (or, more likely, budgetary) reluctance could be observed, the most notable one being the recent attitude of the UK toward CERN and the Space Agency.

These success stories demonstrate that Europe is capable of reaching the top level when the European countries accept the sharing of their human and financial resources. In the case of "big science," they were compelled to do so. The situation was quite different for "small science" or for technological research where, until recently, strong competition—leading to some duplication and waste—has dominated the European scene. The strengthening of European political institutions, namely the European Community, allows now for new types of collaboration and opens the door for better efficiency in the European scientific and industrial worlds.

THE CHALLENGE FOR THE FUTURE

The first and second treaties signed by the (then) six European nations (France, Germany, Italy and the three Benelux countries) were of technological and industrial natures: the European Steel and Coal Community (1950) and the Euratom (nuclear energy) Agreement (1957). The signature of the third treaty, the Treaty of Rome (1958), however, establishing a European Community— the so-called "Common Market"—has cast for years a shadow over the scientific and technological aspects of European cooperation.

Science and technology issues, except for nuclear energy issues and some coal and steel research and development, did not explicitly fall under the legal competence of the Commission of the European Communities (the commission is the executive board for all three "communities" established by the three treaties mentioned above). Yet, through some obscure articles in the Treaty of Rome, which allow for some extension of its explicit objectives, the commission started, some twenty years ago, to launch timidly a few cost-shared incentive programs in academic and industrial laboratories. In those days before 1980, the commission, following the European tradition, had focused its funding on nuclear energy (and, also after the first "oil shock," on non-nuclear energy and on energy conservation).

The revision, four years ago, of the status of the European Communities (known as the "Single Act") has substantially changed the situation in that research and development have become an official mission of the commission. Yet, the size of the science and technology programs are still small, representing barely 2.5% of the total budget, while the Agricultural Common Policy (60%) and the Structural Funds aimed at helping the development of the poorer regions of Europe (20%) consume the lion's share. Likewise, the European research and development budget represented, in 1987, only 2.4% of the total research and development spending of EURO-12.

No matter how small it is (presently about $1.3 billion dollars per year), the funding has already been quite successful in stimulating European collaboration in industrial research and in cross-fertilizing the academic and industrial worlds. The reasons for this success are numerous.

The most important reasons are:

- The "trans-national rule," which imposes on contractors alliances between operators from different countries;
- The "cost-sharing rule," which imposes a 50%–50% split in funding with the contractors, hence doubling the financial impact of the programs;
- A highly selective competition, thanks to the large number of applicants, which insures the quality of the products; and
- Well-focused work plans for each program, emphasizing a limited number of important and topical subjects.

At present, the largest program that has been launched by the commission is ESPRIT (information technology), followed by BRITE (industrial processes and technologies) and RACE (telecommunications), plus some minor ones among which should be mentioned SCIENCE (a scientific exchange simulation plan, allowing for networking among academic laboratories, for cross-exchanges of scientists for seminars and workshops).

THE PRESENT PROSPECTS

The present prospects for future programs are encouraging. A new proposal has been made by the commission to the Council of Ministers of the twelve countries in order to increase by some 60% the current research and development budget, together with a better and more concentrated definition of scientific and technical objectives. Should this proposal be accepted, the share of the commission's funding in EURO-12 would climb to 4% of the total expenditures of the twelve countries and, through the cost-sharing process, represent 8% of the work performed in research and development.

Such a figure begins to be very important for the following reasons:

- The commission's subsidies consist of *incentive* money which is free of any institutional burden (except for a limited amount of funding dedicated to in-house research and development executed in the commission's own laboratories at the Joint Research Center—JCR); and
- The more narrowly focused goals of the European Commission's program which concentrate a larger amount of funds on specific subjects of strategic importance to Europe.

This means that, in such specific fields, the current funding of the commission already matches the incentive credits of the major European nations, and will become much larger if the new proposals are accepted. One should, indeed, remember that some 90% of the national public research and development budgets is appropriated in favor of institutional research organizations (including international bodies), and hence are not freely available for new R&D programs, especially in the private sector.

The consequences of the fast-growing importance of the commission's research and development programs on national policies is obvious: A great fraction of the decision procedures has shifted from the national capitols to Brussels, and this trend will no doubt continue. Furthermore, an intra-European cooperative research mentality is also growing, and tends to supersede the traditional nationalism, thus reducing further the influence of the national authorities.

Indeed, the initial decision-makers are still the ministers of the twelve countries who have to approve, amend, or even refuse the commission's proposals (after further shuttling of the proposals through the European Parliament of Strasbourg which has amendment and some loose vetoing possibilities). But, once the guidelines of a five-year program (a so-called "framework program") have been unanimously accepted, its detailed content is only subject to the approval (according to the recent "Single Act") of a "qualified majority," which—in "Euro-jargon"—means that the majority is weighed according to the economic importance of the various member countries.

But even more important is the fact that the real actors in research and development, namely those who win the calls for tender which are eventually launched by the commission, are selected by commission officials—helped, of course, by experts—and this extremely important decision-making step escapes from any national control. It is fair to say, however, that advisory committees have been set up and that one of them is composed of qualified representatives of the national governments. There are, therefore, "unofficial" means of expressing national views on the final choice of contractors, but the commission is still the only body which has, in principle, the power to make such decisions.

It is also worthy of adding that, in view of the forthcoming opening of the single European market in 1993, the main goal of the commission's research and development programs—with the full agreement of the twelve governments—is now to favor industrial research over academic research (although universities and public research organizations are strongly welcome in joint partnership with industry). In that sense, the research and development tool given to the commission by the "Single Act" can be considered as an important trump of the general policy of Europe of aiming at the establishment of a true economic community of over 300 million people, while waiting for a more remote political community of nations.

Advisory Activities of the German Democratic Republic (East Germany) Academy of Sciences

Claus Grote

THE GERMAN DEMOCRATIC REPUBLIC *(Deutsche Demokratische Republik) (East Germany) was established in the Soviet-occupied zone of Germany in 1949. The constitution in force at present was adopted in 1968. Its land area is 41,768 square miles, and its population was estimated at 16,564,000 in 1989. German is the official language.*

The German Democratic Republic's Academy of Sciences is an institution that unites the potentials of scientists and of highly efficient research facilities. More than 350 leading scientists in the fields of mathematics, the natural, engineering and social sciences, and medicine are members of the academy, in either full, corresponding or associate capacities. These scientists work together in the academy plenum and in ten working groups ("classes"), which are subdivided according to major specialized fields.

The academy includes nearly sixty research institutes dealing with natural, engineering and social science topics. Its staff is made up of about 8,000 scientists and some 16,000 other staff members. Its multidisciplinary composition and the scientific skills and vast stores of experience of its members enable the academy to adopt a high-level, integrated scientific approach—universitas literarum—and to provide advice on a national and international scale.

Through their research work and their general commitments, the members and entire staff of the academy help to further accumulate and deepen the country's knowledge of nature and society. According to the principles of its founder, Gottfried Wilhelm Leibniz, the academy aims to combine theory and practice, to carry out basic research alongside applied research, and to rapidly and efficiently transfer scientific findings into the production sector and other spheres of society's life.

Giving advice is one of a whole range of responsibilities faced by the academy. It must be seen in close relationship to its general societal role, which ranges from the long-term strategic determination of the main trends in explor-

Claus Grote is Secretary-General of the Akademie der Wissenschaften der Deutschen Demokratischen Republik, a post he has held since 1972. Born in 1927, he holds a D.Sc. degree from Humboldt University, Berlin, and is involved in high energy physics and space research. Dr. Grote has been a member of the council of the UNESCO Commission of the GDR and national representative to the International Council of Scientific Unions, as well as Chairman of the GDR Committee for Research and Use of Outer Space.

atory and application-oriented basic research to the active participation of the academy's members and employees in spreading the word of the latest scientific findings to universities, colleges, technical schools, and general schools, as well as to the general public.

This social role also includes carrying out scientific groundwork for technological, economic, social, intellectual, cultural and other development processes; cooperating with combines and enterprises when it comes to transferring scientific discoveries to production; and providing expert advice to governmental bodies concerning the development of science and technology, the combination of scientific and technological breakthroughs with economic, social, intellectual and cultural progress, and the safeguarding of the peace.

WHO RECEIVES ADVICE

The Academy of Sciences gives advice to the following bodies:

- Central bodies of the GDR's leading political party, the Socialist Unity Party of Germany (SED);
- The GDR government, *i.e.,* the Council of Ministers, ministries, and other central governmental institutions;
- Combines and companies;
- Universities, colleges, and other educational institutions;
- Public organizations; and
- International scientific organizations which have intergovernmental or nongovernmental characters.

Depending upon the nature of the issue and the degree and level of competence, this advisory function is performed by:

- The academy's board,
- The plenum of the academy members,
- The academy's classes,
- The institutes,
- The academy's Scientific Councils for research programs and the main directions of research in the fields of natural and social sciences,
- The national committees and scientific associations affiliated with the academy, and
- Individuals.

On a national scale, the quality and efficiency of the academy's advice depends upon both the level and the extent of the members' and staff's store of knowledge and experience and the extent to which they are capable of evaluating and processing their knowledge in such a way that their suggestions and recommendations become socially relevant and acceptable. This requires that the scientist be aware of the complexity of social interrelationships and the specific nature of the respective management and planning processes. Furthermore, he has to have certain political, ethical, sociotheoretical and ideological convictions, attitudes and inclinations.

Scientific advice, especially in politics, cannot be reduced to a purely academic activity, devoid of any moral values and administered from the heights of an ivory tower, an activity that entirely neglects opposing social interests. Rather giving advice forms part and parcel of the political commitment and the social responsibility of the scientist as a member of society and as a citizen. Therefore, the better the scientist combines excellent professional skills with comprehensive insight into interrelated social, economic, political, national and international processes, the more efficient his scientific advice to the different social bodies will be, even though the institutions seeking advice—especially central governmental bodies—will always face situations requiring complex decisions.

This, then, calls for opinions of other experts as well, but the academy's viewpoint will, however, always be taken into account. For the academy members and employees, it is an undisputed rule that they will not only exert influence on the formulation of objectives, strategies, plans, solutions and approaches required by their partners, but also share their partners' responsibilities for the actual management and control processes. This integrated process of accumulating knowledge, giving advice, and assisting in practical affairs is an important manifestation of socialist democracy.

THE LONG-TERM PLAN

Bearing in mind its responsibility in the field of basic research, the Academy of Sciences, together with the Ministry of Higher and Technical Education, is preparing a "Plan for the Long-Term Development of Basic Research in the Fields of Science, Mathematics and Technology Within the Framework of the GDR Academy of Sciences and the Ministry of Higher and Technical Education." At present, this plan covers the period until the year 2000. It is based on analytical and prognostic assessments of the academy's classes, institutes and research departments and the institutions of the higher education system. The plan is being discussed by the Academy Board and the Minister of Higher and Technical Education. It will be used to facilitate five-year planning in basic research.

The plan has been developed and continued alongside the national economic plan, and it covers the same five-year planning period. Through this plan, the Academy of Sciences and the institutions of the higher education system act as advisers to the government. Through its approval by the Council of Ministers of the GDR and its systematic implementation, this plan makes a direct impact on the development of science and technology on a macroeconomic scale.

When it comes to long-term planning in social science research, the social science research unit of the academy, together with the respective departments of universities and colleges, the Academy of Social Sciences and other scientific institutions of the SED, faces a similar responsibility for the preparation of the "Central Plan for Social Science Research in the GDR." This plan is also renewed after every five-year period, and it is passed by the SED Politbüro.

The Ministry of Science and Technology is in charge of preparing documents on the further development of science in the GDR. These documents reach beyond the framework of the "Plan for the Long-Term Development of Basic Research," while bearing its aims and objectives in mind. By preparing papers and opinions, the academy's plenum, classes, scientific councils, institutes and individual members get involved in the formulation of these documents, which include a paper on "Main Directions and Priorities of Science and Technology Between 1986 and 1990 Up Until the Year 2000, As Well As Major Projects of Scientific and Technological Cooperation Between the GDR and the USSR from 1986 to 1990."

The above is part of the "Plan for the Economic and Social Development of the GDR Until the Year 2000." This provides a guideline of how science is to be integrated into society's overall development. Via concrete decisions by the Council of Ministers and other governmental authorities, this integration is, in collaboration with the Academy of Sciences, further specified and put into practice.

In addition, the classes and the scientific councils of the Academy of Sciences have to come up with their own ideas and positions concerning the major tendencies and priorities of scientific and technological development (e.g., memoranda on the development of physics).

These ideas and positions have then to be submitted to the Research Council affiliated with the Ministry of Science and Technology. The role of this body is to provide the government with advice and recommendations as far as the general development of science and technology and their macroeconomic utilization are concerned. In the Research Council itself, the academy is well represented by a number of leading scientists. As a rule, the recommendations made by the Research Council are approved and enforced by the government. In some cases where the government comes down against a Research Council recommendation, the grounds are given.

ANALYSIS AND PLANNING

The analysis and planning activities within the research programs with regard to the major trends of research are performed by the Scientific Councils. Their responsibilities include the identification of research priorities and the nationwide coordination of research undertaken in the various fields. The membership of these Scientific Councils includes experts from the academy and higher education institutions and scientists from industry and other social areas.

There are a total of five research programs and thirty-eight research trends that fall under the responsibility of the Scientific Councils of the academy.

The academy has a coordinating function in the areas of social sciences and medical research as well, and there are also advisory bodies. In the area of social sciences, there are Scientific Councils for the following:

- Economic research,
- Law and political research,
- Social sciences information and documentation,
- Archaeology and ancient history,
- Linguistics,
- General science of science, and
- Others.

Even in areas with mainly interdisciplinary orientations, the academy plays a guiding and coordinating role. The GDR Coordinating Committee for the Peaceful Exploration and Utilization of Space, which coordinates the research activities of GDR scientists within the framework of the Intercosmos Program (with the Institute of Space Research being the central institution) is, for example, based at the academy. The Antarctic base, which was founded in 1987, is run by the academy, too. The academy coordinates the GDR's research activities in polar regions (with the Central Institute of Geophysics being the central institution).

Furthermore, there are advisory bodies for interdisciplinary problems, such as Scientific Councils for the fundamentals of microelectronics, basic research in the energy sector, the fundamentals of environmental management and protection, information and library management, research technology, and instrument production.

ACADEMY/INDUSTRY COOPERATION

Cooperation between the academy and industry includes a wide range of advisory responsibilities and topics performed by the academy on different levels, such as the following:

- Before the GDR Council of Ministers passed the Decree on the Relations Between Science and Production (Research Decree) in 1985, it had consulted the academy about some of the principal issues.
- The work coordination and service contracts which are concluded on the basic of the Research Decree between the academy institutions and industry are negotiated by leading representatives from both the academy and the concerned companies. Within the framework of this cooperation, the academy has to live up to its basic research responsibilities, to inform management in industry of new development opportunities, and to see to it—together with the companies—that the research findings are rapidly and comprehensively introduced into the sphere of production.
- In this context, such forms of cooperation between the academy and

industry as academy-industry complexes (e.g., such complexes as "Pharmacological Research," "Technological Microbiology," "Organic High Polymers," and "Industrial Robots"), joint science parks, and joint transfer teams have turned out to be very useful.

• It has become common practice in the cooperation between the academy and industry for academy institutes to give advice to interested partners from combines and enterprises on scientific and technological issues. Each year, scientists from the academy hold tens of thousands of consultations to pass on their experience and the results obtained in basic and applied research, as well as the latest findings from both their own research and international scientific activities.

THE NATURAL SCIENCES

Natural science research departments and academy institutes perform advisory functions in the form of various services. The geology and space research unit, for instance, carries out observation programs, including the following activities:

• Monitoring the upper atmosphere, especially concerning radio-wave propagation;
• Monitoring the geomagnetic field;
• Recording seismic events, including giving expert opinions concerning seismic hazards, e.g., in mining;
• Generating the time standard (service for time and frequency);
• Recording geodetic and gravimetric parameters;
• Recording oceanological parameters in the Baltic and North Sea regions; and
• Performing tasks included in the Antarctic Treaty.

When it comes to energy issues, particularly the utilization of nuclear power and the safety of nuclear power stations, the academy's Central Institute of Nuclear Research has much the same advisory responsibilities as the National Board of Radiation Protection. Regarding environmental issues, the Scientific Council, which was established for this purpose by the Academy of Sciences, is in permanent contact with the respective national institutions.

Through theoretical studies (e.g., in the economic sciences) or through analyses (e.g., on the demographic situation or the extent to which the population uses democratic rights and performs its duties), which are submitted to the competent central bodies of the SED and the government, the academy's social science institutes help to prepare laws, decrees, etc., on topics such as welfare and family measures.

THE SOCIAL SCIENCES

In addition to its more or less direct advisory responsibilities, the academy, through its extensive social science research work, contributes considerably to the intellectual and cultural life of the country and to enhancing a progressive awareness of the past in the country's people, *e.g.,* by identifying progressive historical traditions, reassessing intellectual trends or political figures of German history (Martin Luther, Frederick II, Bismarck), and by reevaluating the history of the GDR and reviving certain traditions.

Moreover, through their involvement in the work of the Scientific Councils of GDR universities and colleges, the scientists of the academy assist in the training and education of students. Through expert opinions and their direct participation in the commissions run by the Ministry of Education and the Academy of Educational Sciences, scientists from the Academy of Sciences make their impact felt when it comes to formulating basic principles of th e further development of the educational system and preparing curricula and text-books for general polytechnical schools.

THE INTERGOVERNMENTAL ROLE

At the level of the United Nations and its specialized agencies, scientists of the academy help create and implement scientific programs for intergovernmental organizations, such as the UN Intergovernmental Committee for Science and Technology for Development, UNESCO, the World Health Organization (WHO), The International Atomic Energy Agency (IAEA), and the World Meteorological Organization (WMO). Some of the projects involving scientists from the academy are the International Hydrological Program, the Man and Biosphere Program of UNESCO, the Global Atmospheric Research Program (GARP) of WMO, and WHO's MONICA Project.

The academy regularly organizes training courses for junior scientists, mainly from developing countries. These courses, which are held in collaboration with UNESCO or the United Nations Development Program (UNDP), cover geophysics, biotechnology, information processing, etc. The academy's contribution to WHO programs focuses on research into cancer, blood circulation, and coronary disease.

Furthermore, institutions of the academy are engaged in the training of international IAEA inspectors, and they also support developing countries within the framework of the IAEA Program on Technical Assistance and Cooperation, such as holding advanced training courses and assigning academy experts to these countries.

The academy's attitude toward nongovernmental international organizations is also governed by the principle of giving advice and cooperating in international scientific programs and projects. The academy has several national committees which represent it in more than fifty of these organizations, including the International Council of Scientific Unions (ICSU) and the International Federation of Social Science Organizations (IFSSO). On a national scale, they advise, for instance, the organizers of international scientific conferences.

SAFEGUARDING THE PEACE

The GDR Academy of Sciences has made it one of its most important duties to advise and assist the GDR government in all its efforts toward safeguarding the peace. In order to better perform this duty, the Committee for Scientific Aspects of the Safeguarding of Peace and Disarmament was formed in 1983 at the academy and includes forty-seven renowned GDR scientists. As the advisory body of the Academy of Sciences, the committee sees its main task as the coordination of the academy's relations to national and international bodies, institutions and individuals who—with their own specific means and methods—work for peace and disarmament. In addition, the committee encourages GDR scientists to increasingly study issues linked with the preservation of peace and the potential abuse of new scientific findings for warfare.

Academy members are actively involved in the work of the GDR's peace movement and in international bodies, such as the World Federation of Scientific Workers, the GDR section of the Committee for European Security, the National Pugwash Group, Physicians of the GDR for the Prevention of Nuclear War (which was founded in 1982) and the GDR Peace Council.

In 1982, at a meeting held in the academy's Einstein Laboratory of Theoretical Physics (formerly the residence of Albert Einstein in Caputh near Potsdam), leading GDR physicists called upon their colleagues throughout the world to fulfill the hopes of this famous scientist, who is best known for his discovery of relativity theory, to fight against the danger of mankind being wiped out in a nuclear war.

Another case in point in which the advice given by the academy scientists was considered were the negotiations between the GDR's SED Party and the Federal Republic's SPD concerning their joint proposal to create a chemical and nuclear weapon-free zone in Europe. This proposal, in turn, formed the basis for the respective proposals submitted by the GDR and Czechoslovakian governments to the government of the Federal Republic of Germany.

Or there is the case of the National Pugwash Group of the GDR, for example, which is promoted by the Academy of Sciences. This group has been studying the issue of chemical weapons for many years. In 1987, at the invitation of the Academy of Sciences and the National Pugwash Group of the GDR, the 12th International Pugwash Seminar was held in Berlin to deal with the control of the nonproduction of chemical weapons. The seminar's findings were integrated into the negotiations within the framework of the Geneva-based Committee on Disarmament (CD), in particular concerning verification issues and the creation of a chemical weapon-free zone in Europe.

The GDR's disarmament delegation at the Geneva negotiations *(e.g.,* on a chemical weapons ban, a nuclear test halt, a contract restricting the utilization of space to nonmilitary purposes, and a convention on biological weapons) included scientists of the academy. In this context and beyond the scope of the above issues, academy members are increasingly involved in national problems regarding the GDR's policy for disarmament and peace. In the process, the emphasis is on the scientists' expert knowledge in the fields of chemistry, physics, geology and astronomy.

In this context, mention should be made of the academy's peace research responsibilities, which result from its advisory activities. These include both the national programs for peace research (the Council for Peace Research, the GDR Committee on Scientific Aspects of the Safeguarding of Peace and Disarmament), and international peace research programs, such as the one initiated by the Stockholm International Peace Research Institute (SIPRI) and an initiative launched by scientists and aimed at finding a way out of the arms race.

The contributions made by academy members to issues of nuclear and biological and chemical weapons, as well as geological and space-related questions concerning the control of nuclear testing and warfare scenarios based on the use of nuclear, chemical and other means of mass destruction, deserve special mention.

After the Washington agreement between the US and the USSR, which marked the first step in nuclear disarmament, social scientists from the academy indicated to the leadership the new problems to be dealt with under the conditions of a lasting peaceful coexistence between the two different social systems, the worldwide effects of the technological revolution, the aggravation of other global problems, and the ever-closer links between national and international development. The suggestions made in this context will be included in the current Central Plan for Social Science Research in the GDR for the 1986–1990 Period, and they will be used to prepare the next plan covering the period from 1991–1995.

Science Advice to Government in West Germany

Heinz Maier-Leibnitz and Hubert Markl

THE FEDERAL REPUBLIC OF GERMANY *(Bundesrepublik Deutschland) was established under a democratic parliamentary system in 1949. Its land area is 95,987 square miles, and its estimated population in 1989 was 61,352,000. German is the official language.*

In the Federal Republic of Germany, there are the federal government (or Bund) in Bonn and the eleven Land governments. The latter are responsible for education and thus for the universities and research in general, but the Bund has been granted some central competence, too.

After World War II, the reconstruction of universities started without much change in structure or in scope. But it soon became evident that more should be done for a future in which science and technology were expected to play major roles. Adenauer, the first Bundeskanzler, accepted advice from some scientists, such as Heisenberg, in an unofficial, but rather effective way, and the states' support for the universities grew.

There are two classes of science advice to government. The professional activities of scientists lie in teaching and research, and it is evident that they should be heard when decisions about the role and the organization of universities and research institutions are at stake.

The second class concerns problems which are important to society and which require the special knowledge of scientists and engineers to contribute to the preparation of decisions. One often speaks of applications of science and technology, but usually it is not the scientist who proposes or desires the applica-

Heinz Maier-Leibnitz, born in 1911, is a former President of the Deutsche Forschungsgemeinschaft. He was a full Professor for technical physics at the Technical University of Munich from 1952 to 1979, and is now Professor Emeritus of that institution. Holder of a Ph.D. in physics, Dr. Maier-Leibnitz holds honorary doctorates from Vienna, Grenoble and Reading Universities.

Hubert Markl is President of the Deutsche Forschungsgemeinschaft of which he also served as Vice President for a number of years. He is a Professor at the University of Konstanz and a former Professor at the Technical University of Darmstadt. Dr. Markl was born in 1938 in Regensburg, Germany. He spent a year as a visiting researcher at Harvard and Rockefeller Universities, and another in habilitation in zoology at the University of Frankfurt. He is a member of the Heidelberger Akademie der Wissenschaften; the Deutsche Akademin der Natursforscher, Leopoldina, Halle; and the Bayerische Akademie der Wissenschaften, and a Foreign Honorary Member of the American Academy of Arts and Sciences in Boston, Massachusetts.

tions. He contributes his knowledge and sometimes his ideas and warnings about possible consequences, but his part in the actual plans and decisions is necessarily limited.

During the first decade after World War II, science and scientists were held in high esteem, and it is understandable that some of them believed that their advice could be important in many fields. Advice to government from an elite of scientists was one of the major motivations for the founding of the Forschungsrat (research council). One of its projects is the protection of civilians in an atomic war (Zivilschutz), which began hopefully, but now exists only on a very small scale. The Forschungsrat was opposed by many people, including most scientists. In 1951, it became part of the newly reorganized Deutsche Forschungsgemeinschaft (DFG). Later, all the founders of the Forschungsrat disappeared from the new organization.

THE DFG MANDATE

The DFG might be called a republic of the sciences, including all fields of science and the humanities. Legally a private association under the civil law of universities, academies and major research institutions, the DFG has a mandate both for funding academic research in all fields and for promoting scientific cooperation among researchers in Germany and other countries. It also advises parliaments and governments in scientific matters.

It is this latter function which is of relevance when one turns to advice on matters of public concern where science has a specific policy contribution to make. The DFG, from its rebirth as an institution in 1951 (it had a predecessor founded in the Weimar Republic), has offered independent advice, particularly on questions regarding environmental protection and health hazards. Some of its early committees, concerned, e.g., with food additives and food technology, came into existence through the initiatives of the leading German scientists of their time. This tradition is still strong in the DFG and is exemplified in the committee which draws up—and annually reviews—a list of the maximum concentrations of hazardous substances in the workplace.

Some of the advice offered by the DFG was based, to a considerable extent, on special cooperative research projects, e.g., on certain ecosystems, on atmospheric chemistry, on aircraft noise, or on certain health risks. In the majority, however, the DFG's committees base their findings on extensive reviews of research results from all countries on such problems as toxicity and carcinogenic and mutagenic effects of hazardous substances.

What characterizes the work of the DFG is the habit of waiting for proposals from competent scientists, those who do the work before granting or setting up any project. DFG is funded by the governments, who hold back their influence on decisions, even if, officially, they could use it. The President, the scientists in the Senate, and the leading referees are all elected by the members of the scientific community, so advice from the DFG really means advice from science.

This tendency to keep the planning of research within the scientific community was not sufficient when it came to the promotion of modern technology (R&D). This is especially true of nuclear energy where government support, often including planning and control, has been established in several countries, such as the United States, and has taken on such dimensions that politicians in Germany felt that a similar effort was needed there.

DEUTSCHE ATOMKOMMISSION

In 1955, Adenauer named Franz Josef Strauss as the first minister for atomic questions. The Deutsche Atomkommission was organized on the federal level. It was presided over by Strauss, without the other ministers, but with top-level members from industry, representatives of public life, and scientists participating.

There is no doubt that the Deutsche Atomkommission, with its subcommittees for special subjects like nuclear research, power reactors, raw materials, law, and safety, has been very effective during the first years of its existence because of its high status and because of the freedom it had as long as a powerful bureaucracy did not yet exist, and as long as the prominent members found it worthwhile to devote their time to it. The commission could not follow the principle that the members should not have vested interests, because everybody did have them, but there was a pioneer spirit, and the discussions were quite frank and open with no hidden afterthoughts. All ideas were welcome, but were criticized without hesitation. The ensuing body of knowledge was much better than the sum of the individual contributions.

This could, of course, not last and, indeed, after a decade, the Atomkommission was dissolved and, whenever necessary, replaced by *ad hoc* committees with members who had less power to decide and with much more influence from government officials.

Under the nuclear energy program, nuclear research centers were built, programs were created and coordinated, and firms, after initial hesitation, were given more and more support for reactor projects and related programs. The universities contributed fundamental research and personnel, both experts for the many committees and staff with sophisticated knowledge of industry and the administration. The first research reactors and a number of accelerators were built at universities.

It was evident that the role of the universities must become much greater than it had been in the past, not only for nuclear energy, but quite generally if one recognizes that more knowledge is good for all kinds of progress. The need to enlarge the universities (and with them institutions for fundamental research, especially the Max Planck Gesellschaft, with its many renowned institutes) became more and more evident and urgent.

THE WISSENSCHAFTSRAT (SCIENCE COUNCIL)

The Science Council (Wissenschaftsrat), inaugurated in 1958 by the President of the Federal Republic of Germany, for many years had a mandate to draw up a "comprehensive plan for science and scholarship." It played a decisive role in the period of rapid expansion and, sometimes, as one now realizes, overrapid structural change in the higher education system between 1960 and the mid-1970s.

Its advice is still mandatory for the federal and state governments on all matters concerning the joint funding of investment (buildings, large scientific instruments) in universities and polytechnics. Of its thirty-nine members, twenty-two are Cabinet members or government officials from all of the states and from the federal government. The idea is that everybody can present his own knowledge and the interests of his own group or office and, at the same time, can learn and better understand the needs and interests and the possibilities and limitations of all the others.

It is thus a microcosm of those who carry responsibility for science in West Germany, and it has issued authoritative statements, both on the quantitative aspects of higher education and research and on the development of research fields, such as medicine, agricultural research, polymer science, or the social sciences.

The facts that the members come from all the circles that should be heard, that they are changed every few years, and that most of them are personal members, not bound by interests or subject to orders from others—all this combines to make the Wissenschaftsrat an unusually good instrument of advice to government.

During the years that followed, not only the universities grew enormously. The same is true for the new tasks for government in many fields where scientific advice was needed. They range from high technology, health, ergonomics and environment to economic problems, national and international, including assistance to the Third World, mass communications, and social psychology.

Here is another point which becomes more and more important. Advice must be sought not only from science and engineering, but from the humanities as well, from fields such as history, law, economics, psychology, sociology, medicine, of course, and even theology. This is a serious problem which is not well solved in the FRG. It creates frightening problems which become visible far beyond reasonable measure in public discussions.

There are two extremes that should be avoided: One is the scientist who has become an amateur sociologist or moralist and thinks that his superior intelligence in science makes him superior in other fields, too. The second is the sociologist or political scientist who believes that science should be distrusted and must be dominated and guided into directions on which "society" (of course, as represented by himself) decides.

RECIPIENTS OF ADVICE

The number of recipients of scientific advice increased enormously, in part because new ministries were created. The ministry devoted to nuclear energy is now the Ministry of Research and Technology. In addition to aiding technological projects, in industry and elsewhere, and maintaining the research centers which now work on wider fields than nuclear energy, it promotes international projects like space and fusion. A relatively large part of its support still goes to fundamental research, to cooperative projects at universities, and to research centers abroad, and it funds the Max Planck Society. In this way, it fulfills a requirement which the FRG tries to maintain: Applied research should never be done without fundamental research. The Ministry for Education and Science, together with the states, funds research mainly at universities. The fact that its budget is not loaded with big projects, because these are funded by the other ministry, has proved to be an important advantage.

Other new ministries, like Health and Environment, support—as other ministries do—institutions whose provinces consist of—or include—carrying out research. This takes a wide variety of forms ranging from academic research that could equally well take place in a Max Planck Institute or in a university department to strictly mission-oriented and—in part—routine investigations directly serving the purposes of the Executive.

An even larger number of ministries, both at the federal and at the state level and including some of those named above, have permanent and *ad hoc* expert committees from which they draw extensively for all parts of the academic community (universities, Max Planck Institutes, government establishments, national laboratories) as well as industry. Some of these committees have wide mandates with both considerable political influence and high reputations for independence, *e.g.*, the Advisory Committee for Economic Development (Sachverständigenrat zur Beurteilung der gesamtwirtschaftlichen Entwicklung) or the Reactor Safety Committee (Reaktorsicherheitskommission). Parallels to this development can be seen in many ministerial advisory bodies today with independence valued in some and political and/or administrative influence pervasive in others.

COMMISSIONS OF ENQUIRY

Parliamentary Commissions of Enquiry (Enquête-Kommissionen) must be mentioned here as a further example—after the Science Council—of direct and sometimes beneficial interaction between politicians and academics. Psychiatry and mental hospitals (in the 1970s) and, more recently, recombinant DNA technology are subjects on which such parliamentary commissions have produced documents of authority stemming from a consensus—or near-consensus—not only between the political parties, but also between politicians and scientists.

In some cases, the results have been more doubtful. A parliamentary body is not very well suited to judge in cases of scientific or pseudo-scientific controversies.

Finally, in the FRG, as in all countries, there is an infinite variety of government-commissioned policy advice from individuals and groups commenting on a particular policy issue at the need of a minister or his officials. Much of this is prepared using the methods of the social sciences. In contrast to other countries, such as Great Britain, France or the US, little work of this nature is commissioned from university departments or learned societies (reflecting a peculiar weakness, not to say "absence," of policy research in most of FRG academia), and very little is properly published, with the Minister of Education and Science and—recently—the Federal Chancellor's office providing exceptions that deserve imitation.

In the FRG, unlike the US, academies do not have a great role in preparing material for advice. The country has never had a chief scientist and there is not, at least so far, an office of technology assessment for the parliament. There is, however, a great variety of sources of advice, starting with the Research Council, DFG, the National Research Centers, and many scientists from the universities and the Max Planck Gesellschaft, from industry and other organizations, and from individuals.

All this can work if there is a fruitful understanding between the scientists on the one hand and the politicians, the administration, and industry on the other. A scientist's authority may be great in his field, but it is useless if he does not understand the problems of others or if he cannot make himself understood. Too few scientists have really learned this—fewer, for example, than those in the US. There seems to be a lack of what one might call "elder statesmen" in science, persons who, after a successful career in science, have gathered experience in administration and in talking to politicians. Lack of mutual understanding is an obstacle to the process of making good decisions. It is even more harmful in public discussions which, at least in the FRG, now have such great influence on public opinion and, therefore, on choices in politics.

Science and Technology Advice to Government in Hungary

István Láng

THE HUNGARIAN PEOPLE'S REPUBLIC *(Magyar Népköztársaság) was an independent kingdom from the year 1000 until it became a republic in 1946. It was a Communist Republic from 1949 until 1989 when the Communist Party was overthrown by the Socialist Party and the Hungarian Socialist Workers' Party. Its land area is 35,919 square miles, and its population in 1989 was estimated at 10,551,000. The official language of the country is Hungarian.*

Science policy, research management, and advice to government take specific forms in various countries. They are related to the country's cultural and historical traditions, to the structure and function of its political institutions, and to the quality and quantity of its research and development capacity. To enhance understanding, the following is a short survey of the development tendencies of—and also the most important data on—research management in Hungary. The picture outlined reflects the situation in early 1989.

AN OVERVIEW OF RESEARCH MANAGEMENT

In the second half of the 19th century, Hungarian scientific life developed gradually within the Austro-Hungarian monarchy. The so-called "national sciences," most of which belong to the humanities *(e.g.,* linguistics, literary scholarship, history, ethnography), helped the national consciousness to evolve. The natural sciences, mathematics, and the medical and technical sciences all contributed to serve the growing demands of the industrializing society. Scientific research at the time was carried out at universities and at some of the larger museums.

Following World War I, Hungary became an independent state (in 1918). A significant part of its territory was annexed to neighboring countries according to the Treaty of Trianon. Because of this, the basis of scientific research was diminished. During the 1920s and 1930s, conditions of scientific research continued to be developed at the universities. There were also, however, some

István Láng has been Secretary General of the Hungarian Academy of Sciences since 1985, and served as Deputy to the post for the previous fifteen years. Born in Mohács, Hungary, in 1931, Dr. Lang holds a D.Sc. degree in agricultural sciences, and is a member of the World Commission on Environment and Development, the Editorial Advisory Board of the World Resources Report, *and the General Committee of the International Council of Scientific Unions. He is also a foreign member of the All-Union Academy of Agricultural Sciences (USSR) and the Polish Academy of Sciences.*

large industrial firms that had world-famous development departments *(e.g.,* in the fields of pharmaceutical products and light bulb production).

In 1945, after the end of World War II, the territory of the country remained unchanged, but there was heavy damage to buildings and equipment and also to intellectual capacity as many of the intellectual elite left the country. It took from four to five years to repair the war damage. Then, a quarter of a century of extensive development followed from 1950 to 1975. A whole network of universities, colleges, research institutes, museums, and developmental laboratories was built during this time. As a result, compared to the size and population of the country, a significant R&D potential has been created.

Presently, the country's population is about 10.6 million. About 80,000 people work in the field of R&D. Thirty-six thousand of them are researchers, including the teaching staffs of universities, engineers working in industrial development, and those who are able to devote their full working time to science in research institutes.

Since the second half of the 1970s, Hungarian science policy has not considered any more quantitative growth in personnel. Instead, it has aimed at the realization of qualitative development in two respects: first, to increase expenditure per researcher and, second to improve the quality of the research staffs. Unfortunately, neither of these aims has been realized to a satisfactory degree.

The ratio of R&D in the Hungarian Gross Domestic Product (GDP) is relatively high—namely 3%. The value, however, of Hungary's GDP lags behind that of other medium-sized countries in Western Europe, and thus a Hungarian researcher has only about half the budget of his Western European colleagues. The qualitative development of the research staffs has brought about some results, which were, to a great extent, due to the country's widespread international scientific relations developed after 1970. The researchers' methodologies, their knowledge of foreign languages, and the qualitative indicators of the publications have all improved. At the same time, the less productive researchers could be sent to other fields only in limited numbers. This is primarily due to low social mobility in the country which, in turn, is fostered by, *e.g.,* the housing problems that hamper moving from one town to another.

The percentage of distribution of R&D expenditures among the five principal fields of science is as follows:

Technical sciences	74.0
Natural sciences	11.9
Agricultural sciences	6.9
Social sciences	4.0
Medical sciences	3.2

In international comparison, the ratio of the medical and the social sciences is smaller than in most European countries.

Between 1972 and 1988, the government controlled R&D through the activities of the Science Policy Committee, which was headed by one of the deputy prime ministers. This committee dealt primarily with strategic issues; that is, it decided on national priorities in the field of R&D. Regarding financing, the committee only made decisions concerning the so-called Technical Development Fund and that part of the state budget that could be spent on R&D. As a result of the decentralization of government activity, the Science Policy Committee ceased to exist at the end of 1988. Since then, R&D activities have been coordinated by one of the ministers of state.

On the second level of administration, there are the ministries and the other national authorities. The Hungarian Academy of Sciences is also on this level. It has its own network of research institutions, primarily in the fields of the natural and the social sciences.

The State Committee for Technical Development is also on this level. This committee has no institutes of its own; it finances programs aimed at technological development. Various ministries *(e.g.,* in the fields of agriculture, health and industry) finance quite independent research institutes which carry out mainly applied research. These are supervised by three ministries (the Ministry of Culture, the Ministry of Agriculture, and the Ministry of Health). The financing of these institutes is carried out through several channels; that is, their fundamental operating costs are covered by the appropriate ministry, while they contract for specific tasks with organizations or firms which require their research activity and have the funds to finance it.

THE HUNGARIAN ACADEMY OF SCIENCES

This academy was founded in 1925. Its members have been elected from among the eminent personalities in the country's intellectual life. Some of them have also been members of the government. At present, there are two academicians in the government: Kalman Kulcsar, Minister of Justice, and Tibor Czibere, Minister of Culture. The President of the Presidential Council, F. Bruno Straub, is also an academician.

The Hungarian Academy of Sciences as an organization has played an advising role for the government since the early twentieth century by offering its opinions on important questions of education, culture, etc. Since the 1950s, this activity has become stronger and broader, and includes the issues of applying scientific results in practice as well as the proposals for tackling social problems. This latter activity has become regular, especially since the 1970s.

The Hungarian Academy of Sciences has played its role in two ways: It examines specific issues either on its own initiative or at the request of the government. Its advising activity is multidirectional: It has advised the Hungarian Socialist Workers' Party, the leading political power in the one-party system in the country, as well as the government, some ministries, and some government offices.

There are several examples of this. In the mid-1960s, novel ideas about the so-called new economic mechanism—which was intended to decrease the preponderance of central planning and control and pay more attention to market mechanisms—were developed in the institutes of the Hungarian Academy of Sciences. The scientific community has regularly made proposals for the further development of economic reform during the 1970s and 1980s. In the past few years, the idea of economic reform has become connected with that of political reform and this had led to plurality in the political sphere.

Social policy was also re-evaluated in the mid-1980s. It was again in the scientific workshops of the academy that the institutionalization of social security and welfare was initiated; this was later accepted by the political decision-makers.

Protection of the environment as a societal movement was developed in Hungary around the mid-1970s. The Hungarian Academy of Sciences contributed to the scientific founding of its legal regulation.

The academy has dealt with the issue of energy policy several times. The utilization of nuclear energy and the construction of a nuclear power plant have been discussed many times and, on the basis of these discussions, proposals have been made to the government. Hungary, being poor in energy resources, either imports various sources of electric energy or applies nuclear energy; the practical solution is a reasonable combination of the two. There is a quantitative limit to importing energy from the Soviet Union while energy imports from other markets have been hindered by a shortage of convertible currency. As a consequence, the technological and social conditions of the utilization and safety of nuclear energy production had to be created.

The Hungarian government has asked the academy to give its opinion on several issues before it accepted its final decision. Some of these were, for example, the conception of the economic development plan for 1986–1990, the introduction of the new personal income tax and the turnover tax based on added value, and the issue of the construction of the power plant and dam on the Danube, which has led to great public debate. The various committees, as well as the Presidium of the Hungarian Academy of Sciences, have discussed these problems and have given very critical opinions on them. Some of the opinions have been taken into account by the government; some of them, however, have not been accepted.

THE STATE COMMITTEE FOR TECHNICAL DEVELOPMENT

The State Committee for Technical Development was created by the Council of Ministers in 1961. Its main tasks are to put into practice the government's technological development policy, to initiate and prepare government decisions on technological development, and to participate in developing further economic management and planning.

It is this committee that initiates the managing, planning and regulating measures in technological development policy which encourage technological development. It works out the main lines of technological development, and helps to publicize, apply and disseminate in Hungary the most up-to-date technological culture.

To prepare and realize decisions on technological development, the committee works out prognoses and ideas about the expectable and desirable technological development of the economy, participates in shaping conceptions of economic policy, and elaborates on and presents to the government its technological development policy conceptions related to the medium- and long-range national economic plans.

In the field of economic management, the State Committee for Technical Development takes part in making the system of economic management more up to date, in shaping the system of forming and utilizing the financial resources serving technological development activity, in further developing the principles of credit policy and the methods of financing, and in adapting the credit conditions to the technological and economic conditions.

The State Committee for Technical Development has a fund of its own. This is called the Technical Development Fund and is collected by the way of a special tax. The committee finances, from this fund, R&D programs which are directly connected to economic development goals. It also provides financial support for the development of the infrastructure of scientific research.

The State Committee for Technical Development has a wide network of specialists at its disposal. It has expert opinions on about one hundred to one hundred and fifty technological developments per year. It is on the bases of these opinions that Hungarian technological development problems are analyzed, international trends are evaluated, and prognoses on foreseeable developments and studies on the conditions and possibilities of applications are made. These expert opinions are utilized by production firms, ministries, and other state authorities. Development concepts relating to one or more branches or to suddenly and quickly developing fields of specific branches are also often offered to the government.

In the past decade, government-level advising and initiation of development have been especially fruitful and efficient in the following three fields:

- wide-scale application of computer technology and, in this context, the development of the microelectronic industry;
- production, adaptation and dissemination of new materials and technologies; and
- the application of biotechnological procedures in the pharmaceutical and food industries and in agriculture.

The State Committee for Technical Development plays an advising role in international scientific relations and cooperation, too. It gives its opinion of bilateral intergovernmental scientific and technological programs. It evaluates the results achieved in these fields and makes proposals for practical applications. It is also the task of this committee to work out conceptions and action programs for the government on Hungary's participation in the complex development programs organized by the Council for Mutual Economic Assistance (e.g., in the fields of microelectronics, robot technology, nuclear energy, new materials, and biotechnology).

POLITICS, LEGISLATION, AND GOVERNMENTAL IMPLEMENTATION

Since 1949, there has been a one-party system of government in Hungary. At the beginning of 1989, the development of institutions of political pluralism began to be widely discussed.

The Hungarian Socialist Workers' Party, the leading power, is supported in its work by the expertise and advice of representatives of scientific circles. The party has several committees and panels (e.g., in the fields of social, economic, cultural and science policy). Among the members of these committees and panels, there are thirty well known scientists who perform advising roles.

The Hungarian National Assembly (i.e., the Parliament) is a one-chamber legislative body. Its 384 members perform their activities here in addition to their regular occupations. The assembly has four or five sessions a year, usually of about three days each. It has no scientific committee. The issues of scientific research are dealt with in the Committee for Culture, but this discussion is mainly restricted to the annual budget.

The Council of Ministers called into existence its Scientific Advisory Panel in 1988 on the proposal of the Presidium of the Hungarian Academy of Sciences. Its president is the economist and academician Jozsef Bognar. Its members are well-known economists, sociologists and technical experts. The primary task of this panel is to give opinions of the Council of Ministers prior to meetings on propositions which might affect a wide portion of the people.

CONCLUSION

A review of the situation in Hungary shows that scientific advice to governmental activity is given on several levels and in a decentralized way. New ways and means are being discussed, and changes may be expected. Science and politics require each other's support and assistance, but, at the same time, this relationship often means mutual criticism as well.

Science and Technology Advice: The Indian Situation

M. K. G. Menon and Manju Sharma

THE REPUBLIC OF INDIA *(Bharat) has been an independent member of the Commonwealth of Nations since 1947. Its republican system of government has been in effect since 1950. The country's land area is 1,222,480 square miles, and its estimated 1989 population was 828,934,000. The official languages are Hindi and English along with others that are official in certain states. As of December 31, 1989, the US dollar was equal to 16.62 rupees.*

India became independent in 1947. To understand the way science and technology have developed in the little more than four decades since Indian independence, it is important to discuss briefly the scenario at the time that independence occurred.

Innovative ideas relating to science and technology have been a part of the Indian culture and formed the basis of its civilization and its history, going back to the Indus Civilization of 4,000 to 5,000 years ago. Indeed, in 1918, the testimony of the British-appointed Industrial Commission included the following statement:

> When merchant adventurers from the West made their first appearance in India, the industrial development of the country was at any rate not inferior to that in the more advanced European nations.

Thus, unlike many other developing countries, India did have a flourishing scientific tradition in its history and culture. Through various degenerative processes in society, however, and through internecine strife, India came under colonial rule. As a result of these very features, scientific development also came to a halt.

M. G. K. Menon is Minister for Science and Technology in India and a member of the Indian Government's Planning Commission. A physicist whose research has been in cosmic ray, elementary particle, and high-energy physics, he has been director of the Tata Institute of Fundamental Research, Bombay, and Secretary of Electronics, Environment, Science and Technology, and Defense, as well as Chairman of the Science Advisory Committee to the Cabinet. Currently President of the International Council of Scientific Unions, he is a Fellow of the Royal Society, London, and of three Indian academies, a Foreign Member of the USSR Academy of Sciences, a Foreign Honorary Member of the American Academy of Arts and Sciences, and a Member of the Pontifical Academy, as well as an Honorary Fellow of IEEE.

Manju Sharma is Chief (Science), Planning Commission; Scientific Secretary in the Office of the Scientific Adviser to the Prime Minister of India; and Secretary of the Island Development Authority. She has done research in plant sciences at the Universities of Lucknow, Purdue and Copenhagen. She is General Secretary of the Indian National Academy of Sciences and former Secretary of the Science Advisory Committee to the Cabinet.

During the British period, there were developments in science, technology and education, but these were essentially meant to meet the needs and requirements of the existing government. This did result, however, in some major developments, such as the setting up of various survey organizations, and contacts with the fast-moving developments in science and technology in the West that followed the Industrial and Scientific Revolutions.

The real modern awakening in Indian science took place through the efforts of a large number of outstanding Indians over the three-quarters of a century prior to independence. Along with the ferment of the struggle for political freedom, which imbued Indian society with a new elan, there was a renaissance in Indian science, characterized by work of great scientific merit. As a result, at the time of independence, India did possess schools in various disciplines of pure science in the educational institutions and scientists of high quality who had established themselves prior to independence and were available to advise the government on scientific matters.

But, until independence, the Indian economy as a whole had basically languished. The growth of agriculture was only 0.3% and industry was largely restricted to textiles, a few extractive sectors, irrigation, and small hydel projects and a steel plant set up at the instigation of J. N. Tata.

The concept of using science and technology to underpin and to accelerate national development and the creation of the infrastructure needed for this had to await independence and the vision of Jawaharlal Nehru.

THE NEHRU ERA

From his writings, speeches and the way he looked at issues, it is clear that Jawaharlal Nehru had an insight and understanding which was truly visionary of the role of science and technology as a powerful force for social, economic, and cultural development. Economic planning at the national level, which had been started in the USSR in 1927, had made a strong impression on Nehru. Thus he observed, as Chairman of the National Planning Committee, set up in 1938, that

> the three fundamental requirements of India, if she is to develop industrially and otherwise, are: heavy engineering and machine making industry, scientific research institutes and electrical power. These must be the foundations of all planning.

It was those lines of reasoning that led to the setting up of the Planning Commission soon after independence, at the insistence of Nehru in 1950. He was its first chairman and continued to remain in that post until his death in May 1964, and he ensured a scientific underpinning for planning. The Nehru period was characterized by a massive development of infrastructure for science. With this commitment and vision relating to science, Nehru sought and got advice of exceptional quality from the best scientists in the country.

During the years when Jawaharlal Nehru was Prime Minister, scientific advice which had significant impact came from individual scientists of standing who had proposed major new initiatives of a national nature and in whom Nehru had confidence. There was a close personal relationship between Homi Bhabha and Jawaharlal Nehru. Because of this, Homi Bhabha was able to build up the Tata Institute of Fundamental Research as an internationally known center for basic research in mathematics and physics and, thereafter, he built the atomic energy program.

Homi Bhabha also provided major input to Nehru in the framing of the Scientific Policy Resolution put before Parliament on March 4, 1958. Almost twenty-five years later, Prime Minister Indira Gandhi said, ''Our approach to science was eloquently summed up in the Science Policy Resolution of March 1958, which our scientists regard as their charter.'' This resolution constitutes an exceptional statement of the commitment of a government to science and its use for national development.

It was Homi Bhabha who saw the tremendous advances taking place in the field of electronics and, envisioning all the revolutionary and pervasive implications that this would have, persuaded Nehru to set up the Bhabha Committee in 1963 to plan for electronics in India.

Another person with great influence was Shanti Swarup Bhatnagar, who proceeded to systematically set up the chain of national laboratories which constitutes the Council of Scientific and Industrial Research. Today, there are forty-one laboratories under this council.

In 1940, Nehru came into contact with Mahalanobis from the viewpoint of the role of science in planning, particularly the use of statistics. Mahalanobis had set up the Indian Statistical Institute in 1931, and pioneered random sampling in agriculture. Mathematical approaches to data collection, sampling, and analysis became an intrinsic part of the planning regime of the country. The early model of development, which concentrated on heavy industry and infrastructure, is referred to as the Nehru-Mahalanobis model.

Largely as the result of discussions with Patrick Blackett, soon after World War II Jawaharlal Nehru set up the nucleus for defense research in India. The first scientist who headed this effort was D. S. Kothari, who later became very influential in matters of educational policy.

Thus, until Nehru's death in 1964, while there were apex-level structures, the principal inputs at the highest levels for the growth of major areas of science and technology came from individual and influential scientists. Nehru started a tradition, which Indian science has enjoyed ever since, of the Prime Minister of the country being in charge of science and technology with a minister of state for the category in addition.

APEX-LEVEL ADVISORY COMMITTEES

Various apex-level committees, which have functioned since independence to advise government on science and technology matters, are:

Apex Committee for Coordinating Scientific Research (ACCSR)

This committee existed between the period 1948–1956, under the chairmanship of the Prime Minister with eminent scientists and technologists as its members. Its role was basically to advise on the coordination of scientific research in the country.

Science Advisory Committee to the Cabinet (SACC)

This committee was set up in 1956 and functioned until 1968 under the chairmanship of the Cabinet Secretary with several very eminent scientists as its members. The committee advised the Cabinet on the formulation and implementation of the science policy of government. It also helped in the coordination of scientific work between the various ministries and semigovernmental and nongovernmental scientific institutions in the country, including the scientific and technical departments of the universities. In addition, it considered aspects relating to scientific and technical cooperation with other countries. These proposals were put before the Cabinet for approval and implementation. It was during the tenure of this committee that the Scientific Policy Resolution of the Government was placed before Parliament in 1958.

Committee on Science and Technology (COST)

Between the years 1968 and 1972, under the chairmanship of the science member of the Planning Commission, this committee played the role of an advisory body. It had, as members, technologists, industrialists and economists in addition to scientists. It provided linkages between the planning process and the implementation of science and technology programs and activities. The committee was responsible for the formulation and implementation of the government policy on science and technology and the determination of national priorities in these areas. It studied the pace of the development of science and technology, suggested corrective measures—especially for removing imbalances, provided a structure for coordination and cooperation, and ensured the fullest development and utilization of national scientific and technological resources and manpower. It also provided advice on scientific and technological cooperation with other countries. There was a close relationship between this committee and the Planning Commission.

National Committee on Science and Technology (NCST)

In 1972, under the chairmanship of the Deputy Chairman of the Planning Commission and the Minister for Planning, who was also the Minister for Science and Technology, a National Committee on Science and Technology (NCST) was set up with a strong technical secretariat in the newly created Department of Science and Technology. This committee functioned until 1977. Its principal effort related to the preparation—for the first time—of a plan for the science and technology sector; this was prepared in 1974. For this plan, NCST identified twenty-four major socio-economic sectors, in each of which science and technology programs were spelled out that would lead to self-reliance, increased efficiency and productivity, and optimum use of local resources. This exercise involved thousands of scientists from all over the country. The linkages of NCST with the actual departments and agencies concerned with the formulation of plans and the implementation of them in various socio-economic sectors were inadequate, however, and this plan did not succeed. In 1977, with a change of government at the center, NCST was reconstituted. The new body did not pursue the planning effort of its predecessor, but dealt more with specific issues brought before it, and made an attempt to formalize a national technology policy.

Cabinet Committee on Science and Technology (CCST)

In 1981, for the first time, a Cabinet Committee on Science and Technology was constituted under the chairmanship of the Prime Minister. It was to review the progress of science and technology, take an overall view of the scientific effort in the country, and provide policy guidance for the rapid development and application of science and technology.

Science Advisory Committee to the Cabinet (SACC)

The Science Advisory Committee to the Cabinet was simultaneously organized in 1981, under the chairmanship of the science member of the Planning Commission, and consisting of the secretaries of all scientific departments and other eminent scientists and technologists. SACC was created to tender advice on the formulation of the science and technology policies of government, as well as the manner of their implementation, and to identify measures for enhancing the country's technological self-reliance, particularly in reference to policies on foreign collaboration and the import of technology, including filling critical gaps in national competence and promoting technical cooperation among developing countries.

Major achievements based on the recommendations of the SACC were the creation of a National Biotechnology Board, which led to the creation, in 1986, of a separate Department of Biotechnology; a National Science and Technology Entrepreneurship Development Board; a National Council of Science and Technology Communication for the popularization of science and promotion of scientific awareness; improved personnel policies for scientists and technologists; measures to remove regional imbalances; the strengthening of the infrastructure for scientific research in the universities; etc. A major policy document which SACC prepared was the Technology Policy Statement adopted by the government in January 1983. SACC provided a forum for much greater interaction among the scientific departments and agencies and scientists from outside the government system, and discussed many common issues of interest and overall development of science and technology.

Scientific Adviser to the Prime Minister (SA to PM)

In 1986, a Scientific Adviser to the Prime Minister was appointed for the first time to advise the Prime Minister on science and technology matters in general and any other issues referred to him by the Prime Minister or the government.

Science Advisory Council to the Prime Minister (SAC-PM)

Also in 1986, a Science Advisory Council to the Prime Minister was set up for the first time to advise on major issues facing science and technology, the health of science and technology in the country and the direction in which it should move, and to prepare a perspective plan for 2001. SAC-PM consists of scientists from outside the government system. This council has prepared a perspective plan for 2001 and looked at several important thrust areas which require support.

THE PLANNING COMMISSION

Apart from the apex-level advisory structures, the National Planning Commission has a very major role in the planning, investment, monitoring, and other aspects related to the promotion and development of science and technology in India. It has been responsible for preparing and finalizing the National Five-Year Plans which involves:

- Integrating various overall national objectives defined by the political system with the resources available and the investment priorities;
- Allocating responsibilities among the center and the states and between the public and private sectors; and
- Bringing about an integration among the various sectors of the economy.

In these regards, the commission has to deal with many interconnected issues: savings, resources that can be raised, inflows from abroad, import/export aspects and balance of payment, improvements in incremental capital output ratios and efficiency/productivity, the demographic profile and its consequences, material balances, sectoral and macro growth rates, etc.

The efforts in science and technology have to fit into this overall, complex, interlinked planning process. More directly, the Planning Commission deals with programs, investments and priorities of the individual Central Scientific

Departments/Agencies, science and technology efforts under the socio-economic ministries, and the science and technology plans of the state governments. On the bases of the Five-Year Plans, there are discussions each year on the annual plans of each of these entities. There is a total review of the progress by the Planning Commission and, accordingly, investment decisions are made.

OTHER STRUCTURES

In areas of strategic significance, where there is requirement for a high degree of self-reliance and confidence, high-level structures were created right at the start to deal specifically with these. The first of these entities was the Atomic Energy Commission, set up at the suggestion of Homi Bhabha. It was armed with all the powers of government—administrative and financial—to be able to provide policy guidance and support for programs in this sector.

In the resolution setting up this commission, it was stated that this was to free this body from ". . . needlessly inelastic rules of government. . . ." By analogy with the Atomic Energy Commission, at a later date, the Electronics Commission was set up and, still later, the Space Commission. A decade after that, because of the importance of renewable, decentralized, nonconventional energy sources, a somewhat similar commission was set up to deal with "Additional Sources of Energy."

From the very early days, soon after Indian independence, a Science Adviser (SA) was appointed to the Minister for Defense. He was backed up by a Technical Secretariat. Later the Defense Research and Development Organization was created; its Science Advisor became its Director General. Thus, apart from being the head of a large-scale research and development organization with a chain of laboratories, the incumbent also provided scientific advice to the Cabinet Minister for Defense and functioned as Secretary to Government in the Ministry of Defense. This situation has not been implemented in any other area.

For the integration of science and technology in the socioeconomic sector and for the preparation of science and technology plans and the development of capabilities essential for the fulfillment of tasks in these important sectors, Research Advisory Committees and the Science and Technology Advisory Committee have been constituted by the major socioeconomic ministries. For the coordination of these activities, an Inter-Sectoral Science and Technology Advisory Committee has been set up within the Ministry for Science and Technology. A Technology Information Forecasting and Assessment Council (TIFAC) has also been created. These structures are currently being strengthened and operationalized to ensure that science and technology will become integral parts of the overall national development.

Another major development since the Sixth Plan period has been the creation of science and technology structures in all the states and union territories. This is because India—as a large country of subcontinental dimensions—has highly varied, location-specific requirements.

Today, twenty-four states and five union territories have set up State Councils on Science and Technology and Departments of Science and Technology. These councils are chaired by the Chief Ministers/Governors/Administrators, and they are meant to provide policy guidelines to the highest levels of state governments for the development, application and utilization of science and technology in the states. Important programs of relevance to the various states have been initiated under the auspices of these state councils. They also have many experts from outside their own states to ensure that the scientific community of each of the states would get fully involved in policy formulation, implementation, and monitoring of science and technology programs.

THE TRANSFORMATION

With the advice provided by the apex-level structures in government and considering the fact that 80% of the effort in the science and technology sector has so far been through the government, it has been possible to transform the scenario in science and technology from that which existed at the time of independence to that in existence today. The expenditure on science and technology has grown from Rs. 200 million in the First Plan period to Rs. 84,870 million by the end of the Seventh Plan period.

There have been major accomplishments, particularly in the areas of space, atomic energy, defense research, agriculture, industrial research, biomedical research, etc. In many of these, there now exists a strong, self-reliant and indigenous base. The effort in the years to come would be to consolidate and utilize fully the existing infrastructure so that science and technology can be brought to bear on the major development problems of the country so as to become an integral part of the overall socioeconomic development plans and play a major role in removing poverty from the country, providing employment opportunities, and helping the population, particularly the poorer strata, from the viewpoints of better living standards and meeting their basic minimum needs.

THE FUTURE

It can be seen from the foregoing that—from the high-level scientific capabilities in basic research in educational institutions—over the four decades since independence, a large and diversified infrastructure and similar capabilities have been created, encompassing many areas of applied research, technology, and the utilization of science and technology for meeting national objectives. To bring this about, there have been various types of high-level structures for providing advice to the government. From this experience, one can now ask: What of the future?

Science is advancing rapidly and so is technology, and this is expected to continue with even greater rapidity. This is happening in a resonant symbiotic relationship. As a result, science and technology are becoming increasingly intrinsic parts of all aspects of national policies and development. This situation poses challenges in fields as varied as foreign policy, defense, competitive industrial development and exports, and education to prepare future generations for the kind of world into which science and technology are leading us.

There are also major opportunities to leapfrog many steps in the development process. Informatics, the new developments in biology, and space technologies with implications for communications, broadcasting, and remote sensing are examples of areas of opportunity that offer the promise of a "brave new world," if one proceeds the right way.

But these developments will have significant implications for the future. Clearly, the government must know about these implications and not be faced down by situations when they occur. Developing countries are one step removed from these rapid developments which are taking place mainly in the advanced industrialized countries. But these developments have serious implications for the developing countries in terms of advantages and disadvantages, challenges and opportunities. It is, therefore, clear that new structures will be called for, in which scientists and technologists concerned with both pure and applied areas—including those involved in the production and services sectors, those from within and without government, in addition to those concerned with human resource development, foreign policy, defense, the strategic sectors, etc.—are brought together in a continuing dialogue backed by a strong secretariat.

Such a body could commission studies, and provide information in appropriate forms to the decision-making structures, such as Parliament and governments at the center and in the states. It could also assure a much greater public awareness of the development of science and technology on an international basis and the likely implications for the future. Within such a large framework, there will be a need for a smaller executive structure of exceptional quality in terms of scientific ability and vision, as well as administrative, political and societal understanding. The tempo and widespread ramifications of these rapid developments demand such appropriate mechanisms for high-level advice.

Science and Technology Advice for Developing Countries: The View from Indonesia

Bacharuddin Jusuf Habibie

THE REPUBLIC OF INDONESIA *(Republik Indonesia) was established as an independent republic in 1945, and has been under a modified military regime since 1966. The land area of the country is 741,117 square miles, and its population was estimated at 177,956,000 in 1989. The country's official language is Bahasa Indonesian, which is a form of the Malay language.*

As is the case in many other developing countries, the development of science and technology in Indonesia is motivated by—and takes place within—the larger social and political process of nation-building. In the sense used in this essay, a society can only be called a nation if it has developed a common identity and philosophy, the capacity to develop a distinct lifestyle and mode of cooperation, and the ability to realize its economic, cultural and political potential as a distinct, unified entity.[1]

Economically, nationhood involves the ability to produce the goods and services the country itself needs as well as goods and services needed in the world market for exchange for those that the country requires and cannot provide for itself.

The key to this is the capacity to obtain as well as to develop technology. Without this capability, even abundant natural resources will not constitute a controllable asset. On the other hand, with mastery of science and technology, the scarcity of natural resources will not constitute an insurmountable obstacle.

TECHNOLOGY AND HUMAN RESOURCES

People and technology are inseparable. Science and technology are inherent in and are transferred by human beings, who also create them. It is the ability of people to think analytically, systematically, in-depth, and for the long term that produces science, which, in turn, gives birth to technology. It is, therefore,

Bacharuddin Jusuf Habibie is Minister of State for Research and Technology, Chairman of the Agency for Assessment and Application of Technology, and Chairman of the Board of the Batem Industrial Development Authority. He is a member of the Indonesian Parliament and chairman or director of numerous governmental and industrial boards in Indonesia. Dr. Habibie is a member of the Royal Swedish Academy of Engineering Sciences, foreign associate member of the US National Academy of Engineering, and holder of numerous awards and author of many publications, especially in the field of aeronautical engineering.

223

clear that a nation's enduring progress is ultimately based on the knowledge and skills of its people.

This is why the development of human resources is the heart of science and technology development, and why the development of a strong, vibrant science and technology community is the prime concern of science and technology management.

It is now universally accepted that, when developed into an economically viable force, a nation's renewable human resources are its greatest asset and the determining factor in its future progress. The development experience of many countries in Europe, as well as Japan, Korea, Chinese Taiwan, and other areas in Asia, demonstrate that, even without large endowments of natural resources, progress can be attained even in a relatively short time through the well-planned development of human resources and an economic infrastructure—transportation, communication, energy, and science and technology.

High-quality human resources and economic infrastructure become the foundation of the ability to produce and deliver goods and services of better quality and less cost than those of other countries. Such goods and services will find a ready market in the world, giving rise to trade surpluses and the growth of foreign exchange reserves.

In 1988, Korea's official reserves jumped from US$3.6 billion to US$12.4 billion, transforming it from the net debtor country that it recently was into a net creditor country. In late 1989, Taiwan's official reserves exceeded US$80 billion.

ADDED VALUE

People make use of technology to improve added value processes, *i.e.*, processes to transform raw materials and intermediate goods into finished products having higher values. These added value processes are continuous and complex; they are successful only if the use of machinery, the skills of people, and the materials can be fully integrated by technology. Because of this integrative nature, technology constitutes the most decisive element in added value processes.

The more efficient and productive the added value processes, the higher the standard of living of the country. An increased standard of living gives rise to new ways of thinking and even more advanced science and technology. An upward spiral is created between the level of the development of technology due to the standard of living, and the standard of living because of the level of development of technology. Technology means the presence of the possibility of increasing the capability to produce and advance the standard of living.

This is true for all people—in Europe as well as in Asia, Japan, Africa, North America or Latin America, whether in advanced or developing countries. Every society on this earth has the opportunity to develop itself as long as it is provided with technology.

THE IRRELEVANCE OF LABELS

Given the pressure of the concrete problems of life faced by the underdeveloped parts of the world, there is no great point in classifying technology into elementary, intermediate, high, appropriate and sophisticated levels, as is done by people who do not work with technology and base their classifications on the observation of people who do. The subsequent conclusion drawn is that technologies appropriate to primitive countries are also primitive. This does not help these countries very much.

To say that—to map and inventory their natural resources—primitive countries should not use remote sensing is to demand that such countries remain primitive. To insist that, for them, the appropriate technology for fighting disease is primitive health technology is to perpetuate their misery. To argue that, to overcome natural disasters, to forecast the weather, to eradicate pests, to obtain clean water, to raise agricultural productivity, these countries should use primitive technologies is to ensure the vicious circle between ignorance and poverty.

It would be far more useful to ask which technologies can solve particular problems without caring about whether the technologies have been labelled primitive, intermediate, advanced or sophisticated. It would be far more constructive to believe that, through preparation and counseling, the capability of any people can be increased so that they can make the leap in reasoning ability and imagination needed to master even the most sophisticated science and technology to solve their problems and improve their added value processes.

NATIONAL PERFORMANCE PRODUCTIVITY

Increased, improved production gets translated into income and wealth only through the market. Thus nations must compete internationally. Success in the arena of international competition is not measured in terms of countries' sizes, products, or incomes. Success is measured in terms of a country's surplus and reserve in foreign assets relative to its national production and income. The key factor behind this surplus and reserve is, therefore, of crucial importance to policy-makers in any nation.

This key factor is a country's performance productivity, *i.e.*, the productivity of the country in using its assets to generate net trade and current account surpluses leading to the accumulation of foreign assets.[2]

In microeconomics and technology, performance productivity is the combination of multi-factor productivity—productivity of labor and productivity of capital—and other factors.[3] The productivity of labor and capital can be measured, not only on the production floor, but also in design rooms, engineering shops, marketing offices, and administration and management. The combination of labor-capital productivity is called "multi-factor" productivity, while performance productivity is the result of interactions among multi-factor productivity and other cultural factors, such as innovative ability, entrepreneurship, hard work, discipline, professionalism or "sense of workmanship," strategic planning, and a long-term vision of the future.

Labor, capital, multi-factor and performance productivity can be measured in the factory and at the enterprise level. The national performance productivity of a country is the integration of the performance productivity of its enterprises and industrial sectors.

Performance productivity—in the shop, in the enterprise, and at the national level—is thus the measure of the country's human resources participating in added value and added cost processes which generate and deliver goods and services acceptable to consumers in the domestic, regional and international markets competitive in quality and price.

Improvements in labor productivity and capital productivity will thus increase multi-factor productivity, the composite measure of how efficiently a country makes use of its labor and capital. When increases in productivity are combined with innovation, entrepreneurship, and other factors, the end result will be a major improvement in the country's total performance productivity.

The achievement of high-performance productivity requires an economic system in which individual companies are managed innovatively, professionally, and with entrepreneurship.

What is important here is not so much the absolute level of a country's performance productivity. Of far more importance is its rate of growth. For two decades, the United States had a performance productivity growth rate which was lower than those of Japan and West Germany. As a result, today, the US lags behind those two countries in its performance productivity in many areas.

All this means that, if developing countries are serious in their intent to attain the same level as the developed countries, they must attain a performance productivity rate higher than those of Japan, West Germany and Korea. Without this, it will be impossible to increase manufacturing output and exports sufficiently to catch up with the developed and newly industrializing nations.

Improvements in productivity depend upon improvements in the quality of human resources. Entrepreneurship, innovation and long-term vision are all different products of high-quality human resources. In other words, improvement in the total performance productivity of any nation depends on its ability to improve its efforts in human resource development.

INTERNATIONAL COMPETITIVENESS: THE LESSONS OF EXPERIENCE

It is now increasingly recognized that it is the decline in the productivity growth rate, in comparison to Japan and West Germany, that has been at the root of the US trade deficit. Because of this decline, US companies have lost out in the competition to fulfill the demand of the American consumer for better quality at a better price.

It is true that other factors have contributed to the trade deficit of the US. The high propensity to consume evident in both the private and the governmental sectors of the US is one of these factors. The exchange rates of the US dollar, the Deutschmark, and the yen, which—until corrected—favored imports into the US over exports, is another.

Yet, the high propensity to consume cannot alone explain why it was not American, but Japanese and German production that fulfilled the American demand. Clearly, something else was at play. This was the inability of American manufacturing to compete because of its low performance productivity. This, in turn, was rooted in the low proportion of science and engineering graduates or, in other words, the small number of people trained in the application of science and engineering to production.

Over the past ten years, while only 6% of all United States college and graduate school graduates were science and engineering majors, 20% of Japanese graduates and 37% of West German graduates were awarded science and engineering degrees. This may have been a major reason behind the slowdown in the performance productivity rate of the US which caused it to lag behind West Germany and Japan.

All countries—and, especially, developing countries—need to learn from the US experience. This experience shows that more serious attention must be given to science and engineering education. A greater proportion of the national budget must be spent on science and engineering education, and a greater number of scientists and engineers must be produced every year. By the nature of things, even the best managers of manufacturing enterprises cannot turn out good performances unless they are backed by a pyramid of innovative people who are skilled in design, product development, engineering, and production.

All countries must take a bold second look at their educational systems at all levels—primary, secondary and tertiary, general as well as professional—and do more in terms of integrating the needs of industry to produce more people who are better trained in applications of scientific disciplines to production problems. They must also meet the needs of the educational establishment for more funds, facilities, and work-study opportunities.

Developing countries know full well that this will be a great burden. Because of the need for laboratories and scientific equipment, the per capita cost of education in science and engineering is greater than in other fields of study.

But there is no other choice. In preparing themselves for the challenges of the next century, all countries must take heed of what economics teaches and recent history has demonstrated: that increases in wealth and prosperity are rooted in increases in productivity, and that the key to productivity is the use of science and engineering.

Developing countries must keep in mind the two principal lessons of history: first that, if they are to catch up, their performance productivity rates must be higher than those achieved by the leaders in the world economic competition; and, second, that, in order to achieve this rate, the number of persons trained in science and engineering must be increased.

PRINCIPLES AND PRIORITIES IN INDONESIAN POLICY

It is with this conceptual background and with the reality of severely limited resources in mind that Indonesia has approached the question of science and technology for national development. All less-developed countries face problems of limited manpower, scarce funds, inadequate facilities, uncoordinated programs, insufficient societal support, and low income in their scientific communities. Indonesia is no exception.

Severely limited resources have forced Indonesia to optimize and take a pragmatic approach. The country must make a careful selection of the topics and fields in science and technology to be transferred and to be developed at home.[4]

It has been decided that sciences will be developed in Indonesia only insofar as they contribute to the acquisition and development of the technologies appropriate to the improvement of added value production processes or, more generally, to the solution to concrete national development problems. In other words, directly or indirectly, science and technology should contribute to national development within the realities of economics and geography.

Including its Exclusive Economic Zone, Indonesia's territory is 7.1 million square kilometers, on which 5.2 or 73% is ocean. More than 17,000 islands are located in this area along a span stretching 5,000 kilometers from Sabang in Aceh on the west to Merauke in Irian Java on the east. The country enjoys a strategic location on main shipping routes between the Pacific and Indian Oceans.

Indonesia's population in 1989 was about 178,000,000 people. With the annual rate of population growth expected to decline from 2.18% to 1.9%, the population should be 192.9 million in 1993 and increase to 216 million by the year 2000. Java will continue to have the largest proportion of Indonesia's population and labor force (60% in 1980 and 59% five years later), and hence will remain the most densely populated island of the archipelago (800 persons per square kilometer in 1988 and 864 in 1993). At the same time, the largest reserves of energy are found on other islands or off-shore.

In the light of these facts, President Soeharto has defined Indonesia's national priorities for science and technology as follows:

> Economic development—which is at the heart of our national development today—will progress unhindered only if national stability and national resilience can be maintained, if the basic needs of the Indonesian human being can increasingly be fulfilled, and if the economic infrastructure can be provided. Economic structure among others includes land, sea and air transportation, telecommunications, and the supply of energy.

It is because of this that, in addition to the fulfillment of basic human needs such as food, clothing, education, health and life environment, the provision of economic infrastructure continues to have our great attention.

Efforts to fulfill basic human needs and to provide adequate economic infrastructure are never-ending. Both have therefore to be undertaken all the time with maximum use of our own Indonesian products so as to provide employment, increase income, economize on foreign exchange, and raise the quality of life.[5]

Given the scarcity of resources, by far the greatest priority will be given to the applied sciences. To the maximum extent made possible by international and bilateral cooperation agreements, results of basic research will be drawn from the developed countries and international agencies. Indonesian scientists with great interest in and aptitude for, let us say, high energy physics will be enabled to join laboratories and institutes in countries with which science and technology cooperative agreements have been reached, such as the United States, the Federal Republic of Germany, France, Japan, and the United Kingdom. Rather than spending scarce resources on building the necessary facilities in Indonesia, this would be a far better way to use their interests and talents.

Not all basic research, however, would be left to the developed countries and international agencies. Basic research of direct relevance to national interest would be undertaken in-country by Indonesian nationals. This would include, for instance, research related to specific topics in food agriculture—new and improved seeds, foods, etc.; in health—vaccines for hepatitis-B, malaria, and other communicable diseases; in material sciences—effects of salinity, humidity, and other aspects of the climate and environment; in defense, in culture, in ideology, and other areas. While bilateral and international assistance would, of course, be welcome, it would be unwise to rely on others to solve these problems. The initiative to undertake basic research on topics of this kind must be made by Indonesia itself.

Indonesians are also aware that no technology for added value processes has ever been developed by the use of one science alone. Technologies are always based on a minimum of two or three. Indonesia is, therefore, developing national scientific information systems interconnected with worldwide information networks to increase the flow of scientific information generated in-country as well as abroad by other nations and international agencies. The information required to develop particular technologies would be drawn from these systems. This would optimize the information resources.

TECHNOLOGICAL AND INDUSTRIAL TRANSFORMATION

The attempt to increase production through the transfer and development of sophisticated technology requires consistent and thorough efforts to apply particular production programs.[6]

These programs are distinct because they must fulfill two conditions.

The first condition, which is necessary, but not sufficient, is that it must be possible to implement progressive manufacturing plans. This means that it must be possible to break down the production programs into steps which enable the progressive penetration of the technology being used. In this, levels of penetration into the technology are measured by the percentage of domestic added value produced by the technology in the value of the total product. Steps of penetration are measured in terms of production volume by tying the progress of technology transfer to the number of goods produced and not by setting time targets.

Thus successively deeper penetration into technology means that the larger the production volume, the greater the percentage of domestic value-added obtained by the technology receiving firm or country.

The objective of progressive manufacturing plans is to develop the technological capability level of the technology receiving firm so as to be able to produce the same added value percentage obtained by the technology transferring firm.

The second, necessary and sufficient condition which must be fulfilled by the programs is that the products or product groups manufactured must be competitive in the market. For this, several requirements must be met.

First, the scale of production must approach optimum. Second, the quality of production as well as that of after-sale service must be reliable. To meet these two requirements, it is necessary for the producer to be given temporary protection. In other words, the market for the products must be controllable.

It is possible for the scale of production to approach the optimum if the volume of sales is limited. Also, skills in production as well as after-sale service cannot be developed after producing only a few items. Far greater experience is needed. An international market cannot be controlled by the government of the technology-receiving firm. For this reason, if technology receiver firms must compete in the international market from the start of production, the continuity of production and—because of it—the perpetuation of proficiency in the relevant technology cannot be guaranteed. Government can, however, control the domestic market. The continuity of demand for goods can be better guaranteed with such control. The continuity of the production process can be better ensured. The process of transfer and gaining proficiency in technology can proceed with more assurance, and the further development of the technology can be guaranteed.

Because of this, the second condition can only be fulfilled with the existence of a domestic market which can be controlled.

Only programs producing goods and services which fulfill the first requirement will guarantee the transfer of technology in its totality. Only programs which fulfill the second requirement will guarantee a sufficient scale of production to survive in the market. Because of this, only production programs which fulfill both conditions will be able to transform technology receivers into industrial units, societies, and nations with sophisticated technologies. It is for this reason that programs which fulfill these conditions are called "vehicles for technological and industrial transformation."

The philosophy which must be followed in carrying out these programs is the philosophy "to start with the end and end with the beginning," *i.e.,* to commence with the final product and finish up with the initial componen. The process must commence with the assembly and production of final products, not with the production of components. Although perhaps requiring smaller initial investment, the production of components and the establishment of vendor item factories constitutes the final step in this process, not the initial one. It is easier to find controllable domestic markets for final products than for components and vendor items. Components and vendor items must be marketed in domestic markets controlled by competitor countries, and, therefore, the stability of demand and the viability of production cannot be guaranteed.

VEHICLES OF TRANSFORMATION

Given Indonesia's geography and the level of its economic development, the following eight sectors have been identified as the vehicles of transformation. The first five sectors relate to economic infrastructure, *i.e.,* land transport, shipbuilding and maritime industries, the aircraft industry, electronics and communication, and the energy industry.

Growing needs for plants and equipment for the processing of Indonesia's agricultural products and mineral and energy resources point to the engineering industry as the sixth vehicle for Indonesia's industrial transformation. With land on Java becoming increasingly scarce, agriculture on poorer soils and with limited labor on islands other than Java must be increasingly developed. This will require the increased mechanization of agriculture, both preharvest as well as post-harvest, and identifies the agricultural equipment industry as the seventh vehicle.

Eighth and last, given Indonesia's strategic location, its vast reserves of natural and human resources, and its rising wealth, there is greater need for a domestic defense industrial capability.

Rising income and wealth will give rise to greater demand for the products of the construction industry, agroindustry, and all kinds of service industries, including education and health. These together can be regarded as constituting a ninth derivative vehicle.

STAGES OF TRANSFORMATION

This transformation itself will take place in four overlapping stages. Three of these are relevant for developing countries, while the fourth stage constitutes the key to success for countries which intend to defend their technological superiority.

The first and most basic stage is the stage of technology transfer through licensed production, *i.e.*, the stage of using already existing production and management technologies in the production of goods already on the market.

The second stage will be the stage of integrating already existing technologies into the design and production or completely new products, *i.e.*, those not yet on the market. At this stage, new designs and blueprints are developed. Thus there is a new element, that of creation.

The third stage is the stage of technology development itself. In this stage, already existing technologies are developed further. Differing from the second stage, in this stage new technologies are developed. The motivation to undertake this is the opportunity to produce the products of the future.

The fourth and final stage is the stage of large-scale basic research to support the other three stages and to defend the technological superiority already attained.

MUTUAL BENEFIT

Indonesia realizes the crucial importance of creating and maintaining an appropriate environment for technology transfer. While important, agreements, memoranda of understanding, and official decisions are of themselves not sufficient. They must be supplemented by, first, sincere and fair agreements to harmonize the interests of both the technology proprietor and the technology receiver. Second, serious efforts must be made to overcome certain constraints, both on the receiving as well as on the transferring side.[7]

There must be mutual friendship. Sincere steps must be taken to remove suspicion and antagonism. Mutual interests can only be brought into harmony on the foundation of mutual liking and understanding. It is, at best, unrealistic to expect that technology will be transferred by the passing of resolutions at antagonistic international conferences where it is insisted that advanced countries transfer their technologies to developing countries as rapidly as possible and without charge.

It must also be realized that other interests must be acknowledged.

First, to compensate for the expenditure of time, effort, skill and other scarce resources needed to develop their technology, technology proprietors must be given appropriate direct and indirect incentives to transfer their technology. License fees and royalties are the usual forms of direct incentives. Indirect incentives include the opportunity to widen markets, to increase sales volumes, and to raise research and development funds to further advance technology, among others, through research and development cooperative programs between transferor and receiver.

Second, it must be recognized that the property rights of technology owners must be protected. Therefore, Indonesia is strengthening the laws and regulations to sufficiently guarantee intellectual property and patent right protection.

Third, technology transferors hope that technology transfer will not result in job losses. To fulfill this aspiration, it is necessary to undertake a division of labor between transferor and receiver on the basis of the consideration of macro- and micro-economic factors on both sides. In the author's opinion, a fair sharing would be one in which 40% to 60% of value added is carried out by the receiver while the remainder is undertaken by the transferor. This way both parties will complement each other and jointly contribute to the research and development costs of their partners.

Fourth, in addition to the division of labor in added value processes, it is also necessary to share the market. The transferor must be guaranteed that the receiver will not compete with him in his own market, while the receiver must be given sole marketing rights in its domestic market and/or in the region surrounding its domestic market.

Fifth and finally, proprietors will only transfer technology when they are assured of a mutually profitable long-term cooperation between them and the receivers. Only under such conditions will they be induced to share knowledge and economic resources.

INDONESIA'S INTERESTS

On the other hand, due recognition must be given to Indonesia's interests as a technology receiver.

First, the country would like to be guaranteed that the technology received is really state of the art.

Second, Indonesia must be assured that, by paying certain service charges, it will always be in a position to obtain the most recent information on the latest developments in these state-of-the-art technologies.

Third, the economic and human resources of Indonesia must be given the opportunity to be involved in the further development of these technologies.

And, fourth, Indonesia must be as convinced as the technology suppliers that the cooperation will be mutually profitable and long-term.

The adjustment of mutual interests is only one aspect of the careful preparations that must be made for technology transfer to be successful. Equally important are programs to overcome conditions that constrain effective and large-scale technology transfer. Some of these constraints are internal; others are more external in nature.

A major internal constraint faced by the technology receiver is that its labor force has usually just completed its formal education and lacks practical experience. In addition, the added value processes undertaken by the receiver lack the integration usually found in the modern organizations of technology transferors. In advanced countries, workers can usually be relied upon to thoroughly know their jobs and the interconnections between their jobs and the others in the factory. This is not the case in a developing country. Because of this, factories in developing countries have to undertake additional investment in infrastructure, plant facilities, education and training, systems and work procedures, etc., in the effort to change themselves into what are called "technology carriers." All this impacts on the cost of production.

It is usual for developing countries to rely on their own inexpensive labor. It is true that, under certain conditions, labor costs—including overhead—in developing countries may be only 10% of the labor cost in advanced countries. But the productivity and efficiency of labor in developing countries is not so high as that of the experienced labor force in advanced countries. In addition, "just in time" supply systems have not been established in developing countries, and material and vendor inventory levels are necessarily higher: in some cases, up to three months of production.

It is clear that, except when higher material, vendor item, and machine-hour costs can be compensated for by savings in labor costs, there is no economic reason to produce in the developing countries. Prices of goods will be higher than prices of similar goods produced abroad, and firms must be subsidized by the customers.

EXTERNAL CONSTRAINTS

In addition, technology receivers also face the external constraints of societal and governmental attitudes.

Today, through the educational system and the system of articulating the will of society, the institutional structure, the attitude of labor, and the framework of rules and regulations of developing countries still reflect the orientation of their societies toward agriculture, trade and services. There is, as yet, little reflection of an orientation toward industry. Yet the objective is a society which is oriented toward all these fields.

This is the largest external obstacle that technology receivers in developing countries face today.

If government regulations are not properly prepared to support the process of production increase through technology transfer, the struggles of managers, workers, innovators and entrepreneurs and their efforts to create fruitful cooperation with their transferring partners will be in vain. Internal savings in production costs will be nullified by increased costs due to obstacles and delays caused by external factors.

Because of this, it is necessary to also make improvements in the external business environment, especially in the framework of laws and regulations and in the orientation of society in general.

Not only the governments of technology-receiving countries must be improved. Governments of technology-transferring countries should also do more in terms of providing support to technology transfer. Measures which can be taken include the application of appropriate tax, labor and credit regulations; the institution of financial and technical assistance programs; and the provision of incentives for business units seeking opportunities to transfer their technology to firms in developing countries in pursuit of the previously mentioned future world economic scenario.

Incentives must also be provided for developing countries which seek to receive technology, and have policies and views of their economic future which are in agreement with those of the donor countries. These incentives could take the form of educational and technical assistance, the provision of guarantees, and so on.

All of this must be adequately prepared. Without thorough preparation, technology transfer will be like pouring water into leaky buckets.

THE ORGANIZATIONAL FRAMEWORK (IN EXISTENCE AND PLANNED)

In Indonesia, the President is both Head of State and Head of Government. There are three types of ministers in the cabinet, all reporting directly to the President. Coordinating ministers are equivalent to Deputy Prime Ministers in other types of Cabinets. The ministers in charge of departments are heads of departments of government: foreign affairs, the interior, agriculture, industry, mining and energy, etc. Each of these departments has its respective agency for research and development.

Ministers of State are responsible for government-wide functions and, thereby, have authority over all agencies of the government, including departments, with respect to these functions. The Minister of State for National Development Planning, for example, oversees and coordinates the plans and development projects of all agencies of governments, including departments.

Likewise, the Minister of State for Research and Technology oversees and coordinates all research, science and technology activities of all government agencies and is the highest adviser at the Cabinet level to the President for research and technology.

The Office of the Minister of State for Research and Technology was established in 1978 as an extension and expansion of the previous Office of the Minister of State for Research. The minister is charged ". . . to deal with issues and problems of research and technology in order that their development and application shall have more direction and coordination to support the needs of development."

The office of the minister includes the offices of the Secretary General, Assistant I for General Planning, Assistant II for the Development of Research and Technology, Assistant III for Institutional and Manpower Development, Assistant IV for Research and Technology Programs and Project Supervision, and Assistant V, who is also Secretary of the National Research Council.

The Minister of State for Research and Technology is concurrently Chairman of the Agency for the Assessment and Application of Technology. This agency was established by President Decision in 1978 to complement the macro-planning performed by the Minister of State for National Development Planning (concurrently Chairman of the National Development Planning Agency) with the more detailed assessment regarding appropriate and effective technologies to implement development projects. The structure of the agency was expanded in 1982.

The chairman of the agency is assisted by a vice chairman and six deputy chairmen: for basic and applied research, for technology development, for industrial analyses, for natural resources, for systems analyses, and for administration.

The basic conceptual framework for coordination and direction of research and technology in Indonesia is the National Matrix of Research and Technology. This matrix is designed to focus the attention of the scientific community and of society in general on the larger purposes to be served by science and technology to be advanced in Indonesia.

Consistent with the Indonesian belief that a nation's enduring progress is ultimately based on the knowledge and skills of its people and that, therefore, the development of the Indonesian human resource potential is at the heart of science and technology development, all sciences and technologies in Indonesia are directed toward the fulfillment of the basic human needs of the Indonesian people; to the development of the energy and natural resources needed by the nation and its people; to the implementation of industrialization; to the maintenance of national defense; and to the improvement of society, economy, culture, law, and life philosophies.

These five purposes constitute the columns of the National Matrix of Research and Technology, while, to ensure its comprehensiveness, it encompasses the four rows of land, sea, air, and the environment, thus forming a five-by-four matrix of twenty cells or elements of broad research and technology areas, such as, for instance, marine food and nutrition, sea defense and security, etc. Entering all research and development projects and programs into the elements of the matrix thus enables the determination of whether particular areas are being overresearched or are being relatively neglected. Given Indonesia's need to reduce her reliance on natural resources, a slightly higher emphasis is given to the needs for rapid industrialization and the science and technology relevant to it.

To implement and further develop the National Matrix, the Team for the Formulation and Evaluation of National Programs for Science and Technology was established in 1978. By Presidential Decree Number 1 of 1984, this National Team was elevated into the National Research Council as an advisory body outside the government proper chaired by the Minister of State for Research and Technology to do the following:

- Coordinate the formulation of national priority programs in research and technology;

- Continuously observe and evaluate the implementation of these programs; and
- Provide appropriate substantive direction and supervision.

Similar to the National Team, this council comprises five committees, each with the task of directing and evaluating science and technology projects toward one of the five purposes. It performs this task by formulating criteria for relevance, for performance, and for capability; by specifying program objectives; and by evaluating existing laboratories and institutes. Also, through the minister, it advises the National Development Planning Agency on the research and development budgets to be allocated to government agencies and universities.

PROVIDING FOR EXCELLENCE

To provide for excellence in science and technology, preparations are being made for the establishment of the Indonesian Academy of Sciences, the Indonesian National Academy of Engineering, and the Indonesian National Academy of Medicine. Membership in the academies will be by election, and members of these academies will automatically be members of the National Research Council.

For coordination purposes, National Science and Technology Coordination Meetings, organized by the Office of the Minister of State for Research and Technology, and National Science and Technology Seminars, called by the National Research Council, are held every other year, the first to coordinate programs and report on the institutional capabilities of laboratories and institutes, and the second to discuss specific topics relevant to the implementation of the National Matrix of Science and Technology.

The PUSPIPTEK Center for Research, Science and Technology, in Serpong, near Jakarta, is designed to be a centrally located 1,000-hectare area comprising a 500-hectare complex of multidisciplinary laboratories and research facilities, all fully equipped with up-to-date instrumentation which will permit the conduct of research to international standards; a 350-hectare high-technology industrial zone; and a 150-hectare educational complex for the Indonesian Institute of Technology campus, as well as an office complex which will include office facilities for the Indonesian Academy of Sciences, the National Research Council, the Indonesian National Academy of Engineering, and the Indonesian National Academy of Medicine.

The 500-hectare area reserved for research and science encompasses a 30MW multipurpose research reactor, with separate installations for nuclear fuel element fabrication, experimental fuel elements, radioactive waste treatment, nuclear meccano electronics, radio-isotope production, nuclear safety engineering, radiometallurgy, and informatics. In addition, it will comprise five laboratories under the Indonesian Institute of Sciences: calibration, instrumentation and metrology; electro-technical; applied physics; applied chemistry; and laterite metallurgy. It will also include six laboratories managed by the Agency for the Assessment and Application of Technology: construction testing; thermodynamics, engines, and propulsion systems; aerodynamics, gas dynamics, and vibration; natural resources and energy; process technologies; and natural disaster mitigation.

Of these laboratories, the multipurpose research reactor with the research reactor fuel element production installation; the Center for Radio-Isotope Production; the Center for Nuclear Instrumentation and Engineering; the Experimental Fuel Element Production Installation of the National Atomic Energy Agency; the Construction Testing Laboratory and the Aerodynamics, Gas Dynamics, and Vibration Laboratory and the Indonesian Low-speed Wind Tunnel of the Agency for the Assessment and Application of Technology; the Calibration, Instrumentation and Metrology Laboratory; and the Laterite Metallurgy Laboratory of the Indonesian Institute of Sciences are operational. The Applied Physics Laboratory, the Applied Chemistry Laboratory, and the Energy and Natural Resources Laboratory are in partial operation. The other laboratories and scientific installations are under construction and/or in the planning stages.

A Science Demonstration Center and Multipurpose Service Center complement a housing complex, which also includes sports, recreation and shopping facilities, and pre-school, primary and secondary school facilities, a polyclinic, and religious services facilities. A botanical garden for the preservation of rare plant species will be planted over the entire 1,000 hectares and provide for pleasant surroundings for the whole complex.

Science and technology centers similar to PUSPIPTEK have been established and are being planned in other locations to focus on biotechnology and genetic engineering (health and medicine, food and agriculture); and marine science and technology. Other centers in agricultural research and experiment stations established earlier in this century will be further developed following the PUSPIPTEK pattern.

COOPERATION WITH ASEAN MEMBER COUNTRIES

Commensurate with Indonesia's commitment to the development of the Association of South East Asian Nations (ASEAN), the country is active in science and technology cooperative programs with other ASEAN member countries. ASEAN cooperation in science and technology takes place through its Committee on Science and Technology and is monitored by meetings of ASEAN ministers in charge of science and technology. Four such conferences have taken place.

The first meeting was convened in Pattaya in 1980, the second in Jakarta in 1983, the third in Kuala Lumpur in 1986, and the fourth took place in Manila in 1989.

At the Manila meeting, Indonesia confirmed its commitment to regional cooperation, and urged ASEAN member countries to increase the application of science and technology for basic human needs, for human resource development, and for economic infrastructure to secure and advance welfare, peace, stability and resilience in ASEAN, the Pacific Basin, and the world.

Indonesia also stressed the need to establish and advance mutually beneficial cooperative arrangements with ASEAN's more technologically advanced friends and partners, such as nations in western Europe, northern America, Japan, and Australia, on both an individual country-to-country basis and a cooperative basis.[8]

TOWARD THE FUTURE IN THE PACIFIC BASIN

As Indonesia looks into the future in the Pacific, it perceives the 21st century to be shaped by the following three factors.[9]

First is the increase in the world's population around the Pacific Ocean with significant increases also in living standards. For a great many people, their basic needs will have been adequately met. Many more societies will enjoy good quality food and nutrition, low infant mortality, high life-expectancy rates and generally good individual and community health. Good quality education at all levels and in many fields of knowledge will be more widely available. Private and public housing will have ceased to be a major problem. The preservation and improvement of the natural environment will also, it is hoped, have been taken care of better.

The second is the existence of more and better economic infrastructures: transportation modes and facilities (ports, roads, ships, railways, automotive equipment, and aircraft will have been vastly improved). Through satellites and fiber optic transmission and better software and hardware, information and communications services will have been made even more rapid and productive. Because of this, office and factory work will be more productive, data processing and transmission quicker, and recreation and leisure more enjoyable. Through better materials and processes, energy use will have been improved, and the environment better protected and preserved.

True, for a great number of people in the Pacific region, the fulfillment of basic needs and the enjoyment of an adequate infrastructure may, at that time, still be a major problem. Yet the critical mass of people with the skills, motivation and energy to develop the economies of the area and thereby create better conditions for others will already exist.

The third factor is the large expansion of the market for science and technology products generated by the first two factors. Higher living standards and better economic infrastructure create better-quality people: people with better health, more and greater skills, who are better informed; in short, people who can make use of more and better science—established as well as advanced— and better technology—simple as well as sophisticated.

There will be greater demand for science and technology in many national markets around the Pacific, each with its own particular philosophies, conditions, and potential volume of trade. At the same time, higher standards of living and a better infrastructure create better environments for innovation and invention—the foundations of a greater supply of more and better science and technology.

The nature of these markets will, however, change.[10] The higher the skills and the better the information, the less will people in national markets be content to be merely buyers of finished goods. In an increasing number of high-technology items—electronic equipment, aircraft, ships, communications satellites, cement factories, fertilizer factories, etc.—people in national markets will want a larger share of production, both in hardware and in software.

A radically different pattern of the division of labor will be required, not primarily because of political-philosophical reasons, but primarily because of fundamental techno-economic forces. The most important of these will be the rising cost of research and development in high-technology products in developed countries. Because of the rising cost of skilled personnel, software and hardware, the funds for the research and development needed to further develop technology have become very large. Consequently, the market for high-technology products must be widened to include the developing countries. Through their purchases, the low-income populations of the world have to become involved in the funding of research and development for sophisticated technology industries.

But the low-income populations of the world can become a large market and a significant donor of high-technology industry research and development funds only if their incomes and purchasing power increase. Only societies with high productivity and high income will be able to create a demand for science and technology. The increase of purchasing power through the provision of commercial, soft and even very soft loans is not of sufficient significance compared to the increase of income through increases in productivity of added value processes. This improvement of the added value processes can happen only with the enhancement of technology.

This means that technology transfer and trade are not only in the interest of the developing countries. For the sake of widening their market, technology transfer to developing countries is also the advantage of the advanced countries. Raising the standards of living of developing countries will not benefit only those countries. It will be of benefit to the developed countries as well. They must, therefore, not only be concerned with selling science and technology to developing countries, but also must make it possible for people to increase their incomes and wealth through productive employment and thereby add to their ability to acquire science and technology. Doing so will require the use of science and technology to improve the added value processes, as well as for human resource development and development of the economic infrastructure.

The future is here today. The signs of development in this direction can be seen even now. The volume of trade between the advanced countries and between advanced countries and industrializing countries is far larger than that between advanced countries and raw material producing countries. We see new technologies being transferred and productivity and production in developing countries rising. As production increasingly stabilizes, a larger number of component and material producers are relocating to developing countries. Costs are being lowered further and further to approach the material and vendor item costs in advanced countries.

Slowly or rapidly, depending upon the speed of the increase of production planning and control capabilities and the skills of workers, the comparative disadvantage of the developing countries in material and vendor item costs will decrease. On the other hand, slowly or rapidly, their comparative advantage in labor cost will disappear. Their labor will demand higher wages; their level of aspiration will rise. They will be more skilled and experienced. All this will will be reflected in larger remuneration packages. This is precisely the object of development. In time, production costs and the prices of manufactured products will be the same all over the world.

THE DIFFERENCE IN THE FUTURE

But what will be different in the future will be the volume of production, of sales, of employment, and of wage levels. All these will show large increases. The levels of welfare in all nations also will be greater. The international division of labor will be completely different from a few decades ago; it will be vastly more equal and just. No longer will there be countries which serve only as raw material suppliers and markets for manufactured goods while other countries gain the added value of production and the advanced technology upon which it is based. The international division of labor will be based on different political, economic and social considerations. In terms of population, the advanced part of the world will vastly outnumber the so-called underdeveloped part.

Such a world will be a much better place in which to live than our world of today. Relations between nations will be more harmonious. Economic and social integration between countries will be higher. There will be more cooperation between countries—in science and technology, in production, and in economic and social life generally, with each country being able to contribute more to this cooperation.

NOTES

1. B. J. Habibie, "Science, Technology, and Nation Building," address delivered to the International Symposium on Energy and International Cooperation: Choices for the 21st Century, Tokyo, Japan, March 1982.
2. B. J. Habibie, "Some Remarks Regarding the Constraints on Indonesia's Transformation into a Modern Society," commencement address to the ninth graduating class, The Indonesian Institute for Management Development, Jakarta, August 1989.

3. B. J. Habibie, keynote address to the 12th National Congress, Indonesian Engineering Association, Bandung, Indonesia, November 1989.
4. B. J. Habibie, "Science Policy Management in Indonesia," address to the Third Meeting of the ASEAN Ministers for Science and Technology, Kuala Lumpur, April 1986.
5. President Soeharto, address on the inauguration of the commissioning of the G. A. Siwabessy Multipurpose Research Reactor, PUSPIPTEK Center for Research, Science and Technology, Serpong, Indonesia, August 1987.
6. B. J. Habibie, "Some Thoughts on a Strategy for the Industrial Transformation of a Developing Country," address to the Deutsche Gessellschaft fur Luft und Raumfahrt, Bonn, Federal Republic of Germany, June 1983.
7. B. J. Habibie, "The Application of Sophisticated Technologies in Developing Countries: The Case of Indonesia," keynote address at the International Herald Tribune Centennial Conference, "Pacific 2000: Global Challenge," Singapore, November 1987.
8. B. J. Habibie, address on behalf of the ASEAN ministers at the Fourth Meeting of the ASEAN Ministers for Science and Technology, Manila, January 1989.
9. B. J. Habibie, "The Globalization of Technology: The Perspective of the Technology Receiver," remarks at the Pacific Summit on Economic Relations of the Pacific Region, "Opportunities and Challenges of the Next Century," Seattle, Washington, August 1989.
10. B. J. Habibie, "The Challenge of Trading High Technology Products and Services: The Perspective of Indonesia," remarks at the Technology Symposium of the Pacific Summit (see Note 9).

Science Advice for Governments: Ireland and the European Community

Vincent J. McBrierty

THE REPUBLIC OF IRELAND *(Eire) has been an independent state since 1921, and has operated under a republican constitution since 1937. The country's land area is 27,136 square miles, and the population was estimated in 1989 at 3,608,000. The official languages are Irish (Gaelic) and English.*

> Science is subject to human values and beliefs: It is not their master.
> —K. Pinkau

Francis Bacon's famous statement, penned nearly four centuries ago, "nam et ipsa scientia potestas est" (for even knowledge itself is power),[1] has acquired a totally new dimension in this age of unprecedented scientific enlightenment. But history offers repeated testimony as to the manner in which knowledge and the power that derives from it can be used for good or evil. The inherent ambivalence in the way that knowledge is perceived should not be a cause of feigned surprise: knowledge, or, more precisely, the manner of its use is truly a double-edged sword.

Science and technology provide a classic example of this viewpoint. Their influence permeates virtually every aspect of human existence, often in subtle and poorly understood ways.[2] Ambivalence reveals itself in the public perception of science and technology as universal remedies, capable of redressing many current problems, while concurrently holding them responsible for accelerated unemployment, increased health hazards, ecological catastrophe, and so forth. There is unease, too, with progress in fields such as genetic engineering where profound social, ethical and moral questions have been raised.

Developments in communications technology have added an important new dimension through the creation of a "global consciousness."[3] The ease with which information is rapidly disseminated on a global scale has created an informed society, one that needs to be reassured about the ultimate pricetag on the assimilation of new and ostensibly beneficial discoveries. What are the effects on the quality of life, on health, and, of increasing importance, on the

Vincent J. McBrierty is a Fellow and Professor of polymer physics at Trinity College, Dublin, a post which he has held since 1979. In the course of his career at the college, he has held posts at officer level, including Dean of Science (1984–86) and College Bursar (1986–89). He was Vice President of the Royal Irish Academy (1988–89) and is an adviser to the Council of Europe on Science and Technology.

243

environment? Demands for greater public participation in the decision-making process are an inevitable consequence of this new public awareness.

Apart from the direct benefits that new discoveries can confer on society, there is a second consideration that cannot be neglected. Science and technology have emerged as a universal language, linking different nations and spheres of civilization.[2,4] This universality of science constitutes a potent vehicle for international cooperation with the scientists themselves as the prime participants. But this aspect, too, has its downside. The emerging internationalization of science and technology, embodying as it does a growing realization of the importance of transnational cooperation, is greatly moderated by fears based largely on international competitiveness and the need to protect intellectual property, which is the feedstock of technological progress.

Pinkau notes that the transition from science to technology to industrial application parallels a transition from international cooperation to international competition.[5] But bear in mind two related considerations: First, not all the ills that befall society are attributable to scientific discovery. For example, great damage has been inflicted in the past through implementation of distorted and inappropriate theories of education. Second, political will is at least as unpredictable, controversial, and difficult to handle.[6]

Primarily, it is the exercise of judgment on the pursuit, evaluation and implementation of scientific discovery that presents the formidable challenge. Generally, it is not so much the scientific discovery itself as its subsequent management and assimilation that poses the greatest difficulty. No one individual embodies the collective wisdom necessary to analyse the diverse range of sociopolitical, economic, ethical and scientific aspects of the problem. Baker advocates pluralistic policy guidance.[7]

MANAGEMENT AND EVALUATION

The linkage between the knowledge generator and the political decision-maker has, in the past, left much to be desired; traditional approaches have been inadequate to deal with the scale and sophistication of modern developments. This linkage is, nonetheless, crucial to the effective assimilation of scientific discovery into society. It should, therefore, come as no surprise that the management and evaluation of science and technology now form a growing discipline in its own right: the discipline of technology assessment.[8,9]

In the last analysis, in a democratic society, it is the politicians and ultimately the governments with their direct mandates from the people who finally decide. They carry the responsibility for making informed judgments on a pluralistic input of advice which, in turn, implies the need for accepted procedures, necessarily independent and devoid of vested interests, and having the confidence of all concerned. This is at the heart of the problem that has, of late, been taxing many governments throughout Europe and elsewhere, and one that forms the central theme of these deliberations.

The views expressed here are a personal perspective of the developments in Europe and the efforts of nations within the European Community (EC) to meet the challenge of the current technological revolution. These goals are pursued in the general context of Europe's position *vis-a-vis* the United States and Japan, on the one hand, and the Third World, on the other.

Clearly, any meaningful discussion of science advice for governments requires the examination of the fundamental interrelationships involved in the diffusion of scientific discovery throughout society and an elucidation of the context within which government functions, for there is no single solution that can meet the needs of nations of disparate size, wealth, and cultural background. Guided by this view, the way in which advice for governments is formulated through effective technology assessment is examined in the context of fundamental concepts, global considerations, the infrastructure that exists within the European Community as 1992 approaches, and the particular circumstances that prevail at national levels, with particular reference to Ireland. There is, of course, the overriding caveat that no nation can act with full autonomy in the sense that events in one country can have major transnational implications, as evidenced, for example, in recent nuclear accidents and other affronts to the global environment.

THE PROCESS OF TECHNOLOGY ASSESSMENT

Technology assessment is a process (rather than an analytical technique) which addresses the complex interrelationships between three major participants: society, the legislature, and the scientific community, influenced, in turn, by the media and the educational system. Successful technology assessment rests on the establishment of mutual understanding and communication among them. But many factors conspire against harmonious dialogue; in particular, competing interests within and between the three sectors generate tensions that are difficult to accommodate. In the legislature there is often conflicting opinion between the upper and lower houses, the Executive branch, and the majority and minority parties, whereas society invariably comprises an apathetic majority influenced by minority lobbies and vocal sectoral interests. The scientific community embodies specialist technical expertise along with its own complement of vocal sectional interests.

It is difficult for the nonscientific community to reconcile the spectacle of scientists, who are ostensibly practitioners in precise disciplines, indulging in confrontation and disagreement, which, in reality, are essential ingredients in the evolution of scientific understanding. Nor should the public at large be expected to understand specialist concepts such as probability, randomness, or irreversibility, or, indeed, to appreciate the inherent uncertainty of science with its unintended as well as its intended discoveries. A lack of appreciation of these points can generate public disquiet and undermine confidence in scientific expert opinion. However, as Bondi argues, scientists can convey to the general population *how* we do science, *how* it advances (by seeing just how fallible it is), *how* we constantly make mistakes, and *how* we correct each other; *how* scientific argument is not something extraordinary but is the normal progress of science.[10]

By the same token, parliaments are often dominated by those with legal training whose adversarial style differs profoundly from the consensual character of scientific debate. There is general unease, too, among politicians who are concerned by the potential threat of growing technocracy usurping power by making decisions outside the traditional machinery of parliament.

The media exerts powerful influence in dictating the pace of events: on the one hand, important issues can be buried in a shroud of science, while minority viewpoints attract widespread coverage, either because they are inherently controversial or because they deserve to be championed in countering vested interest opinion of powerful lobbies. Here again, there is the spectre of the double-edged sword.

COMMUNICATION AND UNDERSTANDING

Inadequacies in communication and mutual understanding are symptomatic of an educational system that, for whatever reason, has lost sight of its central mission. The provision of a balanced and broad-based education which facilities dialogue and communication has largely been circumvented by a preoccupation with overspecialization. How then can people trained in highly focused disciplines be expected to understand and communicate with those outside their own genre? As yet, scant attention is being paid to training in communication skills in all sectors of the community; there is little dialogue between the sciences and the arts and humanities; and, despite the goal of a borderless Europe by 1992, widespread teaching of language skills still has to gain the necessary momentum in certain regions of Europe. A balanced level of literacy and numeracy in the education process has yet to be achieved.

The current rate of progress in scientific discovery not only stems from a concentration of effort supported by biased funding policies, it is also due to an ability to divide the complex totality of science into less complex parts (aside, perhaps, from certain of the biosciences), each of which is amenable to meaningful analysis and methodology. Other disciplines, such as the social sciences, are not so accommodating and this has created a mismatch between the rate at which scientific discovery proceeds and the development of those nonscientific disciplines that exert the necessary moderating influence on the assimilation of science and technology into society.

Clearly, there is a dilemma for the education sector. On the one hand, the universities and other third-level institutions cannot function in isolation in a way that denies their unique and strategic contributions to modern society. Nor can they succumb to pressures to provide research and training that are "relevant" when that relevance is dictated by outside agencies solely preoccupied with short-term gains. Education is for life and for a career that typically spans four decades; it is not for the lifetime of the present technology. A recent OECD report[11] notes that excessive concentration on short-term commercial activities may compromise the more important longer-term role in education and basic research. The conflicting demands placed upon the education process can only be met through a return to a more balanced and long-term approach that is mindful of prevailing social needs and fiscal constraints. Resources devoted to education and research are not merely expenditure items; they are part of capital investment.

To summarize, the formulation of advice for governments must take account of a number of basic observations, such as:

- The language and perspectives of society, parliament, and the scientific community greatly differ.
- Much greater public participation in the decision-making process is inevitable, but it is ultimately the responsibility of parliament to adjudicate upon the plurality of scientific, social, fiscal, economic and political elements in the decision-making process, presented as a series of options based on well-reasoned scenarios.
- There are tensions both between and within the three principal participating sectors which reflect competing routes of influence. In addition, powerful, selective and, occasionally, irrational influences, which override reasoned argument, can dominate public opinion and, therefore, directly dictate policy.
- Short-term gains at the expense of long-term benefits should not be allowed to distort the educational process.

Elucidation of the major constraints to effective technology assessment in the foregoing discussion has prompted a number of practical observations, as described in the summary findings of an earlier study.[8] From the general perspective, it is recalled that a common model clearly cannot meet the needs of nations of different sizes, wealth, degrees of development, cultural heritages, and parliamentary structures. The ease with which institutional technology assessments, under the guise of an Office of Technology Assessment (OTA) or otherwise, can be interposed between parliament and society is, therefore, dependent upon national characteristics. There is, nonetheless, broad consensus on the need for openness, a minimal level of complexity and separation from decision-makers, lest its independence and objectivity be impaired.[2,8] It is the goal of effective technology assessment to promote political decision-making to a higher plane of understanding and to enhance public awareness of the disadvantages as well as the advantages of scientific discovery.

GLOBAL CONSIDERATIONS

New technologies are changing the face of the world's industrial map on such a scale that innovation is no longer an option for an industrial society—it is an obligation.[12] Certain industries (for example, ship-building and the steel industry) can be stagnant in one country and highly innovative in another. Industrially developed and developing nations form two broad categories that broadly constitute the north/south divide. The developed nations include the three economic superpowers—Europe, the United States, and Japan (along with other rapidly developing nations in the Pacific Basin).

The way in which developed and developing nations relate to one another is a major issue for governments. Despite the obvious disparities in growth and prosperity, there is a strong interdependence between the two and a recognition that the future prosperity of the north must inevitably depend on a secured prosperity for the south. A narrowing of the gap between developed and developing nations requires sustained policies that ensure equitable trading, market access for Third World products, development capital, manageable debt repayment structures, and improved regulation of raw material and commodity markets.

The ways in which Europe, the United States and Japan approach scientific discovery reflect basic differences in philosophy and culture. Japan's vision of the future is formulated in three guiding principles: the promotion of creative science and technology, the promotion of science and technology in harmony with people and society, and the maintenance of an international perspective. By 1985, Japan was involved in twenty-one cooperative agreements with seventeen countries.

The United States has also managed to create an environment in which entrepreneurial flair, responsive to market needs, flourishes. This is reflected particularly in the dynamism of small business ventures that thrive through sensible government procurement policies, flexible attitudes, worker mobility, and so on. The strong interface between government, industry, and the educational institutions which, interestingly, is not so well developed in Japan, along with the economy of scale of the US domestic market, are major contributing factors.

Europe—by contrast—is the weakest link in the tripartite chain. In recent times, there has been minimal job growth in Europe, due largely to the adoption of policies for consolidation, rather than expansion; relative to the US and Japan, with a few notable exceptions, there has been lukewarm support for basic research and a low level of application of high technology (for the period 1987–1992, it is estimated that the EC will spend less than half the amount spent by the United States on research and technological development); governments in Europe have tended to buffer ailing economies and failing industries, often through lobbies of strength and privilege; there has been an inability to direct innovation to market changes, exacerbated, in turn, by fragmented markets; Europe has 30%–40% fewer scientists than the US or Japan, they are aging through lack of adequate recruitment and through emigration, and there is insufficient geographic and thematic mobility; and a serious mismatch exists between what the workforce can do and what it is called upon to do, which adversely affects employment patterns. Unemployment in the EC is currently at 9.7%. These "gales of creative destruction" in the job market have not been adequately anticipated or prepared for.[12] Collectively, the ills that face Europe have been termed "Eurosclerosis."

The Single European Act, signed in 1987, represents an attempted major European response to this rather pessimistic self-assessment scenario. The Act confers formal legal status on European political cooperation with the stated goal of creating, by 1992, a Europe without frontiers and with free movement of people, goods, and services. In short, it seeks greater political, economic, monetary and social cohesion. A consolidated, internal Community market will account for some 37% of the world's commerce, and will constitute the largest domestic market in the industrialized world with more than 320 million customers.

This bold step has generated a diversity of responses ranging from a "fortress Europe" mentality, anticipating a market protected by a multiplicity of trade barriers, to more positive views that recognize challenging market opportunities of enormous proportions. Note, too, that these developments in Europe are paralleled by sustained industrial growth in other parts of the world, particularly in the Pacific Basin countries.

The prevailing unease that a unified Community market poses a threat rather than an opportunity has, in some instances, prompted reactions elsewhere in the form of increased trading restrictions and other actions directed toward technological isolationism. It would be somewhat ironic if attempts to strengthen an ailing Europe turned out to be an impediment to enhanced international cooperation. From the European perspective, "a strong Community is a far more interesting partner for the United States and Japan than one losing its foothold in international competition."[12]

THE EUROPEAN COMMUNITY

The twelve nations that make up the EC account for about 7% of the world's population; by the year 2020, the figure will be closer to 4%. The EC is about one-quarter the size of the USA and one-tenth the size of the USSR. Sectoral employment in European industry and services greatly exceeds employment in agriculture, even in countries like Ireland and Greece with strong agricultural traditions.[13] In essence, Europe is heavily industrialized, and it is revealing to note that the genesis of the EC—the formation of the European Coal and Steel Community (ECSC)—stemmed from an initiative directly related to industry.

The function of the EC is to provide "a framework which supports the actions of Member States, helps to balance out their specific strengths and weaknesses, and eliminates the risk of duplication of effort to the advantage of the whole Community and its regions." The Single European Act formalized the Community's mandate to promote research and technological development

(R&TD) directed toward improved industrial competitiveness and quality of life.[14]

The multi-annual framework programs for research and technological development are the principal instruments for promoting R&TD. They are agreed upon after exhaustive consultation and refinement, and are funded from private, national and Community resources. They are designed to harmonize with the Research and Technology Development (R&TD) activities of the Member States by concentrating on those activities in which European cooperation offers clear benefits.

The specific goal of progressing the training-research-demonstration-innovation cycle is dovetailed into a wider Community framework of industrial, health, environmental, cultural and communications policies.[15] In the 1990–94 program, the commission proposed a budget of 7,700 million ECU (the European Currency Unit—ECU—has specified rates of exchange against currencies within the EC; it roughly equates with the US dollar) to support research in three broad categories: enabling technologies, management of natural resources, and management of intellectual resources.[15]

How are the decisions on Community R&TD policy arrived at? Heretofore, the commission proposed and implemented, the European Parliament and the Economic and Social Committee delivered opinions, and the Council of Ministers from national governments decided. With the advent of the Single European Act, the Parliament exerts a more direct influence on council decisions which may now be taken by majority vote. Formal evaluation of policies and programs is carried out by the Committee for Scientific and Technical Research (CREST), a committee of government advisers on science and technology, and the Committee for Development of European Science and Technology (CODEST), a committee of independent scientists. Despite the size of the Community bureaucracy, these committees function well as evidenced by the fast response to US and Japanese initiatives in magnet technology; within twelve months, a European concerted action program was put into place.

More forward-looking and visionary deliberations are pursued under the FAST (Forecasting and Assessment in Science and Technology) program, designed to "analyze the role of scientific and technological change for the long-term economic and social development of European societies to identify, on that basis, European priorities." Academic, industrial and governmental research groups throughout Europe participate. The most recent report[16] stresses the primacy of human resources and the importance of transectoral considerations to sustained innovation in Europe.

The FAST program, however, is a commission initiative and, therefore, considered by some to be insufficiently divorced from commission influence. Part of the rationale behind the STOA (Science and Technology Options Assessment) initiative of the European Parliament was "to break out of the closed circuit of information recycling which had tended to become a habit in the Community framework," to improve Parliament's own decision-making in Sci-

ence and Technology Development (S&TD) matters, to enhance public awareness, and to facilitate an independent review of the framework as a whole, in
parallel or even in advance of commission initiatives.[8] The commission, with
the support of the European Parliament, recently proposed the formation of a
European Science Assembly of about two hundred scientists with representation
from the humanities to provide strategic advice. There is strong divergence of
opinion among Member States on the overall merits of this proposal.

As outlined in the Appendix, Europe has the benefit of advice from a number
of important sources. The Council of Europe, for example, has focused on the
social dimension of science and technology principally through a series of quinquennial parliamentary and scientific conferences[17] which again rely upon broad-
based, policy-oriented consultative networks. They offer a useful forum for the
distillation of views of other institutions concerned with the broader implications of S&TD, such as the OECD and the European Science Foundation (ESF).
Academia Europaea, formed in 1988, constitutes a growing and independent
body of academics concerned with such issues as education, the environment,
and ethics. These imputs add a necessary social dimension to EC perspectives
which tend to emphasize purely scientific judgments.

Clearly, not all advice and activity on S&TD at the European level is channeled through the EC framework. COST, established in 1969, represents a
committee of senior officials concerned with the coordination of national research in the nineteen participating countries. The EC Commission and the
Council Secretariat do, however, assume an important role within the COST
framework in promoting transnational cooperation in S&TD.

A comparable industrial initiative, EUREKA, was launched in 1985 by a
Conference of Ministers of the seventeen founding countries (now nineteen),
along with members of the European Commission (at about the same time as
the Strategic Defense Initiative (SDI) in the United States) to stimulate cross-
border cooperation in order to heighten Europe's productivity and competitiveness in the world market.[18] It adopts a "bottoms-up" approach, whereby participants exercise full responsibility for defining and implementing their cooperative S&TD projects within the EUREKA framework.

NATIONAL PERSPECTIVES

Member States of the Community are effectively governed by two legal systems—National and Community Law—that are becoming more and more inter-
twined. "The Community constitutes a new legal order of international law for
the benefit of which the States have limited their sovereign rights, albeit within
limited fields, and the subject of which comprises not only the Member States,
but also their nationals."[19] This loss of sovereignty has, on occasion, been
interpreted within Europe as an interference with national sovereignty, and is
often the source of discord, particularly in the formulation of new policy by

the commission. A current topic of intense debate centers on the Social Charter which defines the rights of the citizen in anticipation of a borderless Europe.

That the traditional social dimension of the industrial process (working hours, minimum wage, general terms of employment, and so on) differs greatly from one EC state to another makes the adoption of a common charter difficult and, for some nations, exceedingly unpalatable. Nor can governments act oblivious of Community law in regard to wholly domestic matters relating to science and technology concerning, for example, waste disposal, the environment, and various ethical issues. Advice to governments must, therefore, be framed in accord with the special circumstances of each nation, but always in harmony with community law.

At the national level, mechanisms are required, first, to achieve effective coordination with the complex Community bureaucracy to ensure full participation and integration into the R&TD programs in Europe, and, second, to provide the necessary advice to government on national initiatives. In Ireland, these functions are carried out by EOLAS, a newly constituted agency with statutory powers to administer research budgets and to advise governments on science and technology matters.

In the past, S&TD have not been afforded adequate priority in government planning: Coordination between government departments concerned with science policy has been less than satisfactory and support for R&TD inadequate. In 1985, for example, Ireland's expenditure in this area was about 20% of that of Denmark, making it the third lowest in the Community. This is untenable (even in the absence of military R&D expenditure, which accounts for a major portion of spending in other countries), and is at odds with Ireland's strategy of encouraging growth in the high-technology industry. To counter these deficiencies, a Minister of State for Science and Technology has been appointed to coordinate the management of S&TD, to raise the overall level and quality of S&TD, and to increase industrial innovation. Special funding has been allocated to selected research areas of strategic importance in line with coherent long-term planning.

Within Europe, Ireland is singularly endowed with a high proportion of young people within its population. This reserve of human talent, properly educated, is central to any future policy for the development and effective use of science and technology. Indeed, the most recent and independent OECD report on Ireland's future argued for a doubling of investment in brain power as part of a deliberate and sustained reorientation of resources toward education and R&TD.[20]

EDUCATIONAL APPROACHES

Paradoxically, the past decade has also witnessed a sustained erosion of state support for third-level education, albeit as part of an effort to correct the nation's tenuous economic position. While these measures are underpinning a remarkable economic renaissance, they have, nonetheless, impeded the universities in their ability to fulfill their obligations in providing education and research to the demanding levels that are currently required. On a more positive note, the decreasing level of state funding has encouraged the universities to pursue new and innovative means to obtain alternative funding, largely from contract research. This has been accompanied by a growing appreciation in Irish universities of the value of intellectual property.

Consider the example of Trinity College, Dublin (TCD), a university founded five years before Francis Bacon penned the aforementioned statement. Contract research earnings have grown at a rate of about 20% per annum in real terms since 1981 to a current annual income of US$8.4 million, reflecting participation in some six hundred research contracts, mainly in the fields of computer science, strategic materials, and biotechnology. A sophisticated infrastructure has evolved to accommodate the strengthening interface between the university and the outside world. Of particular note is the joint venture with Hitachi of Japan to develop high-level languages for the next generation of computers.

The university's structured approach to research has revealed clear pathways for the progression of suitable basic research ideas into the marketplace, which is in keeping with the overall national strategy of job creation. Some of the basic research carried out at the university leads naturally to applied research with clear commercial potential and, as such, has the hallmarks of sponsored applied research. It can be developed either in conjunction with an appropriate industrial end-user or by the researcher in question choosing to progress the discovery along the innovation cycle,[21] under the aegis of a campus company which, if successful, will, in time, migrate off-campus into the industrial world.

The creation of science parks through a partnership of regional authorities and financial and academic institutions is an important driving force for directing the industrial structure of a region toward new knowledge-based industries.[11] The Technopoles in France, representing clusters of research institutes and related commercial enterprises, fulfill a comparable role. From the university's point of view, they are the logical next step for the campus company and facilitate those companies involved in industrial innovation which require close ties with the university. They also allow the full commercialization of research off-campus in a way that might not be possible within the confines of the academic institution itself, for it is essential that such developments do not distort the central pursuit of teaching and research in an atmosphere of intellectual curiosity; *commercial goals must not become the university's* raison d'etre.

These developments can only take place with a government imprimatur and, therefore, any advice to government should be appropriately informed and supportive. It is especially important for a small country like Ireland to maximize the benefits to society from its considerable public investment in education.

NATIONAL PROBLEMS/NATIONAL SOLUTIONS

It is clear that, despite Ireland's membership in the European Community, there are still many cases where national solutions are required for national problems. How will this situation evolve with the approach of 1992? The question is best addressed in the context of a recent report on the effects of EC membership on the Irish economy and the likely effects of the completion of the internal market by 1992.[22] It recognizes that Ireland's future lies in full economic integration, but Ireland must adopt a more explicit, coherent, and fully articulated European policy or strategy. There are fears, for example, that the benefits of an integrated market may be distributed unevenly with maximum advantage accruing to those regions where large-scale industry and high innovation are already strongest. In short, full economic integration may well reinforce current advantages and disadvantages. The report also concluded that "a crucial requirement for success in the internal market is maintenance of a domestic economic environment conducive to growth and competitive enterprise."

Many problems have yet to be addressed, in particular, the proposed harmonization of tax rates. Unless the comparatively high income tax rates in Ireland are reduced through substitution of broader-based taxes or otherwise, the incentive for the young, mobile, well-educated worker to remain in Ireland in a Europe without frontiers is reduced.[23] More important, however, is the continued creation of a climate for enterprise, self-reliance, and sustained confidence in Ireland's social and economic future, a process that will be accelerated by additional capital investment of approximately US$4.2 billion from the EC in anticipation of a unified market in 1992.

To conclude, it is doubtful if there will be a single market for every product and service by 1992 and, indeed, there is a body of opinion that suggests that full economic and monetary union will not be achieved during this century. Be that as it may, Europe is in a state of transition undoubtedly toward a position of greater strength on the world's economic stage as 1992 approaches. Science and technology are at the center of these developments, and the extent to which they can be used to enhance the prosperity of Europe and the world at large will depend greatly on the attention given to the deleterious side effects of their implementation and on efforts to redress the current imbalance between the developed and the developing nations. The example of Japan in devising and managing industrial development policies which rest on technological skills suggests that the organization of *science advice* for European government will be fundamental to achieving the goals of the unified Community.

APPENDIX

The European Community (EC)

The EC has evolved from a number of initiatives, beginning with the Treaty of Paris (1952), which formalized the Schumann plan to achieve integration of (at least, part of) the coal and steel industries of Western Europe through the creation of the European Coal and Steel Community (ECSC). Six nations were involved: Belgium, France, the Federal Republic of Germany, Italy, Luxembourg, and The Netherlands. In 1957, the Treaties of Rome effected the establishment of the European Economic Community (EEC) to achieve economic integration, and the European Atomic Energy Community (EURATOM) to foster cooperation in the development and peaceful use of atomic energy.

The original six nations were joined by Denmark, Ireland and the United Kingdom in 1973, by Greece in 1981, and by Spain and Portugal in 1986. The Single European Act (1987) conferred formal legal status on European political cooperation, and clearly anticipated the Community's objectives of achieving a Europe without frontiers. The target date for this is 1992. Special emphasis is accorded to social/regional policy, the environment, scientific research, monetary affairs, and foreign policy. In short, it has set a goal for greater economic, social and political cohesion. This rather simplified synopsis belies a complex institutional system. Fundamentally, the EC represents "twelve independent member countries which retain most of their independence, but which, on certain matters, have yielded up their independence or sovereignty to the Community so that decisions on these matters can be taken jointly."[24]

Responsibility for Community action is principally vested in four institutions, as follows:

- The council,
- The commission,
- The European Parliament,
- The Court of Justice,

with input and advice from a number of other important sources which include the following:

- The European Council, comprising Heads of State, their foreign ministers, the President, and one vice president of the commission;
- The Permanent Representative Committee comprising ambassadors to the EC;
- The 189-member Economic and Social Committee;
- The ECSC Consultative Committee;
- The Court of Auditors, which fulfills the formal auditing function for the Community;
- A range of other committees, including the Committee for Scientific and Technical Research (CREST), which advises both the commission and the Council of Ministers; the Committee for the European Development of Science and Technology (CODEST); and the Industrial Research and Development Advisory Committee (IRDAC);

The Council is composed of twelve ministers representing the Member States.

There are representatives of the commission in attendance, often in the roles of mediators. Laws are made by the council after consultation with the Economic and Social Committee and the European Parliament. Many major decisions of the council can now be taken by majority vote without the risk of veto (the Luxembourg Compromise) by any one nation following enactment of the Single European Act. The presidency of the council rotates systematically between Member States, large and small alike.

The Commission is effectively the executive arm of the EC. The seventeen commissioners act independently of government and the council in initiating and implementing Community policy, often in the form of common policies (in agriculture, fisheries, regional development, monetary matters, the environment, and consumer protection). The commission derives its political authority from the fact that it is answerable to Parliament alone. It administers four major funds: the Social Fund (3,100 in MECU in 1987), the European Agricultural Guidance and Guarantee Fund (24,000 MECU), the European Regional Development Fund (3,300 MECU), and the European Development Fund, which is the principal instrument in the Community's development aid effort. The latter was sent at 8,500 MECU for the period 1985–1990. The commission also administers aid to developing countries not covered by the Lomé convention.

The European Parliament is a 518-member body of directly elected members (MEPs), covering the full spectrum of political ideology. It is a fully integrated Community institution which guarantees the commission's independence, but it is also its watchdog with powers of censure. The Single European Act conferred the *power of assent* on Parliament, permitting the exercise of direct influence on council decisions, even though the final say still rests with the council. It has the final say on all ''noncompulsory'' expenditures (27.5% of the total budget in 1988), and can reject the budget as a whole, as it did in 1979.

The Court of Justice ensures the fair and uniform interpretation and implementation of Community law. It represents an autonomous legal system, independent of the legal systems of Member States. The court is served by thirteen judges appointed for six-year terms and assisted by six advocates general.

The Council of Europe

The Council of Europe is an assembly of nationally elected parliamentarians, representing almost four hundred people from twenty-one countries in Western Europe "committed to democratic systems of government, in accordance with the rule of law, and in furtherance of human rights, individual freedoms, and personal dignity."[25] It comprises a Committee of Ministers, a Parliamentary Assembly, and a Court and Commission of Human Rights. The contribution to the science and technology debate is channeled principally through the series of six (to date) quinquennial Parliamentary and Scientific Conferences.[17]

The European Science Foundation (ESF)

Founded in 1974, the ESF is an international nongovernmental organization based in Strasbourg. Its forty-nine members are the academics and research council members drawn from nineteen countries. Its primary mission is to identify and to stimulate international competition through collaborative programs both in *and between* the humanities, social sciences, biomedical sciences, and natural sciences. The operating budget is drawn from the member organizations. Scientific networks and the use of workshops are integral features of the foundation's approach to such diverse projects as brain and behavioral research, forest ecosystems, transport, problems of migration, and beliefs in government.

The Organization for Economic Cooperation and Development (OECD)

The OECD, according to the Convention signed in Paris in December 1960, was charged with promoting policies designed to achieve proper economic growth of both member and nonmember countries and to contribute to the expansion of world trade "on a multilateral, nondiscriminatory basis in accordance with international obligations."[11] The twenty original members were later joined by four other countries with, in addition, the partial involvement of Yugoslavia. Member countries are distributed worldwide.

Other Agencies

Other agencies contributing to the science and technology development debate include:

- the European Space Agency (ESA);
- the European Centre for Nuclear Research (CERN);
- the United Nations Organization (UN);
- the United Nations Educational, Scientific and Cultural Organization (UNESCO);
- the United Nations Environment Program (UNEP);
- the International Atomic Energy Agency (IAEA);
- the International Energy Agency (IEA);
- the European Nuclear Energy Agency (ENEA);
- the World Health Organization (WHO);
- the Food and Agriculture Organization (FAO);
- the International Federation of Institutes for Advanced Study (IFIAS); and
- the International Council of Scientific Unions (ICSU).

NOTES

1. Francis Bacon, "Meditations Sacrae: De Heresibus" (1597).
2. V. J. McBrierty, ed., *Europe-Japan: Futures in Science, Technology and Democracy* (London: Butterworth's, 1986).
3. H. Cleveland, "The Twilight of Hierarchy: Speculations on the Global Information Society," *International Journal of Technology Management* 2 (1987), pp. 45–66.
4. W. T. Golden, ed., *Science and Technology Advice to the President, Congress and Judiciary* (New York: Pergamon, 1988).
5. K. Pinkau in McBrierty (1986), p. 94.
6. I. Hirvela in McBrierty (1986), p. 142.
7. W. O. Baker in Golden (1988), p. 16.
8. V. J. McBrierty, "Technology Assessment for Governments at the National and European Level," *Futures,* February 1988, pp. 3–18, and references therein.
9. H. Brooks and C. L. Cooper, eds., *Science for Public Policy* (New York: Pergamon, 1988).
10. H. Bondi in McBrierty (1986), p. 112.
11. *Science and Technology Policy Outlook 1988* (Paris: OECD, 1988).
12. U. Colombo in McBrierty (1986), p. 24.
13. Statistics quoted in *About Europe,* cat. no. CC-47-86-874-EN-C (L-2985 Luxembourg: European Community, 1987).
14. *Vade-mecum of Community Research Promotion,* cat. no. CB-PP-88-011-EN-C (L-2985 Luxembourg: European Community, 1987).
15. *Research and Technological Development Policy,* cat. no. CB-PP-88-011-EN-C (L-2985 Luxembourg: European Community, 1988).
16. "Science, Technology and Society: European Priorities," results and recommendations from the FAST II Program (Brussels: 1979).
17. These conferences were held in London, 1961; Vienna, 1965; Lausanne, 1972; Florence, 1975; Helsinki, 1981; and Tokyo, 1985.
18. *EUREKA: Together for the Future,* published by the Central Secretariat, 19H avenue des Arts, Bte 3, Brussels, Belgium.
19. *The European Community's Legal System,* cat. no. CB-NC-84-005-EN-C (L-2985 Luxembourg: European Community, 1984).
20. *Innovation Policy in Ireland* (Paris: OECD, 1987).
21. V. J. McBrierty, ed., *Strategy for Innovation: The Role of the Third Level Institutions,* The Confederation of Irish Industry Business Series no. 8, March 1981.
22. "Ireland in the European Community: Performance, Prospects and Strategy 1989," report of the National Economic Social Council of Ireland, September 1989.
23. *OECD Economic Surveys 1988–9—Ireland* (Paris: OECD, 1989).
24. E. Noel, *Working Together: The Institutions of the European Community,* cat. no. CB-52-88-897-EN-C (L-2985 Luxembourg: European Community).
25. K. Ahrens in McBrierty (1986), p. 3.

The Advisory Situation in Israel

Ephraim Katchsalski-Katzir and Eliezer Tal

THE STATE OF ISRAEL *(Medinat Yisra'el) was established in 1948, operating under a multiparty parliamentary system. Its land area is 8,291 square miles, and its 1989 estimated population was 4,473,000. The official languages of the country are Hebrew and Arabic, but English is widely taught and spoken.*

A discussion of science and technology advice to government must clearly go beyond questions of organization and administration. At a more fundamental level, it involves an analysis of the interface between two systems: the political and the scientific. The first strives for power and authority in order to accomplish things for the good of the people and the country. The second is motivated by the disinterested pursuit of knowledge, both for its own sake and for its technological applications. There are, however, some fundamental and occasionally irreconcilable differences between the two. Israel serves as an interesting case study of the interplay between science and politics in a small democratic state that is poor in natural resources, but rich in the caliber of its manpower.

POLITICAL STRUCTURE

Israel has adopted the basic principles of modern democracy with a clear division of powers among its legislative, executive and judicial branches. The single-chamber parliamentary legislature, the Knesset, consists of 120 members elected according to proportional representation for four-year terms. The official head of state is the President, who is elected by the Knesset for a period

Ephraim Katchsalski-Katzir served as the fourth President of the State of Israel (1973–1978) and has assisted Israeli governments in research and development policy decisions. He participated in establishing the Hemed and Raphael R&D units in the Defense Ministry and was Chief Scientist in that ministry from 1966 to 1968. Dr. Katzir took part in the founding of the Weizmann Institute for Science where he was biophysics department head from 1951 to 1973. He has been guest professor at Harvard University, The Rockefeller University and others, and is a member of the Israeli Academy of Sciences and Humanities and a foreign member of the National Academy of Sciences, US; The Royal Society of London; the Academie de Sciences, France; and the Leopoldina Academy of Sciences, Halle, Germany.

Eliezer Tal was Director General of the National Council for Research and Development, Israel, for thirteen years, and also served as Chairman of the Chief Scientists Committee. Dr. Tal spent three years as Science and Technology Adviser for the Inter-American Development Bank, Washington, DC, and has published papers on science and technology policy in Israel and in Latin American countries and a book (1964) on Naval Operations in the Israel War of Independence.

of five years and may be reelected for an additional term. The office of the President is nonpolitical and carries only limited executive powers. Executive power is vested primarily in the Cabinet, which is also the main policy-determining body. Major decisions of the Cabinet have to be approved by the Knesset, and the government is called upon to resign should it lose the confidence of the Knesset.

Much Cabinet business is done by either permanent or *ad hoc* committees composed mainly of the ministers directly concerned. A Ministerial Committee for Science and Technology, intended to promote and coordinate scientific and technological activities in the different ministries, was first established in 1965, and has been active off and on since then. Because no single political party has ever managed to achieve an overall majority in a general election, all governments—and hence all Cabinets—since the establishment of the state have been comprised of coalitions of a variety of political parties. Thus, while the individual Cabinet minister enjoys considerable authority in his own department, the politically heterogenenous structure of the government makes cooperation and coordination among ministries extremely difficult. Science and technology have often fallen victim to this cumbersome framework which involves a plethora of divergent interests.

Every bill placed before the Knesset must pass through one of the ten Knesset committees, which together cover all spheres of legislative activity. Unfortunately, despite sporadic attempts over the years to remedy this situation, none of these committees has formally been given the responsibility for science and technology. Given the lack of interest that has been shown by the Knesset, science and technology advice in matters of national importance, rather than being directed at the Knesset, has been directed at the Cabinet.

PATTERNS OF RESEARCH AND DEVELOPMENT IN ISRAEL

Israel's expenditure on research and development has shown a steady increase over the years. In 1983, it was approximately $700 million or about 3% of the Gross National Product. This proportion has remained essentially the same since then. An estimated total of 16,000 scientists and engineers (or about 69 per 10,000 persons in the labor force) is currently engaged in various research and development (R&D) activities. Thus, although in absolute terms the numbers are small, in relative terms, the Israel R&D effort equals that of the United States and exceeds that of most other technologically advanced countries.

The strong emphasis on scientific and technological research is not surprising, given the Jewish people's traditional respect for learning. Added to that is the vital need of the State of Israel to ensure its physical security, develop a viable economy, improve the quality of life, and generally hold its own in a world of increasingly sophisticated technology. These were the forces shaping the rapid growth of R&D in the universities, in government-sponsored laboratories, and in industry.

It seems worthwhile to point out some of the significant ways in which the R&D patterns emerging in Israel differ from those found in most other industrialized countries. First, dependence on government funding for research is high—64% as compared with around 50% elsewhere. Second, the contribution of Israeli industry to the national R&D expenditure is only 22%, which is about one-third to one-half that in other industrialized countries.

Industry also employs only a small proportion—about 26%—of Israel's R&D manpower, as compared with 41% in France, 62% in the Federal Republic of Germany and in Japan, and 72% in the United States.

Third, the university sector in Israel accounts for a relatively high proportion of the total national R&D effort with expenditures amounting to 30% of the total, as compared with 15% in the Federal Republic of Germany and 12% in the United States. The relative strength of the university sector probably accounts for the high volume of papers published by Israeli scientists and engineers in international journals. These and other departures from the R&D patterns prevailing in other industrialized countries have had a strong bearing on the framework that has emerged in Israel for science and technology advice to the government.

HISTORICAL OVERVIEW OF THE ADVICE SYSTEM

When the State of Israel was established in 1948, the country already possessed a modest infrastructure of diverse science and technology institutions, manned by scientists and engineers engaged in research, teaching and professional services in a variety of fields. From this nucleus, it was possible to create, in 1949, the Scientific Council of Israel as a first step toward the development and expansion of the country's scientific and technological capabilities.

Although the Scientific Council was intended as a central advisory body for the elaboration of a national policy on science and technology, practical necessities steered its attention mainly toward the setting up of new research institutes in such vital areas of activity as applied physics, fiber research, geological surveying, and arid zone research. At the same time, the government Ministries of Agriculture, Development and Defense involved themselves, to varying extents, in research and development within their own specific purviews.

The first decade of statehood can thus be described as a period of largely spontaneous and uncontrolled growth, characterized on the one hand by initiative on the parts of bodies within and outside the government ministries, and on the other hand by the absence of overall planning and coordination. Many of the institutions established during that time now constitute the foundations of basic and applied research in Israel.

Public criticism came to be voiced regarding the lack of a national policy on science and technology, its haphazard development, and the emphasis on the basic sciences to the neglect of applied research. A formal reassessment of the situation in 1959 led to the replacement of the Scientific Council by the National Council for Research and Development (NCRD), which was charged with two distinct tasks: to develop a national science and technology policy while coordinating all R&D activities under a government agency, and to administer such government institutes as the National Physical Laboratory and the Negev Institute for Arid Zone Research.

Within a few years, however, the feeling among the scientific community was that, although the establishment of the NCRD was a step in the right direction, it did not go far enough. The dual responsibility proved far too onerous for the NCRD, especially as the problems connected with the day-to-day management of the institutes kept it from its main task of developing a national science and technology policy. Moreover, the interest of the NCRD in securing a realistic budget for the institutes weakened its position as an impartial adviser to the government.

Like its predecessor, the Scientific Council, the NCRD was granted only very limited executive powers. Its effectiveness was thus almost wholly dependent on its powers of persuasion, which proved inadequate to bring about the implementation of a comprehensive national policy. In practice, very little was achieved in regard to defining national priorities, securing budgets for R&D activities in the various government ministries, coordinating research programs, or developing applied research.

It was, therefore, obvious that more radical changes—in policy as well as in organization—were essential to enable Israel to cope with the new military, economic and social challenges that lay ahead. Accordingly, in 1968, the Prime Minister appointed a committee, under the chairmanship of Ephraim Katchsalski-Katzir, to determine the future direction of science and technology and to advise the government on how best to pursue programs of research and development.

The committee's report revolutionized the government's attitude toward science and technology, and laid the foundations for its systematic organization. Taking into account the wide powers enjoyed by Cabinet ministers in their own departments, the committee proposed that each ministry be made responsible for R&D policy and practice within its own sphere of activity. At the same time, the committee placed responsibility for the design, coordination and implementation of national science and technology policy on the government as a whole.

A THREE-LEVEL R&D STRUCTURE

As a result of the Katchsalski-Katzir Report of 1968, the government set up a three-level structure to handle R&D in the following manner:

- At the level of R&D performance, all government research institutes were regrouped into specialized research organizations, such as the Agricultural Research Organization, the Industrial Research Organization, and the Earth Sciences Research Organization, and each was affiliated with the appropriate government ministry.

- At the ministerial level, a chief scientist was appointed in each of the ministries interested in R&D (Health, Transportation, Defense, Education, Commerce and Industry, and Agriculture) with the object of formulating and implementing R&D projects of major national importance. The chief scientist functions as the principal science adviser to the minister and is expected to promote applied research in government institutions, in institutions of higher learning, and in industry.
- At the national level, planning and coordination of national science and technology policy is handled by two bodies: the Ministerial Committee for Science and Technology and the NCRD. The former was intended to be the government's decision-making instrument on matters related to science and technology. The NCRD, in its revamped form, was no longer directly in charge of the setting up or running of R&D institutes; its functions were as follows:

To propose a comprehensive national government policy for scientific research and technological development; to advise the government on scientific and technological matters of national importance; to encourage R&D in subjects of national importance, even if they are not directly under the aegis of a specific government ministry; to advise the government on the detailed structure of ministerial budgets for R&D; to coordinate the R&D activities of different government ministries; to advise the government on the setting up or the closing down of government research institutes; to collaborate with the Foreign Ministry in promoting contacts with bodies engaged in R&D in other countries with a view to encouraging binational projects; to plan a nationwide information network on matters concerning science and technology; to counsel government ministers on the appointments of chief scientists in their ministries; and to advise the government on the recruitment, management and advancement of research personnel in the government research network.

The NCRD was also designated the professional secretariat of the Ministerial Committee for Science and Technology with the NCRD's director serving as secretary of the committee. Board members of the NCRD include university professors, members of the Israel Academy of Sciences, representatives of industry and agriculture, and the chief scientists.

THE ROLE OF THE ACADEMY OF SCIENCES AND HUMANITIES

To complete the picture, mention should be made of the role of the Israel Academy of Sciences and Humanities in the system of science and technology advice to the government. Established by an Act of the Knesset in 1961, the academy is an independent body whose members are drawn from among the country's leading scholars. One of its functions is to "advise the government on activities relating to research and scientific planning of national significance." Such advice may be either unsolicited or given in response to a specific request. To minimize overlap, an understanding was reached whereby the academy would concern itself with basic research and the NCRD with applied research and technology. In its early efforts to stimulate basic research, the academy adopted a policy of noninterference with regard to content and subject matter. More recently, however, the academy has undertaken to assist the scientific community in defining priorities for basic research and has published "Guidelines for a Master Plan for Basic Research."

In 1982, a Ministry of Science and Development was established. The NCRD was absorbed intact into the new ministry, and constitutes its principal department. On the initiative of the new minister, the Ministerial Committee for Science and Technology appointed an *ad hoc* committee to reassess the organization and management of government research in light of the changes over the fourteen years since the Katchsalski-Katzir Committee had presented its findings.

The recommendations of the *ad hoc* committee (1984) did not include changes in the system of advice to the government, which, therefore, remains to this day essentially as proposed by the Katchsalski-Katzir Report. The system is a pluralistic one, incorporating several channels of advice: the NCRD, the Israel Academy of Sciences and Humanities, and the chief scientists. The effective distillation of advice received from the various sources into a cohesive national policy is heavily dependent on the decision-making talents of the Ministerial Committee for Science and Technology. This committee, however, meets infrequently and does not function as effectively as had been desired.

STRENGTHS AND WEAKNESSES OF THE SCIENCE ADVICE SYSTEM

The scientific community of Israel is one that is well aware of its own potential and does not hesitate to offer advice on the steps it believes necessary to advance R&D and promote the utilization of the products of R&D for the benefit of the country. The activities of this community may be described as a "push" mechanism, which is particularly pronounced in contrast to the weak "pull" mechanism exerted by the Knesset and the government.

The setting up by the government of the three-level structure for handling R&D outlined above resulted in a considerable increase in the resources placed at the disposal of R&D. It thus led to an overall increase—from the time the state was established—in the proportion of national funds expended on science and technology—to the point where Israel today ranks as a country with one of the highest proportional expenditures on R&D in the world. Individual ministries, under the guidance of their chief scientists and motivated by their specific sectorial needs, have developed their own expertise in R&D management and policy. This approach has effectively shifted the dynamic center of scientific activity from basic to applied research.

In this connection, it is pertinent to note a report of the Israel Academy of Sciences and Humanities, published in 1986, showing that changes in the national distribution of research funds have resulted in a marked drop in government support for basic research. Predictably, this decline has led to a deterioration of the research infrastructure in Israel.

It should be pointed out that, on the whole, the handling of science and technology at the ministerial level has had positive results, particularly in bringing government-supported research more closely into line with ministerial goals. The success of this system can be attributed to two main factors: the adoption by the ministers of sectoral R&D policy as an integral part of their ministerial responsibility, and the effectiveness of the chief scientists—deriving from their high status, strong influence, and direct participation in the work of their respective ministries.

Nevertheless, there is still room for streamlining the professional operation of the chief scientists and their bureaus—for example, by the participation of selected scientists and engineers in advisory committees attached to the various ministries. These committees would assist each chief scientist to shape ministerial science policy by identifying problems and defining priorities within his sphere of sectoral responsibility.

In spite of the success of the chief scientists acting in their ministries, the Cabinet has failed to develop a comprehensive policy for science and technology, and has demonstrated its inability to act beyond the limited frameworks of individual ministries. The Cabinet has likewise failed to appreciate the essential interdependence that exists between basic and applied research, technological development, and higher education. These failures highlight a conceptual gap between the Cabinet and its science and technology advisers.

On the one hand, the Cabinet appears to be incapable of evaluating the significance of science and technology needs in a postindustrial society, and has, therefore, failed to come up with a workable master plan for national R&D. On the other hand, science advisers to the government may need to take hold of the dictum that counsel, even of the highest caliber, is hardly useful if it is consistently ignored. One possible solution might be to extend the function of science and technology advice to include active assistance in its implementation. The advisers (*i.e.,* the scientific community) would then participate directly in the decision-making process and play a role in priority definition, planning and control.

Among the problems of science policy that the Cabinet, as a whole, might well tackle are the following: the search for new sources of energy—solar, shale, wind, and local oil; water desalination; and waste disposal and decontamination. The government must decide which of the important new areas of research—superconductivity, space research, biotechnology—it most keenly wishes to pursue. It also needs to pay detailed attention to the following: the elaboration of rules and regulations necessary to facilitate the development of science-based industry and agriculture; the absorption of highly qualified professionals, including immigrants from the USSR; and the drafting of legislation that will protect the utilization of local, original discoveries, as well as encourage the acquisition of essential foreign technology.

AN UNINTERRUPTED DIALOGUE

The continued successful development of science and technology in Israel requires, as in many other countries, an uninterrupted dialogue among academia, industry and government. Israel is rapidly approaching a postindustrial era and, as industry is still not highly developed, the support of R&D by the government will continue to play a major role in determining the rate of Israel's socioeconomic development. A successful working relationship between the country's scientific leadership and its political decision-makers seems, therefore, to be of paramount importance. Unstinting efforts are needed to promote—among members of the Knesset, the government, the political parties, and other public organizations—an understanding of the important role of science and technology in determining the social and economic well-being of the country.

A long-term educational mission has to be undertaken—by the universities, the Association for the Advancement of Science, professional societies, and the Academy of Sciences and Humanities—to inform the public of the achievements and the potentials of modern science and technology. Such a mission, if unsuccessful, will spur the government to strengthen the existing means—such as the Ministerial Committee for Science and Technology—and to establish new ones to tackle the problems of scientific and technological policy with which it has to cope. Such a mission will also help to enhance awareness of the benefits to be derived from a fruitful dialogue among policy-makers, scientists, and engineers.

The Postwar Evolution of Science Policy in Italy

Umberto Colombo

THE ITALIAN REPUBLIC *(Repubblica Italiana) was designated as a unified state in 1861. Its status as a republic dates from 1946, and it operates under a parliamentary constitution, which was established in 1948. Its land area is 116,303 square miles, and its estimated population in 1989 was 57,552,000. The official language is Italian.*

Any attempt to analyze the institutional framework within which Italian scientific and technological research takes place must, first of all, explain the peculiar circumstances affecting all aspects of public life that have been derived from the perennial political instability in Italy. There have been forty-eight governments since the end of World War II with consequent discontinuity in the country's decision-making and strategic planning. It has to be said, however, that this instability is often more apparent than real. Italy is governed by coalitions, and the major partner in all postwar Cabinets has always been the Christian Democrat Party.

While administrations fall with great frequency, certain key figures remain in the government, and there is a recognized hierarchy of office which rotates both men and parties in ministerial positions according to the current make-up of the government coalition. In this, as in other areas, Italy can be compared (within OECD) only to Japan. Years of consensus politics have taken Italy from an essentially agricultural economy in southern Europe to its position today as one of the five leading Western industrial economies. This has taken place, however, with such rapidity that there has not been time for a real industrial culture to radicate in the country with the result that many people in Italy retain an almost miracle-like faith in science, coupled with a diffused feeling of diffidence toward technology.

Economic development was not without trauma. In the northern part of the country, technologically advanced industries compete on world markets. In the still backward south and the islands, an essentially rural economy struggles against age-old lacunae in infrastructure and outdated ideas.

Inevitably the situation regarding science policy reflects the contradictions of

Umberto Colombo is Chairman of ENEA, the Italian Commission for Nuclear and Alternative Energy Sources. After receiving his doctorate in physical chemistry, he made his career at Montedison, where he became Director General for Corporate Research and Strategic Planning before assuming his present position. An expert in science and technology policy, Dr. Colombo has been chairman of the relevant committees at OECD, the European Community, and the United Nations. He is a member of several Italian and foreign scientific academies.

Italy's postwar history. Advanced institutions vie for public funds with others that are far less prepared. The pattern of corporate investment in R&D is extremely patchy and even some large companies do not have separate R&D budgets to this day. Geographically, the majority of researchers and most of the funding are concentrated in the northern and central parts of the country. Despite certain exceptions, the south and the islands still show a lamentable incapacity to undertake really high-level research.

SCIENTIFIC EXCELLENCE

Italy has always produced examples of scientific excellence. Epoch-making discoveries abound from the time of the Renaissance onward. Figures of global standing in all disciplines, such as—to cite at random—Galileo, Volta, Torricelli, Galvani, Spallanzani, Marconi, Volterra and Levi-Civita, are to be found in every generation. This century has been marked by the Rome School of Physics in the nuclear field under the leadership of Fermi, Amaldi, and Segré.

But this teamwork is an exception, rather than the rule. In general, contributions have all too often been the outcome of individual brilliance, rather than of concerted team effort. Single figures, of whatever stature, cannot substitute for a solid basic research capability, and that has been lacking in Italy.

The Italian domestic market was delayed in opening up to foreign competition in comparison with other major industrial economies. This delay was also accompanied by a tradition of buying know-how—through licenses and patents—rather than of developing it "in-house." That, then, this know-how is improved or adapted to suit particular market conditions—in the process often generating considerable market advantage—does not alter the fact that scientific and technological dependence on foreign sources poses a strategic threat to the health of the Italian economy, besides distorting the career prospects of thousands of Italian scientists and engineers.

Standards inevitably suffer as the best brains tend to go where facilities, funding and centers of excellence are most plentiful. This is a problem shared by many European countries, but there are reasons to believe that the "brain-drain" in Italy is more serious than elsewhere and that the lack of prospects may act to dissuade even the best students from embarking on careers in science and technology.

Research still tends, by and large, to be an academic exercise, carried out in universities and specific institutions with insufficient contact with the real worlds of industry and the public services. In the United States, Japan and West Germany, the needs of the latter are at the forefront in the design of research plans and in allocating resources.

Nevertheless, the Italian picture is not entirely bleak. Valid examples of cooperation between industry and academia do exist. Joint work in the 1950s between the Milan Polytechnic and Montecatini created the groundwork for

Natta's discovery of polypropylene, using the Ziegler catalyst. The local universities in the Industrial Triangle formed by Milan, Genoa and Turin are increasingly being brought into more direct touch with the requirements—in terms of both research and skills—of the companies in that region. But much more must be achieved in this direction.

It was not until the 1960s, in fact, that the government recognized the need to pay official attention to scientific research. The experience of the United States and other major industrialized countries had already signalled to Italian policy-makers and industrialists the role that government could play in financing and coordinating R&D. Even before the appointment of a minister without portfolio to oversee research in 1962, the financing and reorganization of R&D had begun to reflect the wider goals of national economic policy.

By the end of the 1960s, pressure was mounting to give the minister wider responsibilities, more authority within the Cabinet, and greater access to funding in order, specifically, to increase the industrial relevance of research. Industry itself was taking the lead in putting forth proposals to modify the institutional framework along these lines.

Ministers appointed advisory groups of independent experts from academic life and from industry to assist in establishing a coherent approach to science policy. Each time a minister changed, however, the groups were dissolved and reformed, often with different memberships, with the result that advice lacked continuity and the same ground was covered again and again.

CREATING STABLE LINKS

Despite this lack of efficiency, some moves were made. A series of laws was passed in the early 1970s with the intention of creating stable links between the bodies governing research activities in Italy and the various mechanisms for economic planning. The approach was either across the board or specifically directed at just one sector of research. The problem was that, paradoxically, while R&D was brought to some extent into the planning mechanism—in a country where the real capacity for planning is weak—planning was not brought into R&D and thus the legislation failed to have any decisive impact.

The acceleration in the pace of technological innovation—science-based and often indistinguishable from the science itself—and the emergence of the global economy during the late 1970s and 1980s further highlighted the inadequacies. Italy's R&D problems and an increasingly critical situation in all branches of education made it essential to make a radical attempt to redraw the institutional patterns in both fields.

There has never been a real ministry for scientific research. The minister's staff was often chosen from industry, the universities, and the research institutes—that is, from the very places where funding, coordination and regulation are required, and his available logistical support was poor. Data was fragmented and outdated; interdisciplinary rivalries were intense. The more active ministers tended to see this post as merely a stepping stone to more powerful positions, and there was no continuity of direction. Despite all the fine words and good intentions, all in all, the results were modest. Research policy remained in the hands of the various bodies which traditionally had carried it out, above all in the hands of the National Research Council (CNR).

The structure that CNR had assumed after World War II was not conducive to effective strategic thinking about research. Dominated by university academics, jealously safeguarding the sectional interests of their disciplines and specific fields of study, CNR was unable to surmount factionalism and achieve a global view of Italy's research requirements, despite higher funding and an expansion of its responsibilities to embrace the humanities as part of the council's reform of 1963.

The greater number of apparently autonomous research laboratories and other units depending solely on CNR did not mean that the bias in favor of the universities was reduced, as their directors were almost always chosen from the universities themselves. In spite of increased spending on research, one negative effect of this expansion of research capability was higher dispersion and ensuing lack of coordination.

A similar effect resulted from the reform of the university structure, which was undertaken in 1965, which reinforced the corporativist tendencies already present and increased the compartmentalization of research to the detriment of an interdisciplinary approach.

This lack of strategic vision has long been recognized. In the debate sparked by the publication, in 1967, of Servan-Schreiber's *Le Défi Americain* on the technological gap opening up between the United States and Europe (seen as a brake on Europe's prospects for autonomous growth), the Italian response was a package of government measures in 1968 setting up a fund to finance applied research. Management of this fund (initially of 100 billion lire—a sizeable sum for the country's slim research budget) was entrusted to IMI (the Instituto Mobilare Italiano), which already enjoyed a fine reputation in investment banking. The fund was designed to provide incentives for applied research, above all in industry, and includes specific assistance for innovation, diversification, the upgrading of services, improvement in international competitiveness, the expansion of small firms, and also the development of southern Italy and the islands.

Via subsidies and soft loans, financing was made available to specific high-risk projects in key applied research areas. The fund gave IMI the potential to assume minority stakes in specifically set up research and development companies in partnership with industry. Several of these ventures have produced remarkable results, such as Tecnomare, a company operating in marine technologies; others have been less successful: the cases of Tecnotessile and Tecnocasa in the textile and housing sectors, respectively.

WANING SUCCESS

There is no doubt that, in the 1960s, European success in science and technology seemed to be on the wane. The need for a strong link between science and technology policy on the one hand and economic growth on the other was underscored in the series of reports from OECD covering most of its member states. The report on Italy, produced in 1969, was especially critical, pointing out the total lack of coordination in research activities. Severe structural problems still existed in Italy's scientific base, and there was inadequate feedback to the socioeconomic needs of the country. Such criticism appeared at the same time as violent student unrest (in Italy, a phenomenon of 1969–70), reflecting dissatisfaction with the state of education and a widespread loss of confidence in the impact of science on society.

There was some response to increasing calls for better use of Italy's excellence in science and technology. In 1970, the Interministerial Committee for Economic Planning (CIPE) established a series of priority areas, such as health, transport, housing and town planning, the environment, and automation, in which it called upon CNR to undertake targeted research. The instrument to achieve this was defined in 1973 as specific projects, termed Finalized Projects (Progretti Finallizzati) with *ad hoc* financing approved by CIPE.

In 1975, the first eighteen projects were launched in a variety of fields, including energy, the environment, oceanography, biomedical sciences, geodynamics, air traffic control, and agricultural mechanization. As can be seen, the initial intentions had grown to embrace far more sectors than the first key priorities.

Furthermore, the financing was given to all institutions engaged in research in specified fields in an attempt to integrate research programs and generate synergies. The pattern resembled, in some respects, the "actions concertées" of the Délégation Générale à la Recherche Scientifique et Technique in France and the programs of the Deutsche Forschungsgemeinschaft in West Germany, yet the solution was, in large part, novel and it bore fruit. Much of the financing went into the hands of companies which were already active in the areas concerned with almost no international cooperation at either the corporate or the university level but, despite this, there was some expansion of Italy's research capability. Even so, Italian R&D spending still only accounted for about 5% of the Gross National Product (GNP) even as late as 1975, and the significance for industry remained at an unacceptably low level.

THE NUCLEAR POWER PROGRAM

The difficulties encountered in aligning research capabilities and industrial needs had long been widely recognized. When the time came to establish a nuclear power program in Italy, the decision was made to create, in 1960, a National

Commission for Nuclear Energy (CNEN), separate from the CNR and entrusted not only with nuclear research and applications, but also specifically with stimulating the emergence of a techno-industrial structure with the ability to design, build and manage nuclear power plants.

Despite good intentions, the combination of political and financial interests did not allow the Italian nuclear program to get off the ground, and CNEN's efforts remained largely unproductive.

The lack of strategy continued to affect the energy field throughout the 1970s and much of the 1980s. Awareness that a more farsighted policy was required led, in 1982, to the reconstitution of CNEN into the National Commission for Nuclear and Alternative Energy Sources (ENEA). The objective was to overcome dependence on foreign oil by the adoption of a new energy strategy with greater attention being paid to nuclear and renewable sources, energy conservation, and the protection of the environment.

These goals led ENEA to work more and more closely with industry on targeted interdisciplinary projects in which ENEA's contribution is, first of all, its scientific resources and, secondly, financing. The diffusion of innovation initially developed in the energy field has gradually broadened into a general technological upgrading of industry. Side by side with initiatives in high-tech sectors, wide-ranging activities have been started, aimed at the rejuvenation of mature industrial sectors in close collaboration with the small- and medium-sized firms which predominate in such areas of the economy. Through the introduction of advanced technologies into the existing industrial fabric, the scope is to revamp these mature sectors and so restore their international competitiveness. Great interest has been shown internationally in this aspect of ENEA's work, which has achieved some significant successes.

Despite the absence of any precise framework from a coordinated science policy, there are some indications that increasing use is, at last, being made of Italy's research capabilities to further the economic development of the country. The chief merit of this has to be ascribed to the flexibility, the resilience, and the willingness to innovate that has been shown by Italian industry when faced with the restructuring imposed by the recession of the late 1970s and early 1980s. A sound background of research is now recognized as an important factor in international competition, and one that will become ever more important as the 1992 deadline for the creation of a single European market approaches.

The new role of research has also called forth a political response. In 1980, a further reform of the university structure created a higher university degree, the research doctorate. Meanwhile, a national archive of all research which receives public funding was created. The reforms also laid down the rule that 40% of university funding must be set aside for research work and, by this, ended a situation in which financial resources for academic research came only from CNR.

This was followed, two years later, by another law which was designed to foster industrial innovation. This established the first direct contracts given by the government to finance private research, new programs to stimulate technology transfer to small- and medium-sized firms, and research grants to small firms, particularly in the south, to help meet the costs of R&D commissioned from outside sources. The same act refinanced the IMI Fund for applied research, and set up a new fund for technological innovation covering downstream phases up to final commercialization of new products and processes. During the same period, special legislation, since amended, was passed concerning the promotion of the industrialization of southern Italy and the islands. This included provisions for the creation of research infrastructure with the use of public subsidies and facilitations.

INTERNATIONAL RECOGNITION

The time was ripe for an increased public commitment to science policy. Italian science received international recognition with the Nobel Prizes awarded to Carlo Rubbia in physics and Rita Levi-Montalcini in medicine. Partly as a result of these successes, the attention paid by the mass media to scientific research dramatically increased during the course of the 1980s. Renewed popular interest was coupled with growing diffidence, stimulated above all by environmental, health and safety issues, toward certain key technology areas which hitherto had dominated public and private sector R&D investment in Italy, in particular in nuclear power and chemicals.

The first socialist-led coalition government, in 1984, recognized the strength of this feeling and attempted to bring science and technology policy into the mainstream of political decision-making, somewhat along the lines of that which had been done in neighboring France. The Prime Minister then set up an advisory panel of independent experts to report back directly to his office with an assessment of the state and the future potential of Italy's technoscientific structure, together with an analysis of policies followed in the past, both in the public and the private sectors, and suggestions and proposals regarding the reinforcement of measures to encourage innovation.

The panel reported in early 1986, putting forward three key recommendations: an increase in Italy's research capability both qualitatively and quantitatively; a parallel increase in research spending over five years to reach 3% of the Gross Domestic Product (GDP), concentrating funding on a few selected advanced sectors of industrial interest and on key existing areas of excellence; and the creation of incentives aimed at increasing the commitment to R&D in the private sector via financial contributions and tax facilitations.

The necessary condition for attaining these goals was identified as the creation of an effective governing system for Italian research, linking efforts with results. This would involve improving the universities and their research skills, strengthening the research agencies—particularly CNR and ENEA, and expanding international collaboration in the research field—above all, inside the framework of the European community.

In addition, the advisory panel called for increased prestige and influence to be invested in the Ministry for Scientific Research. This was pursued in the subsequent Law 168 of May 1989, which gave the ministry full status and expanded its responsibilities to include the universities, in this way providing the new Minister for Scientific Research and the universities with an autonomous budget and administrative structure.

Other significant changes also took place at this time. Presentation of the annual report on the state of research in Italy passed from the Chairman of CNR to the Minister for Scientific Research. Coordination between the various public sector research agencies was improved, and a discussion of the reform of CNR was started. In this framework of possible reforms, the creation of a specific agency for innovation and technology transfer is being considered. In 1988, the Italian Space Agency (ASI) was established to take over the responsibility for the whole of Italy's space effort from CNR, including links with the European Space Agency.

INTERNATIONAL INVOLVEMENT

One ever more important aspect of Italian research is the increasing involvement in international projects, particularly those within the European framework. Italy is an active participant in EUREKA, the advanced technology program launched by President Mitterand of France in 1985, which includes participation from the twelve European Community member states, plus Austria, Finland, Norway, Sweden, Switzerland, and Turkey, and in a series of European Community programs, such as ESPRIT, BRITE and RACE, programs in the fields of biotechnology and the stimulation of basic scientific research. Other joint international efforts include the European nuclear fusion program and a strong Italian presence in CERN for research into high energy physics.

Italy has thus set itself an ambitious goal: to double its research effort in just five years in terms of cash and human resources in an attempt to bridge the gap separating it from the three other major Western European powers—France, the United Kingdom, and West Germany. This must be achieved while maintaining research standards and tight control over spending targets, against a background of economic stringency imposed by attempts to deal with Italy's enormous budget deficit. There is, however, a general consensus within Parliament and industry that this is vital to keep the creation of the 1992 single European market results from disrupting the still fragile Italian research structure, with inevitably negative consequences on the competitiveness of the whole economy.

Italy's forte has always been individual initiative and a free rein on creativity; it does not excel in the discipline of planning. Bottom-up governance of research is, therefore, more likely to bring rewards. The previous system, which relied upon advisory groups and informal or *ad hoc* panels of experts, often proved chaotic and evanescent.

There is now the basis for an institutionalized and stable structure in place. Provision for such a structure is specifically made in Law 168 for the establishment of the Ministry for Scientific Research and the universities, which, after a quarter of a century, gives official recognition to the strategic value of research. The ministry is charged with direction, coordination and planning. Its structure marks an innovation compared with other ministerial organizational patterns, adopting a departmental system as opposed to directorates general, thus permitting greater flexibility and speed of decision-making.

General policy will be elaborated in conjunction with a new body, the National Council for Science and Technology, which is unprecedented in Italy. The council is composed of members who are, in part, elected by the scientific community and, in part, appointed by the minister. Funding will not be the direct responsibility of the ministry, but is assigned to the research institutions and universities which independently decide upon its allocation and utilization. The new council should ensure that progress will continue and, at last, be more strategically directed to serve the wider goal of preparing Italy for the 21st century.

Organization of National Science Administration in Japan

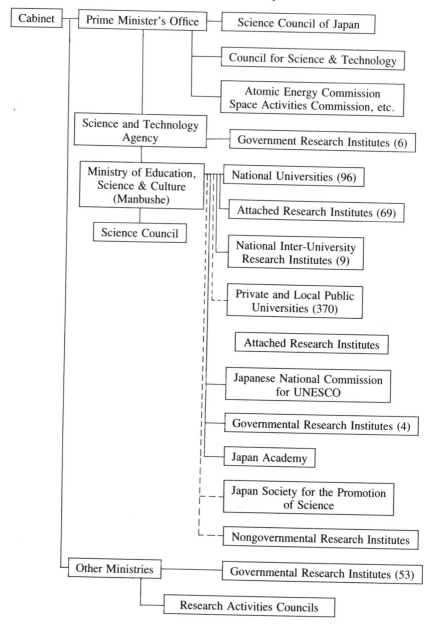

The Activities of the Science Council of Japan

Jiro Kondo

JAPAN *(Nippon) has operated under a multiparty parliamentary system of government since its constitutional monarchy was established in 1947. Its land area is 143,750 square miles, and its estimated population in 1989 was 123,298,000. The official language of the country is Japanese. As of December 31, 1989, the US dollar was equal to 143.72 yen.*

The Science Council of Japan (JSC) was established in 1949 as a body representing the scientists of the country, both internally and internationally.

The council itself is made up of 210 members and has oversight of 180 research liaison committees, made up of 2,370 members, and academic societies, which have memberships totaling 490,000. Eight hundred and thirty-six societies were registered with the JSC in 1988.

The Science Council of Japan engages in the following activities:

- Conducts discussions, independently, on important matters concerning the sciences, and makes efforts to implement any decisions reached; and
- Coordinates scientific research as a means of enhancing the efficiency of research efforts.

The government may seek opinions from the Science Council of Japan, and the council has the right to take the initiative in making recommendations to the government.

The council sends delegations both to important international meetings overseas and to foreign countries for the purpose of bilateral scientific exchanges. It also organizes and supports important international conferences in Japan.

The main feature of the JSC is that it represents all the qualified scientists in the country. Candidates for membership are nominated by academic societies, and the 210 members of the council are selected by the research liaison committees.

Finally, the Prime Minister appoints the candidates to membership in the JSC. The president and two vice presidents are elected by a vote of the mem-

Jiro Kondo is President of the Science Council of Japan (JSC) and is an ex officio member of the Council for Science and Technology of the Prime Minister's Office. A member of the Science Council of the Ministry of Education, Science and Culture, he holds an undergraduate degree in mathematics and a doctorate in engineering. His specialties are applied mathematics and aeronautics. Dr. Kondo has been Dean of Engineering at the University of Tokyo and, from 1980 to 1985, he was Director of the National Institute for Environmental Studies. He has served in other governmental capacities, and has published many books and papers and received numerous awards.

bership. Members of the JSC serve as special government employees, working on a part-time basis. The majority of members are university professors; the others are directors of public or private hospitals, managers of private companies, and directors of governmental or private establishments.

THE RESEARCH LIAISON COMMITTEES

The Research Liaison Committees (RLCs), in order to study, as necessary, those fields and problems relating to scientific research, as well as to examine the present state of achievement and the consolidation of research conditions, maintains close contact with concerned scientists, research institutes, and academic societies, and serves as liaison to international organizations.

Some of the 180 Research Liaison Committees work as national committees for the respective international unions to coordinate the activities of Japanese scientists and academic societies and to examine future plans for certain specialized fields of science.

Committees consist, usually, of ten to thirty members who are suggested by academic societies. Senior scientists who are members of RLCs work together, side by side, with the members of the RLCs and are associate members of RLCs.

THE PROCESS OF APPOINTMENT OF MEMBERS

Until the twelfth term of the Japanese government, members of the Science Council of Japan were publicly elected by eligible voters. From the beginning of the thirteenth term, this has been changed to a selective system, based on the academic societies. In this new system, the scientific research organizations are asked to choose candidates and to appoint persons to make recommendations. In the final stage, a group from the RLCs nominates 210 people as qualified to be members of the Science Council of Japan; these are formally appointed by the Prime Minister.

The JSC is directly connected to the Prime Minister's office as the Council for Science and Technology (CST). The CST, however, does not include the social sciences or the humanities. The Prime Minister is the Chairman of the CST, and the President of the Science Council of Japan automatically becomes a member of the CST. He is chairman of a liaison committee with the JSC in the CST.

CST is responsible to the Prime Minister if the government consults it about science policy. As a practical matter, however, the government does not consult the CST, since each ministry has its own science council, the members of which are appointed by the respective ministers. For example, the Science Council is attached to the Ministry of Education, Science and Culture, which is responsible for national higher education, promotion of scientific research, etc. The president of the CST is appointed by the Minister of Education.

The Japan Academy is also attached to the Ministry of Education, Science and Culture. Membership in the Japan Academy is a prestigious post, and members can stay for life. The academy awards prizes to scholars who have made outstanding contributions to research.

Research Activities Councils are attached to other ministries. The president of the JSC is appointed President of the Central Council for Environmental Pollution Control, which is connected with the Environment Protection Agency of the government.

THE HISTORY OF ACTIVITIES OF THE JSC

The Science Council of Japan has built a record of many achievements since its foundation, such as recommendations, reports, and opinions on scientific research projects which have been submitted to the government.

Almost 670 separate recommendations and requests concerning research funds, the establishment of research institutes, the university system, the promotion of the sciences, and international scientific exchanges have been made.

The most important of these are the following:

- In 1965, comprehensive recommendations concerning the "First Five-Year Plan for Scientific Research" were made. As a result, Joint-Use Research Institutes were established and Supercomputer Joint-Use Centers were established in seven universities;
- Considering the important role that universities play in the conduct of scientific research, the Science Council of Japan, since its founding, has deliberated subjects concerning universities and made many recommendations;
- In recognition of the fact that basic laws relating to scientific research should be established to effect the promotion thereof, proposals were drafted and recommendations made to the government, in 1962, "Regarding the Establishment of Basic Laws for Scientific Research;"
- In 1954, "Three Principles for the Peaceful Use of Atomic Energy," stipulating the principles of open public scrutiny, democratic management, and autonomous development, were proposed to the government. These principles were later incorporated into the provisions of the Basic Act for Atomic Energy.
- A proposal, "Regarding the Establishment of a Cultural Properties Protection Act," was made in 1973, and one entitled "Regarding the Foundation of the National Museum of Ethnological Research" (tentative name), in 1965, resulted in the founding of the National Museum of Ethnology.
- A recommendation, "Regarding the Prevention of Dispersion and Loss of Archives," in 1959, resulted in the founding of the National Archives. Through a recommendation on "The Establishment of Laws for

the Preservation of Historical Documents,'' in 1965, the founding of regional archives in each of the prefectures was promoted.

STATEMENTS AND APPEALS

The Science Council of Japan researches and deliberates on subjects concerning the sciences and publishes the results thereof, as well as making known the council's own views; these take the form of statements and appeals to scientists at home and abroad, as well as to the citizens of Japan. The purpose of this is to promote the just progress of science and to fulfill the social responsibilities of the scientific community, the following in particular.

In 1949, the first General Meeting, "Resolutions on the Occasion of the Inauguration of the Science Council of Japan" were determined. In this statement, the past attitude of the scientific community was discussed. A resolution was made to contribute to the peaceful rehabilitation of Japan and the promotion of the welfare of mankind on the conviction that science provides the basis for a cultural and peace-loving nation. It was further resolved that government would render whatever services possible for the protection of the freedoms of thought, learning and speech, as guaranteed in the Constitution of Japan, as well as for the advancement of science for the peace of all humanity in collaboration with the scientists of the world.

In 1961, the "Views of the Science Council of Japan Regarding International Scientific Cooperation" were made public. These consisted of five principles:

- That the purpose of international scientific cooperation shall be to contribute to world peace;
- That international scientific cooperation shall be worldwide;
- That independence shall be respected in the event of international cooperation;
- That international scientific cooperation shall be conducted on equal terms among scientists; and
- That the results of international scientific cooperation shall be made public.

In 1980, a "Charter for Scientists" was adopted. Its purposes were to establish an obligation to work for the sound development of scientific research and to clarify before the citizens of the nation the responsibilities of scientists in the form of a code of ethics. The Science Council of Japan expressed its determination to observe this charter and appealed to a wide sphere of scientists for cooperation.

In 1988, on the occasion of the amendment of the agreement between the government of Japan and the government of the United States on Cooperation in Research and Development in Science and Technology, the Science Council of Japan expressed its great concern about the amendment and insisted that the spirit of the appeals of 1961 and 1980 should be respected. The appeal had been issued before the treaty was signed by the Prime Minister.

In 1987, a special committee on therapeutic technology and human life tried to make public its opinion on brain death. After heated discussions at the 102nd and 103rd General Assemblies, the JSC did not admit the opinion, since the majority of the members thought that more time might be needed before brain death would be accepted as actual death in the country.

THE PLAN OF ACTIVITIES FOR THE FOURTEENTH TERM

The Science Council of Japan adopted the Plan of Activities for the fourteenth term (1988–1991) at its 106th General Assembly in October 1988. The plan defines the basic standpoints, objectives and problems to be emphasized during the fourteenth term of the JSC up to July 1991.

Three priority objectives are the guidelines for the activities of the JSC, both domestically and internationally. They are:

- *Promotion of science in consideration of its relationship to welfare, peace, and the natural environment.*
  The remarkable development of science and technology has made human life richer, but sometimes it seems to have caused adverse effects on human society and the natural environment. It is recognized that it is very important to promote science in consideration of its relationship to the welfare, peace, and natural environment, and it is proposed that there be established a practical plan for promotion and development of science, taking into account its contributions to and undesired effects upon human beings, society, and the environment as well as the guidelines for completing the social structure correspond to it.

  Also, the council will encourage existing disciplines to cooperate with each other to achieve reforms in the quality and organization of research, and to seek more scientific methodologies, since interdisciplinary researchers will be necessary to solve the complicated problems of the contemporary world.
- *The promotion of basic research and coordinated progress of science, i.e., basic research is indispensable for the development of science, particularly in present-day Japan.*
  Also, an effort has to be made to foster individual scientific fields as well as to develop various domains of science in coordination. In the thirteenth term, the Third Standing Committee studied the trends of science in Japan and submitted a report entitled ''The Trend of Scientific Research in Japan'' to the General Assembly of the council. This report surveyed the trend of research subjects, the present status of research activities, the levels of research compared with the international research standards, and bottlenecks in the progress of science.

In the fourteenth term, on the basis of this report, work will be done to strengthen the progressive research projects with emphasis on creative individual thought and bearing in mind the elimination of any negative factors which prevent creativity. Suggestions will also be made in regard to practical measures for the progress and development of science.

· *Emphasis on international scientific exchanges and the strengthening of contributions to world science.*

Scientific research is an intellectual activity aimed at searching for truth, and its fruits are the common property of mankind. Consequently, it is basically of an international nature, and concern must always be shown about international scientific exchange.

There have been increased requests for Japanese scientists to strengthen their contributions to international collaboration, especially on world-wide issues, such as peace and the solution of global environmental problems.

The council well recognizes the importance of international scientific exchange and cooperation, so—on the basis of the principles and achievements which have been established—Japan will endeavor to strengthen its international activity significantly and to open the academic systems of Japan to the world.

CONCRETE SUBJECTS

In accordance with the three major objectives described above, the council has selected fifteen subjects to be deliberated upon by members representing various fields of science, and fruitful results are expected regarding these subjects during the fourteenth term. These subjects are:

· Ethics and the social responsibilities of scientists;
· The long-range prospects for scientific research;
· The training of scientists;
· The reinforcement of research foundations and the activation of research projects;
· Measures for well-organized systems of scientific information and materials;
· Measures for the expansion of international scientific exchange and cooperation;
· Review and activation of the international activities of the JSC;
· Peace and solutions to international conflicts;
· Problems regarding nature and the existence of human beings (integrated science for human beings);
· Therapeutic technology and society;
· Bioscience and bio-engineering;
· Agriculture and rural communities;

- Resources and energy;
- Human activities and the global environment; and
- The high-technology society.

Among the subjects above, the first seven will be mainly deliberated upon by standing committees; the rest will be handled by *ad hoc* committees.

STANDING COMMITTEES

The activities of the standing committees are as follows:

First–Deliberates upon the activities of the Research Liaison Committees and the organization of the Science Council of Japan.

Second–Discusses matters relating to the freedom of learning and thought, ethics, and the social responsibilities of scientists, and the improvement of the status of scientists.

Third–Analyzes the present situation and studies the long-term programs of science.

Fourth–Deliberates upon the academic organizations for creative research and cooperation with other scientific institutions.

Fifth–Reviews topics related to science information and data.

Sixth–Studies international scientific exchange and collaboration.

SPECIAL COMMITTEES

The 106th General Assembly established seven special committees to study the concrete subjects mentioned in the Plan of Activities. The names and the terms of reference of these committees are:

- *Special Committee on Peace and International Conflicts*
  This group examines the problems regarding international conflicts arising in such fields as culture, ethics, and technology, and measures for the promotion of comprehensive research on peace and conflict resolution.
- *Special Committee on Therapeutic Technology and Society*
  This group examines the social aspects of the progress of therapeutic technology which raise many questions and issues of concern to various fields of science.
- *Special Committee on Bioscience and Bio-engineering*
  This group examines measures for the promotion of bioscience and bio-engineering and the impacts of their rapid progress on mankind, society and nature.
- *Special Committee on Agriculture and Rural Communities*
  This group examines—on the bases of domestic and international circumstances—the multiple functions of agriculture and rural communi-

ties, such as food production and environmental preservation and their
links with culture, the economy, nature and urbanization.
- *Special Committee on Resources and Energy*
This group examines the development and utilization of resources and
energy as well as negative influences on the natural environment and
society.
- *Special Committee on Human Activities and the Global Environment*
This group examines the problems of human activities and the global
environment in consideration of their serious influences and their links
with culture, the economy, etc.
- *Special Committee on the High-Technology Society*
This group examines the impact of the remarkable developments of high
technology on society as well as measures to bring into harmony information and technology oriented toward human beings, and to bring about
the proper relationship between huge technological systems and the human factor.
- *Special Committee on Integrated Science for Human Beings*
This group is to be established in the near future because it is necessary
for all disciplines to study what it means to be a human being. Some
time is needed for a pre-examination of the issues.

THE FUTURE OF THE SCIENCE COUNCIL OF JAPAN

The Science Council of Japan is a unique, semi-governmental organization which
came into existence after World War II. The members represent the active
scientists of the country. At times, however, their recommendations are not
accepted because they are contrary to the policies of the government.

It is important, therefore, for the JSC to be always concerned with the intentions of scientists. The council should carefully analyze the trend of scientific
research throughout the world and be able to issue timely recommendations.

In Japan, the system of administration for science is complicated, since several advisory bodies to the Prime Minister are in existence. The author believes, however, that the Science Council will maintain its authority in the
future.

The Council for Science and Technology: Its Contribution to Japan's Science and Technology Policy

Michio Okamoto

The current status of science and technology policy in Japan can be examined from several different viewpoints. Since this author has been involved in science and technology administration—as a standing member of the Council for Science and Technology (CST)—for the past ten years, it would be best to begin with a description of the principal functions of CST activity.

The Council for Science and Technology was established in February 1959 as a standing advisory body in the Prime Minister's office. Its mission is to organize the development of comprehensive science and technology policies for the government. The original goals and principles for carrying out its mission, which have remained unchanged for the past thirty years, are the following:

- To establish a fundamental and comprehensive framework for science and technology policy;
- To delineate comprehensive and long-term research objectives;
- To outline fundamental policy promotion programs for carrying out important areas of research; and
- To provide advice and guidance to the government through special inquiries and reports to the Scientific Council of Japan.

Furthermore, it is explicitly stated that the Prime Minister "shall esteem and follow" (*i.e.*, he cannot refuse) the recommendations from the CST's reports and findings.

The current membership of the CST is shown in Table 1. The Prime Minister presides as chairman of the council, and the members, ten in all, consist of four Cabinet ministers, the chairman of the Science Council of Japan, and other scholars and men of experience representing the three sectors: government,

Michio Okamoto, M.D., is Senior Member of the Council for Science and Technology in the Office of the Prime Minister and Chairman of the Committee on Policy Matters of the council, as well as President of Kobe City General Hospital. He was Dean of the Medical School of Kyoto University (1970–73) and President of that university (1973–79). Born in 1913, Dr. Okamoto served as a member of the Science Council of the Ministry of Education, Science and Culture (1968–86) and was President of the National Council on Educational Reform.

Table 1. Membership of the Council for Science and Technology

Chairman:	The Prime Minister	Toshiki Kaifu
Members:	Minister of Finance	Ryutaro Hashimoto
	Minister of Education	Kazuya Ishibashi
	Minister of the Economic Planning Agency	Sumiko Takahara
	Minister of the Science and Technology Agency	Eizaburo Saito
	Chairman of the Science Council of Japan	Jiro Kondo
	Executive Member	Michio Okamoto
	Executive Member	Yoshimitsu Takeyasu
	Member	Yasusada Kitahara Executive Advisor, Nippon Telephone & Telegraph
	Member	Seiichi Saba Advisor, Toshiba Company
	Member	Seiji Morii President, Kansai Electric Power Co., Inc.

academia, and the industrial community. Recently, as rapid developments in science and technology continued to impact on the greater issues of social, economic and international activity, the importance of developing coordinated science and technology policies aimed at maintaining national harmony has been of primary importance to the council.

In order to achieve the objective of a more comprehensive science and technology policy and in view of the suggestion to the CST of the Provisional Administrative Council, the organization of the CST was strengthened in March 1983 by the establishment of a Policy Committee. This group consists of eight outstanding experts from various fields in addition to the current members of CST in the academic fields and has the purpose of facilitating decisions on important issues at appropriate times for the CST. This author has been chairman of this committee since its inception.

THE MISSION OF THE CST

The Prime Minister's statement at the first meeting of the CST in 1959 most adequately describes the mission of the council; he stated:

> Utmost in carrying out objectives in S&T promotion should be policy which seeks to maintain systematic linkage between each related organization. In other words, a balanced policy which integrates and incorporates all areas in related organizations is fundamental. For policy integration, it is imperative that we secure an S&T level of performance that is suitable to the country's capabilities. Complementary to this statement is the acknowledgement that each relevant government agency exerts effort in carrying out its related tasks. But these efforts alone will not suffice to

develop a balanced and comprehensive S&T policy. The CST, therefore, is established to compensate for any shortcomings. Thus the CST's mission is of great importance as an integrating and energizing factor in achieving cohesive national S&T policy efforts. Needless to say, every effort will be made to appropriate the requisite financing and I will endeavor to follow the distinguished council's recommendations.

It is plain that the role of the CST began with the presentation of the direction of Japan's science and technology policy and its purpose, accordingly, is to assist the activities of government agencies for promoting priority issues and efficient policy implementation under a well-coordinated plan.

DEVELOPMENT OF BASIC POLICY AND GOVERNMENT APPROACHES

It would now be appropriate to describe the development of the CST's basic science and technology policies and to explain some of the background of the government's approaches to facilitate the understanding of the functions of the council.

Published in October 1960, the council's first report outlined a ten-year prospectus for science and technology policy promotion. At that time, Japan was in the midst of its "income doubling" policy; thus economic growth policies and science and technology promotion policies were interdependent.

In 1966, the council proposed 102 issue areas, which were to be stimulated in Japan, under the report title, "Opinions on the Overall Basic Policies for Science and Technology Promotion," and showed a continuous direction for the advancement of science and technology as the key issue for the enhancement of economic power.

In 1971, however, the fifth report of the council, titled "Basic Science and Technology Policy in the 1970s," stressed the harmonization of nature and society and the need to seek out the more humane aspects of science and technology from the background of a serious environmental situation.

In the sixth report, "Basic Principles for Long-Term Prospects in an Integrated Science and Technology Policy," published in 1977, the country was showing higher levels of science and technology policy achievement. Thirty years after the end of World War II, Japan's science and technology had reached comparable levels *vis-a-vis* most Western countries through the absorption of technologies from advanced countries.

The effort to bring Japan from a "catch-up" phase toward developing more autonomous technologies was shown in this report. The report, however, placed emphasis on the promotion of science and technology to solve individual problems, such as constraints from limited resources due to the energy crisis; thus the promotion of basic science was treated secondarily.

Furthermore, in order to strengthen the CST's coordinating function and aid in its leadership role in science and technology policy implementation, the Science and Technology Promotion Adjustment Fund (started in 1981 and receiving funding in the amount of 10.1 billion yen in 1989) was established. This fund serves to implement the promotion and coordination programs in vital selected areas of research following CST's policy direction.

In November 1984, the CST published its eleventh report, entitled "Long-Term Perspectives on the Promotion of Science and Technology: Basic Integrated Policy in the Light of Changing Circumstances." This report outlined the basic view for science and technology policy promotion for the next ten years.

The government articulated its "Fundamental Principles for Science and Technology Policy," based on this report, in December 1987. The report considers three essential policy issues: "Highly Creative Science and Technology," "The Development of Science and Technology in Harmony with Individuals and Society," and "The Development of Science and Technology Focused on Internationalization."

Recent activities of the CST are based on these principles.

CURRENT CST ACTIVITIES

In addition, the main current activities of the CST include the following:

- Deliberation of the sixteenth CST report, "Basic Guidelines for Preparing the Promotion of the Science and Technology Infrastructure;"
- Deliberation on the seventeenth CST report, "Basic Planning for R&D for Earth Sciences and Technology;"
- Discussion meeting on life sciences and human civilization; and
- Discussion meeting on global issues relating to science and technology.

The first point is based on Japan's self-awareness that basic science is important and has been neglected in the past because the promotion of technology was emphasized.

The second point is based on an awareness of the shadow aspects (e.g., public safety hazards) to civilized society, such as disharmony between science and society. The importance of this point can be understood when one looks at the current activities addressing global environmental issues. The final point is reflective of Japan's present international situation which has been economically developed.

THE POLICY DECISION-MAKING PROCESS

The Provisional Committee on Administrative Studies of the government was organized in March 1981. Its final report indicates that independent and creative research processes are not sufficiently developed in Japan. Moreover, interministerial and interorganizational sectionalism hinders the efficient promotion of research and development.

To overcome these problems, this report further points out the necessity for establishing well-defined rules for utilizing industrial research and development activities in both the public and the private sector; promotion of cooperation among industry, academia and government; the flexible management and organization of universities and national research institutes; the promotion of international science and technology cooperation; the improvement of planning and coordination functions of the CST; and the promotion of integrated science and technology management and a desirable organization plan for program administration.

Furthermore, the Provisional Administration Reform Promotion Council, following the points above, stated—in regard to science and technology administration—that, in Japan, where government activities are assigned to different ministers and agencies, it is necessary to clarify the basic directions of research and development programs from the overall government viewpoint.

Also, it notes that it is important to establish a management system that can facilitate the integrated and efficient promotion of Japan's science and technology in a program which emphasizes both basic science and advanced technology. It was the CST that assumed this overall responsibility.

The representative approach to administration that is taken by the CST is the formulation of recommendations in response to inquiries from the Prime Minister. Namely, the Council for Science and Technology Establishment Act stipulates that, when the Prime Minister recognizes that there is the need to adjust the policies of the related administrative organizations regarding the establishment of a basic overall policy for science and technology, the minister is required to consult with the CST. Whenever the Prime Minister receives such a recommendation from the CST in response to such an inquiry, he must follow the advice of the council.

Upon receiving an inquiry, the CST organizes a sectional meeting, under the general meeting, to be in charge of the problem and further organizes divisional meetings and working groups with the cooperation of a number of experts; then the sectional meeting prepares a draft recommendation as a result of discussions held over a period of one to two years.

To bring about realistic reflection of the nation's policy, the draft recommendation of the sectional meeting is released at an early stage to the relevant ministries, including the Ministry of Finance, which is in charge of funding in the Science and Technology Agency through the secretariat of the CST. This step is carried out to obtain the understanding of each ministry and to arrange for any necessary adjustments. After adjustments have been made, the draft recommendation is finalized and decided upon at a general meeting involving the relevant ministers and is submitted as CST's recommendation to the Prime Minister.

WHO PARTICIPATES

The ministers present at such a general meeting include the Ministers of Education and Science and Technology, the central enforcement agencies for science and technology policy, as well as ministers from the Economic Planning Agency and Finance. In addition, any ministers having interests in the subject may participate in the meeting.

For example, the Minister of Health and Welfare participated in the general meeting which discussed "Ten-Year Overall Strategies for Fighting Cancer," and the Minister for International Trade and Industry participated in the discussions on "The Human Frontier Science Program."

As mentioned earlier, as ministry officials in charge of the pertinent matter have already consented to the draft recommendation (which is amended, if necessary) during the preparation process, ministers are also admitted to the final discussions when the recommendation is approved at the general meeting. The Prime Minister then has the obligation to accept the recommendation.

These recommendations generally deal with long-term and comprehensive planning. Each member of the CST usually offers his opinion at this time on administrative issues important to the Prime Minister. Since the ministers present also hear these opinions, this meeting is an important opportunity for council members to present their views.

Each year, the important issues are decided by the Policy Committee prior to the finalization of the national budget as "Important Guidelines for Science and Technology Promotion." These guidelines represent the CST's annual direction prior to the submission of the individual ministries' budget requirements. Individual ministries require science and technology funding within these guidelines to develop programs for science and technology promotion.

In order to decide the important issues for each year, the Policy Committee collects information by asking the individual needs of the ministries, as well as the business community, for science and technology policy. The committee then decides upon the budgetary requirements based on the information presented and expert opinions offered by the committee members.

ISSUES IN 1989

Following are important issues that were decided upon for 1989:

- Promotion of basic science and advanced technology and the development of creative human resources;
- Enhancement of international exchange programs and cooperative systems; and
- Strengthening of the infrastructure for science and technology promotion and facilitating research exchange.

In addition, the importance of formulating timely policies, such as fostering human resources in developing countries and active participation in global environmental problems, were also pointed out. The Policy Committee has requested support for the important guidelines from the ruling party and the concerned ministries, and has been following up on these programs with hearings involving the individual ministries.

The Council for Science and Technology also indicates the directions of the individual ministries' science and technology administration and makes substantial adjustments by effectively utilizing the Science and Technology Promotion Adjustment Fund, which is appropriated for the budget of the Science and Technology Agency, since the CST has the authority for the allocation of such funding.

The CST holds hearings for the requirements of the individual ministries' science and technology administrations which are prepared annually in conformance with the guidelines mentioned earlier. As a result, the CST selects the requirements, such as the covering of plural administrative agencies, cooperative research by industry, academia and the government, and advanced research in essential areas, and disburses the funding on a priority basis. For this purpose, the assessment is carried out by the Research Investigation Subcommittee of the Policy Committee.

Moreover, the Science and Technology Promotion Adjustment Fund includes the budget for promoting basic research in ministerial research institutes and expenses for overseas trips, those for inviting researchers from foreign countries as well as those for studying the basic principles of science and technology policy. The current total budget is about ten billion yen per year.

In regard to studies on science and technology policy, the National Institute for Science and Technology Policy, established in 1988, continues significant activities in this field in addition to the CST's own studies, this taking a leading role in policy decisions.

THE CST'S OWN POLICIES

The CST sometimes develops its own policies for specific science and technology problems which involve plural administrative agencies by addressing the relevant ministries at the initial stages. Typical examples are "Ten-Year Overall Strategies for Fighting Cancer," which was proposed six years ago, and "The Human Frontier Science Program" started in 1989.

After the CST completes a review of the implementation plan, the actual implementation is assigned to an individual ministry. This CST function is essentially designed to obtain the cooperation of the Ministry for Education in plans involving research activities in the universities. This is because only the CST can coordinate joint research efforts involving plural ministries, including the Ministry of Education, which has jurisdiction over research projects in the universities. The Science and Technology Agency can also coordinate joint research involving plural ministries, but its responsibility does not extend to research carried out in the universities.

Individual agencies formulate policy plans along the guidelines laid down by the CST through the above-described method, but, in addition, each ministry has individual councils to establish its own plans. In any case, these science and technology policies of the individual ministries are brought directly to the ruling party's Science and Technology Divisional Committee. This committee discusses and studies the problems, after which the approved subjects are submitted to the Science and Technology Committee of the Upper and Lower Houses of the legislature where they are again reviewed and finally laid before the Diet.

The results of these deliberations depend, of course, on the subject of the particular policy, but also on the efforts of the officers in the concerned ministries during the process.

There is no science and technology adviser to the Prime Minister in Japan, but the Prime Minister sometimes asks for specialists' opinions on specific subjects to help in the promotion of policies, or specialists may offer their opinions on science and technology through informal channels. Because of the difference in form of the authority between Japan's Prime Minister and the President of the United States, there is no science adviser in Japan, but this role is carried out by the CST through its direct relationship with the Prime Minister.

CONCLUSION

As previously stated, the Council for Science and Technology aims at formulating long-range plans by seizing the current status of trends of science and technology throughout the world, and, at the same time, assuming responsibility for the overall coordination of the individual ministries' implementation plans. This objective is believed to be met on the whole through the annual presentation of important guidelines and the allocation of the Science and Technology Promotion Adjustment Fund. The programs of the individual ministries, however, in their own scientific and technological fields, have recently become more intensified. In view of the current trend, each ministry concentrates its energies on these programs, and there is competition between them.

Thus the status has still not been reached where the CST takes the initiative in all the science and technology policy decisions in Japan, makes adjustments to avoid duplications, and effectively allocates funds. In this regard, activation of the CST's overall coordinating power has been disputed, but, on the other hand, the competitive mindset of the ministries is, in a sense, recognized as a motivating force for promotion of the policies. Thus the role of the CST should not be rejected without reservation.

The CST ensures reliable judgment in establishing an overall plan based on long-term perspectives, and believes that adjustment by indicating the principle

Figure 1. Organization Chart of the National Institute of Science and Technology Policy (NISTEP)*

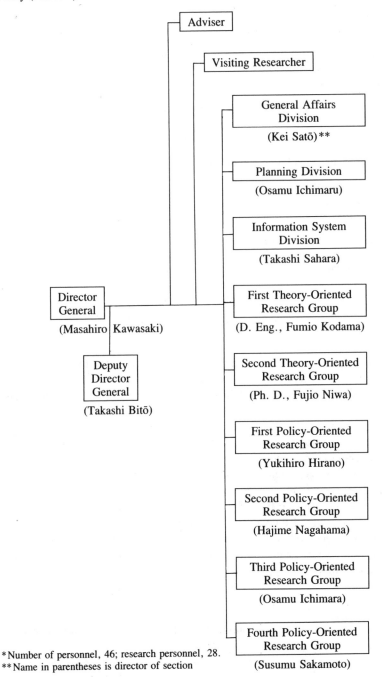

```
                                    ┌─────────────────┐
                                    │     Adviser     │
                                    └─────────────────┘

                                    ┌─────────────────────┐
                                    │ Visiting Researcher │
                                    └─────────────────────┘

                                    ┌─────────────────┐
                                    │ General Affairs │
                                    │    Division     │
                                    └─────────────────┘
                                       (Kei Satō)**

                                    ┌─────────────────┐
                                    │ Planning Division │
                                    └─────────────────┘
                                      (Osamu Ichimaru)

                                    ┌──────────────────┐
                                    │ Information System │
                                    │     Division     │
                                    └──────────────────┘
                                      (Takashi Sahara)

  ┌───────────┐                     ┌────────────────────┐
  │ Director  │                     │ First Theory-Oriented │
  │ General   │                     │   Research Group    │
  └───────────┘                     └────────────────────┘
  (Masahiro Kawasaki)                (D. Eng., Fumio Kodama)

      ┌───────────┐                 ┌─────────────────────┐
      │ Deputy    │                 │ Second Theory-Oriented │
      │ Director  │                 │   Research Group     │
      │ General   │                 └─────────────────────┘
      └───────────┘                   (Ph. D., Fujio Niwa)
      (Takashi Bitō)

                                    ┌─────────────────┐
                                    │ First Policy-Oriented │
                                    │  Research Group │
                                    └─────────────────┘
                                      (Yukihiro Hirano)

                                    ┌─────────────────┐
                                    │ Second Policy-Oriented │
                                    │  Research Group │
                                    └─────────────────┘
                                      (Hajime Nagahama)

                                    ┌─────────────────┐
                                    │ Third Policy-Oriented │
                                    │  Research Group │
                                    └─────────────────┘
                                      (Osamu Ichimara)

                                    ┌─────────────────┐
                                    │ Fourth Policy-Oriented │
                                    │  Research Group │
                                    └─────────────────┘
                                      (Susumu Sakamoto)
```

*Number of personnel, 46; research personnel, 28.
**Name in parentheses is director of section

Table 2. Organization of the National Institute of Science and Technology Policy (NISTEP)

Hiroshi Inose
Director General of the National Center of Science Information Systems
Hiroyuki Ōsawa
President of the National Space Development Agency of Japan (NASDA)
Sōgo Okamura
Professor, Denki University
Shinroku Saitō
Former President of the Technological University of Nagaoka
Yōichi Sandō
Executive Director of the Asahi Research Center Co., Ltd.
Eiji Suzuki
President of the Japan Federation of Employers' Associations
Minoru Nagaoka
President of the Tokyo Stock Exchange
Yujirō Hayashi
Vice Chairman of the Institute for Future Technology
Noboru Makino
President of the Mitsubishi Research Institute, Inc.
Takashi Mukaibō
President of the Japan Society for Science Policy and Research Management
Isamu Yamashita
Chairman of the East Japan Railway Co., Ltd.
Shigeru Watanabe
President of the Tokyo Metropolitan Institute of Technology

---

direction is appropriate, except in providing extreme duplication in reviewing the policies of the individual ministries.

The activities of the National Institute for Science and Technology Policy (NISTEP), established in 1988, are expected to provide the basis for science and technology in Japan and, therefore, have great significance.

NISTEP was established on July 1, 1988, as a central organization of research on science and technology policy. It conducts research activities in coordination with the Council for Science and Technology and other related governmental organizations.

In order to prepare the basis for appropriate and effective science and technology policies, NISTEP conducts systematic and quantitative analysis research and studies, concerned with both theory and policy, in all relevant areas. In addition, it cooperates with overseas organizations in the US, the UK, the Federal Republic of Germany, the Republic of Korea, and the People's Republic of China.

Its goals include the following:

· The harmonization of continuous technological innovation in a global society;
· Competition and cooperation in the field of science and technology;

- Realization of "centers of excellence";
- Changing dynamics of the progress of science and technology;
- Relationship between science and technology and society; and
- Interrelationship of science and technology with resource utilization and global environmental concerns.

Policy Mechanisms and Development Strategy for Science and Technology: The Approach of the Republic of Korea (South Korea)

Hyung-Sup Choi

THE REPUBLIC OF KOREA *(Taehan-min'guk) has been operating as an independent republic since 1948 and since 1988 under its present constitution. Its land area is 38,025, and its estimated 1989 population was 43,127,000. The official language is Korean.*

Since national governments are the leaders of economic and technological development in developing countries, its planned promotion is an extremely important issue. Government direction is absolutely essential in overcoming an underdeveloped economic and social structure and in promoting the capacity for development.

Hence the most important activity is to first establish a firm national science policy mechanism. In general, science policies and administrative mechanisms may be classified into two types: first, the case of unified planning carried out at the ministerial level, as in Japan and Korea, and, second, the case of planning carried out by a special advisory body, such as a science or research council.

A given country must choose the type which better suits its unique circumstances and level of development. Moreover, it is important that scientific and technological planning should have organic linkages with the overall national development plan. It is necessary to preserve these linkages from the time that the plan is established right through its execution.

In addition, attention must be paid to the distribution of scientific and technological investment capital among the various sectors. It is also important that a system for overall coordination be set up to determine how to regulate most efficiently—in accordance with the national science policy—the diverse projects related to science and technology that are being carried out by each government ministry.

The first task to be undertaken in the area of scientific and technology de-

Hyung-Sup Choi was the founding President of the Korea Institute of Science and Technology and served as the Minister for Science and Technology of the Republic of Korea from 1971 to 1978. In these capacities, he contributed greatly to the formulation and implementation of Korea's science and technology development policies and strategies. He is a member of the National Academy of Sciences, Korea.

velopment in developing countries is the establishment of the planning mechanism mentioned above. This must be consistent with the building of the foundation or basis for development. Urgent matters also include devising laws and regulations for the efficient promotion of science and technology on a national scale through systematizing latent capabilities, establishing R&D systems for fostering research capabilities, and creating policies and systems for scientific and technological manpower development.

In the case of Korea, it took at least ten years after the initiation of the effort in the early 1960s to build the bases for science and technology development. It only became possible to promote technological innovation through its own technological capabilities in the mid-1970s. Thus, the rate of scientific and technological development can be accelerated only if a firm foundation for it has been laid.

ORGANIZATION OF THE MINISTRY OF SCIENCE AND TECHNOLOGY

Along with a strong desire to develop science and technology in a national dimension, the Ministry of Science and Technology (MOST) was founded in Korea in 1967 as the central policy-making, planning, coordinating and promotional body in science and technology. It is headed by a minister of state who is directly under the Prime Minister.[1]

The major functions of the ministry include the establishment of a long-term policy for science and technology, the framework of five-year plans for the development of science and technology, policy implementation decisions in all fields, and the establishment of an appropriate system for all of the foregoing. The most important element of the policy for science and technology is that, from the planning through the implementation stages, there must be a close linkage with the long-range national development plans.

For this purpose, all those policy planners from other government ministries must be persuaded to raise the appropriate consciousness about the importance of science and technology, and they must understand the priorities of investment in science and technology. If a nation's science policy—made public as part of the policy plans—is called an "explicit policy," there may also exist an "implicit policy" which efficiently influences and executes the policy behind the scenes. This means that the implicit policy is also an important element that should certainly receive attention.[2]

One special feature of modern science and technology is the dualistic trend of ever-subdividing specializations versus an ever-increasing scale. For this reason, activities connected with science and technology cannot be implemented under a single ministry or a single research center. Under the plans for execution, duties are entrusted to specific government offices and related agencies according to their primary specialties. But, as these activities are closely related to long-term policies for science and technology, it is necessary that there be unified regulation at the national level. The Ministry of Science and Technology coordinates activities related to science and technology in the relevant ministries and research institutions according to the Law for the Advancement of Science and Technology.

POLICY CONSULTATIONS AND DECISION-MAKING MECHANISMS

The development of science and technology transcends short-term and fragmentary efforts, and does not rely only upon the power of a single ministry or coterie of scientists and engineers. Because of the need for integrated activities on the panministerial level, the Federal Council for Science and Technology was founded in 1973, and is composed of the relevant ministers and members prominent in science and technology. The Prime Minister serves as chairman. This is the highest authority on science and technology development in the country.

There are many examples in other countries of this type of policy-making organization. Nevertheless, there is a danger that the council's functions may become confused with those of a council of ministers, in which case many difficulties could arise in achieving the primary objectives of the federal council. The reason for this stems not only from the duplication of or similarity between proposals presented to this council and the Economic Ministers Meeting or to the Cabinet, but also because there is a major tendency for government to concern itself with the interests of the individual ministries or offices rather than taking a panministerial view.

The Federal Council for Science and Technology, however, rather than promoting prior discussions of how problems should be resolved, should clarify for the relevant ministers the nature of the problems and what the Ministry of Science and Technology proposes and will practice in order to solve such problems. Problems such as these are usually interrelated with the work of other ministries and cannot be tackled single-handedly. Therefore, the major functions of the council is to confirm the policies and the plans proposed by the Ministry of Science and Technology in order to ensure cooperation and coordination at the national level.

The Committee for the Promotion of Science and Technology was founded to answer policy inquiries from the Minister of Science and Technology. The committee is composed of distinguished members of industrial and academic fields, and the minister himself is its chairman. The committee is in charge of the advisory function for policy-making and planning in science and technology, and controls the budgets of major projects. Its most significant role is that of facilitating cooperation among government, industry and academia regarding the examination and selection of policies to be promoted for science and technology.

In addition to the above, various other committees—needed for the promotion of matters related to science and technology—have been established and are in operation.

An indispensable factor in the development of science and technology in a developing country is for the political leaders to clearly recognize the vital roles of science and technology in development. Consequently, the Republic of Korea held its first Technology Promotion Meeting in January 1982, presided over by the President of Korea and attended by Cabinet ministers and representatives from the relevant segments of the administrative, business and academic sectors of the country.

The main purpose of such a meeting is to coordinate and formulate technology development policies on the national level, as well as to report on advanced technology trends and introduce successful cases of technology development in both private and government sectors. This meeting, which is held quarterly, provides guidance and nationwide support for the development of science and technology. In addition, a Science and Technology Advisory Committee, consisting of representatives and experts from both the industrial and academic fields, will be established soon in accordance with Article 172 of the Constitution with the purpose of recommending to the President the most desirable science and technology policies.

SCIENCE AND TECHNOLOGY DEVELOPMENT STRATEGY

The Korean government has formulated intensive policies and strategies for the development of science and technology which include many innovative supportive measures.

The major elements of the policy guidelines for the 1970s were as follows:

- The provision of a secure foundation for scientific and technological growth and the nurturing of a cadre of high-caliber scientists;
- The strategic development of industrial technology, providing an intermediary agent for technological development; and
- The creation of a favorable climate for science and technology through nationwide promotion of science.

These guidelines were followed by concrete planning for the execution of these policies.

In this plan, Korea adopted a three-pronged approach, emphasizing capability build-up—particularly manpower development at various levels, the accelerated introduction of advanced foreign technologies, and the stimulation of domestic R&D activities. To this end, an implementation plan was formulated, considering—among others—both the institutional and the legal factors.

THE INSTITUTIONAL FRAMEWORK

The institutional framework of the Korean approach was somewhat daring. It included the establishment of the following:

- The Korea Institute of Science and Technology, created by a special law (the KIST Assistant Act) in 1966 as an autonomous, multidisciplinary, industrial research institute, chartered as a contract research organization to make researchers aware of technology marketing;[3]
- The Korea Advanced Institute of Science (KAIS), which was established in 1971 to be a mission-oriented, post-graduate school in selected applied science and engineering to meet the emerging needs of Korean industries;
- Many specialized research organizations which are specific to each industry and problem area in which technological requirements have increased in level and diversity with the growth of industry;
- The Daeduk Science Town, which houses research organizations, both public and private, as well as institutions of higher education, forming an intellectual complex to contribute to the development of science and technology;
- The Korea Science and Engineering Foundation, set up in 1976 to act as the primary agent for strengthening research in the basic and applied sciences; and
- A great many vocational training institutes and technical high schools, which were established to meet the rapidly rising—almost explosive—demand for skilled workers and technicians.

LEGAL SUPPORT

Next came the legal support for the promotion of technology development, particularly in private industry. A number of legal measures have been enacted to stimulate industrial technology development. Examples include the Law for the Promotion of Technology Development, the Engineering Services Promotion Law, and the Assistance Law for Designated Research Organizations. Of these, the Law for the Promotion of Technology Development has played the most crucial role in advancing the technological level of the Korean society.[4]

Furthermore, Korea has launched a national movement for the popularization of science and technology as an integral part of its long-range science and technology development plan. The movement is aimed at motivating a universal desire for scientific innovation among the people in all aspects of their lives. The basic goal of the movement is to reorientate public attitudes. It is not intended to focus attention solely on major scientific or technological advances, but rather on a vast number of small advances made by the people in every segment of society. In all aspects of this movement, the primary emphasis is on rationality, creativity and workability.

CONCLUSION

In striving toward the realization of national goals for industrialization within the context of the global and regional economy, Korea has made substantial achievements—through trial and error—in improving national scientific and technical capabilities, in innovations in its administrative and support systems, and in increasing—as well as orienting—its R&D investment.

The total science and technology effort was intended to effect a structural change in the economy, turning it from a simple labor-intensive one into a more viable technology-intensive structure and, later, into a brain-intensive structure. In other words, these efforts have been directed toward accelerating the transition of sciences and technology's roles from supporting national economic development to leading such development on the foundation of a technologically self-reliant economy.

It is appropriate here to underscore the statement of Stevan Dedijer that positive involvement of the chief executive of a nation in the development of science and technology for economic growth and social development is not merely desirable, but essential for developing countries if they are to develop their science and technology and apply them efficiently to their development.[5] Korea has been most fortunate in the understanding of and support of science and technology by its chief executive.

NOTES

1. Hyung-Sup Choi, *Bases for Science and Technology Promotion in Developing Countries,* Chapter 6 (Tokyo: Asian Productivity Organization, 1983).
2. Maximo Holty Carrere, "Technological Strategies for Developing Countries," paper presented at the Regional Conference on Science and Technology Policy Instruments, Manila, November 1978.
3. Hyung-Sup Choi, *Industrial Research in the Less Developed Countries* (Bangalore, India: The Regional Center for Technology Transfer, ESCAP, 1984).
4. Hyung-Sup Choi, "Science and Technology Policies for Industrialization of Developing Countries," *Technology Forecasting and Social Change* 29:3 (1986).
5. Stevan Dedijer, "Underdeveloped Science in Underdeveloped Countries," *Minerva,* Vol. 1 (1963).

Science and Technology Advice to the President in Mexico

Guillermo Soberón and Graciela Rodriguez

THE UNITED MEXICAN STATES *(Estados Unidos Mexicanos) has been an independent nation since 1810; the federal constitution adopted in 1917 is presently in force. Its land area is 761,600 square miles, and the estimated population in 1989 was 84,460,000. Spanish is the official language.*

Science and technology advice to the President is a brand-new function in Mexico. It was established in January 1989 and, therefore, there is no experience to report. Rather, this discussion will be concerned with perspectives and descriptions of the way this mechanism is being organized and projected.

The approach will be better understood, however, if the situation of science and technology in Mexico in recent years is briefly described.

Science and technology in Mexico started to receive some attention from government in 1960. At that time, the federal government created the National Institute of Scientific Research (INIC), which—while oriented to funding and the promotion of research projects as well as enhancing scientific high-level education—was almost limited to providing scholarships.

In 1970, INIC, through the influence of the scientific community, was transformed into the National Council on Science and Technology (CONACyT). This new agency conserved the financial and scientific promotion functions of the previous organization, but new aspects were introduced.

CONACyT and the Ministry of Budget and Planning (SPP) have been involved in national scientific planning and the promotion of technological de-

Guillermo Soberón is Executive President of the Fundación Mexicana para la Salud and General Coordinator of the Consultative Council of Science. He has served as the Mexican Secretary of Health, Head of the Research Division of the National Institute of Nutrition, and Rector of the University of Mexico. Dr. Soberón received his Ph.D. in physiological chemistry from the University of Wisconsin. He was in charge of a group studying the health system in Mexico for the Presidency, and has been widely published. He was recently elected a Trustee of The Population Council. Dr. Soberón was born in Iguala, Guerrero, Mexico, in 1925.

Graciela Rodriguez has held the posts of Director General of Human Resources for the Presidency of Mexico, Preventive Health Services Official at the Institute of Social and Security Services for Government Employees, and PAHO Consultant on Women's Health. She has served as Chief of the Experimental Psychology Laboratories, Research Coordinator, and Dean of the School of Psychology at the National University of Mexico, and is a member of the university's Council and Board of Governors. Dr. Rodriguez received her doctorate in general experimental psychology from the National University, and is consultant to a number of Mexican and American scientific societies.

velopment. Thus 1970 really is the point at which the federal government showed a definite interest in science and technology, although, previously, scientists had been occasionally consulted about plans and progress related to the furthering of science.

The national interest in scientific and technological development and its relationship to the country's independence were frequently the subjects of political speeches. Before and during the oil economic boom in the late 1970s, however, the idea that scientific expenditure was a luxury was in the minds of many. Furthermore, other groups felt that there was no need to develop technology nationally since Mexico had the money to buy it elsewhere.

THE IMPORTANCE OF S&T

In the year 1981, with the drop in oil prices, the economic crisis that has equally affected other Third World countries began. The enormous burden of external debt was revealed, and, as a consequence, greater concern was placed on science and technology practices. Stress has been placed on the importance of science and technology to economic and social improvement. No longer are scientific and technological activities considered luxury expenditures, but they are, rather, the basis for a middle- or long-term process that is expected to alleviate some of the phenomena that have led to financial difficulties.

Nevertheless, monetary resources for science and technology activity have been strongly reduced, as has much of the federal budget. Financial support to specific projects has been meager and difficult to obtain; scientists' incomes have been affected by the inflationary process (as a matter of fact, the income of scientists has steadily declined over the past few years to near 50% of its 1982 figure); and scholarships have been greatly reduced in number and in size, causing high-level educational opportunities to diminish.

Indeed, the national scientific and technological panorama looks somewhat gloomy. Scientific expenditure is low (0.35% of the Gross National Product), mainly coming from the federal budget. Scientists constitute a small community, which is geographically concentrated in Mexico City where it is easier to find at least minimal conditions for accomplishing their purposes.

Private funding and industrial participation in science and technology development has virtually not existed up until the present time. The social image of science and technology, furthermore, does not allow researchers an important place in the national life of the country.

IMPORTANT ADVANCES

Important advances, however, have been achieved within the past administrations: As mentioned before, science and technology were recognized by the government as important factors that will contribute to the national economic and social development. Also, it has been conceded that scientists need higher incomes in order to continue with their work as well as to diminish the so-called "brain drain." A mechanism has been implemented to provide extrainstitutional economic support to productive scientists by means of special supplementations of their salaries granted through academic evaluation of their work. A mechanism has been established for this called the National System of Researchers, more commonly "SNI" (Sistema Nacional de Investigadores).

Precise requirements must be met to enter this system as well as to remain in it; an annual elevation of each scientist already accepted is carried out in order to confirm the nomination.

Initial efforts have been carried out in order to interest industrial enterprises in scientific and technological potentials and products. Some results have been obtained in this area. Also, private and public non-profit research funding in specific areas, such as the health sciences, has been promoted through particular philanthropic institutions, such as the Fundación Mexicana para la Salud.

SCIENCE AND TECHNOLOGY IN THE NATIONAL DEVELOPMENT PLAN

President Salinas's administration last May presented the National Development Plan for the next six years. The plan's major goals center on promoting Mexico's interests externally, broadening democracy, reaching economic recovery without inflation, and productively improving the standard of living.

These objectives, among others, will be met by means of national modernization, which has as its key element economic growth. Great advances have been made recently on the economic scene; in order to maintain these advances, however, without going into a recessive economy, wide transformations had to occur.

High levels of economic competitiveness must be reached internally as well as on the international level. This can only be accomplished through production efficiency.

Economic modernization implies a public administration that is able to provide high-quality public services, higher levels of external competitiveness in the production apparatus, an economic regulatory system that stimulates private economic activity, better education and job training programs, and the efficient use of national or foreign technologies according to their appropriateness.

In this way, science and technology development is considered to be an important issue in the economic structural changes ahead. The National Development Plan considers that it is urgent to reform the national policy on science and technology, recognizing that this area has been neglected in the past and that this neglect has resulted in the considerable underdevelopment of these activities. It is clearly stated that the strengthening of science and technology is urgent, and must be greatly promoted in the near future in order to support the national economy, especially the international participation of the Mexican economy. Thus future economic growth will depend to a large extent on technological modernization. Scientific and technological activities have different roles in this process. Scientific research is expected to contribute to technological modernization on a long-term basis; meanwhile, technological development will have an immediate impact on production activity.

Both of these areas will be reinforced during the present administration, based on the concept that they are inevitably linked together. There is no technological development without scientific progress, and this cannot be achieved without technical competence.

Out of the National Plan of Development, some twenty-one so-called "midterm programs" have to be formulated. Science and technology is one of these programs. CONACyT is responsible for this particular task, and a Commission for Science and Technology, presided over by SPP and composed of twelve other federal government secretariats, and CONACyT will review and approve it.

The promotion of scientific development will include greater financial support from both public and private sources, which is intended to increase the human and material resources available to this area. Science-oriented education, as well as postgraduate programs, will be reinforced, including the active incorporation of postgraduates into research institutes and scientific production groups.

Highly productive groups will be especially supported, as well as new groups appointed to work on priority areas and projects.

The federal government is also interested in promoting the return of Mexican scientists living abroad through the establishment of incentives that will make it easier for them to join national research groups.

The reinforcement of technological development will include further financial support through public-private cooperative financial efforts in technological areas and closer relationships between technological development institutions and production facilities. Industrial technological modernization will be promoted through financial support.

Another important aspect of the promotion of technological development concerns technical education and training.

Regulation of patent registration and technology transfer must also be modified in order to promote national innovation and help business organizations buy accessible technologies.

THE CONSULTATIVE COUNCIL ON SCIENCE

Federal government structure includes several mechanisms related to the promotion of science and technology, mainly the Ministry of Budget and Planning (SPP), CONACyT, and two major areas at the Ministry of Education. There is also a commission for the furthering of science and technology, presided over by the SPP and composed of twelve ministries and CONACyT.

Scientists, however, have had limited participation in decision-making, since their opinions usually do not reach the highest levels of government.

Considering that scientists can provide useful information and opinions on national matters, particularly in regard to science and technology issues, President Salinas has invited all National Science Award recipients to become members of the Consultative Council on Science (CCC). Having received the award makes a person eligible, but it is up to the individual to accept.

The council was created to directly advise the President on science and technology and related issues, including national priority selection, as well as policies and the mechanisms needed to implement them.

Furthermore, the council members can suggest and eventually undertake specific studies about scientific and technological programs underway or planned for the future.

Finally, the council can convey to the federal Executive the opinions and proposals which have been expressed by those members of the science and technology community who wish to use this conduit. It is clear, however, that the council is not and cannot be representative of the interests of the science and technology community.

The council can establish collaborative relationships between public and private institutions connected with the different aspects of science and technology in the country and abroad, particularly the science-related offices in the federal ministries.

The Consultative Council on Science has fifty-two members at the present time; to function efficiently, the number cannot be smaller than twenty-five. National Science Award recipients become members as soon as they formally accept their memberships in the council. In order to maintain independent opinions about any matters submitted to them, the participation of the members is not remunerated.

THE ORGANIZATION OF THE COUNCIL

A general coordinator is elected by the majority of votes within the membership. This officer holds this position for a three-year period with the possibility of being re-elected once. The general coordinator is in charge of the overall conduct of the council's activities. This does not, however, imply that this officer holds any administrative or hierarchical preeminence over the other councillors. He is the direct link between the council members and the President, and is also the chairman of the council's plenary meetings.

In order to accomplish their tasks, council members decided to create five separate committees to handle different issues, depending upon their nature. In this way, various topics are studied by one or several of the following committees:

- social sciences;
- physics, chemistry and mathematics;

- natural sciences;
- technology; and
- multidisciplinary.

The council has also established temporary or *ad hoc* working groups in order to cover specific demands. At the moment, four groups have been formed. These groups deal with the diagnoses of existing scientific resources and strengthening strategy, human resource formation policy, the establishment of links between the council and the public, private and social mechanisms related to scientific and technological development, and strategies for the dissemination of scientific knowledge.

The councillors may invite other scientific and technical community members who are experts on specific matters to support the tasks of the committees and working groups.

The members are free to withdraw and to re-enter the membership of the council at any time. A formal acceptance or letter of resignation is sufficient to announce their intentions.

Administrative support to the council's activities is provided by the President's office through an executive secretary, who is appointed to this charge by the President himself.

The Consultative Council on Science was legally constituted on January 24, 1989. By May 1989, the first recommendations of the council were presented to the President. It was decided to restrict them to measures whose implementation might be effective in preventing further deterioration of the science and technology capability.

THE PROPOSALS OF THE COUNCIL

The following items were included among the proposals:

- Implementation of a national campaign to explain to the country the importance of scientific and technological research and its great potential in terms of national development.
- Extension (up to three times the present level) of the budget assigned to scientific and technological research activities. In the recent past, many projects did not receive financial support from CONACyT although they were considered to be technically and methodologically adequate.

   The council also recommended that projects be examined by disciplinary committees whose members are acknowledged active scientists.
- Increase the real income of scientific and technological research personnel by increasing the SNI scholarships or by raising the salaries of the academic staffs in the science and technology institutions, and by covering travel expenses related to research activities, including assistance in attending scientific meetings.
- Establishment of a system similar to that already existing for researchers

(SNI) for research technicians and auxiliary personnel, based on excellence criteria of technical activities within research projects. The council also recommended that some mechanisms be designed to stimulate higher education teachers to dedicate part of their time to research activity.

- The councillors considered it to be necessary that the President explicitly instruct Cabinet members and the heads of other government organizations to collaborate in the tasks of the CCC, among other things, by providing all necessary information requested by the council's committees or working groups. For this purpose, the CCC has started to create close and formal relationships with the appropriate areas of the above-mentioned institutions.
- Implementation of tax deduction benefits for scientific and technological researchers, including the purchase of equipment, materials, scientific journals, and books. Tax deduction programs should also be applied to benefit those public or private businesses (industries or services) who give financial support to science and technology development.
- Simplification of import procedures for scientific and technological research information.
- CONACyT must be instructed to promote the participation of scientists and potential "knowledge consumers" (mainly industrials) in the process of the strategic design of scientific research and technological development programs.

All the items on this list need urgent attention, according to the CCC's view. Most of them are oriented toward the immediate stimulation of scientific and technological research, but some of them are necessary conditions for the council's short- and medium-term activities.

The effectiveness of the council's activities in scientific and technological policy determination through assessment for the President is a real possibility. It will be important for the role of the CCC to be consolidated so that some of the already mentioned recommendations on science and technology and others to be formulated in the near future are evaluated and implemented.

"PASTEURIZATION"

Up until August 1989, nothing had yet happened as the result of these efforts. This introduced skepticism among the members of the CCC; a common saying among the research community is that Mexican science and technology have been "pasteurized," because they are periodically warmed up and then cooled. The President himself has emphatically stated that this will not happen during his term, but money is scarce in the country.

The President has expressed the view that the CCC recommendations should be taken up in the context of the science and technology mid-term program. Accordingly, the general coordinator of the CCC has been invited to participate in the commission presided over by the SPP that will review the draft of the mid-term science and technology programs prepared by CONACyT.

During 1989, the CCC decided to carry out the following activities:

- Identify priority research areas through the study of the state of the art of each discipline and thus detect the major limitations affecting them. At the same time, the council must estimate the size of the financial resources required to solve the most urgent problems. In this way, the council can establish an overall diagnosis of the science and technology research activities, mainly by consulting the various sources of information that already exist and analyzing their findings.
- Design project evaluation models and criteria in order to have objective bases for resource allocation.
- Propose various mechanisms for improving the capabilities of scientific and technological personnel.
- Establish a permanent dialogue with both the institutions producing and those consuming science and technology knowledge, particularly those related to production activity.
- Establish appropriate criteria to evaluate the science and technology promotion efforts that have been carried out in the past.
- Study and propose mechanisms that can stimulate public, social and private investment in science and technology development.
- Appraise the different science and technology policies formulated in the country with the idea of collecting relevant information to improve science and technology policy design in Mexico.

CONCLUSION

In short, the situation is still uncertain as to the feasibility of a ''turn for the good'' with respect to the encouragement of science and technology. On one hand, there is no question that the President means well and will do everything within his power; on the other, the shortage of money is a definite obstacle.

Recent negotiation of the external debt offers a ray of hope, and it should not be forgotten that science and technology development is a powerful tool for helping the country reach a higher standard of living.

It is strongly felt that, through the opinions and the recommendations of CCC's scientists to the President of Mexico, a supportive policy could be formulated, one that is oriented toward expanding scientific and technological activity and can link it to economic and social development.

In the medium and long terms, the country would benefit from the efficient application of scientific knowledge and technical development, and find the solution to problems that, at the present time, pose serious difficulties for such programs.

Science Advising to the Government in The Netherlands

Hendrik G. van Bueren

THE KINGDOM OF THE NETHERLANDS *(Koninkrijk der Nederlanden) has been a constitutional monarchy since 1814, and operates under a multiparty parliamentary system. Its land area is 13,103 square miles, and the 1989 estimated population was 14,859,000. Dutch is the official language. As of December 31, 1989, the US dollar was equal to 1.91 guilders (florin).*

External advice to the government, preferably by experts, constitutes an essential component of any democratic national science and technology policy system. The Netherlands' system is no exception to this. Indeed, as was pointed out by Stuart Blume in a report[1] to the Dutch Advisory Council for Science Policy (RAWB), in most OECD countries, advising stood at the root of actual policy-making.

In the 1950s and 1960s, science policy advisory bodies were established in several countries with the explicit aim of preparing the way for national science policies. In The Netherlands, an independent council of experts in various branches of science and technology (RAWB) was established in 1966. This council was soon to be followed by an interdeparmental committee (IOW), made up of civil servants who were charged with providing the government response to the propositions of the RAWB and were to help with the preparation of a national science budget. In 1972, the first minister charged explicitly with science policy was included in the Cabinet (without a budget of his own, though).

In the first few euphoric years of its existence, the RAWB made a great many suggestions as to how Dutch science policy should be developed and run. It thereby concentrated on the concepts of a coordinated national science policy, a flexible fund for governmental research, and the great significance of basic research at the universities (which the council then considered to be in an unsatisfactory state).

Later, when the euphoria had vanished and made room for political realism, the first Ministerial Report on Science Policy appeared (Nota Wetenschapsbel-

Hendrik G. van Bueren is former Chairman of the Advisory Committee for Science Policy in The Netherlands, and has served as Chairman of that country's Scientific Council on Nuclear Affairs and Committee on Nuclear Fusion. A former research scientist at the Philips Laboratories, he studied astronomy at Utrecht and Leyden, and holds a doctorate in solid state physics from the latter university. Born in Rotterdam in 1925, Dr. van Bueren is a former Professor of material physics and Scientific Director of the Nuclear Reactor Institute at Delft and Professor of astrophysics at Utrecht.

eid, 1974). In it, political support was requested (and obtained) for the so-called coordination model after the Canadian example. In that model, the Minister for Science Policy himself has hardly any money to spend. His task mainly consists of coordinating, by persuasion, the various departmental plans, programs and budgets on science matters in such a way that one coherent national science policy is created, with an accompanying budget to which the relevant departments contribute in proportion to their efforts. This is called the Homogeneous Expenditure Group (HUG).

From then on, the government and the RAWB went their separate ways. The latter gradually developed from mainly an inspirator to, rather, a critical companion of the former. The RAWB never had much faith in the coordination model, but gave it the benefit of the doubt until it was clear that it did not want to subject their own science and technology activities to the approbation of another minister and, therefore, HUG became only nominally a national science budget. *De facto*, it was just the sum of a number of individual budgets which took an inordinate amount of time to add up. The Dutch Constitution does not provide for such a far-reaching limitation of departmental competence and independence.

THE PRESENT BUDGET

The present situation, which evolved from developments over a number of years, is that the minister charged with science policy (who is no longer a separate individual, but the Minister for Science and Education, who disposes of an enormous budget for his many tasks) still prepares a national science budget (WB) every year, reviewing and commenting on the planned expenditures of all relevant departmental budgets, except that for technology. This latter is described in a separate document, the Technology Policy Review (BOT), for which the Minister of Economic Affairs is responsible. The RAWB publishes its annual report in which it comments on the state of the art of the moment, and these three documents form the input for the yearly parliamentary debate on science and technology policy.

This situation is not entirely satisfactory. Whereas the WB contains much material on the departmental plans and interesting considerations on the aims and goals toward which Dutch science can be put to good use politically—such as development aid or environmental protection—technology plans proper are—rather artificially—left to the BOT.

This is the consequence of a split in responsibilities: the separate Minister for Science Policy has disappeared and his portfolio has been passed on to the Minister of Science, but technology policy was removed first and transferred to the Minister of Economic Affairs, who has now been saddled with the task of coordinating it. The separation of science and technology illustrates, on the one hand, the demise of the original optimistic hopes for an all-embracing national science policy—of which technology forms a natural part—and, on the other, the growing emphasis in The Netherlands on the economic component of science policy in general. In fact, it marked the beginning of a new era: that of market-oriented science policy.

This way of political thinking, introduced in 1982 with the coming of the Cabinet that proudly calls itself a "no nonsense Cabinet," has since involved not only science policy, but also scientific thinking in general in The Netherlands. Managing and planning have made their entries into the universities and other scientific organizations, and seem to be there to stay.

The RAWB is soon to be dissolved and will be succeeded by an Advisory Council for Science and Technology (AWT), which will put much more emphasis on the market aspects of advisory work. Its advice will no longer be directed to the whole Cabinet, but to the two responsible ministers mentioned above.

Science Budget and BOT will form the main input components for the new council to comment upon, and this commentary will probably be much more project-oriented in style than that of the present RAWB, which aimed primarily at in-depth studies and analyses of the parts of the research system, with emphasis on long-term development, and did not, properly, comment on WB and BOT, but on the course of government science policy in general.

"CULTURAL SCIENCE"

The advisory function for "cultural science" has, in the past been divided between the RAWB and the much older Royal Dutch Academy of Sciences, which, in general, have worked well together. Since the academy presides over only a small secretarial office and most of its members are primarily interested in science and abhor politics, the political role of the academy has, thus far, been mainly symbolic.

Recently, however, the academy's secretariat has been reinforced and its political significance as a national advisory body has been once more underscored. It is to be hoped that these developments will ultimately lead to a cultural compensation in the increasingly more economics-oriented Dutch science policy. In order to carry out its task effectively, though—also in another and equally important direction, *i.e.,* the evaluation and promotion of the intrinsic quality of Dutch science—a complete functional reorganization of the present old-fashioned structure of the academy is going to be required. It is not clear at the present time whether the academy, as an organization proud of its independence, will easily submit to this requirement.

A third advisory council which has to do, if only obliquely, with matters of science is the Scientific Council for Government Policy (WRR). This provides the Cabinet with the scientific background of its future policy-making in the form of lengthy studies and background reports of civil and political interest. The reports are mostly aimed at analyses of social and industrial developments,

Figure 1. Advisory Structure of The Netherlands Government

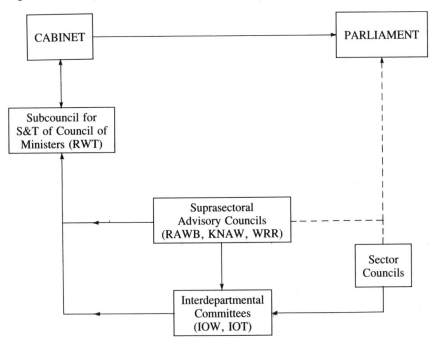

such as employment and labor, minorities, housing, and the future of technology in today's complex society.

These reports receive much attention from politicians, social scientists, and economists. In the immediate implementation of the present science and technology policy, they are of lesser significance. The structure of the WRR resembles that of the RAWB: a fairly small council of experts aided by a competent staff of scientific collaborators who carry out much of the groundwork and the writing.

The three advisory organizations mentioned together provide the government of The Netherlands with advice from the highest levels on science and technology (see Figure 1). Before discussing the procedures by which the recommendations are discussed and implemented (or not), it is necessary to consider the system and the structure in which Dutch research is actually carried out.

In The Netherlands, much political effort is expended on maintaining this small country's favorable position among the vanguard of the highly developed, technologically advanced, and economically prosperous nations of the world. This had strong effects in recent times on the executive organs of (governmental) science. These are, first, the independent state universities and connected research institutes. Next, there is The Netherlands Research Organization (NWO), which subsidizes fundamental and "strategic" research projects and programs and also maintains by itself a number of research institutes.

Figure 2. Research Funds in The Netherlands*

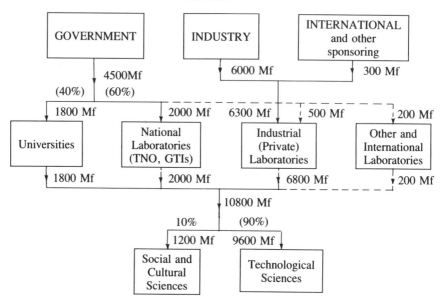

*Total: f9000 million guilders in 1989

NWO works closely with the universities, especially in providing personal research grants, which, these days, have been extended to all sorts of applied research also.

For the latter, there exists also a number of quasi-independent national research institutes (GTIs) that carry out applied research on demand, and the organization for Applied Scientific Research (TNO), which operates thirty-five institutes in all possible fields of applied science. This picture is completed by thirty or so agricultural research institutes constituting the departmental organization for agricultural research (DLO) and a number of other research laboratories belonging directly to other individual ministries, such as the National Institute for Health and Environmental Research (RIVM).

GTIs and TNO, as well as DLO, work partly on a commercial basis. NWO is, as yet, fully government subsidized, and RIVM works mostly on government contracts; together, they employ about 15,000 workers, one-third of whom are graduates, and they cost the state about two billion guilders a year, about as much as is spent on university research (see Figure 2). All these organizations should be mentioned because they all perform in a more or less legalized way some advisory functions to the government, and they are all immediately affected in the execution of their research by the policy vagaries of the government.

The most striking phenomenon resulting from the latter influence is, again, the strong emphasis on market-oriented research that the government compels the institutions to yield to. TNO, as well as the universities, is prone to it nor do any of the other organizations escape the pressure. In simple words, the current science-political attitude in the country toward research organizations tells them to earn as much as they can *themselves* of the money they need for their research.

In practice, the responsible ministries have severely pinched basic subsidies which were meant to promote the long-term basic research to support the applied research. The result of this has been that even the most fundamentally oriented institutes have to do their best to obtain contracts on a necessarily short-time market. This national short-term science policy is stressed politically by the presumed economic need of society for continuing technological innovation and the necessity for Dutch science to participate in as many of the fields as possible that contribute to the development of new and technologically advanced applications. Only in this way does the government consider it feasible for Dutch industry to remain internationally competitive.

The prospect of a "Europe without frontiers" serves only to intensify the foregoing opinion. Whether or not such considerations are valid in theory, it should be realized that the present urgency to serve the needs of marketable technology is, in practice, more or less dictated by the political need felt by the government to economize on its own expenses! That long-term basic research suffers disastrously under such a policy, in the institutes as well as in the "enterprising universities" (as some of them proudly call themselves), and that this has economic consequences, too, nowadays appears to be slowly being recognized again by politicians (and, consequently, a shift of emphasis back to fundamental research is to be expected sooner or later).

OMINOUS PROSPECTS

The prospects of such a strongly market-oriented science policy—equally opposed by the academy, WRR and RAWB—are ominous. The universities tend to neglect their primary tasks to educate scientists and the cultural vanguard and to perform free basic research. They increasingly favor brief professional education schemes instead and prefer contract research. In this way, the students may learn ingenuity and commercial alertness, but they do not become scientists.

TNO and most other national institutes have quickly learned how to provide for more than half their budgets from commissioned research, but this is what they were meant to do in the first place. It can thus be considered a healthy development that keeps the institutes away from private hobbyism. But what to say of equally subsidized departmental institutes, national institutes, TNO and universities, all competing in the same short-term private market?

The principal profiteer from a good climate for science and technology is, of course, industry. In The Netherlands, the peculiar circumstance prevails that five very large and about as many moderately large multinational companies dominate the industrial scene. They all have their main research laboratories in this country. All the complicated, very advanced applied research and most of the basic research that goes with it that are required by these companies are carried out by their own laboratories. The only support they need from the government in this respect is that good care is taken to educate the many clever scientists that they will need now and in the future.

For the actual science and, in particular, the applied science that is produced within the national organizations, they have little use and, consequently, little interest; it is scientists they want, not science (other than fundamental science).

If, therefore, the Dutch government stimulates the production of applied science and technology results and even products within the universities at the expense of long-term basic science and the education of excellent researchers, this is not in accord with the requirements of the multinationals. The effort is certainly more useful to the smaller Dutch enterprises that, on the whole, are not very research-minded. Indeed, Dutch technology policy of the moment is clearly aimed at fostering the national economy in terms of helping the medium-sized and small businesses. A very difficult step on this road is, of course, the transfer of knowledge from research institute or university to a firm, followed by its implementation as a new product.

It is, therefore, not surprising that the Dutch Ministry of Economic Affairs has for many years laid heavy stress on the solving of the many problems related to the "diffusion of science." Indeed, much of the science and technology policy of the 1980s is devoted toward this end, as is clear from the agendas of the meetings of committees like that for Science and Technology Policy of the OECD.

Meanwhile, the research climate for the large multinationals does not improve with the decreasing standards of university education in the country, and one can observe another percolative process gradually getting underway: the shifting of the research activities of the multinationals to other countries, for instance, the newly industrialized nations in the Far East. True, the shift is not yet very significant, but the evidence of it sheds doubt on the infallibility of the Dutch technology policy priorities, given the actual Dutch situation.

THE INTERNATIONAL SCENE

In order to prevent misunderstanding, it is necessary to say a few words about the international dimension of science, which is so important to a small country like The Netherlands.

First, the many multinationals already mentioned play an important role in maintaining the bond between Dutch and international technology progress. Participation by these multinationals in bilateral, as well as multilateral (precompetitive) research and development agreements—notably in the framework of the European Community—is much favored by the Dutch government and strongly supported, either financially or otherwise. Although not all multinationals appreciate such support, it nevertheless forms an equilibrating counterpart to the national small-business line mentioned earlier.

The prospect of a Europe without frontiers after 1992 gives the economic politicians much reason for concern. Will The Netherlands be able to keep a reasonable share of the European technological effort in their own hands with so many freely competing, but much larger countries? Is specialization necessary and, if so, on which domains of technology should The Netherlands concentrate? Will the Dutch institutes for applied research maintain a share of the European contract? Will they be able to compete in quality? And what about the universities: their students and their graduates? The Dutch reputation for sound quality in education is at stake and will be severely tested.

The Minister for Science and Education has recently published a white paper on the intended science policy of the 1990s, in which the "international question" figures conspicuously. (Other notable discussion themes are science in the complex modern society and science and technology in private and public frameworks.) This paper is to be discussed under the auspices of the RAWB in as broad a forum as possible of research workers, civil servants, and users of science. The outcome of the discussion will be implemented in the form of a second Ministerial Report on Science Policy (Tweede Nota Wetenschapsbeleid) that will appear in 1990.

In the meantime, The Netherlands scientists and especially the national institutes and TNO are preparing themselves for the coming situation by participating as much as they can in Community activities in science and technology. In particular, the Dutch contributions to biotechnology, informatics and agricultural research must be noted. It is found, however, that, among university scientists, the awareness of the various European Community opportunities is still regrettably low.

Much scientific attention is traditionally given in The Netherlands to hydrotechnological and agricultural research, both considered to be of use to developing nations. In both, Dutch scientists enjoy good reputations. It is remarkable that these fields are nearly exclusively managed by self-contained small governmental organizations: the DLO mentioned earlier and the National Hydrographic Department (Rijkwaterstaat), a rather independent division of the Ministry for Transport. Might this mean that, in a small country like The Netherlands, national political arrangements in science are less efficient than self-grown specialized units where internationally competitive research is concerned?

CONCLUSION

This discussion is concentrated on the highest level of science policy advising in The Netherlands. Therefore, there has been no description of the lower echelons, such as, for instance, the typically Dutch construction of sector councils. These are advisory bodies based on the three-party concept: Members are scientists, civil servants, and potential users of the relevant science, respectively.

At the moment, five such councils exist (*e.g.*, for environmental research), which report to their respective ministries about concrete research projects in the form of annual review reports. Their advice is strictly limited to their own sectors of scientific application.

The RAWB hopes that the system of sector councils will ultimately develop into the infrastructure of a system of departmental science coordinators, which together will constitute a kind of national applied research council, something that does not yet exist in The Netherlands (not any more than a national university council). Such a system might make the IOW superfluous. For the positions of the sector councils in the system, see Figure 2.

The Dutch Parliament sadly lacks regular means through which it can obtain high-level advice on science policy. Before the annual debate on the subject, the RAWB is invited to present its views in a parliamentary hearing session. Political interest in this sort of policy is rather low and confined to the few tens of Parliament members who have active scientific backgrounds of some sort.

Therefore, science policy is somewhat neglected terrain, certainly when compared with economic or health politics to which science and technology contribute so much! This situation is to be deplored, but it differs little from that in other western countries. It should be realized, however, that, if a government wishes to use science and technology on an extensive scale for political purposes—be they economic or military, then the public discussion of such plans had better be equally extensive. The general neglect of science politics as an important instrument in decision-making has, until now, been a nuisance, but may well soon become a danger. One cannot direct a technological society without appropriate attention to the ins and outs of its driving force. This does not apply only to the situation in The Netherlands!

For one section of science policy only, political attention is usually considerable: the public acceptability of science. Technology assessment of and public information and instruction about the ever more powerful products of science and technology and the eventual protection against their consequences have received much political attention recently. Fear provokes better than admiration.

In The Netherlands, an independent advisory organization for technology assessment (NOTA) has been established by the government and is working well. Public information about the progress of science, so popular in other countries, leaves much to be desired, however. No "interactive" science museums exist nor is there a serious science park to be found in the country. This is regrettable, because the lack of political interest in science and its consequences rests, in large part, on unfamiliarity with it.

Contacts between science policy makers, government executives, and advisers is better than that between the latter and Parliament. The chairmen of the RAWB and of the WRR are members of a ministerial subcouncil on science and technology (RWT) and can, therefore, vent the opinions of their organizations directly to the ministerial level. The chairmen of the three main advisory bodies are regularly invited to provide ministers with advice on special problems, mostly related to priorities in the financing of science.

Finally, these bodies are increasingly made use of by the relevant ministers to disseminate new political concepts having to do with science in the scientific world and to incite discussion on them, to evaluate the state of research in specific fields, and even to organize public debates on science policy.

All in all, the situation with respect to science and technology policy in The Netherlands gives cause for hope and for fear: fear, because after more than a quarter century of science policy, this is still a politically neglected subject, and big chunks of it are now and then chopped off and absorbed by other sectors of politics as soon as their political significance becomes obvious. Moreover, it is to be deplored that the scientists themselves have not yet been convinced of the importance of science policy, however tiresome it may appear to them. The science advisory organs have still to produce the necessary enlightenment here.

As far as hope is concerned, there are signs that the relevance of science policy is being increasingly recognized by at least the executive levels of government. This process has accelerated with the approach of the "Europeanization" of the national economies in this part of the world and the realization that the "technological society" has begun in earnest and is here to stay. It is to be hoped that the one-sided emphasis on the economic aspects of science and technology, so characteristic of the present Dutch situation (and not only of the Dutch), will soon be widened to include political attention to the "cultural" aspects in a comparable manner. Science and technology are of much more relevance to society than as only economic factors.

NOTE

1. S. Blume *et al.,* "The Development of Dutch Science Policy in International Perspective, 1965–1985," RAWB Background Studies Series, no. 14 (December 1985).

Concerning Research Policy Advisory Functions in Norway

Francis Sejersted

THE KINGDOM OF NORWAY *(Kongeriket Norge) has been operating as a constitutional monarchy since 1905 under a multiparty parliamentary system. The land area of the country is 149,282 square miles, and its estimated population in 1989 was 4,236,000. The official language is Norwegian.*

Norway is, at present, the only country in the OECD region that does not have an independent central agency for advising the government on questions of research policy. This is hardly a field where one should swim against the tide. At a time when the importance of research is increasing faster than ever before, the importance of good research policy is growing with it. But research policy is difficult, with conflicting priorities and uncertainty as to the best organizational solutions.

The absence in Norway—since February 1988—of any advisory body of this type is, first and foremost, a reflection of a serious crisis in the field, although that would seem to be precisely the kind of situation in which such a body would be needed. Experience has shown, however, how difficult it is to build up an advisory service which can satisfy all needs. There may, indeed, be no truly satisfactory model. In a situation of extreme uncertainty, it seems—paradoxically enough—as if the very problems themselves make it difficult to establish any agency at all.

Three types of problems, familiar enough to anyone with experience in research policy, appear to have led to the present policy deadlock in Norway. One is that fundamental uncertainty makes it difficult to listen to advice; coordinated advice, in such a situation, can create the impression that policy is being dictated to the political authorities from the outside. For advice to serve its purpose calls for a certain level of competence on the part of those receiving it. The Ministry of Cultural and Scientific Affairs may have seen a threat in an independent science policy council.

This is accentuated by the second problem, which is that any body offering advice on research policy is bound to appear, to some extent, to be representing special research interests. It is difficult to imagine completely independent ad-

Francis Sejersted served as Chairman of the Norwegian Science Policy Council from 1983 to 1988, and is a Professor in economic and social history at Oslo University. Born in 1936, he has been Chairman of the Scandinavian Association for Economic and Social History (1979–1982), and member of the Nobel Peace Prize Committee (1982–   ). Dr. Sejersted has also been a member of the Norwegian Academy of Sciences since 1976 and has been widely published.

vice. In a situation marked by a vague faith in the importance of research, combined with a high degree of uncertainty as to strategy, there can be considerable scope for special research interests. One way of preventing these, in the short term, from having too much play is to discontinue systematic advice altogether. It is not inconceivable that the Ministry of Finance may have lent its support from such motives.

The third problem is of a different nature, although just as familiar in research policy as the other two. This is the tension between sector interests and the need to coordinate research. In Norway, the responsibility for coordination has lain with the Ministry of Cultural and Scientific Affairs. The Science Policy Council, which was abolished in 1988, was established under that ministry, whose minister was, at the same time, the Chairman of the Cabinet Research Board. Ministries responsible for special sectors and, especially, the important Ministry of Industry, may find their interests best served by undermining the science ministry's efforts at coordination. Such special interests, too, have more elbow room when uncertainty is rife.

Pressure from sector interests, in all probability, played an important part in the decision to discontinue the Science Policy Council. One natural consequence of its abolition was a reduction in the authority of the Ministry of Cultural and Scientific Affairs as the coordinating agency in research questions. The absence of any coordinating authority in research policy is probably just as questionable as the absence of systematic advice at the highest level of the government.

THE ORGANIZATION OF RESEARCH

Since World War II, the organization of Norwegian research has, on the whole, developed along the same lines as in other OECD countries. Research councils and a number of institutes of applied research were established relatively soon after the war. This was the result not of overall planning, but of a number of relatively independent ventures in separate sectors. Behind them, there was, generally speaking, a new faith in the importance of research to the development of society. Such general faith in the significance of research, however, still falls a long way short of the systematic utilization of research in the various sectors. In the Norwegian context, this can be illustrated by pointing to the two closely interrelated features.

Consisting mainly of small enterprises, Norwegian industry is not research-intensive. The many measures aimed at strengthening industrial research after the war largely originated outside the industrial sector. That meant, for one thing, that the research councils, notably the Council for Scientific and Industrial Research, acquired a "push" function in relation to industry. There was only a limited need for research funding: The demand had to be created. One can see from this the fact that, until well into the 1980s, more public than private funding went into Norwegian research.

Besides, a large protection of the public money for industrial research went to more or less independent semi-public research institutes, which were to play a very important part. This unusual structure—with "autonomous" research institutes in the intermediate zone between the public and the private spheres—thus reflects the predominance of the "push" element in Norwegian applied research.

The second feature is that the public sector, too, failed to coordinate research policy with industrial policy. The public sector invested considerable amounts of money in Norwegian industry after the war, but the investments were not geared to research-based industries. At the same time that the government was investing in the development of new technologies for industry, it was itself investing in old technology.

So, whereas the system was marked by a general belief in the importance of research to modern society, it proved difficult in particular cases to win support for the application of research as an instrument in specific sectors. To put it differently, society's long-term objectives called for more research, while research was difficult to realize in the short-term. And, in a structure consisting of many small units in industry and with a public administration divided into many sectors, short-term objectives carried more weight.

A SECOND BREAKTHROUGH

In the 1960s, there was what amounted to a second breakthrough for the importance of research to the development of society. The OECD played a major part in it, especially in raising levels of research policy awareness. The Piganiol Report, published by the OECD in 1963, recommended the establishment by every country of a central agency to evaluate and advise on research policy.

Under the direct influence of this report, Norway set up a Central Committee for Norwegian Research and the Cabinet Research Board. The former consisted chiefly of researchers, especially from the universities, and the latter exclusively of politicians. The idea of a mixed body was considered, but rejected. Mixed committees are, on the whole, foreign to the Norway Administration. When the question arose as to whether the Central Committee's secretariat should be in the central government administration or independent, the latter course was chosen.

The new Central Committee thus found itself working at arm's length from both the political leadership and the administration. Such independence can be an advantage, provided one has sufficient authority to make oneself heard, but can also lead to isolation.

In 1971, the Central Committee proposed that a separate ministry be established for research, but this was turned down by the Bratteli government, which emphasized that individual ministries would retain the responsibility for research in their respective sectors—underlining the sector principle. Generally speaking, the new advisory organization established in 1965 cannot be said to have resulted in improved coordination of public investments in Norwegian R&D.

Sector interests are traditionally very strong in the Norwegian Administration. The Central Committee did become relatively isolated, and lacked the real authority required to coordinate the Norwegian research effort.

The 1980s have seen increased investment in research by both the public and the private sector, and a corresponding increase in the attention that is being paid to research policy. In 1982, the government asked that OECD carry out a review of Norway's research policy (as it had done in 1969). The report was highly critical. One of its main points was that, despite the large numbers of research policy reports and studies, little ability had been demonstrated in following up proposals in practice.

In 1982, the Central Committee was reorganized and given a more appropriate name: "the Science Policy Council." The terms of reference were not very different from those of the former Central Committee, but the reorganization did indicate that the government wanted to make a more systematic use of the council than it had of the Central Committee. Until the change of government in 1986, the practice of inviting the chairman of the council to attend meetings of the Cabinet Research Board was also adopted.

There appears to be agreement that the Research Policy Council worked well in the years after 1982. Numerous initiatives were launched, the most important being the establishment of target sectors for research. The general trend has been to organize sector research in large programs. The establishment of a separate Research Council for Applied Social Sciences was important in that connection. There was also a breakthrough for participation in international research programs.

The council carried out an evaluation of the institute system, and took steps aimed at improving its structure. It became an advocate for greater emphasis on basic research and of regarding science also as a culture. One result of the latter approach was the designation of the mediation of culture and traditions as a separate target sector.

The council also insisted that the university system be put on the agenda. In a society where demand for research was steadily increasing, the university system was, paradoxically, running into difficulties. This problem was widespread, as can be seen in OECD's 1987 report, *Universities Under Scrutiny*. The council proposed that its terms of reference be extended to research and higher education. The government responded favorably. An *ad hoc* committee (the Hernes Committee) was appointed to study the system of higher education and propose reforms. Its report attracted a great deal of attention and paved the way for several reforms. The committee also supported a wider mandate for a permanent Science Policy Council. The outcome, as indicated to begin with, was the opposite: The council was abolished.

THE ADVANTAGES OF THE COUNCIL

Since 1982, the most important work of the Science Policy Council had been not the more spectacular initiatives mentioned above, but the day-to-day contacts with political leaders. One very important element was the proposal that it submitted every January concerning the following year's research budget, which was sometimes followed up at meetings between council members and political representatives in connection with concluding budget preparations. The council's proposals carried considerable weight. What was equally important, however, was that the contacts that the council achieved with the political leadership at a number of more informal meetings of a generally informative nature helped to raise the level of awareness of research policy among politicians. A forum began to take shape in which the politicians in charge could discuss general questions of research policy.

It is important for such discussions to take place with a responsible council, which is obliged to base its advice on overall considerations. No government is ever short of advice, but, unless the advisory structure has had certain general considerations and obligations built into it, it can be difficult to know which advice to listen to. Having too many or too few councils both can give headaches to the authorities.

Along with its contacts with political leaders, the Science Policy Council also attached great importance to developing contacts with the whole of the research system, so as to be able to communicate its needs and moods. To function well, a system must give the impression that the advice being given is both informed and coordinated. A science policy council ought to be capable of functioning as a confidence-building intermediary between the research system and the political authorities. There were signs that some progress had been made in that direction beginning in 1983.

When a labor government replaced the nonsocialist government in 1986, contacts with the political authorities became more difficult. No members of the council were replaced. The ensuing loss of contacts must have been the beginning of the end for the council. Officially, it was an apolitical agency, in accordance with Norwegian administrative principles. In practice, however, the chairmanship had been a semi-political appointment. The situation reveals how vulnerable contacts with political authorities can be, at least, when they rest on such insecure governmental foundations. Political and also perhaps personal confidence between the council chairman and the minister can have an important impact on how well the council functions.

THE RESEARCH POLICY DILEMMA

The preparation of research budgets brought the Science Policy Council face to face with the classic research policy dilemma: whether research funds ought to be distributed centrally or by sector. In a system of centrally allocated funds, limits are set on the total research budget, and funds are then allocated within those limits. A relatively large allocation to one sector means a smaller one to another sector. Distribution by sector, on the other hand, means that research as an instrument within a given sector has to compete with other expenditures in that sector.

During the Science Policy Council's period of operation, research was definitely centrally financed, inasmuch as the point of departure was a given total amount in the research budget for distribution to sectors. The council warned against this system on several occasions, but it remained unchanged throughout the period.

It needs to be borne in mind, however, that the adoption of such a procedure does not, in itself, necessarily imply that the distribution of resources will be strictly coordinated in accordance with an overall evaluation. The preparation of a research budget can resemble a tug of war between strong sector interests, and that was, to some extent, what took place. The tendency on the part of sectors to compete for each other's research funds was the regrettable aspect of the attempt to conduct a coordinated research policy, but did not mean that the efforts to achieve coordination had been without significance.

It is necessary in any system of research policy to weigh the need for coordination against the need of each sector to relate its research to its other activities. It is important to strike a balance between the two principles. That, in itself, is difficult enough, and calls for skill on the part of the advisory body; and, as mentioned, the Science Policy Council did advise against excessive coordination. A central advisory agency is not synonymous with strong central coordination. On the contrary, a healthy balance between the two principles depends on good overall advice.

It is clear today that the establishment of the Science Policy Council in 1982 and the general attempt to improve coordination were closely related to a general increase in research resources. In a situation where an overall and long-term policy makes it desirable to promote research as an instrument across a broad front, it is natural to give preference to a more centralized system. One of the main points, which was made as long ago as 1971 in the influential Brooks Report, published by OECD, was that there is a tendency in the sector system to disregard long-term goals in favor of short-term ones.

As it turned out, the activities of the Science Policy Council were mainly directed at long-term objectives. Short-term goals would, in any case, be catered to by the vigorous agencies of the respective sectors. Most of the new target sectors span a number of areas, and considerable competence in coordination was required to bring them into existence. The research councils, three of which represent distinct sectors, would not have been able to realize programs of that type.

The strongest argument in favor of coordination may be that, in a system so marked by its division into sectors, basic research, too, can come to be regarded as the responsibility of a separate factor. It was not merely because it included a majority of university people that the Science Policy Council so strongly stressed the importance of basic research, the universities, the recruitment of scientists, and science in its cultural and not merely its instrumental aspect. The main reason was that it found it necessary, in taking an overall view, to compensate for the lack of support for basic research among sectoral bodies. An advisory body has to learn to play by the rules of the political game. In other words, it must take an overall view, adjust imbalances, and defend those legitimate interests which have difficulty in gaining a hearing in a sectoral system. The outcome, however, was that strong sectoral agencies made it difficult to win the necessary support for basic research and a general build-up of competence. The council, therefore, adopted an alternative strategy.

THE FINAL REPORT

The last report issued by the council states that the sector agencies must, to a greater extent than before, *themselves* assume the ultimate responsibility for building up basic competence in their respective sectors. They must find ways of taking their shares of responsibility for fundamental training and for the institutions of basic research. This strategy appears to have produced some results. Universities and research training have been given prominent places on the research policy agenda, despite the slight coordination possible in the present situation.

The responsibility of the sectors for basic research and for building up competence has also been emphasized in the government's 1989 Report to the Storting (Parliament) on research. This can be seen either as reflecting a traditionally favorable attitude to the sector model or as a second-best alternative in a system which makes coordination difficult.

It can be argued that the relatively sharp increase in research funds during the 1980s and the number of organizational measures adopted during those same years called for a period of institutional consolidation. If so, that would mean evaluating the measures with a view to adjusting them if necessary. A number of evaluations have begun, some on the initiative of the Science Policy Council before it was abolished. Such a process would mean setting grand visions aside in order to concentrate on getting the existing system to work as well as possible. During such a phase, a relatively large share of responsibility would devolve on the intermediate-level bodies, chiefly the research councils, and relatively less on the top-level institutions. Such steps would have been reasonable and understandable.

What has happened, however, is that the government, in the very report in which it abolishes the Science Policy Council for good, gives notice of a radical restructuring of the research council system, with no indication of the kind of structure that is intended to replace it. This confronts the country, for one thing, with the paradox that, at a time of changes intended to be so sweeping that even the advisory bodies are to be reformed, there will be no advisory bodies. For another, the signals transmitted have created a high degree of uncertainty at every level of the system. Foundations had been laid for rational research policies. The latest report on research has demolished them. The situation is wide open, and the outlook for the 1990s is unsettled.

Science and Technology Advising and Policy Formulation in Pakistan

M. A. Kazi

THE ISLAMIC REPUBLIC OF PAKISTAN *(Islami Jamhuria-e-Pakistan) has been independent since 1947 and withdrew from the Commonwealth of Nations in 1972. It was established as a republic in 1956, and operates under a constitution adopted in 1985. The land area of the country is 310,402 square miles, and the population was estimated at 108,683,000 in 1989. The official language of the country is Urdu.*

The history of scientific and technological effort in Pakistan has been a story of both successes and failures. On one hand, the science and technology system of the country has produced well-trained and qualified manpower, which today not only provides key personnel for research and industry within the country, but also participates in the development of other friendly countries. On the other hand, the system has not succeeded effectively in translating the ongoing science and technology (S&T) effort into lasting socioeconomic gains for the country. Successive governments in the past have tried to place increasing emphasis on science and technology and, consequently, there has been visible growth in the S&T sector, but this effort has lacked the momentum and speed so vital for any emerging country in the early stages of its development.

At the time of its independence, Pakistan received a very meager heritage in terms of scientific and technological institutions and manpower. The major S&T institutions were located in other parts of the subcontinent. Pakistan had to start from scratch, and new institutions had to be established and the necessary manpower trained to man these institutions. A concerted effort has been made during the forty years since independence and, as a result, Pakistan's scientific and technological effort has steadily grown and progressed despite many difficulties and constraints that were faced from time to time.

Pakistan is a development country. It is passionately devoted to the development of its resources and the advancement and welfare of its people. Its

M. A. Kazi, born in 1928, is a former adviser to the President and Prime Minister on science and technology (1980–88), and has been President of the Pakistan Academy of Sciences (1984–88), Chairman of the Pakistan Council for Science and Technology (1980–88), Chairman of the University Grants Commission (1973–79), and President of the Pakistan Chemical Society (1978–present). He is the President of the Islamic Academy of Sciences and Coordinator General of COMSTECH, the Organization of Islamic Conference Committee on Scientific and Technological Cooperation in the Islamic World. Earlier, Dr. Kazi was Merit Professor of chemistry at the University of Sind (1955–72). He has also been a member of the United Nations Advisory Committee on Science and Technology (1984–89). His chief interests are science education and science policy formulation and management.

goals for national development clearly warrant an extensive and sustained use of science and technology in its development process. Although the basic infrastructure for science and technology is available in Pakistan, it is neither large enough nor strong enough to bring about the much-cherished scientific and technological revolution in the country.

Pakistan, therefore, needs a strong base of science and technology to solve its problems of food and shelter, fuel and energy, health and population, exploitation of mineral resources, boosting of agricultural and industrial production and, above all, problems arising from the defense needs of the country. Fortunately, there is considerable realization at the decision-making level in the government today and, consequently, a renewed effort is being made to enhance and upgrade the domestic S&T capability and research potential to deal with these problems within the country.

It could further be mentioned that Pakistani society, by and large, is a progressive society. There are not many social or cultural constraints on development. Qualitatively, the human element—on an individual as well as a collective basis—is not averse to development, and likes to adopt new technologies, provided they are properly explained and demonstrated, and the community feels convinced that such developments are actually beneficial to the people at large.

In fact, the Pakistani nation today realizes, far more than ever, that the country's progress and prosperity depend on how quickly and effectively it can mobilize science and technology to improve the living conditions of its people.

The size of science in the country, however, is rather small, and is unable to adequately meet the increasing developmental requirements of the country which has over one hundred million people. Like other larger developing countries, there are so many competing claims on the national resources that it is difficult to give priority consideration to the development of science and technology. Scientific and technological development in the present-day world demands heavy investment, and Pakistan just does not have the resources at present.

Consequently, it has not been possible to make fixed allocations or quantitative apportionment of resources on the basis of Gross National Product (GNP) or Gross Domestic Product (GDP) or percentage of national budget. Allocations are made on the basis of the needs and priorities of the development programs. Often the quantum of allocation is quite substantial, but is not visible as it is subsumed in the development programs of the nation. Nevertheless, it is far below the 1% recommended by the Vienna Plan of Action for the application of science and technology in developing countries.

INSTITUTIONAL STRUCTURE

The institutional structure of science and technology, which presently contributes directly or indirectly to development in Pakistan, consists of twenty-two universities, eight full-fledged research councils, over 175 science and technology institutions, and some five hundred field stations. Besides, some of the major public sector industries have set up research and development (R&D) units for quality control and design improvement of their products. Nongovernmental science has also been growing, and a number of professional societies and learned bodies have been established. The Pakistan Academy of Sciences, the Pakistan Association for the Advancement of Sciences, the Pakistan Association of Scientists and Scientific Professions, and the Scientific Society of Pakistan are the leading nongovernmental fora for the promotion of science and technology in the country.

Pakistan is basically an agricultural country. Agriculture is the largest single sector of its economy, accounting for nearly 30% of the GNP. It sustains 72% of the population, and employs 55% of the labor force. In the past decade, the country has witnessed a "green revolution," and has become self-sufficient in food and most of the important agricultural commodities. This has been the result of increasing scientific and technological input into the agricultural sector. It is expected that the present export potential in agriculture will be doubled within a few years' time.

On the other hand, the industrial base of Pakistan is neither varied nor very large. Heavy industry is not sufficiently developed, and the country has to live on imports from outside for its major requirements, including military hardware. Most of the imported industrial plants are two or three generations lower in technology and, therefore, high technology is almost nonexistent at present. An effort is underway to develop some capability in high technology areas, and, for this, adequate manpower is being trained. For the past few years, about four hundred scientists have been sent abroad every year for their Ph.D. degrees in selected fields of high technology.

SCIENCE AND TECHNOLOGY POLICY

In 1983, a comprehensive science and technology policy was launched by the government to provide a blueprint for action for long-term development of national resources. The main objective of the policy was to provide a clear sense of direction and purpose to the national scientific and technological effort and to make the S&T system an integrated and coordinated one in order to assure that it is functional and effective. The policy is presently under implementation and, despite the paucity of financial resources, considerable headway has already been made.

The policy proposals that have evolved are realistic and practical, and the approach adopted is selective and goal-oriented in content. Emphasis has been placed on the concentration and consolidation of the national effort and the reorganization and upgrading of the science and technology structure. Only where glaring gaps existed in the system have new proposals been made. Greater autonomy and intellectual freedom have been proposed with a view to providing full scope and opportunity to the creative minds in science in the country. While the objective has been self-reliance, it has been clearly recognized that science is an international activity and must be acquired through the sharing of knowledge, cooperation, and collaboration with those who have it. The policy proposals have been projectized and reflected in the five yearly development plans and programs of the nation.

A number of initiatives have been taken as a consequence of policy proposals. For a quantum leap, however, large inputs are required, which the country can ill afford at the moment. Therefore, a selective approach has been adopted. Certain thrust areas have been identified, and major consideration has been given to them. These areas include reorganization of the present science and technology structure at the decision-making level, strengthening of the R&D effort, building of high-level S&T manpower, incentives to scientists and technical people, the popularization of science, resource surveys, science-support services, and the participation of the private sector in the national scientific effort.

In the light of the major problems facing the nation, the following have been identified as current priorities: food and agriculture, irrigation and water resources, energy, industries, mineral resources, electronics, biotechnology, health and population planning, housing and environment, and education and training of manpower. It has been recognized that these priorities have to be pursued in the perspective of overall balanced and harmonious development of all sectors of the national economy, keeping in mind that the majority of the population lives in the rural areas of the country.

SCIENCE ADVISING

Pakistan's advisory structure on science and technology has been built steadily over the years, and is now fairly well institutionalized. With increasing public consciousness of science and technology, the emergence of a vigorous scientific community, the establishment of a network of S&T institutions, the development of nongovernmental science and technology, and the increased use of S&T input into agriculture and industry, a certain kind of national demand has been created for making the S&T system of the country more effective and efficient. This situation has necessitated, in turn, the need for regular science advising at the decision-making level for strengthening the S&T capability of the nation in order to help solve the outstanding problems.

The Prime Minister of Pakistan is the chief executive of the country. The Cabinet, which is presided over by the Prime Minister, finally approves all science and technology policy issues and program actions. The Prime Minister has contacts with the public at large through the elected representatives. Both houses of Parliament have science and technology committees which advise the Prime Minister on national issues. The Prime Minister has also appointed a science adviser who is a professional with the rank and status of a minister.

Figure 1. Organizational Structure for Science and Technology

PAKISTAN
FEDERAL GOVERNMENT

MINISTRY OF EDUCATION
· Quaid-I-Azam University
· University Centers of Excellence (7)

MINISTRY OF INDUSTRIES
· Cotton Textile Industry R&D Center
· Pakistan Industrial and Technical Research Center

MINISTRY OF COMMUNICATIONS
· Telecommunication Research Center

MINISTRY OF RAILWAYS
· Railway Research Center

MINISTRY OF PLANNING & DEVELOPMENT
· National Transport Research Center

MINISTRY OF PETROLEUM & NATURAL RESOURCES
· Geological Survey of Pakistan
· Hydro-Carbon Development Institute

MINISTRY OF SCIENCE & TECHNOLOGY
· Pakistan Council for Science and Technology
· Pakistan Science Foundation
· Pakistan Medical Research Council
· Pakistan Council of Scientific and Industrial Research
· Pakistan Council for Research in Water Resources
· Council for Works and Housing Research
· Appropriate Technology Development Organization
· National Institute of Silicon Technology
· National Institute of Electronics
· National Institute of Oceanography
· National Institue of Power
· National Center for Technology Transfer

PAKISTAN ATOMIC ENERGY COMMISSION
· Pakistan Institute of Nuclear Science and Technology, Islamabad
· Nuclear Institute of Agriculture and Biology, Faisalabad
· Nuclear Institute of Food and Agriculture, Tarnab
· A. E. Agricultural Research Center, Tandojam

MINISTRY OF FOOD AGRICULTURE COOPERATIVE
· Pakistan Agricultural Research Council
· Pakistan Central Cotton Committee
· Pakistan Forest Institute
· Zoological Survey of Pakistan

MINISTRY OF DEFENSE
· Defense S&T Organization
· Survey of Pakistan
· Space & Upper Atmosphere Research Council
· Geophysical Research Center
· Institute of Meteorology and Geophysics

MINISTRY OF HEALTH, SOCIAL WELFARE & POPULATION
· National Institute of Health
· Ennah Post-Graduate Medical Center
· Drug Research Laboratories
· National Institute of Fertility Control

MINISTRY OF WATER AND POWER
· Flood Control Laboratories

332

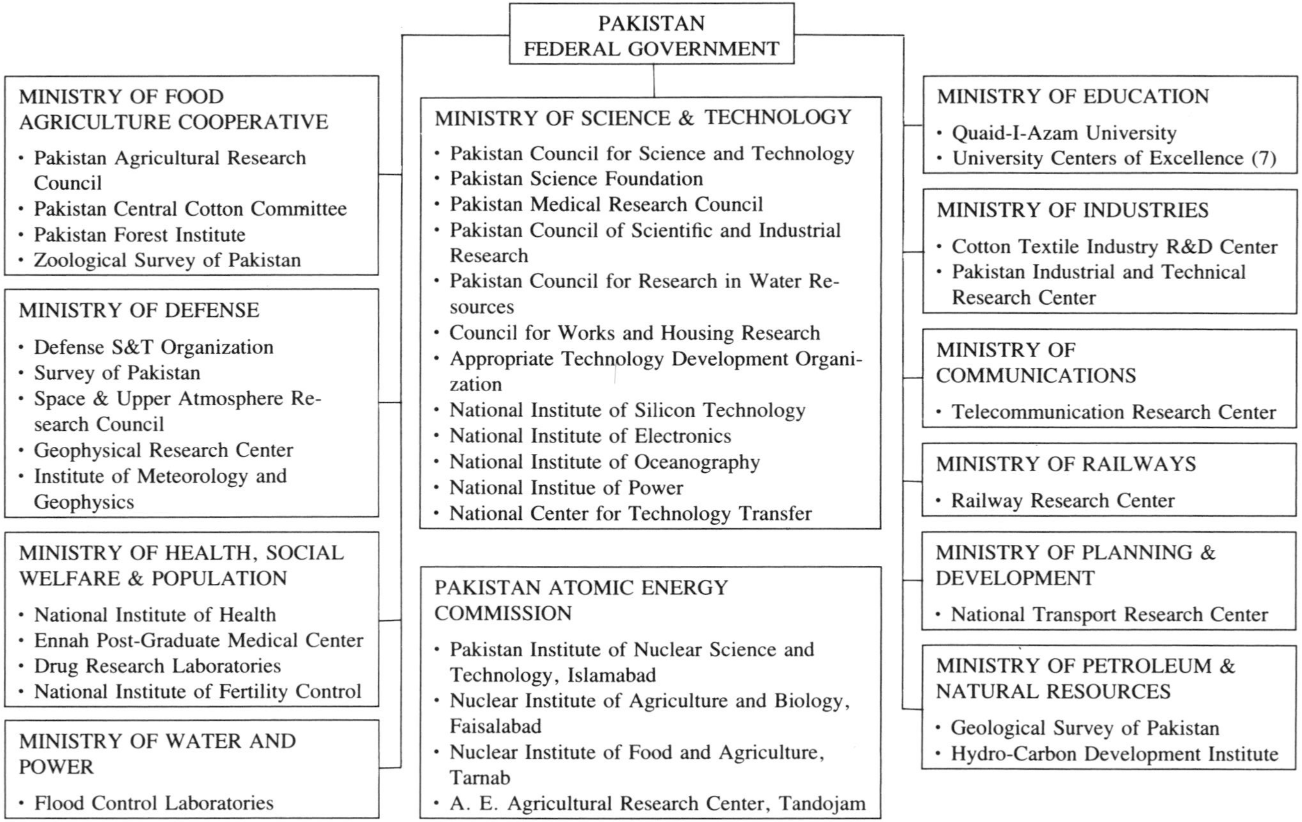

Figure 2. Advisory Structure on Science and Technology in Pakistan

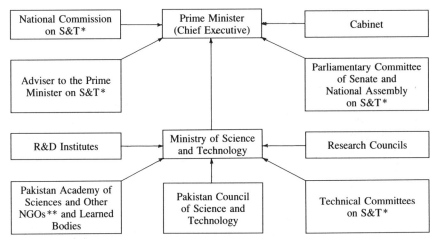

* Science and technology
** Nongovernmental organizations

The adviser advises the Prime Minister regularly on all matters of science and technology. There is also a Ministry of Science and Technology which regularly prepares proposals, after consulting professional people, for the consideration of the Cabinet and the Prime Minister.

NATIONAL COMMISSION ON SCIENCE AND TECHNOLOGY

In order to provide the requisite political will and authority for the promotion of science and technology and its applications to development, a high-powered National Commission on Science and Technology (NCST) has been established as an apex decision-making and coordinating body for science and technology in the nation. The commission, which is headed by the Prime Minister, provides the leadership and overall guidance for S&T programs, and ensures the proper linkage of the science and technology effort with the production sector.

The membership of the commission extends to federal and provincial ministers dealing with S&T financing and planning and the heads of the leading scientific organizations, such as the Atomic Energy Commission, the Space and Upper Atmosphere Research Organization, the Agricultural Research Council, the Pakistan Council of Scientific and Industrial Research, the University Grants Commission, the Pakistan Council of Science and Technology, the Pakistan Academy of Sciences, the Pakistan Engineering Council, and others. Representatives of users' organizations and leading scientists are also members of this body.

MINISTRY OF SCIENCE AND TECHNOLOGY

The Ministry of Science and Technology is the main executive machinery for the implementation of the S&T programs and the oversight of the performance of various S&T and R&D organizations in the country. It has also been charged with the responsibility for formulating S&T policies and programs, coordinating S&T organizations and the production sector, training and utilizing manpower, evaluating and regulating imported technologies, coordinating interprovincial S&T, providing international liaison in S&T, and promoting science in society.

The ministry seeks advice on science and technology matters from the organizations working under its umbrella, which are technological committees that have been set up on different subjects. It also makes recommendations on the national, regional and international seminars and conferences which are held in the country by nongovernmental bodies and professional scientists. The adviser to the Prime Minister on Science and Technology is also available to the ministry for advice and guidance.

THE PAKISTAN COUNCIL FOR SCIENCE AND TECHNOLOGY

The Pakistan Council for Science and Technology, although administratively linked with the Ministry of Science and Technology, is an independent forum for giving advice to the government. It performs these advisory or consultative functions through undertaking, *inter alia,* futuristic, scientometric, and other technological studies, and provides an objective assessment and independent advice to the government on all matters pertaining to the S&T sector.

The present democratic government is fully committed to using science and technology in increasing agricultural and industrial production in the country and in raising the standard of living of the people. In fact, the development of science and technology is high on the list of priorities of the present government. Accordingly, the Prime Minister has been taking a personal interest in the development of science and technology in the country, and has directed the relevant scientific and technological institutions to provide appropriate responses to the requirements of the country through increasing input of science and technology. Additional allocations are being provided for this purpose to the S&T sector. It is hoped that, with the increasing patronage of the chief executive and greater political will in support of science and technology, Pakistan science will further progress and make a quantum jump in the near future.

Science and Technology Advice in Poland

Zbigniew Grabowski

THE POLISH PEOPLE'S REPUBLIC *(Polska Rzeczpospolita) has been an indepen-dent state since 1918. The Communist People's Republic was established in 1947, and the present constitution took effect in 1952. In 1989, nonCommunists were first elected to offices in the government. The land area is 120,725 square miles, and its population in 1989 was estimated at 38,274,000. The official language is Polish.*

Changes which took place in Poland in the mid-1980s in the sphere of national economy management and science and technology control have modified and adapted the system of advising on science, as well as the whole organization of scientific life to the new requirements created by economic reforms.

The system of advising on science consists of activities of the central admin-istration supreme bodies, the Polish Academy of Sciences, scientific and tech-nical societies associated with the Polish Federation of Scientific and Technical Associations, and other scientific and technical societies.

The supreme body of the central administration in the field of scientific and technological progress is the Committee on Science and Technology Develop-ment of the Council of Ministers, of which the executive body is the State Office for Science and Technology Development. The committee is presided over by the Prime Minister or, in his absence, by the Minister-Head of the State Office for Science and Technology Development. The Committee is the highest advisory body for the Polish Government on scientific and technologi-cal matters.

The committee consists of approximately seventy members: ministers, direc-tors of leading scientific and research institutes, directors of the largest indus-trial enterprises, representatives of the Polish Academy of Sciences, and presi-dents of some scientific and technical societies. Its activities are concentrated mainly on planning, organization, and supervision of research and development work and scientific investigations directly serving the industrial enterprises, as

Zbigniew Grabowski is Professor at the Warsaw Technical University and, until very re-cently, was Minister-Head of the State Office for Science and Technology Development and First Deputy to the President of the Committee on Science and Technology Development of the Council of Ministers. A member of many national and international scientific societies, he is former President of Warsaw Technical University. Dr. Grabowski has served as Pres-ident of the Polish Committee on Geotechnics and Underground Works and a member of the Executive Board of the International Association for Ground Mechanization and Foun-damentation. He has also been a member of the Consultative Board for the President of the Council of State. Dr. Grabowski was born in Warsaw in 1930.

well as facilitating the practical utilization of their results in the national economy.

The committee, in cooperation with other bodies, elaborates directives of policy for science and technology, and participates in the planning of research activities and the elaboration of educational programs for the preparation of highly qualified personnel for industry as well as initiating research and development work and implementing the results.

ADVISORY FUNCTIONS

The committee carries out its advisory functions by expressing opinions on the following matters:

- The directions and scope of fundamental research having significant influence on scientific and technological progress;
- Research and development projects which are particularly important to the social and economic development of the country;
- Starting production which requires the introduction of new technology under so-called ''governmental orders'' included in the five-year National Social and Economic Plan and the Central Annual Plan;
- Investments related to the development of science and technology;
- The financing of research and development work;
- Legal instruments which help to optimize research and development activity, raise its effectiveness, and facilitate the dissemination of its results and their implementation in the production process;
- The development of information systems in the fields of science and technology;
- Scientific and technical cooperation with other countries, particularly licensing policy and the exchange of scientific and technical achievements;
- Inventiveness, rationalization, and industrial design;
- Important undertakings in the field of standardization, metrology, and the quality of products;
- The level of Polish science and technology compared to world standards; and
- The dissemination of technical culture among the population.

The president and vice-presidents of the committee—who are the Minister-Head of the State Office for Science and Technology Development, the Minister of National Education, the Minister of Industry, the Minister-Head of the Central Planning Office, and the Scientific Secretary of the Polish Academy of Sciences—constitute the so-called ''presidium'' of the committee.

The presidium defines the need for the preparation of prognosis and expertise, establishes and cancels—according to the opinion of the committee—central research projects of great importance to the development of the country, allocates financial means from the central funds for scientific and research activities, and awards prizes for outstanding achievements in the field of scientific and technological progress.

The committee has established, among its members and with the participation of other outstanding representatives of science, sixteen topical groups for the consideration and evaluation of different problems. These groups are links between the committee and scientists, engineers, scientific societies, and organizations, and constitute the intellectual base for the committee.

In addition, the committee or its presidium can establish, in case of need, *ad hoc* advisory groups, for instance: a Commission of Awards for special achievements in science and technology; a Coordinating Council for supervising selected projects being realized in cooperation with foreign institutions; and an Expert Group to evaluate the results of projects executed within the framework of science and technology development programs for 1981–1985.

THE CENTRAL QUALIFICATION COMMISSION

The Central Qualification Commission for Scientific Manpower, which is made up of over 200 outstanding scientists representing the main scientific disciplines, is another advisory body to the Prime Minister. The commission expresses its opinions in cases relating to:

- The granting, suspension, limitation or withdrawal of rights of scientific institutions to confer scientific degrees;
- The evaluation of the activities of institutions authorized to confer scientific degrees; the standards and procedures for granting degrees of doctor and doctor habilitacja; and oversight of dissertations and examinations. (The doctor habilitacja—commonly abbreviated as "habil."—is the examination that grants the right to teach at a university as an associate professor, and to ultimately be appointed as a professor);
- Conferring titles of extraordinary professor and professor; and
- Appointment to a post of associate professor of a person not having a doctor habil. degree (exceptional cases).

Another body performing advisory functions in the field of science is the Polish Academy of Sciences. The academy participates in the planning and coordination of scientific research in the country; expresses its opinions concerning the organization, present status, and future needs of Polish science, including the need for manpower training; and performs expertise ordered by the government or other governmental bodies.

The academy is a permanent advisory body for the government on scientific matters. The scientific secretary of the academy has, in turn, his own advisory bodies: the Scientific Secretariat and the College on Scientific Institutions.

Several divisions of the academy have their own advisory bodies in the form of scientific committees composed of members of the academy, recognized scientists from outside the academy, and leading representatives of industry in given fields. Opinions and advice on matters not belonging to any particular division are prepared by scientific committees organized directly at the presidium of the academy. Those committees are mainly involved in the coordination of scientific and research activity.

The Polish Academy of Sciences holds periodic so-called "congresses" of Polish Science. These congresses are fora for the discussion of the most important problems in science.

At the ministerial level, there are also several organizations which serve as advisory bodies. For the Minister of National Education, the main advisory body is the Central Council on Science and Higher Education. This council consists of seventy members, mostly representatives of universities from throughout the country. The council gives opinions on the short- and long-term plans of the higher education system; the development, organization, and curriculum of study; personnel policy in the higher education system; the financing of scientific research conducted in universities; cooperation of unversities with other scientific institutions; proposals concerning changes in the structure of universities, including closing and opening universities and branches; and drafts of legislation concerning, to any extent, the higher education system.

There are also branch councils acting in the respective sectors of higher education, *i.e.,* the Council on Higher Medical Education, serving mainly the Minister of Health and Social Welfare; the Council on Higher Artistic Education, serving the Minister of Culture and Art; and the Council on Higher Physical Culture Education, serving as the advisory body to the President of the Committee on Youth and Physical Culture.

OTHER ADVISORY BODIES

The Minister of National Defense has the Council on Higher Military Education and Science as his advisory body on education and the development of science and scientific research in the military forces.

The Minister of the Interior has his own advisory body, the Council on Higher Education and Science in International Affairs.

The National Mining Council, in turn, is an advisory body for the Minister of Industry on matters concerning the following:

* The development of the mining industry, including the introduction of new technology and organization in the mining process;
* The principles of rational exploitation of fossil deposits;
* Geological surveys necessary to assure the proper balance of fossil reserves and the proper use of resources;
* The social and health care of miners; and
* Legal acts and safety regulation in the mining industry.

The council may, in case of need, establish commissions or working groups composed of its members or persons from outside the council to initiate or conduct necessary analytical work.

An advisory and opinion-making body for the Minister of Environmental Protection and Natural Resources is the National Council on Environmental Protection. It expresses its opinions on problems relating to any aspect of environmental protection and makes proposals concerning the conditions necessary to preserve or to improve the environment. In particular, the Council does the following:

- Gives opinions on drafts of the National Social and Economic Plans regarding environmental protection;
- Gives opinions on state policy on environmental protection;
- Comments on the activities of ministers of other branches relating to environmental protection;
- Remarks on the siting of large construction projects;
- Initiates undertakings oriented toward environmental protection and the rational use of natural resources;
- Participates in the elaboration of legislation and regulations concerning the protection of the environment;
- Stimulates research activity on problems relating to the environment and its protection; and
- Gives opinions on the use of financial means from the Environmental Protection Fund.

The Council also cooperates with other domestic and foreign organizations operating in the environmental protection area.

The National Atomic Energy Agency, which is the supreme authority in the country on problems connected with the utilization of atomic energy, has its own advisory body, the Council on Atomic Energy. The council consists of sixty persons, who are specialists in the theory and practical use of atomic energy, and representatives of central administration bodies, various organizations, and social groups. The domains in which the council serves as the advisory body are as follows:

- The utilization of atomic energy and the application of nuclear methods, as well as the development of research activity in the field of atomic energy;
- Nuclear safety and radiological protection;
- The social impact of the utilization of atomic energy;
- Public information policy in connection with the utilization of atomic energy; and
- Cooperation with foreign partners in the field of the peaceful uses of atomic energy.

The council prepares reports, which are presented to the National Atomic Energy Agency or directly to the government. The council may, in case of need, invite specialists from outside its membership to consider particular problems.

THE PATENT OFFICE

The Patent Office is another central administration body which serves, to some extent, as an advisory body for the government on scientific and technical matters. The Patent Office prepares drafts of legislation and regulations concerning the invention and protection of industrial properties; initiates research activity on and testing of innovative products, especially those of an interdisciplinary nature; provides information on all domestic inventions and the most important foreign ones; and offers, when necessary, explanations of invention regulations. The activities of the Patent Office are supported by the Council on Inventions, which is the advisory and opinion-making body for the office.

The Polish Committee for Standardization, Measures and Quality is yet another advisory body for the government on problems concerning theory, methods and techniques of standardization; research activity in metrology and quality assurance; and the exchange of experience with foreign organizations. The committee prepares proposals on national standards, evaluates proposals of branch standards, and provides information on standards and metrology within the national system of scientific, technical and economic information.

THE POLISH FEDERATION

A special place within the Polish system of science and technology advice is occupied by the Polish Federation of Scientific and Technical Associations. This federation is composed of several societies of engineers and technicians from various branches, covering almost all the technical professions and specializations. By virtue of a resolution of the Council of Ministers, all central and local (down to the voievideship level, or mayors of towns and cities and governors of provinces) administrative bodies are obliged to cooperate in the process of elaboration and execution of projects stemming from the multi-year social and economic development programs of the country with the federation and its respective scientific and technical associations.

This cooperation is, most of all, connected with joint efforts oriented toward the conservation of raw materials, energy and fuels; the utilization of waste materials; raising labor efficiency in industry, transportation and services; raising the quality and standards of products; the orientation of scientific and research activity along the lines defined by the present and future needs of the national economy; and raising the qualifications of technical manpower and the utilization of the knowledge and skills of engineers and technicians.

Representatives of the federation and its branch associations take part as advisers, experts and consultants in the process of the preparation and elaboration of legislation and various decisions concerning all sorts of scientifically related matters. They are also invited to participate by advisory vote in the governing boards of the central administration bodies and various working groups and commissions dealing with the problems of technology, work organization, and economic progress.

PERIODIC CONGRESSES

Congresses of Polish engineers, sponsored by the federation, are held periodically, and constitute fora for the exchange of experience and views on technology development in the country. Their resolutions help the government to better define the necessary steps and actions which should be taken to assure proper investments in and development of branches that are the most important to the national economy.

The Council on Industrial Design is an advisory body for the government which has recently become more and more important. This is mainly due to the fact that the production from domestic industry is becoming market-oriented, which was not always the case. The council, therefore, has been asked to express its opinions on all problems related to industrial design, the planning of research activity in the field, and the elaboration of necessary legislation.

The Polish Economic Society actively participates in the elaboration and execution of national economic development plans. It also works on the improvement of planning and management methods, the promotion of economic and organizational development, the development of the scientific and research base for economic sciences, and the initiation and coordination of research activity in the field.

The Popular Science Society is an organization involved in educational and cultural activities concerning the popularization of culture, the dissemination of knowledge about scientific and technical achievements, and the promotion of new ideas. It operates through popular universities and clubs of science and theory, and organizes editorial activity, among other tasks. It cooperates with schools, universities, scientific societies, and other organizations.

The lowest level of science and technology advice for the governmental bodies in Poland is based on the activities of the Scientific, Technical and Economic Information Center, which, together with the Institute of Scientific, Technical and Economic Information and other branches and local institutions of this kind, provides necessary scientific and technical information.

The Council of Ministers has strongly recommended that the central and local administrative bodies take scientific advice when deciding on the most important problems. They are strictly obligated to take into consideration every comment or opinion offered by members of scientific committees or institutes of the Polish Academy of Sciences, universities, branch scientific and research institutes, and scientific and technical societies.

In Poland, there is some activity at the present on the problems of science and technology management, including scientific advice. The greatest attention is being paid to this problem, and Poland is very keen on making use of the experience of other countries.

Science Advice in Portugal

Fernando Gonçalves and João M. G. Caraça

THE PORTUGUESE REPUBLIC *(Republica Portuguesa) is an independent republic operating under a constitution that was established in 1976. Its land area is 35,553 square miles, and its estimated population was 10,459,000 in 1989. The official language of the country is Portuguese.*

Historic evolution and cultural traditions are major determinants of societal configurations. Thus, the status and modes of operation of national scientific and technological systems and the endeavors in scientific fields are bound by the powerful influences of past memories.

The present is the context in which both the actions decided in the past are executed and the future actions are projected. Our sole intervention is through the generation of feasible projects for the future. For them to be credible, they must be seen to reinforce national identity and patrimony.

What, then, are the basic vectors of Portuguese identity? Portugal was among the first countries in Europe to achieve linguistic unity within its frontiers (which have remained virtually unchanged since the thirteenth century), but the last to relinquish its colonial possessions. It was the first country to experience (by the end of the fourteenth century) a form of "bourgeois" revolution, but was also the last in Europe to abandon an archaic method of farming.

Portugal was the leader in the discovery of new ocean routes and overseas territories (in the fifteenth century), but one of the last to begin to industrialize and modernize. The Portuguese were forerunners in the construction of a new culture (in the sixteenth century) with experimental basis and critical tendency that enabled the geographical unification of the planet; however, four centuries later they were seen trailing in education and enduring poverty under a backward political regime.

It was as though the constraints of smallness (an overall scarcity of resources) had imposed their grip on the country. It was as though the universalist vocation and the experiences of dealing with so many peoples in the world

Fernando Gonçalves has been special adviser to the Secretary of State for Science and Technology, and is associated with the Portuguese National Board for Scientific and Technological Research (JNICT). He holds degrees in economics and business administration from Lisbon Technical University.

João M. G. Caraça is Director of the Department of Science of the Calouste Gulbenkian Foundation in Lisbon, and is also coordinator of the project, "Portugal 2000." He serves as a member of the High Council for Science and Technology (CSCT), and has been a special adviser to the Portuguese Government on matters of science policy. Dr. Caraça holds a Ph.D. in nuclear physics from Oxford University.

meant very little. It was as though the Portuguese autonomy, creativity and fecundity were dormant.

But, then, in the past fifteen years, a succession of mutations has been staged in Portugal with significant impacts at the cultural, economic, political and social levels. Structural effects were induced in the country by momentous events: the revolution of 1974 and decolonization, the adaptation of public life to the new democratic conditions, and the integration into the European Community from 1986.

A mood of change has been imprinted on societal activities which promotes some necessary adaptations, although not always successfully. New organizations appear, sometimes of an elusive nature. Enterprises are being systematically pushed toward an attitude of constant change and adaptation to new market conditions, both internally and externally. Many have already succumbed to international competition, while others have wisely yielded to foreign ownership of their assets.

The use of technology in a societally beneficial way has thus been under scrutiny. The receptivity and resistances on the parts of different sectors of the national community should also be analyzed from the perspective of the social and political constraints prevailing in the country. Although it may be true that the process of inflexion and change is underway and that acceptance of this phenomenon is spreading at the societal level, the basic task the country is confronted with is centered in the increase of the value-added in industry.

To accomplish this goal, the incorporation of manpower with better and higher qualifications in the processes that lead to the final products is required. Knowledge-intensity is the critical parameter in this struggle.

But, if one looks closely at the Portuguese scientific and technological system, one can still observe characteristic scars and traces of the past: low levels of financial and human resources, poor coordination and lack of coherent planning efforts, and the existence of inadequate bridges between universities, research institutions, and the production sector. Portugal carries a high degree of dependence on foreign technology, particularly of the package type, which has discouraged autonomous development of technology.

INSTITUTIONAL OVERVIEW OF R&D IN PORTUGAL

The top political level of the Portuguese scientific and technological system is occupied by the Council of Ministers for Science and Technology, a restricted section of the Council of Ministers where the Prime Minister sits together with the ministers who are in charge of scientific and technological activities developed through specific organizations in the vertical areas of the Executive branch. The Minister of Finances is also a member of this restricted council, and the Minister for Planning and Territorial Administration has an important role in responsibility for national scientific and technological policy.

In the Ministry for Planning and Territorial Administration, a Secretary of

State for Science and Technology has been appointed with the duty to develop and promote science and technology and their applications in Portugal.

Only since the second half of 1987 has the Secretary of State had this precise title. In fact, the previous designation was "scientific research" (this portfolio was created in 1986). This is the first time that it occurs in Portugal (with the sole exception of a brief period of one hundred days in 1979).

The change described above is in the Portuguese point of view which is a very important one in qualitative terms because it opens the space for actuality on the one hand and, on the other, it reveals an important evolution in the way the problems of science are envisaged in the country.

Concerning legislative power, the Assembly of the Republic (the national Parliament) has a Special Commission for Education, Culture and Science, in which all matters linked with the national scientific and technological policy are discussed, previous to discussion in plenary.

Beyond the global coordination functions of the Ministry for Planning and Territorial Administration (MPAT), most sectoral ministries have their own co-ordination functions in whatever their specific areas of intervention are, managing research and development (R&D) laboratories and institutions with objectives and goals related to their sectoral preoccupations (industry, agriculture, fisheries, defense, communications, public works, and health).

In this context, special reference should be made to the Ministry of Education which, beyond overall responsibility for education and training, is also in charge of R&D at the university level, and which carries important weight in the Portugese scenario of science and technology activities.

Coordination of university research in the Ministry of Education is achieved through a public institution called the Instituto Nacional de Investigação Cientifica (INIC).

THE HIGH COUNCIL FOR SCIENCE AND TECHNOLOGY

For political advice in the global coordination of the science and technology system, the MPAT has appointed a special advisory council called the Con-selho Superior de Ciência e Tecnologia (CSCT), the High Council for Science and Technology, with a collegiate profile, in which all public departments and institutions concerned with science and technology activities are represented, together with members of the private sector (from the confederations of indus-try to the big foundations). Some personalities of undisputed scientific merit also sit in the CSCT.

As a matter of fact, the science and technology sector has been experiencing an important evolution recently, and an acceleration of this trend can be ex-pected in the near future. By this is meant the emergence of a considerable number of private, nonprofit institutions, the creation of polytechnical educa-tion, a growing favorable environment to innovation and, above all, an impor-tant increment of funds for financing R&D, especially from the European Economic Community (EEC). All these facts justify—from the governmental point of view—a reformulation of the CSCT to create, in particular, a special unit of the council dedicated to the evaluation of science and technology policies and programs.

The Secretary of State for Science and Technology exerts political tutelage over the Junta Nacional de Investigação Científica e Tecnológica (JNICT), the National Board for Scientific and Technological Research, a public agency that supports the global coordination of the system, intervening also in the financing of science and technology activities in Portugal and coordinating the national participation in the European Community programs of R&D.

The importance of the JNICT in the science and technology panorama in Portugal justifies the existence of an inner Consultative Council, in which highly respected scientists and other personalities linked to science and technology participate. In addition, the membership of the council includes the presidents of the national Coordinating Commissions for R&D (nine in all) that operate within JNICT.

In terms of "weight" in the national science and technology system, mention must be made of the Conselho de Reitores das Universidades Portuguesas (CRUP), the University Rectors' Council, a body that has as its members the fourteen rectors of the Portuguese universities. By its nature and functions, the CRUP has a direct say in the level and processes of research and development in the universities.

All these structures are important sources of scientific advice in the national context.

MECHANISMS OF SCIENTIFIC ADVICE TO GOVERNMENT

The Portuguese science and technology system has as fundamental vectors the diversity of institutions and sources of funding, even if one considers solely the government sphere. A proper science and technology budget, integrated into the national budget, is still waiting to be implemented.

This profile implies that many different entities can organize themselves into powerful lobbies that influence the levels and mechanisms of funding of science and technology activities which are the true indicators of political will.

It is easy to understand that the function of scientific advice in Portugal occurs at different levels of intervention, and that it is many times protagonized by the performers themselves. As in other countries, in Portugal, no critical mass in most scientific areas (or in the science and technology policy area) exists which might be used as a mediator in the process.

In Portugal, one finds a strong informal component of advice, which concurs with the established channels for obtaining scientific opinions and statements.

At the governmental level, the most important role is fulfilled by "special advisers to the Cabinet," who are in close contact with the Minister for Planning and Territorial Administration and the Secretary of State for Science and Technology.

Looking at the institutions (and at their linkages) in the science and technology system, one observes that, on the one hand, the scientists and engineers themselves and, on the other, the final users of their products are those in whom more advice (and influential power) is concentrated. In the users are included both the recipients of know-how applicable to the production of goods and services and the universities and other educational institutions that are active in the diffusion of knowledge. One must also mention the role in advice (a reduced one still) of learned societies and of associations of members of the scientific community which can, at times, induce significant impacts.

In terms of institutional (formal) advice, the most relevant comes from the CSCT, because of its placement, status and membership. The CSCT is a special forum for the confrontation of different points of view and specific interests, which can carry out the task of compatibilization and consensus in the light of the governmental scenarios and political orientations. The minister in charge of the coordination of science and technology (the MPAT) is the chairman of this council.

At the second level, one finds the JNICT, which is, by definition, the scientific adviser of the government. For this purpose, the JNICT uses also its own Consultative Council (as mentioned above) which has as members the presidents of all national Coordinating Commissions for R&D. In this context, it is very clear that the performers of R&D activities have direct roles in advice.

At a third level, one finds, in each public science and technology agency or department, a Scientific Council which, in most cases, is composed exclusively of scientists, although sometimes industry leaders and experts in science and technology are also members. At this level, one may say that advice is mainly "judgment in own cause."

In conclusion, it is apparent that the state-of-the-art science advice in Portugal is probably not markedly different from those in many other countries around the world. In fact, only very recently, it became clear that the development and implications of science and technology activities impose specific constraints in matters of advice. The role and influence of the media in decision processes have been acknowledged, but not properly analyzed yet. The Portuguese feel that this is an area of utmost importance and that international cooperation mechanisms are the proper channels through which it should be addressed.

Science and Technology Advice to the Government of Saudi Arabia

Saleh A. Al-Athel

THE KINGDOM OF SAUDI ARABIA *(al-Mamlakah al-Arabiyah al-Su'udiyah) is an absolute monarchy which was established as a unified kingdom in 1932. Its land area is 829,995 square miles, and the 1989 estimated population was 13,513,000. The official language is Arabic.*

For Saudi Arabia, the process of socioeconomic development means accelerated changes in three main dimensions:

- Changes that increase society's understanding and material control over its natural environment, especially as regards the utilization of the available natural resources;
- Changes that contribute to the building of an economic structure that is viable both in the sense of being able to generate and diffuse new wealth and in having a longer-term capability of sustaining itself in its interactions with other economies.
- Changes that strengthen the fabric of society, increase the level of welfare, and contribute to the development of socially responsible individuals by the creation and continued support of cultural, educational and welfare institutions and organizations.

The overall organizational framework for introducing and coordinating these changes on a national scale is provided by the sequence of events in the kingdom's five-year development plans. These plans define the specific objectives and priorities of the development process for each period, and provide mechanisms to mobilize the necessary resources for their implementation. The essential feature of the plans is the integration of the numerous individual projects planned for the various sectors of the economy.

OBJECTIVES OF THE PLANS

The two general objectives of the development plans have, therefore, been the following:

Saleh A. Al-Athel has been the president of the King Abdulaziz City for Science and Technology (KACST) since 1984 and a member of its board of directors since its inception. He was Vice Rector for Graduate Studies and Research at King Saud University from 1976 to 1983. Dr. Al-Athel completed his Ph.D. in applied mechanics at Stanford University in 1971.

- To transform the material conditions of the society by the application and incorporation of science and technology, while preserving cultural values; and
- To develop the kingdom's natural and human resources so as to reduce the extreme dependence upon the depletable hydrocarbon reserves. Financial resources would be converted into domestically available physical assets.

The inception and implementation of viable science and technology policies are, therefore, basic prerequisites for the success of the national development plans. To achieve this, the government of Saudi Arabia has formalized advice on science and technology by creating "King Abdulaziz City for Science and Technology" (KACST). KACST is an autonomous government organization governed by a board of directors which is composed of the ministers of the major ministries to which science and technology are of greatest relevance, such as the following: Defense, Agriculture, Petroleum and Mineral Resources, Industry, Planning, Higher Education, and Finance and National Economy.

KACST is headed by a president who is a member of its governing board of directors, which, in turn, is chaired by the Prime Minister (the King).

THE OBJECTIVES OF KACST

The following objectives have been assigned to KACST:

"KACST is entrusted with the responsibility of promoting and encouraging applied scientific research and coordinating the activities of scientific research organizations and centers in accordance with the kingdom's development requirements. To achieve its objectives, but without limiting its functions, KACST is to undertake the following:

"(1) Conduct applied scientific research programs in the fields that serve the economic and social development objectives of the Kingdom.

"(2) Establish and manage an information center which collects and disseminates data on the scientific and technological manpower resources in the Kingdom in order to utilize this labor force in implementing scientific and technological development policies.

"(3) Establish and operate laboratories for applied scientific research in areas of importance to the Kingdom.

"(4) Provide assistance to the private sector in the development of productive agricultural and industrial research that will help increase the gross national product (GNP).

"(5) Support joint research programs between the Kingdom and international scientific institutions in an effort to keep pace with scientific developments in the world by awarding research grants and undertaking joint research projects.

"(6) Establish and manage an information center maintaining data on national and international scientific institutions. It will also organize seminars and publish research papers as a means of furthering KACST's objectives.

"(7) Formulate a scientific research plan which will specify national objectives for achieving scientific advancement.

"(8) Award scholarships to develop the necessary skills for conducting research work.

"(9) Award grants to individuals and scientific organizations to undertake applied research work.

"(10) Coordinate with government agencies, scientific organizations and research centers in the Kingdom to enhance research, information and expertise exchange, and to avoid duplication of effort. To achieve this goal, a liaison committee shall be formed, consisting of experts from government agencies and organizations associated with KACST's activities. This committee will provide KACST with advice in developing the framework of the national scientific plan.''

From its inception in 1977, KACST has been carrying out its mission in the promotion of science and technology in the kingdom by coordinating and cooperating with the various universities, agencies and institutions concerned with research and technology, and encouraging Saudi experts to undertake research that will help promote the development and evolution of the society. Toward this end, KACST has been organizing grant competitions (mostly in applied research) designed to promote the objectives of social development by utilizing the talents and resources available in the kingdom's academic and scientific institutions.

Besides this, KACST, through cooperative agreements with international science and technology institutions/organizations, encourages closer ties with friendly nations through mutual interests in scientific research and development. It also provides the opportunity for its researchers/scientists to become acquainted with the latest developments related to scientific research and state-of-the art technology. The cooperative research programs have successfully completed several solar energy research projects, the establishment of a Saudi Center for Remote Sensing, the conducting of studies toward establishing a national observatory, the establishment of an aquaculture research station, and other projects.

OTHER KACST RESPONSIBILITIES

KACST monitors and evaluates domestic and global scientific and technological literature. Efforts are then made to disseminate such information to the researchers/scientists by several channels of communication between KACST and other scientific organizations for the exchange of data and information relating to various research fields.

KACST's responsibilities, among others, include the establishment of national research institutes and assuring their proper interface with researchers at universities and other research institutions. Among the institutes are the Institute for Petroleum and Petrochemicals Research, the Institute for Energy Research, the Institute for Natural Resources and Environmental Research, the Institute for Arid Lands Research, the Institute of Astronomy, and the Institute of Space Research.

KACST provides advice to several official agencies of the government and hence contributes to the rationalization of decision-making regarding science and technology. In addition, KACST awards scholarship and research grants to Saudi students in an attempt to form a new generation of experts and researchers capable of keeping pace with the rapid developments in the fields of science and technology. Through these and other channels, KACST's intention is to enhance society's appreciation and understanding of science and technology.

South African Science Planning: Western-Styled to Africa-Specific

C. F. Garbers

THE REPUBLIC OF SOUTH AFRICA *(Republiek van Suid-Afrika) has been an independent state since 1961. Its republican system took effect in that year upon its withdrawal from the Commonwealth of Nations. Its land area is 471,879 square miles, and its estimated population was 38,006,000 in 1989. English and Afrikaans are the official languages.*

Part of the technologically aware First World, but also inextricably involved in the plight of Africa as a whole, South Africa is experiencing a growing awareness of the revolutionary impact of technology internationally and of the role that it can play in alleviating the massive problems of South Africa specifically and southern Africa generally. The typical symptoms of Africa also prevail in South Africa: explosive population growth, underdevelopment, unemployment, and violence.

The resulting massive demands on the treasury to improve the quality of life have accentuated the need for accelerated economic development, job creation, and population development. Hence the interdependence of economic development and the successful exploitation of the excellence achieved in science and technology are receiving unprecedented attention in South Africa as in the rest of the world.

Endeavors to devise an approach to science and technology exploitation which is more specific to Africa have resulted in rapid and sustained changes in the government's science policy. To understand these changes and the coordination of advisory systems requires a brief review of historic developments.

ESTABLISHING AN R&D CULTURE

Until 1945, attempts by a variety of advisory and research councils to stimulate research and development (R&D) in the sciences and applied sciences at universities and in government departments had little effect in developing an R&D culture in South Africa. The founding of the Council for Scientific and Industrial Research (CSIR) in 1945, however, represented a watershed for science

C. F. Garbers was appointed Chairman and President of the Council for Scientific and Industrial Research of South Africa in 1980. He served on the Scientific Advisory Council (1980–1987) and is a member of the Advisory Council for Technology (1987–present). Past President of the South African Chemical Institute, past Chairman of the South African Academy of Science, and holder of a Ph.D. from the University of Zurich, Dr. Garbers serves as chairman/member/trustee on the boards of several organizations.

and technology. The council was created to apply science and technology, to assist the fledgling industries which had been created during World War II, and to stimulate research with the training of high-level manpower. Modeled on similar organizations in the British Commonwealth, it indeed served as an added stimulus for industrial development and for the establishment of a Western-styled education and R&D infrastructure.

The wide involvement of state departments, research councils, and universities in scientific R&D led to the introduction of the Scientific Advisory Council of the Prime Minister in 1962, with the Scientific Adviser to the Prime Minister as chairman. The main tasks were the coordination of the entire state-funded research and development effort, meaningful advice from the scientific community to the authorities, and informed input regarding the allocation of funds. Since it was the scientific adviser's responsibility to advise government on research priorities, the council devoted its energies primarily to the formation of a national science policy.

In 1980, the Office of Scientific Adviser was converted to the Science Planning Branch, followed by the abandonment of the scientific adviser's post. The renamed Scientific Advisory Council, which had acted under an independent chairman from 1982, no longer directly advised the Prime Minister, but reported to the Minister of Constitutional Development and Planning until 1985 and, since then, to the Minister of National Education. These changes not only extended the science advisory channels to the highest authorities, but placed the final authority for science coordination in the hands of the respective ministers, who are the political heads of departments in the country.

This compelled South Africa, quite inescapably, to select between those areas of scientific inquiry which it could afford to follow up and those which were to be left, quite deliberately, without encouragement or support. This was particularly applicable to the state's investment in R&D, where many state departments, which were confronted with major problem areas, did not obtain the required answers despite the considerable state investment in R&D.

MAJOR POLICY CHANGES

Because of this problem, the government introduced major policy changes, such as:

- A new process of priority determination was formally introduced with the establishment of the State President's Committee on National Priorities. (As a result of a constitutional change, the Prime Minister was replaced as executive head of state by the State President in 1984.) The committee functions under the chairmanship of the State President. It is composed of representatives at the ministerial level, provided with input from the Central Economic Advisory Service, and mandated to advise on the allocation of the resources which are under the state's control.

- R&D, as funded by the government, became a line-function responsibility of the individual departments, which had to decide on R&D priorities and funding from their budgets, which were allotted from government resources. This was in line with the government's declared commitment to the largest possible measure of privatization of public activities, as well as the devolution of decision-making.
- In the budgets of the statutory science councils (*i.e.,* CSIR, Human Sciences Research Council (HSRC), the Council for Mineral Technology (MINTEK), the Medical Research Council (MRC), and the South African Bureau of Standards (SABS), the government decided upon the baseline budget that it was prepared to fund, placing greater pressure on these councils to earn a larger portion of their funds through contract research and services. Hence, for survival purposes, these councils had to become more market-oriented in order to secure contracts from clients in the public and private sectors.
- Whereas the Scientific Advisory Council has acted as a mouthpiece to government for the scientific community in general, that role was delegated to umbrella professional associations and other groups of interested parties. These associations and groups now have to address presentations directly to the minister responsible regarding matters in which the state could or should play a role.
- The Scientific Advisory Council, now smaller in size and consisting mainly of experts appointed in their personal capacities, continues to advise the Minister of National Education on matters of science policy and the functioning of the science system generally.
- An Advisory Council for Technology was instituted to advise the Minister of Economic Affairs and Technology on the optimum utilization of South Africa's resources.

These policy decisions are not yet fully operative.

SCIENCE ADVICE: AN ASSESSMENT

Figure 1 summarizes the administrative structure for science in South Africa. Science advice takes on many forms and guises:

- Each ministry's administrative infrastructure is headed by a director general, who is a person in high standing in and knowledge of the mandate of the particular department. He serves as a confidant and first-line adviser to the minister concerned. Some ministries have a series of boards and councils of experts in relevant fields to, quite apart from their knowledgeable staffs, provide advice to the minister.
- *Ad hoc* boards or commissions of inquiry are appointed to study and to report to the minister on vexing problems, after which the board/commission is disbanded.

• A number of independent statutory institutions conduct R&D under their own councils, which are composed of elected individuals who are highly qualified and experienced in relevant areas. The respective ministers do not intervene in their functioning, but frequently request advice or contact the specific institutions to investigate issues pertinent to the particular department or minister.

South Africa has at its disposal a well-developed infrastructure, not only for training in the sciences and applied sciences, but also for R&D and the practice of science and technology. In general, the best advice is mobilized from what-

Figure 1. The Administrative Structure of Science in the Republic of South Africa

State President (SP) ....
    Office of the SP .... SP's Committee on National Priorities
Cabinet* .... :
    Ministry of Finance (Treasury)   . . . Central Economic Advisory Service
    Ministry of National Education   : . . Scientific Advisory Council
        Science Planning   : . . Universities and Technikons Advisory
        Education Policy   :   Council
            : . . South African Council for Education
            : . . Natural History Museums
            : . . Human Sciences Research Council**

    Ministry of Economic Affairs and Technology
        Department of Commerce   : . . Advisory Council for Technology
           and Industry   : . . Council for Scientific and Industrial
            :   Research (CSIR)
            : . . South African Bureau of Standards
            :   (SABS)
            : . . Board of Trade and Industry

        Department of Mineral and   . . . Atomic Energy Commission
           Energy Affairs   :
             | :
        Geological Survey   : . . Council for Mineral Technology**
             | :
        Minerals Bureau of SA   :
             | :
        State Mining Engineer   : . . National Energy Council
    Ministry of Agriculture
        Botanical Research Institute
        Horticultural Research Institute
        Veterinary Research Institute
        Plant Protection Research Institute
        Animal and Dairy Sciences Research Institute
        Etc.

Figure 1. (*Continued*).

Ministry of Environment Affairs and of Water Affairs
Forestry Research Institute   . . . Council for the Environment
Sea Fisheries Research   : . . Forestry Council
   Institute   : . . Council for the Habitat
Weather Bureau (Antarctic   : . . Water Research Commission
   Research)
National Botanic Gardens of South Africa
Hydrological Research Institute

Ministry of National Health and Population Development
National Institute   : . . Medical Research Council **
   for Virology   : . . SA Institute for Medical Research

Ministries for Education and Culture .
                                    . . . Committee of University Principals
   Universities
   Technikons

*The list of ministries is not exhaustive; there are selected line-function responsibilities; advisory bodies have varying degrees of autonomy.
**These statutory research councils each has its own independent Act of Parliament. They are autonomous, presided over by an independently appointed council/board with fiscal independence, even though funds are derived partially from a parliamentary grant.

ever sources are available for specific tasks. Many institutions which are geared to South Africa's particular problem areas are now well established and have a wealth of information at their disposal, *e.g.*, the Small Business Development Corporation, the Development Bank of South Africa (modeled on The World Bank), and the Industrial Development Corporation.

Generally, South Africa is going through a phase in which every activity in the generation of high-level manpower and those related to science and technology are being reassessed. The statutory research councils have emerged leaner from restructuring and have reformulated their missions. The universities, technikons and other "parastatals" are in the midst of major rationalization exercises as part of the government's policy of curtailing its expenditures. Generally, a system of decentralized management and centralized macro-financial and macro-administrative control has been developed. Simultaneously, every effort is being made to deregulate and encourage free enterprise in close collaboration with the private sector.

The overriding significance attached to finding political solutions in a multicultural and multiracial developed society, however, has resulted in a burgeoning highly fragmented bureaucracy. This, together with the drive toward the devolution of decision-making, in part complicates the effective practice of science and technology. Moves are afoot to effect rationalization.

Be that as it may, science coordination now takes place mostly at the ministerial level through the ministers in a line-function responsibility for the practice of science and technology. The greater emphasis on the exploitation and application of research findings has already brought about exciting results. There is growing support, however, within the scientific community for a science council, not only to foster coherent planning, but to ensure the long-term viability of the R&D effort. This is particularly critical if the important role which South Africa is destined to play in the development of southern Africa is considered.

Science and Technology in Spain

Eduardo Punset

THE SPANISH STATE *(Estado Español) was reestablished as a monarchy in 1975 after having operated under a system of personal rule since 1936. Its parliamentary monarchy was confirmed by the constitution that went into effect in 1978. Its total land area is 194,896 square miles, and its estimated population in 1989 was 39,226,000. The official languages include Spanish, Basque, Catalan, Galician and Valencian. As of December 31, 1989, the US dollar was equal to 109.14 pesetas and .84 European Community Units.*

Spain's scientific and technological development, with the exception of a few examples of individual technological excellence in the pre-World War II years, has traditionally been negligible. What was lacking was a structured effort due to a mixture of lack of vision and cultural prejudices that historically relegated science to the bottom of the list of national priorities.

This cultural attitude was best summarized by one of the most influential Spanish intellectuals of our time, the writer and philosopher Miguel de Unamuno (1864–1936) in his famous "que inventen allos" (let them innovate), referring to the most advanced European countries.

Uncoordinated, fragmented, uneven and underfinanced efforts of a few idealistic pioneers—in permanent struggle for a change of attitudes and strategy— were among the factors which historically explain why Spain was unable to develop its own system of research and development (R&D).

The modernization path which radically transformed the Spanish economy in the past thirty years was, not surprisingly, supplemented—as in Japan and, later, in South Korea—by a parallel strategy in R&D encouragement. This can be explained by several factors. Comparatively cheap labor and a well-settled protectionist environment practice nurtured an inefficient—import-substituting—manufacturing sector in which industrialists opted for dependence on foreign licensing. It left domestic production with no room for innovation and opened the gateways for brain-drain, mainly to the United States. Agricultural exports, tourism, and remittances from over one million EEC-based migrant workers carried the burden of offsetting current account deficits and yielding surpluses of the balance of payments.

In the early 1980s, it became increasingly clear to all political forces in the

Eduardo Punset is Minister in charge of relations with the European Economic Community, and Professor of innovative policies and technology at the Instituto de Empresa. He is also President of the Instituto Technologico and a member of the European Parliament. Dr. Punset, born in 1936 in Barcelona, is a law graduate of the University of Madrid and holds a master's degree in economics from the London School of Economics. He has been an economics editor of The Economist.

newly restored Spanish democracy that a radical public policy was needed in order to integrate science and technology as a major input of industrial restructuring. This policy involved a dramatic departure from past ''leave-it-for-tomorrow'' attitudes, while preserving the variety of fragmented ministerial and regional competences in the field of R&D.

The trade-off consisted in pooling all existing and new public resources into a centralized system which would guarantee efficient intervention in the planning and coordination of public funds. All ministries responsible for research, in liaison with the Parliament, autonomous governments, and the private sector, were to be coordinated by an interministerial body to assure a more effective response to R&D needs. The instrumental goal was to thrust expenditure in R&D as a percentage of the Gross National Product from a sluggish 0.4% registered in 1980 to 1.2% by 1991, *i.e.,* an accumulative annual increase of 0.1 percentage points.

The final step was taken by the new socialist government (1982–   ) which adopted a science policy emphasizing the role of public guidance and funding as the catalyst for private involvement in this R&D plan. The resulting system of science and technology is set up in the law of science *(Ley de Fomento y Coordinacion General de las Investigacion Cientifica y Tecnica),* which was formally passed by the Spanish Parliament in April 1986. Its main objectives are:

- To set up a National Plan of R&D, and
- To coordinate all research activities in Spain.

PROMOTION AND COORDINATION OF RESEARCH

Law 13/86 for the promotion and general coordination of scientific and technological research pools thirty-six public research centers ascribed to the following nine governmental departments:

- Ministry of Education and Science,
- Ministry of Industry and Energy,
- Ministry of Defense,
- Ministry of Agriculture, Fisheries and Food,
- Ministry of Public Works and Urban Planning,
- Ministry of Health,
- Ministry of Economy and Finance,
- Ministry of Transport, Tourism and Communications,
- Ministry of Culture.

These departments each have a representative in the Interministerial Commission for Science and Technology, known as CYCIT, which is the highest-level decision-making governmental institution for R&D policy. Its chairmanship is held by the Minister of Education and Science.

CYCIT is assisted by a standing committee, the Permanent Commission for Science and Technology, which prepares its agenda and holds a meeting every month. It is chaired by the Secretary of State for Universities and Research, and its members are directors general from the other departments.

The permanent commission has two dependent agencies which are:

- the General Secretariat of the National Plan, and
- the National Agency for Evaluation and Perspective.

The first is the support unit for CYCIT with direct responsibilities for coordination of the programs and activities, budget management, and administrative tasks. The second is responsible for the assessment of bodies and research groups participating in activities covered by the National Plan.

CYCIT also has two advisory bodies which are:

- the General Council of Science and Technology, and
- the Advisory Council for Science and Technology.

The first is responsible for the coordination of R&D efforts between the state and the autonomous communities, while the second is composed of representatives from the scientific community and the economic and social sectors and is empowered to draft R&D policies.

Besides CYCIT, there is a third body, the Joint Committee Congress-Senate of the National Parliament, composed of representatives from both Houses, and responsible for the control of policy, particularly the implementation of the National Plan.

THE NATIONAL PLAN

The National Plan for Scientific and Technological Research was devised as the central instrument for scientific and technical policy coordination. It consists basically of the national and sectoral (implemented by the relevant ministerial institutions). The programs are financed by the National Fund, of which most financial resources are directly fixed each year in the national budget, the rest being assumed by other public bodies.

The current First National Plan (1988–1991) is one year old at this writing and covers eleven areas of socioeconomic priorities. These are:

- Progress of knowledge and advancement in technological innovation and development;
- Conservation, strengthening and the optimal exploitation of natural resources;
- Economic growth, employment promotion, and the improvement of working conditions;
- Development and strengthening of the competitive position of industry, trade, agriculture and fisheries;

- Development of public services, in particular those relating to housing, communications and transport;
- Promotion of health, social welfare, and the quality of life;
- Strengthening of the national defense capacity;
- Promotion of artistic creativity and the spread of culture in all manifestations;
- Improvement of quality in education; and
- Efforts in adapting Spanish society to scientific development and technologically induced change.

The plan reflects the government's policy of balancing technological development with social policy without restricting the ministries' powers in the definition and implementation of the R&D effort. This approach weakens the role of the centralized planning authority and paves the way for a situation where sectoral views and interests can prevail over a comprehensive response to the strategic needs of the Spanish economy.

The plan is reviewed annually and can be extended if the evaluation results so advise. In this respect, the government also has to address an implementation report to the Parliament every year.

RESEARCH ACTIVITY PRIORITIES

The research activity priorities cover both basic and applied research through national, sectoral, regional and international programs and activities which are mainly carried out by means of projects of technological development and infrastructure (45.6%), concerted projects with industry (22.2%), training of R&D staff (21.6%), and other activities (10.6%).

Basic research is mostly implemented through the National Plan's horizontal program, General Promotion of Knowledge, which is entirely devoted to basic research. Basic research activities, however, are also included in other sectoral programs at the national and the regional levels.

Applied research, like basic research, is also implemented through the national, regional and international programs and activities. Total funds allocated in the National Fund for the national programs for the period 1988–1991 amount to 119,932 million pta or 940 MECU. Total funds for sectoral programs for the same period amount to 227,562 million pta or 1,777.9 MECU. The latter include the General Promotion of Knowledge Program and the sectoral programs of the CSIC (Higher Council for Scientific Research), IAC (Astrophysics Institute of the Canary Islands), and PEN (the National Energy Plan).

The national programs are concentrated in the following five areas:

- Communications and production technologies (44.7%)
  Microelectronics
  New materials
  Robotics

Space
Information and communication technologies
· Natural resources and agricultural and food technologies (18.5%)
Agriculture
Stock breeding
Aquaculture and marine resources
Food technology
Environment
Forest systems and their preservation
· Quality of life (14.3%)
Biotechnology
Health
Pharmaceutical research
Social aspects of science and technology
· Special programs
High-energy physics
· Horizontal programs (combined with special programs, 22.5%)
Training of R&D staff
Linking of information networks

Training activities are a fundamental element of this scheme. A total amount
of 25,899 million pta or 202 MECU is allocated for these for the period 1988–
1991 in the National Plan.

The basic objectives of this action are as follows:

· To increase the number of scientists and technical staff in R&D;
· To ensure the distribution of staff according to the National Plan priori-
ties;
· To facilitate training abroad in understaffed fields;
· To encourage short-term visits by leading foreign scientists to Spanish
research groups; and
· To facilitate exchange programs of staff bidirectional mobility and re-
search collaboration between public and private centers.

Among the major European multilateral cooperative activities, Spain participates in the following plans (in approximate percentages of the total costs):

· EEC framework programs of R&D   (7.5%)
· COST   (5.9%)
· EUREKA   (17 .0%)
· CERN   (5.8%)
· ESA   (3.5%)
· EMBL   (4.5%)
· CIHEAM   (21.0%)
· ORPHEUS   (4.0%)
· ESRF   (4.0%)

- ODP   (4.0%)
- AIRBUS   (4.2%)
- ICA (Canary Islands Astrophysics (20.0%)

PARTICIPANTS

Participants in this research and development plan can be grouped into three main categories: public research institutions, industrial firms, and universities.

Universities provide a permanent reservoir of human resources and installations. Spain's thirty-one public and four private universities were made up of 868,444 undergraduate students and 36,018 professors and lecturers during the academic year 1986–87. Private universities accounted for only 3.38% of the total figure.

Public research institutions participate in the sectoral programs of their respective ministries as well as in the national programs.

With industry accounting for only half of R&D activity (0.4% of the Gross National Product, representing on the average 0.7% of their turnover), R&D promotional activities in industry are a top priority of the National Plan. It offers industrial firms a fundamental role in this strategy. Its basic goal is to increase R&D activity in enterprises—public and private—by means of participation in programs, the use of R&D centers, and access to the results of their research.

The Center for Industrial Technological Development (CDTI), under the Ministry of Industry and Energy, is responsible for steering this participation. Enterprises may receive public financing for up to 70% of the total cost of the project through interest-free loans. They include a technical risk clause by which the enterprise is exempt from repayment if the project is not viable, with the exception of the sale value of the fixed assets financed by the plan.

Besides cost-sharing, firms engaged in R&D may benefit from tax incentives consisting of tax cuts of up to 30% of R&D capital investment and up to 15% of other related expenditure, such as subcontracting to universities or public research institutions. Small- and medium-sized enterprises—in particular, small specialized firms with highly qualified staff—represent over 50% of CDTI beneficiaries. Firms of under 500 employees received 84% of the total funding, with the remaining 16% going to firms with workforces of over 500. This is according to Article 90(2) of the Budgetary Law *(Ley de Presupuestos)*. Small firms, often grouped in research associations, quite efficiently pool their resources by jointly participating in R&D projects.

APPRAISAL

In the first year of the National Plan (February 1988–March 1989), eighteen programs were adopted, representing a total investment of 13,043 million pta. These programs covered training activities, scientific infrastructure, research projects, concerted actions, and other investments, including space, new materials, information and communications technologies, and biotechnology.

A total of 362 research projects were selected, involving 2,680 researchers. In programs, universities received 47% of the funding. In concerted projects (60% of total funds available), 73% went to the area of production and communications technologies. The main beneficiaries were small- and medium-sized enterprises. OTRI (Office for the Transfer of Research Results) began to channel the transfer of technology from universities and OPI (Public Research Institutes) to enterprises.

More experience will be necessary before an adequate evaluation can be made of the system of R&D in Spain. Nevertheless, a few comments can be made.

- There should be greater emphasis on coordination between national priorities and European Community R&D. More participation in the EEC Framework program is paramount for redirection and proper orientation of the Spanish domestic efforts in R&D. Authorities and planners should emphasize this aspect in their future policy definition and encourage greater participation in European programs. Spain's large share in the European Community's structural funds should provide an additional opportunity to reinforce this strategy through investments in R&D infrastructure.
- Equal importance should be given at a proper stage to private initiative and guidance. Innovation is at the bottom of any sound and far-reaching R&D policy. Most of the initiatives should, therefore, be taken in consultation with the private sector, which plays a secondary role in the present R&D framework.
- In addition to these efforts aimed at strengthening the national R&D base and if competitiveness is to be increased, policy should also be directed—well ahead in time—to attracting foreign capital, know-how and human resources through adequate incentives, particularly in view of the Internal Market after 1992. Specialization would, in this regard, be of major consideration. Spain, with the youngest population in the European Economic Community and its privileged climatic conditions and renewed dynamism, could become—with proper communications and infrastructure investments—an attractive base for R&D activities.

Government Science Policy in Sweden

Bert Bolin

THE KINGDOM OF SWEDEN *(Konungariket Sverige) has operated under a consti- tutional monarchy system since 1809; its present constitution has been in effect since 1975. The land area of the country is 173,731 square miles, and the estimated popu- lation in 1989 was 8,463,000. Swedish is the official language.*

The importance of science to the development of a country, its technology and economy was recognized by many industrialized countries during and soon after World War II. Sweden was no exception in this regard. A set of Research Councils were formed in the late 1940s, and have been in operation ever since. Some changes have, of course, taken place over the years. The rapidly increas- ing role of both applied research and technical development in the 1960s led to the creation of the first major institutions for more directed research, *e.g.*, the Board for Technical Development (Styrelsen för teknisk utvëckling—STU), the council for environmental research within the Swedish environmental protec- tion agency (Forskningsnämnden vid statens naturvårdsverk). Further, the ini- tial division of the responsibility for research in the fields of natural sciences into one council for atomic and nuclear physics and another for other fields of science was abandoned in 1977.

But science policy is more than just creating a set of granting agencies charged with the task of supporting the best researchers with project money over and above the regular funding supplied through the universities and their faculties. Science policy addresses questions of how to develop a funding structure that fosters good basic research across the whole range of academic disciplines, how to build bridges between university institutions and industry to assist in the exploitation of scientific findings for the further development of industry, how to ascertain that the advancement of society builds on the increased knowl- edge that research can supply, how to consider simultaneously scientific quality and societal ambitions when setting priorities, how to attract the good students to graduate and postgraduate studies and work, etc.

Bert Bolin was Scientific Adviser to the Prime Minister of Sweden from 1986 to 1988 and is currently Science Adviser to the Vice Prime Minister. He is Professor of meteorology at the University of Stockholm and Chairman of the Intergovernmental Panel on Climate Change (IPCC). Born in 1925, Dr. Bolin was the first President of the Joint Organizing Committee (JOC) that was in charge of the Global Atmospheric Research Program (GARP). He has received several international awards, and has published numerous papers on meteorology and on the role of the greenhouse gases on the climate of the earth.

INITIATIVES IN THE 1960S

The political interest in the role of research for the development of society increased in Sweden during the 1950s, not the least because the Prime Minister, Tage Erlander, had a solid academic background and the leader of the liberal party, Bertil Ohlin, was a world-renowned researcher in the field of economics. In 1962, Olof Palme (later Prime Minister of Sweden; then assistant to Tage Erlander) suggested to the Prime Minister that a group of scientists be asked to advise him on scientific matters. An Advisory Board on Science was formed, and a smaller group of its members was selected as a preparatory body for the board as a whole.

In retrospect, there were three aspects of the arrangements for this advisory committee that turned out to be of principal importance for the role it was going to play:

• The existence of the small preparatory group was essential to the planning and implementation of the work of the advisory board.
• Those chosen as members of the committee and, in particular, of the preparatory group were scientifically very well recognized in academic circles and most of them were well established internationally in their respective fields of research: Hannes Alfven, Sven Brohult, Torsten Gustafson, Bror Rexed, Ingvar Svennilsson and Arne Tiselius, in this way, played key roles during the formative steps of this advisory body; two of them were actually, later, awarded Nobel Prizes.
• Although the Prime Minister served as chairman of the board, the board made no formal decisions and had no responsibility for implementation by the government.

The rather informal role of this advisory body was met with some skepticism within the Social Democratic Party, and there were motions in Parliament to change its formal status. More surprising, however, were the views of the Liberal Party which strongly maintained that more formal arrangements were desirable for the development *and* implementation of a science policy by the Parliament and the government.

A DECADE OF DECREASED ACTIVITIES

As the 1970s approached, the government's policy on technology and industry was charged to a newly created government agency, the Board for Technical Development (Styrelsen för teknisk utvëckling—STU). As Tage Erlander retired from the post of Prime Minister, in 1970, the importance of the Advisory Board on Science Policy decreased.

In 1976, the Social Democratic Party, under Olof Palme, lost the general election, and a coalition of conservatives and liberals formed the new government. The Advisory Board on Science Policy remained, was expanded, and met regularly as before, but still had only a marginal influence on the way research in the country was organized and developed. In 1979, the Parliament decided, however, that a bill on research and development (R&D) should be presented by the government to Parliament every three years. Some preparatory steps were taken by the ruling government at that time, but this new procedure was not fully implemented before the general election in 1982, when the Social Democratic Party returned to power with Olof Palme as Prime Minister.

THE ADVISORY BOARD ON SCIENCE IS REORGANIZED

During the 1970s, the more directed research, for which the responsibility was given to a number of government agencies, had grown rapidly. Industry also increased its involvement in research and development. Now, when addressing the question of how to develop a longer-term science policy for the country as a whole, Prime Minister Palme decided to reorganize the Science Advisory Board.

In 1983, the size of the board was was reduced to a mere eleven members. Its composition now consisted of the Vice Prime Minister (Ingvar Carlsson, who is now Prime Minister), the Minister for Education and Research, the Minister for Industry, the Chief of Planning Research Policy in the Prime Minister's Office, and six well-recognized scientists. The scientists are appointed for a period of three years, and this term cannot be renewed.

In 1986, when Ingvar Carlsson was appointed Prime Minister after the assassination of Olof Palme, he charged the Vice Prime Minister (the Minister of Finance, Kjell-Olof Feldt) with the position of chairman of the board and appointed the Science Advisor in the Prime Minister's Office as a member of the board.

DEVELOPING SCIENCE POLICY IN THE 1980s

The main responsibility of the board is to organize meetings (about four per year) on key issues in science and to select, on occasion, eight or ten additional scientists—perhaps a few additional ministers of the government and heads of government agencies—to take part in a full-day meeting with the board on the particular topic chosen for discussion. Until 1987, these meetings were held on the government estate, Harpsund, about one hundred miles outside of Stockholm, with the Prime Minister as the host. They lasted from three o'clock in the afternoon on one day until eleven o'clock in the morning on the following day and, accordingly, provided ample time for informal discussions. During the past few years, the Haga Castle in the immediate neighborhood of the city of Stockholm has served as the meeting place.

During the past seven years, a great many topics have been dealt with. Some examples include:

- Physics of today,
- Chemists build tailored molecules for use in medicine and industry,
- Biotechnology,
- Medical research and developing countries,
- Environmental sciences,
- Research in the agriculture and sylviculture sciences,
- Peace research,
- The role of religion in the world of today,
- Social sciences.

The board also meets to advise the government in the course of the preparatory work for the tri-annual bills to Parliament on science policy. Thus, the board, in the autumn of 1988, agreed to a proposal to bring together more detailed information on the development of science and science policy in a number of key countries of the world.

Some fifteen well-known scientists were engaged, a few of whom were members or former members of the board. They were asked to travel for two to four weeks and to report back to the board on their findings and impressions. A series of essays on science policy matters in Canada, the Federal Republic of Germany, France, Japan and the newly industrialized countries of the Far East, the United Kingdom, US, and USSR were presented, discussed by the board, and served as the basis for the preparation of the bill on science policy which was presented to Parliament in February 1990.

The creation of a planning office for research and development in the Prime Minister's Office and an Advisory Board on Science raises important organizational questions for the government. Setting priorities is not only judging the relative importance of research in different fields of science. To place research and development in the proper perspective relative to other social activities, of course, also implies the judging of the relative importance of research and development on the one hand and other activities in each specific sector of society on the other. This is a central and important function of each ministry and government agency.

A clarification of the degree of coordination that is useful—or even meaningful—at this level, therefore, is required. A general impression from the work of the past seven years is that a detailed planning effort at the level of the Prime Minister's Office may be counterproductive, but that the provision of an overview of ongoing research and development activities in society and agreement on a set of general priorities is essential. The role of science in the further development of society becomes more obvious and is brought up for explicit discussions at the highest possible level. The procedure used in Sweden has undoubtedly contributed significantly to the increased government funding for research and development that was agreed upon during the 1980s.

The board has been of importance in building confidence between politicians and scientists. A few hundred scientists have met with key politicians during the past seven years and have been given opportunities to present their views on the role of science in modern society. They have also learned about the difficult roles of politicians in deciding on complex issues, often without full knowledge of all aspects of the problems.

The politicians, on the other hand, have become acquainted not only with the leading scientists themselves and their achievements, but also with their scientific ways of approaching problems. Certainly full agreement and harmony have not always been reached in meetings of this kind, but mutual respect has increased. It should also be stressed that the fact that the board does not decide on matters of implementation has been most important in defining the role of the board as an advising body.

PRESENT TRENDS IN SCIENCE POLICY IN SWEDEN

The past five years have seen a clear change of government priorities for research and development in Sweden. While directed and applied research expanded rapidly during the 1960s and 1970s, the past decade has shown more emphasis on fundamental research. This is primarily due to the recognition by industry that broad basic knowledge in a research field much better services the specific needs of industry, since the particular specialties that are needed often can be taught to the newly graduated researcher by the industry itself. This is, however, not so for the fundamental concepts and theories that provide the long-term basis for further advancement.

It has also become clear that long-term development of an industry must be based on high-quality research, which, again, requires knowledge in adjacent fields of science and a good understanding of the key scientific issues.

There is general political agreement on these two important issues, which also means general agreement that increased funds should be provided to the universities, not necessarily directly, however, but rather via research councils that can provide the most careful and objective analyses and scrutiny in the process of granting funds. There is also general agreement that research in Sweden should be viewed from an international perspective. The Natural Science Research council has developed a plan for international assessment of research in Sweden, which undoubtedly has provided the politicians with the confidence that the scientists themselves can find the means to maintain high quality in their profession.

As a matter of fact, Sweden provides a larger share of its Gross National Product for funding research at universities than any other of the leading countries in the world, and the bill presented to Parliament in 1990 has even further reinforced this basic policy.

Science and Technology Advice to the Government of Thailand

Sanga Sabhasri

THE KINGDOM OF THAILAND *(Prathet Thai) is an independent monarchy, and has been operating under its present constitution since 1978. Its land area is 198,455 square miles, and its estimated population in 1989 was 55,562,000. Thai is the official language.*

In recent times, Thailand has been recognized as a new Asian tiger by foreign observers. This implies that the status of the country is undergoing a change from an agricultural country to one of the newly industrialized countries (NICs). Although many of the Thai people are still reluctant to accept this status, the change has, nevertheless, come about—albeit slowly and with great differences in pace from one location to another.

The development of technology can be traced since the mid-17th century when Thailand was heavily engaged in trade with the Western countries. This paved the way for the development of work in the medical sciences, traditional medicine, the public water supply, printing, and metallurgy.

Thailand did not embark upon industrial development until the end of World War II. In fact, there was an existing State Policy, defined in Article 65 of the Constitution of B.E. 2492 (1949), which stipulated that the state should support research into art and science. The National Research Council of Thailand, however, which is responsible for research promotion and coordination, was not established until ten years later, in 1959.

At that time, the council was under the jurisdiction of the Office of the Prime Minister, and was the main body for advising the Cabinet on science and technology activities. A revised version of its mandate appeared in the current Constitution of B.E. 2521 (1978), Article 61, which reads: "The State shall promote research in various fields of knowledge and intensify the application of science and technology for the country's development."

Then, in 1979, the Ministry of Science, Technology and Energy (MOSTE) was set up. This is one of the major breakthroughs in the organization of science and technology, and now serves as a major planning and implementation body for various activities in these areas.

Sanga Sabhasri is the Permanent Secretary of the Ministry of Science, Technology and Energy of the Kingdom of Thailand. He has participated in extensive international scientific activities and has numerous honorary degrees from several countries. Born in Chiang Mai, Thailand, in 1933, Dr. Sabhasri holds a Ph.D. in forest ecology from the University of Washington. His work has been widely published.

EMERGENCE OF THAI SCIENTISTS

The early 1960s saw the emergence of Thai scientists who began to be much better organized for serious scientific work. Various activities, such as conferences, seminars, panel discussions, and public debates on science and technology were frequently held at that time. Competitive and original research, however, did not gain ground until the late 1960s and early 1970s. Such activities received a positive response from the government which, in 1972, appointed an Advisory Committee on Science Policy under the Advisory Board on the Administrative System. Unfortunately, due to the change in government in 1973, the committee had only two opportunities to meet, and, therefore, no specific advice was registered. From that time until 1988, there was no advisory group in science and technology at the government level.

In the past, political leaders have been disinclined to embrace the application of science and technology for national development. This is a common phenomenon in developing countries where the values of science and technology are often underestimated. Developing countries are many times more concerned with national security and economic issues, and are not familiar with the applications of science and technology except in the sense of the commercial products that arise from them.

Not until recently was it widely recognized that science and technology play vital roles in national potential and that they are necessary and appropriate for the country's development. The country has also come to realize the wisdom of strengthening the manpower and capabilities of the science and technology infrastructure in order to cope with new science and technology advances.

The present situation also indicates the need for the establishment of a National Science and Technology Council. In Japan and Korea, where heads of science and technology are appointed as Cabinet members, there are National Science and Technology Councils which formulate the government's science and technology policies.

Chaired by the Prime Ministers of the respective countries, these councils are channels which provide opportunities to the heads of the Cabinets to become involved in formulating science and technology policy at the early stage. Although the councils may meet only a few times a year, the attendance and decisions of the Prime Minister and some Cabinet ministers in the council can help to promote the integration of science and technology policy into the process of national development.

THE PRESENT SITUATION

Thailand has not yet begun a practice similar to Japan and Korea in this respect. Even though many Thai scientists have voiced support for the concept, the council has not yet been established. In 1988, however, the Prime Minister appointed a new committee to give advice on matters pertaining to science and technology policy. The committee is composed of six members from academic circles who have past experience in policy and management of science and technology.

The assigned functions and authority of the committee are as follows:

- To study and propose guidelines and strategies for the development of science and technology in the country in line with both the short- and long-term socioeconomic development efforts, reporting directly to the Prime Minister;
- To call for data, documents and commentary from government agencies, public enterprises, and individuals concerned with science and technology when this advice is needed;
- To invite individuals concerned with science and technology to give briefings or comments pertaining to the functioning of the committee; and
- To carry out other relevant tasks as assigned by the Prime Minister.

Since its appointment, the committee has embarked on a number of major issues in science and technology policy. One example is a recommendation for the government to embark upon new programs in science and technology manpower development. This includes a plan, in addition to indigenous building of such manpower, to send a substantial number of students overseas to study new areas of science and technology which will be required for the predicted industrial and agro-industrial development of the country. This plan was recently approved by the Cabinet.

Another example is the recommendation, also approved by the Cabinet, to set up a data-processing zone in order to utilize and upgrade information and electronic technologies in the service of trade and industry.

The committee reached these recommendations through extensive studies and consultations with the agencies and individuals concerned, so that these recommendations are both realistic and capable of implementation.

NATIONAL SCIENCE ADVISERS

As science and technology activities at present comprise a societal expectation and their roles are played by various ministries and representatives of the private sector, it may be beneficial also to consider the appointment of science advisers to the Prime Ministers, as practiced in the United Kingdom or similar to the Presidential Science Advisor in the United States. By this means, science and technology policy and planning can be effectively carried out among the responsible agencies. It is expected that only experienced and well-recognized scientists can fulfill these tasks. The scientists and technologists as such, with access to the top decision-makers in the government, would help to accelerate the implementation of science and technology policy and other new initiatives.

In conclusion, Thailand already has committed itself to strive ahead in the application of science and technology for development. Thailand's present Constitution states, in Article 61, that the state shall promote the application of science and technology for development. Thailand established in 1979 the highest administrative organization, the Ministry of Science, Technology and Energy; its minister is a voice in the Cabinet and the ministry in general implements a number of projects. It is generally well recognized that science and technology serve as instruments that can systematically solve the country's most pressing problems, indicating how problems can be tackled at the minimum cost and with maximum benefit.

Organization of Scientific Research in the USSR

I. M. Makarov

THE UNION OF SOVIET SOCIALIST REPUBLICS *was established in 1922, and operates under a constitution adopted in 1977 and amended in 1988, and currently under review. The land area of the country is 8,649,489 square miles, and its population in 1989 was 286,717,000. The official language is Russian, but eighty-seven other languages are recognized.*

The general supervision of scientific and technological activities in the Union of Soviet Socialist Republics is exercised by the Soviet government, the Council of Ministers of the USSR.

A nationwide organization, which ensures the implementation of a consistent government policy in science and technology, is the State Committee of the USSR for Science and Technology, headed by a deputy chairman of the Council of Ministers of the country. One of the responsibilities of this committee is organization and coordination of the development of major government scientific and technological programs and the formulation of other scientific problems that are transmitted to the research institutions of various ministries and organizations.

The state committee evaluates the state of the art in the development of science and research in the different branches of the national economy. An important area in the activities of the committee is the development of ways to ensure a timely realization of the achievements of science and technology in the national economy. The committee, jointly with ministries and agencies, proposes measures on the practical implementation of scientific discoveries, inventions, and advanced research and development (R&D) results.

The Academy of Sciences of the USSR is the highest-ranking scientific institution in the Soviet Union and, as a nationwide government center, it is responsible for the formulation of national basic research policies. The Academy of Sciences is directly accountable to the USSR Council of Ministers. It works out general policy lines for the development of basic research in the country; it also formulates programs for developing the most important areas of research and consistently implements into practice these programs by drawing upon the results of research work obtained in its institutes.

I. M. Makarov, Academician, is Chief Scientific Secretary, Presidium of the USSR Academy of Sciences; head of the major research project, All-Union Institute of Systems Research; and Chairman of the Scientific Council for Robotics and Automated Manufacturing of the Academy. Born in 1927, Dr. Makarov is the author of more than 140 research papers.

THREE SECTORS

The traditional system of organization of scientific research in the USSR comprises three sectors—academic, higher educational, and industrial—which differ among themselves with respect to their tasks, affiliations with ministries and agencies, and specific structural and functional features.

Academic science in the Soviet Union develops within the framework of the USSR Academy of Sciences and fourteen academies of sciences in constituent republics of the USSR. The main task of the academies is the promotion of basic research in the natural, technical, social and humanitarian sciences. It is within the academies that basic research is primarily concentrated, although, to some extent, it is also done at the higher education establishments at several branch academies of sciences and scientific institutions.

The most outstanding scientists of the country are members of the USSR Academy of Sciences. At present, the composition of the academy's membership is 308 full members (Academicians), 570 Corresponding Members, and more than one hundred Foreign Members, representing scientists from twenty-five countries of the world.

Its main objective being the development of basic research in the major areas of the natural, technical and social sciences, the USSR Academy of Sciences, according to its statute, exercises general scientific supervision of the research work in the major areas of these three sciences, carried out in the academies of sciences of constituent republics of the USSR, in higher educational establishments, and in other research institutions. The Academy of Sciences of the USSR coordinates the progress of basic research, which is carried out in institutes under ministries and agencies, branch academies, and higher educational establishments.

One of the basic tasks of the academy is the identification of fundamentally new opportunities for technological progress and rendering assistance to the branch ministries and agencies in the fullest possible utilization of scientific achievements in practical applications.

A MAJOR SCIENCE CENTER

The USSR Academy of Sciences is a major science center, not only on a national scale, but on the world scale as well. It has more than two hundred scientific institutions whose research work it has to supervise and coordinate. More than 60,000 researchers work in these institutions (this figure does not include the laboratory assistants and technical staff). A great number of research institutes under the USSR Academy of Sciences are located in Moscow and in science centers around the capitol. The academy has a wide-ranging network of scientific institutions that are located in the Russian Federation: the Siberian, Urals, and Far-Eastern regional branches of the academy; the Leningrad, Kola, Saratov and Kuibyshev science centers; and a number of branch offices of the USSR Academy of Sciences and of its regional divisions in the autonomous republics and districts.

Regional branches, science centers and branch offices of the USSR Academy of Sciences are all comprehensive in their natures with respect to their research efforts in the various areas of science. The scientific institutions that comprise them implement—parallel to what is involved with the general academic research effort—projects which have a direct bearing on the development of the economy and culture in their respective regions.

Members of the management bodies of the USSR Academy of Sciences are all comprehensive in their natures with respect to their research efforts in the various areas of science. The highest management body of the academy is the General Meeting of full members and corresponding members of the academy. General supervision and administrative support of academic research is the single most important function of the Presidium of the USSR Academy of Sciences. There are also several science-oriented branches of the academy which are essentially science and science-administration centers, whose members are academic scientists specializing in one or several branches of science. At present, there are eighteen such branches.

Academic research institutes, according to the statute of the USSR Academy of Sciences, are its main scientific institutions. Many of these institutes have made outstanding contributions to the advancement of world science and technology, and are widely known throughout the world. Among these institutes are the following: the V. A. Steklov Mathematical Institute, the P. N. Lebedev Physical Institute, the A. F. Ioffe Physical and Engineering Institute, the A. N. Nesmeyanov Institute of Organo-Metallic Compounds, the M. M. Shemyakin Institute of Bio-Organic Chemistry, the I. P. Pavlov Institute of Physiology, the O. Y. Schmidt Institute of Physics of the Earth, the Institute of Russian Literature (the Pushkin House), and many other institutes.

The Academy of Sciences of the USSR also carries out important work within the scope of its educational effort by training highly qualified researchers in practically all areas of science.

ACADEMIES IN THE CONSTITUENT REPUBLICS

Academies of sciences in the constituent republics of the Soviet Union—Ukranian SSR, Byelorussian SSR, Georgian SSR, Uzbek SSR, etc.—are major centers of Soviet science. Contributing to the fundamental research effort in all the most important areas of science, these academies place regional problems at the tops of their agendas and actively promote the economic and cultural development of their republics. Both the structure of these academies and the organization of the scientific work under their auspices are generally similar to those of the USSR Academy of Sciences.

Significant results have also been obtained in the academies of sciences and universities of the constituent Soviet republics; major schools of science have appeared in some of them.

The work of the republican academies is coordinated by the Council on Co-ordination of Scientific Activities of the Academies of Science, a body which is accountable to the Presidium of the Academy of Sciences of the USSR. The council strives to unify academic science. All the republican academies of sciences are represented on this council at the highest level, and the council is headed by the President of the USSR Academy of Sciences.

The universities and other higher educational establishments are also engaged in doing both basic and applied research. Great attention is paid to the development of science at Soviet colleges and universities. There are more than nine hundred higher education establishments in the Soviet Union today, including sixty-nine universities. Many of them are also major science centers, *e.g.,* the M. V. Lomonosov University in Moscow and the Leningrad, Kazan and Kiev Universities, among others.

Enormous scientific potential is concentrated in Soviet colleges and universities. To illustrate this point, it is enough to mention that approximately one-quarter of the total number of full members and corresponding members of the USSR Academy of Sciences and more than 50% of scientists having Ph.D. and/or M.Sc. diplomas are employed in the colleges and universities of this country. It is not only the permanent staffs of the colleges and universities—professors, faculty members, teachers, and lecturers—but post-graduate students and a great number of other students who are actively engaged in research work.

Research work is concentrated in the departments of the colleges and universities, at several dozen research institutes that are affiliated with such colleges and universities, and at numerous problem-oriented and branch laboratories. Research work which is done at these higher educational establishments is inseparable from the curriculum training, which determines its substance and organization.

The North Caucasian Research Center of higher educational establishments of the area was established in 1970. This center has made possible effective utilization of scientific potential in a number of regions, districts and autonomous republics in the southern part of the Russian Federation. The development of direct long-term relationships between higher education establishments and industries has become much more productive since the establishment of the North Caucasian Research Center.

GENERAL SUPERVISION

General supervision of research work at higher educational institutions is exercised by the USSR State Committee on Education and by appropriate ministries and committees in Soviet republics through special management apparatus and science and technology councils of these ministries.

The branch academies of sciences are engaged primarily in the coordination of applied research and development work for the various sectors of the national economy. Thousands of institutes and laboratories of the respective branch ministries and agencies are engaged in this kind of applied research. They are responsible for the management of scientific and technological projects in their respective branches, and also for the execution of projects that are connected to comprehensive interbranch scientific and technological problems. By drawing upon the resources of their own administrative and management units, ministries and agencies exercise general supervision of research institutions and of design and development organizations, which are under their authority, including R&D planning and coordination.

Some of the USSR ministries supervise the activities of above-mentioned branch academies of sciences, which are the highest-ranking research institutions in each particular branch of the national economy. Among them are the All-Union Academy of Agricultural Sciences, named after V. I. Lenin (VAS-NIL), the Academy of Medical Sciences of the USSR, and the Academy of Pedagogical Sciences of the USSR. Prominent scientists and specialists in these respective fields are full members and corresponding members of the branch academies of sciences. A General Meeting of academy members is the highest body of the academy. All activities of the branch academies are governed by their statutes, just as in the case of the USSR Academy of Sciences or the academies of the constituent republics of the Soviet Union; members of all governing bodies of the branch academies are also elected. Branch academies have their own research institutes, laboratories, and other facilities corresponding to their areas of specialization in various fields of science; they also have regional offices and affiliates.

It must be emphasized that all sectors of Soviet science are not isolated nor closed upon themselves, but are interconnected and develop in continuous interaction with each other. For example, in recent years, we have witnessed the consistent strengthening of the ties between the USSR Academy of Sciences and the higher educational establishments. New, concrete forms of such ties have appeared, such as science education centers and affiliates of college and university departments in academic institutions. Interbranch scientific and technological complexes have been established to promote practical implementation of the results of R&D projects completed at academic institutes, colleges and universities. There are twenty-three such complexes now, including such well-known complexes as Eye Microsurgery and the E. O. Paton Institute of Electrical Welding.

MAJOR INTERNATIONAL RESEARCH CENTERS

A number of major international research centers have been established and successfully operate in the Soviet Union, including the Joint Institute for Nuclear Research in Dubna. Recently, the L. Euler International Mathematical Institute was inaugurated in Leningrad.

Insofar as the organization of research work in the Soviet Union is concerned, there is a definite trend toward greater concentration of the research effort with a view to solving major scientific problems of fundamental significance. Program- and target-oriented approaches to planning scientific research have been steadily gaining in popularity in the USSR since the 1970s.

The advantage of programs lies in their comprehensive nature: They cover the entire range of activities that are involved in a project, from basic and applied research to actual large-scale industrial production of all kinds of articles that are needed to make the economy run smoothly. The practical implementation of the programs requires a committed effort and the direct participation of research institutions and industrial enterprises, irrespective of their ministerial or organizational affiliations, the only incentive in this being that they should have a common task to solve.

It is envisaged in the programs that problems of great economic significance should be solved as the result of program implementation. Last year, fourteen nationwide government scientific and technological programs were formulated under the aegis of the State Committee of the USSR for Science and Technology. The Academy of Sciences of the USSR put forward eighteen academic programs of basic research. The practical implementation of most of these programs involves the participation of research institutions of different ministerial or organizational affiliation.

Some of the scientific and technological programs are essentially regional or branch-oriented, *i.e.*, their objectives are either to solve certain tasks of general nature and give them concrete applications within a certain branch of the national economy or to solve sets of tasks, all of which have applications within a certain region. The Sibir program—a program of development of this rapidly progressing region of the Soviet Union—is an example of a regional program involving the solutions to a great number of economic, scientific and technological tasks.

PREDICTING THE FUTURE

The prediction of future trends of the scientific and technological revolution is a task to which great significance is attributed in the system of science and technology development planning which currently exists in the USSR. With this purpose in mind, a comprehensive program of scientific and technological progress in the USSR, covering a period of twenty years, is regularly prepared and updated every five years. Many research institutions in the country actively participate in developing this program. The general supervision of the program development is exercised by the Scientific Council on problems of the scientific, technological, social and economic forecasts at the Presidium of the USSR

Academy of Sciences and the State Committee of the USSR for Science and Technology.

Data contained in this program—which cover the period from 1991 to 2010— are used, at present, to develop guidelines for the economic and social development of the USSR until the year 2005 and to develop the national plan for the thirteenth five-year period.

In recent years, the USSR Academy of Sciences has significantly raised the status of a practice whereby all major projects that are marked for implementation on a national scale should undergo examination by an independent academic commission of experts. As a result, the Academy of Sciences of the USSR is receiving an increasing number of government orders for theoretical substantiation, by academic commissions of experts, of various proposals for national economic development.

The USSR Academy of Sciences pays great attention to issues relating to its international ties and to international division of scientific labor. Academic scientists represent the Soviet Union in a number of major international scientific projects, such as environmental protection, energy for the future, and the human genome problem, as well as in a number of various international scientific associations and organizations, such as UNESCO, ICSU and IAEA.

With the process of perestroika now underway in the Soviet Union, many institutes of the USSR Academy of Sciences are taking active parts in preparing drafts of new political and economic laws and new methods of managing the country's development.

An important role in planning, organization and coordination of scientific research in the country belongs to the problem-oriented research councils. Members of these councils work on a voluntary basis and without remuneration. They are scientists, specialists, production experts, educators, social and cultural workers, etc. They serve on these councils irrespective of their own organizations' affiliations, and are interested in the theoretical and practical aspects of the same scientific problems they are solving.

Problem-oriented research councils are set up under the State Committee of the USSR for Science and Technology, the Academy of Sciences of the USSR, and academies of sciences of constituent Soviet republics, as well as the State Committee of the USSR for Public Education. Heads of these councils are prominent scientists. The research councils analyze the progress and results of scientific research in their respective problem areas, discuss these topics at sessions and conferences which they organize, and work out recommendations concerning the practical applications of the obtained results. Thus, more than three hundred research councils, commissions, and other bodies representing the scientific community function today in the Academy of Sciences of the USSR.

VOLUNTARY SOCIETIES

The overall picture of the organization of scientific research in the USSR would not be completed if we omitted mention of the activities of the voluntary scientific and techno-scientific societies, which are grass-roots public organizations, offering to their members excellent opportunities for gaining better understanding of various scientific disciplines and insight into scientific creativity. More than two dozen scientific societies and associations have been established at the USSR Academy of Sciences alone.

Techno-scientific societies, which are established in a number of industries, have very large memberships among technicians, blue-collar workers, inventors, and authors of production rationalization proposals. The total number of members of such societies is about twelve million. All these societies are supervised by the Council of Scientific and Engineering Societies of the All-Union Central Council of Trade Unions.

CONCLUSION

In such a vast, multinational country as the Soviet Union, efficient and precise coordination is very much needed to assure the smooth running of the existing ramified system of scientific institutions, higher education establishments, and public organizations in scientific, technological and cultural spheres, as well as their mutual interactions and diverse interconnections.

All issues relating to further improvements in the organization of research in the USSR are constantly kept in the focus of attention at all levels of power in the Soviet Union in recognition of the growing importance of science in socio-economic, sociopolitical, and technological development of the country, in its social renewal and in improving the well-being of the Soviet people.

Science Policy in the United Kingdom

John W. Fairclough

THE UNITED KINGDOM OF GREAT BRITAIN AND NORTHERN IRELAND *is a constitutional monarchy which operates under a democratic parliamentary system. Its land area is 94,249 square miles, and its population in the 1981 census was 55,775,650 (England and Wales), plus 5,130,735 (Scotland) and 1,562,775 (Northern Ireland, estimated in 1988). The official language is English, but Gaelic and Welsh are also spoken in parts of the country. As of December 31, 1989, the US dollar was equal to .62 pounds sterling and .84 of the European Community Unit (ECU).*

The role of the Chief Scientific Adviser, the position which is presently held by this author, is a heady mixture of freedom to speak up on any science and technology issue across the full range, coupled with a lack of specific budgetary responsibility and no direct control over laboratories in which to test out his advice.

This is mentioned, not to enlist the reader's sympathy or to attract his or her envy, but because it illustrates the most important feature of the British Government's approach to science and technology and, indeed, to many other areas of policy as well, *i.e.,* that decisions, whether they concern basic research by the universities and research councils or applied research in support of government policy, regulation and procurement, should wherever possible be delegated to those who have the depth of knowledge and understanding of the subject in question to recognize scientific excellence, on the one hand, and to understand the contribution science and technology can make to improving the quality of life and international competitiveness, on the other.

The year 1992 will mark the 20th anniversary of the Rothschild Report, which set out the customer/contractor principle on which UK policy for expenditure on applied R&D is based. This requires a clear customer to commission research and development (R&D) from a contractor, so for applied R&D there are as many ministers responsible as there are customer departments: energy, agriculture, and the rest. On the other hand, basic science does not have a true customer, and the Department of Education and Science is responsible for funding

John W. Fairclough has been Chief Scientific Adviser to the United Kingdom's Cabinet Office since 1986. He was formerly Director of Manufacturing and Development for IBM UK Ltd. and Chairman of IBM UK Laboratories Ltd. Dr. Fairclough also served as Vice President of the System Development Division of Raleigh Development Laboratories, USA, and was Managing Director of Hursley Laboratory, UK.

The views expressed in this essay are those of the author and not necessarily those of Her Majesty's Government.

virtually all of this. The UK believes most strongly in supporting "curiosity science" conducted by the most able scientists, but science push and market pull are both important.

Thus, applied science and technology is very much a means to an end and not an end in itself. The responsibility for making decisions on how much to spend and what R&D to spend it on is for those who are responsible for the policies and objectives that that R&D is designed to serve. Different departments of state have their own science and technology budgets and make decisions on them. A list of these departments is shown in Table 1, together with their 1988 annual expenditures on R&D.

There are, however, two risks in pursuing this philosophy too simplistically. First, there is the problem of pre-empting resources. All countries, including the United States, have insufficient scientists to excel in all fields. How are the priorities to be set to get the best out of limited resources? Second, there is the problem of duplication of effort. The question is how to get the most out of our science and technology programs. Work to develop technologies relevant to the defense industries, for example, could be of enormous significance to a range of civil applications. How do we get different customers for research and different teams of scientists to share and collaborate so as to see the results of the research exploited for the widest benefit?

THE MECHANISMS OF SCIENCE POLICY IN THE UK

In a White Paper (Cm 185),[1] published in July 1987, the British Government announced a number of changes to strengthen the central machinery for dealing with science and technology policy.

It stated that particular emphasis would be given to the determination of priorities for science and technology across government. This would be done, each year, as part of the Public Expenditure Survey process.

A new Advisory Council for Science and Technology (ACOST) was set up with membership drawn from the private and higher education sectors. It has terms of reference to advise the Prime Minister across the whole range of science and technology from basic science through industrial exploitation. The Prime Minister herself meets with the council from time to time.

ACOST's work falls into two categories. First, it offers advice to ministers on priorities, so as to inform the annual budgeting process. Second, it reports on specific issues. It is responsible for choosing the topics to study, but takes account of the current issues to which the government is giving particular attention. A recent example is *Defence R&D: A National Resource,* published in May 1989.

ACOST meets six times a year as a full council. Most of its business is done by small study teams whose work ranges from a few weeks for current issues to in-depth studies of specific subjects lasting many months. In addition, there are three standing committees: one dealing with international matters, a second

Table 1. Expenditure on R&D by Departments (1987–88)

Department	£Millions
Civil Departments	
Ministry of Agriculture, Fisheries and Food	113.8
Department of Education and Science	72.8
Department of Energy	176.4
Department of the Environment	62.1
Department of Health and Social Security	47.3
Health and Safety Commission	5.1
Home Office	14.2
Overseas Development Agency	32.5
Department of Trade and Industry	324.4
Department of Transport	26.4
Northern Ireland Departments	16.8
Scottish Departments	51.6
Welsh Office	1.9
Department of Employment	2.2
Training Agency	23.9
Other Departments	31.2
Total Civil Departments	1,002.7
Research Councils	
Agriculture and Food Research Council	49.4
Economic and Social Research Council	21.6
Medical Research Council	139.1
Natural Environment Research Council	70.8
Science and Engineering Research Council	334.5
Total Research Councils	615.5
University Grants Committee	760.0
Total Civil R&D	2,378.1
Ministry of Defence[1]	2,237.5
TOTAL	4,615.7

[1] Includes £1,759.5 million for expenditure, mainly with industry, on development of specific weapons and equipment.

with the annual review process, and a third which monitors key areas of science and technology.

THE ADVISER'S TERMS OF REFERENCE

The Chief Scientific Adviser's terms of reference as are follows:

1. The Chief Scientific Adviser, Cabinet Office, is responsible for providing or organizing the provision of advice to the Prime Minister and the Cabinet Office on scientific and technological matters or scientific and

technological aspects of other issues. He is concerned with influencing postively the economic contribution from government spending in science and technology. He sits on the principal interdepartmental committees which deal with the scientific and technological issues that come before government. He also has a general responsibility for the coordination of international scientific and technological relationships, and is the government's scientific representative on many international occasions.

2. The Chief Scientific Adviser, Cabinet Office, attends meetings of the Advisory Council on Science and Technology (ACOST) and acts as the prime link between ACOST and the government. He is a member of the Advisory Board of the Research Councils, the Advisory Council on Research and Development for Fuel and Power, and the Defence Scientific Advisory Council. He is a *membre titulaire* of CREST (the committee that advises both the European Community Council of Ministers and the Commission on Research Issues) and UK member of the Board of Governors of the Joint Research Centre of the European Community.

The adviser is supported in his task by forty professional and administrative staff members, organized in three groups. The first deals with the scientific business of government and supports the Prime Minister and her colleagues in their consideration of science and technology policies and priorities. This group also includes the Science and Technology Assessment Office, which has led the introduction of the best practice in evaluation and assessment in government departments' research and development programs and projects. The second provides the secretariat for the ACOST, and the third deals exclusively with the UK's international—particularly European—interests in science, such as support for the minister who represents the UK at the European Research Council where the European Framework program of collaborative research and development is agreed upon.

Work with the departments is organized through meetings chaired and arranged by the author as adviser. All departments that have an interest in and spend money on research and development are represented by their most senior individuals dealing with R&D; a number of departments have chief scientific advisers. A subgroup focuses on international issues, dealing particularly with the European collaborative research and development programs.

Additionally, the Departments of Energy, Trade and Industry, Education and Science, and Defence each has an advisory body dealing with research and development and providing independent advice to each department's Secretary of State. As adviser, I am a member of each of these bodies, which gives me the opportunity to influence and be influenced by their work. Also, the chairman of each of these bodies attends meetings of ACOST, and this enables overall policy advice to be effectively coordinated.

Table 2. International Comparisons 1987[1]

	GERD[2] (percent of GDP)	Percentage GERD Financed by Government
UK	2.3	38.7
USA	2.7	50.8
Japan	2.9	21.7
Germany	2.8	33.6
France	2.3	52.9
Italy	1.3	54.2

Notes
[1] OECD data.
[2] GERD is the OECD measure of total R&D activity in a country.

THE MECHANISMS AT WORK

The emphasis in the United Kingdom on establishing priorities means that we are ready to reduce expenditure—not just increase it. Some of the recent increases in expenditure on more fundamental science have been funded by reductions in other areas, in particular, in research for which, we judge, it is more appropriate for the private sector to pay.

A growing proportion of the UK's science and technology budget is being directed to basic and what we call "long-term strategic research" by universities and research councils. This is not "strategic" in any military sense, but in the sense that there are certain areas of research which, by their very nature, are pervasive and potentially of wide application.

Table 2 compares the 1978 R&D activity, as a percentage of Gross Domestic Product, from the public and private sectors of the major industrialized nations. It shows that the UK's performance is broadly comparable with other countries.

THE SCIENCE BASE

To examine the specific area of fundamental science, it should be explained that the United Kingdom Science Budget is administered by the Department of Eduation and Science. The £800 million for the Science Budget in 1989–90 is distributed by the Secretary of State for Education and Science on the basis of advice from the Advisory Board for the Research Councils (ABRC). ABRC, in turn, avoids detailed decisions on projects, leaving those to be decided by the five separate research councils.

In addition to this £800 million, a similar sum is spent on research out of funds allocated directly to the universities; much of this goes on equipment and other overhead to provide "well-found" laboratories for research projects funded by research councils. The vast majority of British fundamental science is funded as the result of decisions made by other scientific experts—peer review is the central mechanism. This contrasts with applied science, which is funded by those who are the customers for the research. "Intelligent customers," *i.e.,* those with the resources to properly assess the scientific options available, are best placed to judge the contributions science and technology programs can make in achieving their objectives.

So many of the interesting challenges and opportunities in science lie on the boundaries between traditional academic disciplines. The challenge to be the first in the race for high-temperature superconducting materials needs the experience of both the chemists and material scientists to experiment with new materials and of the physicists to understand why different materials perform in different ways. As we learn more about the fine structure of the physical and living world, we increasingly find ourselves in border regions between chemistry, physics and biology. These separate domains were created by us for our own convenience, but nature does not recognize such boundaries.

In a country like the United Kingdom, where much of the basic research goes on in universities and is tied closely to particular teaching disciplines, this has meant that we have needed to rethink the way in which such interdisciplinary research is carried out. The UK is not alone in this. The National Science Foundation in the United Kingdom has an ambitious program of interdisciplinary research centers. The UK is embarking on a similar program.

Seventeen interdisciplinary research centers have either been established or are in the process of being established. The subjects on which these centers are focusing cover a wide range from superconductivity at Cambridge to transgenic animal biology at Edinburgh, from surface science at Liverpool to molecular sciences at Oxford. The intention is that each center should be located in a university under the leadership of a scientist who has an established reputation of excellence in his particular field. The centers are not institutionalized, making it easier to focus on and follow areas of scientific excellence, adapting—as necessary—to change.

A DIFFICULT BALANCING ACT

There is always a difficult balancing act between the need to concentrate resources and establish centers of excellence without, at the same time, creating a rigid structure which excludes the individual scientist. There is much to be said for critical mass, but it can too easily become set into rigid structures which outlive their usefulness. This is a challenge for everyone concerned with supporting long-term curiosity-driven science. The task of the director of the center is a difficult one, providing leadership, selecting the key people, and ensuring an atmosphere of communication and cooperation, while avoiding the stultifying of science by overmanagement.

The ABRC is reviewing the process of selection of both subject and location of interdisciplinary research centers so that the country can draw the appropriate lessons and improve the process. The centers currently account for about 3% of the Science Budget.

These are exciting times for scientists in the United Kingdom, both because some important changes are being introduced and because of an increased budget for basic science. The Prime Minister, herself a Fellow of the society, spoke to The Royal Society in September 1988 and explained her deep conviction as to the importance of basic science. She also urged British scientists to do more to communicate the enthusiasm and importance of their scientific work to the general public.

Science, like any other activity, has to argue its case in a democracy, and there is no point in scientists complaining that they are unloved or misunderstood if they do not go out to earn that admiration and explain the importance and relevance of their scientific successes. It is not an easy matter. If the public is to understand science, it needs to have a sufficient degree of scientific literacy and interest itself. But the primary responsibility for achieving this lies with the scientific community.

THE EXPLOITATION OF SCIENCE

One of the best ways of communicating success is to have highly visible commercial exploitation of scientific work. This is a difficult area in which to determine the respective responsibilities of government and industry. Of course, government is critically involved through its responsibility for the patent system and for a framework of protecting intellectual property. That is intrinsically an international activity, and the UK policy is to encourage the uptake of European rather than national patents.

Beyond that, the government has to have policies for the exploitation of the research that it has funded itself, including the universities and the research councils. There have been major changes in Britain in the past few years with much more responsibility being devolved down to the individual institution, the individual researcher, and industry to play greater roles. The government believes that a centrist approach to this important issue is dangerous, because there is a significant risk that directions will be picked without hard commercial tests being applied; there also seems to be a temptation for government to support the weak, because it is they who have their hands out, asking for help. One could argue that it is better to reinforce success, this being consistent with the view that science funding should be based on excellence.

The UK government believes that the most effective way to select national priorities for strategic science and technology is to rely on the good judgment of both science and industry to come together in fields of common interest and for the government to create an environment for this to happen in by providing support to enable more of these collaborations to occur than would happen otherwise. Intellectual partnerships between the creators of knowledge and the exploiters of knowledge is the goal that we have set ourselves.

This is particularly important for the UK because the private sector is not investing enough in longer-term strategic science and technology. This is also important for a second reason: The transfer of technology from the university to industry is not just a one-way process. Through its collaboration with academic research, industry can help set the agenda for science, supporting fields where there is confidence in the people carrying out the research and endorsing its relevance.

THE CREATION OF CEST

More recently, the government has welcomed the establishment of the Centre for the Exploitation of Science and Technology (CEST), an idea originally proposed by ACOST. This center is primarily funded by industrial companies and financial institutions with some government funding as well. Its aim is to bring science, industry, business investors, and government together to do four things, as follows:

- To monitor R&D developments worldwide;
- To form judgments on what holds out the best promise of commercial exploitation, which means looking at social and demographic developments and society's changing needs, as well as the technology needed to satisfy them;
- To seek better ways to link scientists, manufacturers and commerce so that ideas are translated into saleable goods and services; and
- To encourage industry, investors and scientists to stay in touch not only with each other but with the market.

As Chief Scientific Adviser, this author also advises on the coordination of the government's international scientific and technological relationships. The UK attaches significant importance to this. Britain can never hope to do more than a small proportion of total world science. Therefore, its researchers need to stay in touch with the developments in other countries. But this does not mean that we believe in international collaboration for its own sake; it is the quality of the resulting science which matters. Nor are we ready to be less tough with waste and inefficiency in international projects than we are prepared to be in the UK.

That said, the UK has demonstrated its support for international collaboration over the years, most recently with the allocation of an extra £9.3 million for its CERN subscription in 1989–90. The country's most important contribution, however, remains in the intellects and abilities of its scientists and researchers. This is as true of its participation in the European Community's research programs as elsewhere.

THE EUROPEAN DIMENSION

A wide range of science and technology is sponsored by the European Commission. The present five-year program is worth 5.5 billion ECUs and its overall theme is aimed at enhancing European industrial competitiveness. European collaboraton on research and development is set to become increasingly significant.

To start with the basics, at the very heart of the program for 1992 is the Single European Act, which also lays the foundations for the European Community's Framework Program of research. The Single Act makes it plain that the crux is to support the research efforts of companies, research institutes, and universities, both individually and cooperatively. Action by the Community must, therefore, complement and not undermine these efforts.

The single market agenda is, of course, largely focused on trade and related issues, but there are some close links with R&D. The most obvious of these is the harmonization of technical standards. Some research programs, such as RACE and ESPRIT, have already contributed to the formulation of standards which will help European industry compete on the world stage. Others have the creation or administration of standards as a major goal. The Community Bureau of Reference is the obvious example.

A second feature of the single market of importance to research is mobility, both of people and of resources. It is expected that young people—whether at the undergraduate, post-graduate or post-doctoral level—as well as qualified professional people, will move around the Community much more freely in the future. How will this affect where research is carried out? Will we see concentrations of expertise and specialization in the various universities and institutes, or will we see a more general spread of talent? And what about the mobility of resources, both money and research facilities, will they be the main attraction or will they chase after the people and lower overheads?

Another important area is that of regulation. The conduct of scientific experiments will clearly be affected by the harmonization of regulations on animal welfare, safety, and so on. R&D will also be affected by—as well as contribute to—the harmonization of technical standards for products.

There will also be consequences for customers of research. For example, in a freer, more competitive market, will governments be able to turn to any research institute in Europe for guidance on questions of relevance to policy? Will private companies commission more of the research from outside institutions?

THE FUTURE DIRECTION

Finally, how will the direction of research policy in the Community be determined in the future? Clearly, any extension of top-down planning must be fiercely resisted as being quite at odds with the development of science policy in the UK and in other member states of the Community. We should, rather, as with the single market, be seeking to reduce barriers and make it easier for researchers to collaborate and compete across national boundaries. At this stage, there are far more questions than answers to be given about the place of research in the Europe of 1992. Faced with such uncertainties, there are a number of broad principles which will continue to be valid.

First, government-funded R&D, whether at the national or the Community level, should be directed—above all—toward basic and strategic research or in support of governments' policy-making, regulatory and procurement requirements.

Second, international collaborative research is not an end in itself, but—under the right conditions—properly assessed and selected projects can offer real advantages. So there must be an environment in which such collaboration can flourish. This does not mean that they have to be invented and directed by the center. Rather, we need an environment which will facilitate flexible solutions to differing research problems and encourage key individuals to remain in contact with each other. And here the diversity of expertise in the Community should be regarded as one of its strengths.

RESPONSIBILITY AND ACCOUNTABILITY

The next principle is that it is essential for all concerned with collaborative research to feel directly responsible and accountable for the resources they will be using. Community funding for R&D ultimately comes from the taxpayer, and we set out to ensure that only the most worthwhile projects are supported. In the UK, there is not a separate budget for international and European Community collaboration. These and national projects are treated as coming out of the same pot. This ensures that the same standards apply to both. That is as it should be.

Finally, let us not forget that, as we consider action at the government or the Community level, the main research effort must continue to be shouldered by companies, and the wider economic benefits which will result from the single market may help their research efforts far more than anything we do in terms of R&D policy.

It has been said:

> There is nothing more difficult to carry out, nor more doubtful of success, nor more dangerous to handle, than to initiate a new order of things.
>
> For the former has enemies in all who profit by the old order, and only lukewarm defenders in all those who would profit by the new order.
>
> This lukewarmness arises partly from fear of their adversaries, who have the law in their favour; and partly from the incredulity of mankind, who do not truly believe in anything new until they have had actual experience of it.

Who wrote that? you may wonder. Keynes? Friedman? Drucker? It was Machiavelli—in 1513! He knew a thing or two!

NOTES

1. Both the White Paper (Cmd 185) and the ACOST publication mentioned in the text are available from Her Majesty's Stationery Office through its agent, Unipub, Lanham, Maryland 20801, USA.

The Importance of Access and Knowledge to the Science Adviser to the President of the United States

David Z. Robinson

THE UNITED STATES *(United States of America) declared its independence as a nation on July 4, 1776, and has operated as a federal republic since 1789. Its land area is 3,615,122 square miles, and its estimated population in 1989 was 247,732,000. The primary language is English.*

> The President's Science Adviser is *not:* (1) a lobbyist for the scientific community; (2) an uncritical salesman for the President's policies; or (3) a wizard who personally covers all of science and technology in depth.
> —David A. Hamburg[1]

The role of Science and Technology Adviser to the President of the United States, established in 1951 in response to the demands of the Korean War,[2] has broadened with the postwar explosion of scientific knowledge and technical innovation and a growing recognition of their collective impact. Meanwhile, the real power of the adviser has waxed and waned, depending on Presidential style, personal chemistry, staff support, political tides, and external events. This essay is a status report on a dynamic situation.

D. Allan Bromley, the Assistant to the President of the United States for Science and Technology, has three major functions:

- To advise the President on issues of direct concern or interest that have significant scientific or technological content;
- To review and coordinate the activities of the federal government that involve science and technology; and
- To enlist the help of scientists and engineers outside the government in solving problems identified through the first two functions and in examining potential future problems.

These functions are conveniently represented by the adviser's three titles: Assistant to the President for Science and Technology, Director of the Office of Science and Technology Policy, and Chairman of the President's Council of

David Z. Robinson was appointed Executive Director of the Carnegie Commission on Science, Technology and Government in 1988. In 1961, after ten years as an industrial physicist, he joined the staff of the Science Advisor to the President of the United States. In 1967, Dr. Robinson became Vice President for Academic Affairs at New York University, and, in 1970, he joined the Carnegie Corporation of New York, first as Vice President and later as Executive Vice President and Treasurer. He has also been a trustee or adviser to academic institutions and nonprofit agencies, as well as government agencies.

Advisers on Science and Technology. In practice, there is a good deal of overlap in these assignments.

The Office of Science and Technology Policy (OSTP) carries budget and
personnel to support all three functions. Its Fiscal Year 1990 budget is $2.8
million (up from $1.4 million in 1989), and it includes thirty-three full-time
staff positions (up from fifteen). Fifteen of these are senior professional positions. Two additional staff members are assigned from other federal agencies.

Dr. Bromley has filled all four associate director positions that were authorized by the enabling legislation. One is James Wyngaarden, former Director
of the National Institutes of Health. Although OSTP is a relatively small agency,
it can have a great deal of influence, and the changes in budget indicate President Bush's interest in the office. What will determine this influence? As with
previous advisers, success or effectiveness will turn on access and knowledge.

ACCESS TO THE PRESIDENT

Unless the adviser can see the President of the United States when he feels he
needs to, he will have little influence—not only because his primary role will
be circumscribed, but because access to the President is critical to securing the
cooperation and help of people in government and the help of busy scientists
outside. While the access does not have to be frequent, it must be real, and it
should include being "in the loop" when the President deals with problems
that have technological content and political saliency, such as global warming
or the space program.

President Bush gave an important signal about access by upgrading the adviser's formal title. Dr. Bromley's predecessors had the title of Special Assistant to the President. Dr. Bromley has the higher rank of Assistant to the President, at the same level as the Directors of the National Security Council and
the Domestic Policy Council. In his first year in office, Dr. Bromley has had
substantial access to the President.

ACCESS TO THE EXECUTIVE STAFF

The President's staff is roughly divided into the White House staff, which deals
with political and policy issues, the public, the press, and the President's schedule,
and the Executive Office staff, which is involved in continuing issues of policy,
management, and oversight. To be effective, the adviser must have ready access to both.

The key person on the White House staff is the Chief of Staff. The present
chief, John Sununu, is an engineer who understands quantitative thinking and
technical issues. Although the Science Adviser reports to the President, it will
be natural for him to deal directly with Dr. Sununu on many issues.

The key person in the Executive Office of the President is Richard Darman,
Director of the Office of Management and Budget (OMB). When OSTP was

established in 1976 (three years after its predecessor, the Office of Science and Technology, was abolished), the enabling legislation mandated its participation in the budget process. Since budget tends to determine program, the close interaction of the staff members in formulating the budget can be OSTP's most important day-to-day activity.

Although at least three recent Presidents have talked about revitalizing "Cabinet government," experience has shown that the Cabinet is too large for effective deliberation and that most policy decisions—even major decisions—involve only a few Cabinet members in a significant way. One way of dealing with this problem has been to establish "councils" in major areas of Presidential concern that involve more than one agency in a significant way. These councils include the relevant agency heads and Presidential staff.

The National Security Council (NSC), which deals with many foreign policy issues, was established after World War II. In the 1970s, the Domestic Policy Council was established, and the Economic Policy Council was formed in the 1980s. In the mid-1960s, a senior staff person served half-time with the OSTP and half-time as a member of the NSC staff. While this level of interaction with the NSC is no longer in place, the Adviser participates in the deliberations of all three councils when an issue involving science and technology is involved. Vice President Quayle chairs the Space Council and the Competitiveness Council, which are relatively recent additions in their present forms. Dr. Bromley is a member of these councils as well.

ACCESS TO THE GOVERNMENT AGENCIES

Government agencies (the term "agencies" here covers both Cabinet-level departments, such as Defense and Agriculture, and independent agencies, such as NASA and the National Science Foundation) have the responsibility, staff and budgets to carry out a variety of missions. If the Adviser is to understand and review aspects of their programs from the President's perspective, he needs to have comfortable access to agency staff and leadership. That access is aided by the perception that the Adviser is in contact with and is trusted by the President.

In dealing with agencies on particularly significant issues that should be of concern to the President, the most effective means of access is budget review. Because the Science Adviser and his staff get involved with individual agencies during the budget cycle, agency heads and staff will respond to calls from the Adviser and will often try to enlist his support.

In addition to access on high-priority individual issues, there needs to be some way to deal with scientific or technological issues that involve more than one agency. The Federal Coordinating Council for Science, Engineering and Technology (FCCSET, informally and perhaps erroneously pronounced "fix it") is made up of the highest level science administrators in thirteen government agencies with major research and development programs. Chaired by the science and technology adviser, FCCSET works primarily through *ad hoc* or standing subgroups. For example, its Committee on Earth Science has examined the nation's program of research and development related to climate, and attempted—with some success—to coordinate the work of the eight agencies involved.

While individual specialized committees of FCCSET can be very effective, FCCSET itself—like the Cabinet—is too unwieldy and unspecialized a group to work very effectively in meetings of principals. One participant in a previous administration described FCCSET meetings as "time sinks." While FCCSET has been set up by statute and, therefore, will continue until the law is changed, Dr. Bromley will be challenged to make the FCCSET process more useful or to develop other mechanisms for coordination.

ACCESS TO PUBLIC SUPPORT

If the Adviser is to be fully effective, the public must care about using science and technology to better defend, cure, protect and enhance the society. They must feel that scientists and engineers are important and that increasing their quality is a legitimate public policy concern. In addition, the press and at least some portion of the country's leadership outside government need to be reasonably well informed about how science can be brought to bear on public policy. Not only is this useful in its own right, but, if general public interest were felt to exist, political leaders would pay serious attention to scientific advice.

One example of this interest is the establishment in 1988 of the Carnegie Commission on Science, Technology and Government. David Hamburg, President of the Carnegie Corporation of New York, an educational foundation founded by Andrew Carnegie in 1911, has been increasingly concerned about improving government organization and capability for decision-making as it relates to the use of science and technology. He approached a number of distinguished individuals—both scientists and nonscientists—to see if they would be willing to serve on or be advisers to a national commission to make recommendations on that subject. He did not ask sitting government officials to serve so as to avoid conflicts of interest.

As a result, the commission was establishing under the co-chairmanship of Joshua Lederberg, President of Rockefeller University, and William T. Golden, a corporate director and trustee, who, as special consultant to President Truman, had recommended, in 1950, the establishment of the post of Science Adviser to the President and of a Presidential Science Advisory Committee.

In addition to distinguished scientists and engineers who have served the government, the commission members include former President Jimmy Carter, former US Senators Charles Mathias and Dan Evans, former US Congressman John Brademas, former Cabinet members William Coleman and Shirley Hufstedler, and President Eisenhower's Chief of Staff, General Andrew Goodpastor. In addition, former President Gerald Ford, Admiral James Watkins and former Governor Richard Thornburgh, who later joined President Bush's Cabinet, agreed to serve on the commission's Advisory Council.[3] The commission is expected to complete its work in 1992.

An independent, bipartisan commission of this kind is more common in the United States than elsewhere. Recommendations of such bodies are usually considered seriously by people with the responsibility to govern. The Carnegie Commission, in its first report, made a set of many recommendations about the way that the White House should deal with science and technology, in particular, upgrading the title of the adviser, establishing a White House-appointed council of scientific and technical advisers, filling all the associate director positions in OSTP, and developing mechanisms for liaison on technical matters within the Executive Office. Some of these recommendations were also made by other important independent bodies, such as the National Academies of Sciences and Engineering, the Council on Competitiveness and a group established by the Miller Center of the University of Virginia. As this document shows, President Bush adopted many of the suggestions.

THE NEED FOR KNOWLEDGE

Access is essential. But access without knowledge can be dangerous. When people with technical training are called on for advice on technical matters, politicians and nontechnical governmental policy-makers give that advice a great deal of weight—too much weight, in fact, if the advice is based on inadequate technical resources or off-the-cuff judgments.

The issues that confront a President and his staff are wide-ranging, and scientists and engineers can make important contributions on many of them. Military research budgets, AIDS and health care costs, environmental degradation, technology policy, earthquake prediction, gene manipulation, nuclear testing, and Moon and Mars missions are among the current candidates.

But the Science and Technology Adviser is *not* "a wizard who personally covers all of science and technology in depth."[1] He needs a mechanism to reach out to members of the scientific and technical community for a wide range of independent advice.

From 1957 to 1973, a key mechanism for such advice was the President's Science Advisory Committee (PSAC), which had been created with a different title in 1951, reporting through the Office of Defense Mobilization, but with direct access to the President as well. PSAC was a group of about eighteen academics and industrial scientists and engineers which was chaired by the Science Advisor and reported to the President. The committee was abolished by President Richard Nixon, who made the Director of the National Science Foundation also his Science Adviser.

President Ford re-established the full-time Adviser, but not the PSAC. President Carter's Adviser used *ad hoc* groups of experts, rather than a committee.

Under President Ronald Reagan, a White House Science Council was appointed that reported to the Adviser, rather than the President.

President Bush has appointed a President's Council of Advisers on Science and Technology (PCAST), chaired by the Science and Technology Adviser reporting directly to him. This upgrading of the council will give extra credibility to its recommendations and ensure maximum participation of first-quality scientists.

Even the best advisory council, however, does not substitute for an ongoing professional staff. The Science and Technology Adviser needs staff members who have knowledge and experience in the major areas of science and technology that will be relevant to the President and the Office of Management and Budget. They must work with the councils and agencies within the Executive Office and the Executive branch. They must also staff the PCAST if its work is to be really useful and effective. Given the range and depth of the problems, a full-time professional staff of thirty is minimal. Dr. Bromley's present professional staff is about half that size with two members borrowed from other government agencies.

Dr. Bromley will also need to find ways to make full use of PCAST. In the 1960s, the President's Science Advisory Committee met for two days every month, and had as many as six additional task forces or study groups at one time looking into particular areas.[4] In recent years, the White House Science Council met for an evening and a day every two months, and seldom had more than one study group at work.[5]

CONCLUSION

The office of the President's Science and Technology Adviser has evolved into a crucial part of the management structure of the US Government. That structure itself is complex, involving many government agencies and coordinating groups. With access to the President, his immediate staff, and government agencies, the Science Adviser has the opportunity to influence crucial government decisions on the many matters that have scientific and technological content or implications.

With an enlarged budget, a professional staff of adequate size, and a working and supported President's Council of Advisers on Science and Technology, the Adviser can obtain the knowledge he or she needs to use that opportunity wisely and effectively.

The Adviser and the President's Council must have the courage to tell the President what is not known as well as what is known. They must, however, understand that the political process requires action and has its own deadlines. On issues of consequence and complexity, there is seldom sufficient knowledge to act with complete certainty. And, even when technical analysis of an issue is needed and feasible, there may not be sufficient time to carry it out. The nation would be better served if longer-term anticipatory studies on critical issues were undertaken or commissioned by the Adviser and the Council, and the power of science and technology were not limited by the calendar of the political and budgetary process or the short fuse of public attention.

NOTES

1. David A. Hamburg in William T. Golden, ed., *Science and Technology Advice to the President, Congress and Judiciary* (New York: Pergamon Press, 1988), p. 161.
2. See Detlev W. Bronk, "Science Advice in the White House: The Genesis of the President's Science Advisers and the National Science Foundation," *Science*, Vol. 186 (October 11, 1974), pp. 116–121; reprinted in William T. Golden, ed., *Science Advice to the President* (New York: Pergamon Press, 1980), pp. 245–256.
3. The full list of members of the commission and the advisory council are given in Appendix A. Admiral Watkins resigned January 20, 1989, after his nomination as Secretary of Energy.
4. The topics include military technology, basic science, the environment, energy, the world food problem, science education, health research, aircraft hijacking, and many others.
5. White House Science Council topics included the use of government laboratories and high-temperature superconductors.

Appendix

MEMBERS OF THE CARNEGIE COMMISSION ON SCIENCE, TECHNOLOGY, AND GOVERNMENT

William T. Golden, Co-Chair
   Chariman, American Museum of Natural History
Joshua Lederberg, Co-Chair
   President, The Rockefeller University
David Z. Robinson, Executive Director
Richard C. Atkinson
   Chancellor, University of California, San Diego
Norman R. Augustine
   Chairman and Chief Executive Officer, Martin Marietta Corporation
John Brademas
   President, New York University
Lewis M. Branscomb
   Director, Science, Technology, and Public Policy Program, Harvard University
The Honorable Jimmy Carter
   Former President of the United States

Theodore Cooper
    Chairman and Chief Executive Officer, The Upjohn Company
Eugene H. Cota-Robles
    Assistant Vice President, Academic Affairs, University of California
William Drayton
    President, Ashoka Fellowships
Thomas Ehrlich
    President, Indiana University
Stuart E. Eizenstat
    Partner, Powell, Goldstein, Frazer & Murphy
The Honorable Gerald R. Ford, Jr.
    Former President of the United States
Ralph E. Gomory
    President, Alfred P. Sloan Foundation
Theodore M. Hesburgh, C.S.C.
    President Emeritus, University of Notre Dame
Walter E. Massey
    Vice President of Research, University of Chicago
Rodney W. Nichols
    Executive Vice President, The Rockefeller University
David Packard
    Chairman of the Board, Hewlett-Packard Company
The Honorable Lewis F. Powell, Jr.
    Former Associate Justice, US Supreme Court
Charles W. Powers
    Partner, Resources for Responsible Management
James B. Reston
    Senior Columnist, *The New York Times*
Alice M. Rivlin
    Senior Fellow, The Brookings Institution
Oscar M. Ruebhausen
    Former Presiding Partner, Debevoise & Plimpton
Jonas Salk
    Founding Director, Salk Institute for Biological Studies
Maxine F. Singer
    President, Carnegie Institution of Washington
The Honorable Richard L. Thornburgh
    US Attorney General
Admiral James D. Watkins (Ret.)*
    Former Chief of Naval Operations US

---

*Through January 20, 1989

Herbert F. York
Director, Institute on Global Conflict & Cooperation, University of California, San Diego
Charles A. Zraket
President and Chief Executive Officer, The MITRE Corporation

Vatican City State: The Pontifical Academy of Sciences

Maxine F. Singer

VATICAN CITY STATE *(Stato della Città del Vaticano) is an ecclesiastical state which is the seat of the Roman Catholic Church, the largest Christian church in the world. Situated in Rome, Italy, its independent sovereignty has been administered by the Pope of the Church since the Lateran Treaty of 1929. The land area of the enclave is 108.7 acres, and its estimated population in 1990 was about 1,000. Italian and Latin are the official languages.*

Every two years, a group of natural scientists from all parts of the globe, representing different scientific disciplines, nationalities, races and religions, joins the morning crowds entering the Vatican. They quickly separate from those entering the churches, office buildings, museums, and libraries on the main streets and make their way up the hill into a quiet section of the Vatican gardens. There, in a small, jewel-like 16th century building, the Casino Pio IV, they join in the biennial plenary session of the Pontifical Academy of Sciences.

The present academy was established in 1936, but the history of scientific academies in Rome goes back to 1603, when Federico Cesi formed the short-lived Academia dei Lincei (or lynx, said to have the sharpest vision of all animals). The academy was weakened by Cesi's death in 1610, and ceased to function by 1651. In the meanwhile, the academy became famous in Europe, to a large extent because it encouraged and supported its most illustrious member, Galileo Galilei. Indeed, it has been concluded that "The Galileo trial in 1633 would not have occurred if Federico Cesi was living."[1]

The next centuries witnessed abortive attempts to re-establish the Academia dei Lincei, but it was not until 1847 that the academy was firmly re-established under Pius IX as the Pontifical Academy of the New Lincei. The scope of activities was to promote science and advise the (Vatican) government about the new technologies and even about the approval of industrial patents.

After the political changes in Italy in the second half of the 19th century, the

Maxine F. Singer is President of the Carnegie Institution of Washington and is a member of the Pontifical Academy of Sciences. She is Chief of the Laboratory of Biochemistry in the National Cancer Institute, National Institutes of Health, where she retains her title of Scientist Emeritus and her laboratory. Holder of a Ph.D. in biochemistry from Yale University, Dr. Singer is a member of the National Academy of Sciences of the US, and of the American Philosophical Society. She has served as Chairman of the Editorial Board of the Proceedings of the US National Academy of Sciences, *is a Fellow (trustee) of the Yale Corporation, and is a member of the Governing Board of the Weizmann Institute of Science. In 1988, Dr. Singer received the Distinguished Presidential Rank Award, the highest honor given to a civil servant.*

academy split into two bodies. One, the Royal Academy of the Lincei, became the national academy of sciences of Italy, and the other, the Pontifical Academy. Finally, following the reconciliation of the Italian Government and the Holy See in 1929 and under the leadership of Pius XI, the contemporary academy began to take shape in the mid-1930s. The academy then became truly international; its scientists included both clerics and nonclerics. At present, the membership is overwhelmingly nonclerical and, notably for Vatican organizations, includes both men and women.

The first layman to be President of the academy was the distinguished Brazilian biophysicist, Carlos Chagas, who served from 1972 to 1989. The current President is Professor Giovanni Battista Marini-Bettolo.

MEMBERSHIP IN THE ACADEMY

Candidates for seats in the academy are nominated by the academy on the basis of their original scientific studies and their acknowledged moral personality—without any ethnic or religious discrimination—and are appointed for life by the Pope. Regular membership is set at a maximum of eighty. In addition, five individuals are members for their terms of office, including the Chief Librarian of the Vatican Library and the Director of the Vatican Observatory; honorary academicians may also be appointed.

The gardens and the fountains that ring the Casino Pio IV and the stuccos, frescoes and mosaics within provide an unusually quiet and beautiful setting for lively interdisciplinary scientific discussions.[2] The themes of the plenary sessions during the past decade were:

- Science and the Modern World (1979);
- Biotechnologies and Their Impact on Society (1981);
- Science for Peace (1983);
- Scientific Progress and the Future of Mankind (1986);
- The Responsibility of Science (1988).

These meetings also include talks by newly elected members on their own histories and research, and thus offer a rare chance for discussion among physicists, biologists, chemists and mathematicians. The culmination of the plenary session is the opportunity for the members to communicate with the Pope. A formal audience in one of the Vatican's splendid halls is an opportunity for the President of the academy to report to the Pope on the discussions and for the Pope to respond in speeches that are generally published. Informal conversations with the group and with individual members take place when the Pope visits Casino Pio IV. In this way, the Pope is informed about the major current scientific questions and the scientific community is reminded of its obligation to serve the planet and its inhabitants in a positive way.

The aim of the Pontifical Academy, as stated in its constitution, is "to promote the progress of the mathematical, physical and natural sciences and the study of epistemological problems relating thereto.'' This objective is carried out through the biennial plenary sessions of the academy membership and through an active program of Working Groups and Study Weeks.

The Working Groups and Study Weeks bring to the academy many accomplished scientists from around the world. The proceedings of these meetings are published. The meetings often end with a Papal audience at which the President reports to the Pope about the discussions and the Pope responds, frequently with statements of high significance for the Church and the world.

SCOPE OF ACTIVITIES

The scope of the activities can be summarized by a list of a few of the recent Study Weeks and Working Groups:[3]

- 1970   Nuclei of Galaxies
- 1980   Mental Deficiency
- 1982   Modern Biological Experimentation
- 1983   Chemical Events and Their Impact on the Environment
- 1984   Immunology, Epidemiology and Social Aspects of Leprosy
- 1984   Impact of Space Exploration on Mankind
- 1985   Developmental Neurobiology of Mammals
- 1985   The Interaction of Parasitic Diseases and Nutrition
- 1986   Persistent Meteo-oceanographic Anomalies and Teleconnections
- 1987   A Modern Approach to the Protection of the Environment
- 1987   Large-Scale Motions in the Universe
- 1989   Future Trends in Spectroscopy

Many scientists are surprised to learn that there is an active Pontifical Academy of Sciences at the Vatican. Indeed, the history of the relation between science and the Church engenders serious concern among scientists. The treatment of Galileo is, of course, a prime matter. A contemporary issue is the position of the Church on various matters related to research on human reproduction.

Nevertheless, members of the academy welcome the opportunity to discuss such issues openly within the Vatican. And it is clear that they are welcome to do so. At the 1986 plenary session, a live broadcast from Casino Pio IV brought to Italian audiences a lively discussion that included the expression of strong views about population control as a way to deal with worldwide problems.

My summary of a 1982 Study Week on Modern Biological Experimentation, which included the following statement, was published in full:[4]

> . . . [he] described to us the process, within the Church, by which positions on moral questions are reached. It is self-evident that the ethical quality of the decision process itself is critical to the worldwide perception and evaluation of any final position. With great respect then I would point out a severe difficulty in that process, as it relates to questions of

human reproduction. Without full and equal participation of women at
every step of the process, the Church's position on these matters will
continue to be seen as ethically compromised by me and by millions of
others, Roman Catholics and nonCatholics alike.

It is appropriate to ask whether the discussions at the Pontifical Academy are
effective in building understanding between the Church and the worldwide scientific endeavor. The academy provides a mechanism whereby the Church and,
in particular, the Pope, because of his direct involvement, are informed about
scientific achievements. Pope John Paul II has often affirmed his encouragement and trust that science will continue to assist in the amelioration of human
problems. He has also said

> For the truth of the matter is that the Church and the scientific community
> will inevitably interact; their options do not include isolation . . . The
> only question is whether they will do this critically or unreflectively, with
> depth and nuance, or with a shallowness that debases the Gospel and
> leaves us ashamed before history.[5]

RESULTS OF THE ACTIVITIES

There is also direct evidence that the activities of the Pontifical Academy can
lead to remarkable results. In 1979, President Carlos Chagas initiated, in discussions with academy members V. Weisskopf and L. Leprince-Ringuet, a
series of events that culminated in the publication of the Declaration on the
Consequences of the Use of Nuclear Weapons (1981) and the Declaration on
the Prevention of Nuclear War (1982). Pope John Paul II participated in the
deliberations leading to these documents and took a strong hand in arranging
for communication of these documents to the governments of the nuclear powers.

Thereafter, John Paul II continued to encourage the role of scientists in com-
mitting the world for peace:

> It is an irreplaceable task of the scientific community to ensure, as is
> your intention, Mr. President of the Pontifical Academy of Sciences, that
> the discoveries of science are not placed at the service of war, tyranny
> and terror. The intention to direct science to the promotion of justice and
> peace demands a great love for humanity.[6]

In quite a different context, during a Study Week in 1981 on Cosmology
and Fundamental Physics, Pope John Paul II spoke to the assembled scientists
about a subject that is frequently a source of dissension between science and
formal religions.

> Cosmogony and cosmology have always aroused great interest among
> peoples and religions. The Bible itself speaks to us of the origin of the
> universe and its make-up, not in order to provide us with a scientific
> treatise, but in order to state the correct relationships of man with God
> and with the universe.[7]

Thus, the scientific understanding of the origins of the universe, the planet, and its inhabitants are clearly separate from Biblical explanations.

These and other constructive activities have eased some past tensions between the Church and the scientific community. The Church's official position on Galileo, however, remains a difficult concern for academy members and scientists worldwide. In 1979, John Paul II presided over the academy's commemoration of the 100th anniversary of Albert Einstein's birth.[8] Carlos Chagas's address mentioned only one scientist besides Einstein:

> Einstein is compared to the greatest minds in the field of universal thought. I might mention among his predecessors only Galileo Galilei, who applied the keen edge of his genius to the development of science and, like Einstein, became the symbol of an era.

John Paul II responded:

> . . . I hope that theologians, scholars and historians, animated by a spirit of sincere collaboration, will study the Galileo case more deeply and, in loyal recognition of wrongs from whatever side they come, will dispel the mistrust that still opposes, in many minds, a fruitful accord between science and faith, between the Church and the world.

As a result of this dialogue, a commission was appointed to clarify the history of Galileo's trial and condemnation. The Pontifical Academy, in collaboration with the Vatican archives, supervised publication, in 1984, of the entire proceedings of the Galileo trial.[9] This fine, scholarly document was welcomed and critically well received. The mistrust has not been completely dispelled, however. To accomplish this, the Vatican archives will need to be freely open to all interested scholars.[10]

CONCLUSION

The Vatican, replete with religious and historical symbols, is an unexpected setting for scientific discourse. Yet an arresting sight at the 1986 plenary session seemed to symbolize the interest of the Church in fostering science in the service of humanity. One of the pleasures of attending a scientific meeting at the academy is the private tour of the Vatican museums arranged for members and their families. During the 1986 tour, each time a set of stairs barred Stephen Hawking's progress through the galleries, four Swiss Guards, resplendent in their Michelangelo costumes, gracefully raised the wheelchair and lifted it to the next landing.

ACKNOWLEDGEMENTS

In preparing this paper, I made extensive use of several documents published by the Pontifical Academy of Sciences: notes 1, 2 and 3 below. I am grateful to C. Chagas and G. B. Marini-Bettolo.

NOTES

1. G. B. Marini-Bettolo, "Historical Aspects of the Pontifical Academy of Sciences," *Pontificiae Academiae Scientiarum Documents* no. 21 (1986).
2. G. D. Filippi, *The Pontifical Academy of Sciences: The Building* (Vatican City: 1986).
3. G. B. Marini-Bettolo, "Outlines of the Activity of the Pontifical Academy of Sciences, 1936–1986," *Pontificiae Academiae Scientiarum Scripta Varia* no. 67 (1986).
4. C. Chagas, ed., "Modern Biological Experimentation," *Pontifical Academy of Sciences Scripta Varia* no. 51 (1982).
5. Address by John Paul II, published in R. J. Russell, W. R. Stoeger, S. J., and C. V. Coyne, S. J., eds., *Physics, Philosophy and Theology: A Common Quest for Understanding* (Vatican City State: Vatican Observatory, 1988).
6. Document 15 (1983), *The Pontifical Academy of Sciences Scripta Varia* no. 65 (1986).
7. Discourse of His Holiness John Paul II published by the Pontifical Academy of Sciences (1981).
8. Einstein, Galileo: Commemoration of Albert Einstein, 1980, Pontifical Academy of Sciences, Libreria Editrice Vaticana.
9. S. M. Pagano, "I document: del Processo di Galileo Galilei," *Pontifical Academy of Sciences Scripta Varia* no. 53 XII-280 (1984).
10. P. Corsi, a review of the book *Galileo Heretic* by P. Redondi, *New York Times Book Review,* November 15, 1987, p. 13.

Science Policy Advising to the President of Venezuela

Raimundo Villegas

THE REPUBLIC OF VENEZUELA *(Republica de Venezuela) was part of Gran Colombia when its independence was established in 1811. It became an independent republic in 1830, and a federal government took effect in 1958. The land area is 352,143 square miles, and its estimated 1989 population was 19,273,000. Spanish is the official language.*

The essay examines the giving of advice on science policy at the highest level of government in Venezuela. I will differentiate several ways in which the President has been advised with regard to science policy: by friends or persons known to him; by cabinet ministers in areas related to aspects of applied science, mainly medicine and agriculture; by individual scientists or scientific societies through public mass media in times of dictatorship; by heads of scientific institutions; and, more recently, by the Minister of State for Science and Technology. With some overlap, these different ways represent successive stages of the general process.

CASUAL PERSONAL ADVISING DURING THE PAST CENTURY

Like many other Latin American countries, scientific research in Venezuela started gaining some social significance during the present century. Casual personal advising was given by scientists to Presidents during the 19th century. For example, José Maria Vargas, a naturalist and physician, gave advice to Simón Bolivar, the Liberator and first President, as to the writing of the Republican By-Laws of the Central University of Venezuela, promulgated in 1827.

Similarly, Calixto González, Professor of Medicine at the Central University, advised the then-President of the Republic, Juan Pablo Rojas Paúl (1888–1890), to send to Paris José Gregorio Hernández, a young physician. The aim was to allow Venezuela to have access to the most advanced experimental medical sciences at that time. Physicians have played important roles in scientific development in Venezuela.

Raimundo Villegas is a Venezuelan neuroscientist. Director of the Venezuelan Institute of Scientific Research, IVIC (1969–1974), he was Acting Vice President of the National Council for Scientific and Technological Research, CONICIT (1970–71); Minister of State for Science and Technology (1979–1984); and President of the International Institute of Advanced Studies (IDEA) (1980–1985). He is currently Chancellor of the Latin American Academy of Sciences (ACAL), and Professor at IDEA.

ACADEMIES AS ADVISORY AGENCIES

During the course of the late 19th and early 20th centuries, groups of professionals, most of them university professors, encouraged the creation of "national academies;" their creation preceded scientific research as a professional activity. State-created and formed by a reduced, fixed number of members, these academies have had among their functions government advising on their particular specialties.

MINISTERIAL DECISIONS AND IMMIGRANT SCIENTISTS: FIRST HALF OF THE 20TH CENTURY

In Venezuela, the 20th century started in 1936, after the death of the dictator, Juan Vicente Gómez. After his death, possibilities for political, social and economic progress opened up for Venezuela. Enrique Tejera, a medical researcher in the field of tropical diseases, was Minister of Health for short periods during these new times; he also was Minister of Education.

In the late 1930s, one of Tejera's decisions was to invite a physiologist from Spain, Augusto Pi Suñer, and other European university professors to take up residence in Venezuela. Pi Suñer created the Institute of Experimental Medicine (IME) within the Central University of Venezuela in 1939.

Francisco De Venanzi and Marcel Roche, medical researchers initially associated with IME, later played key roles in the process of transforming scientific research into a profession in Venezuela.

ADVISING UNDER DICTATORSHIP: THE PRESS AS A LINK BETWEEN SCIENTISTS AND GOVERNMENT

A new military dictator ruled from 1948 to 1958. In 1950, a group of professors from the Central University, headed by De Venanzi, created the Venezuelan Association for the Advancement of Science (AsoVAC). After the Central University was placed under the military regime's control in 1951, De Venanzi continued his work in a private agency, the Institute of Medical Research, headed by Roche. De Venanzi was Associate Director. A small group of researchers and students—myself included—most of them coming from the university's Institute of Experimental Medicine, worked at the Institute of Medical Research until the dictator was overthrown.

AsoVAC members, as well as the personnel of the Institute of Medical Research, tried to advise the dictatorial government on science policy, although they maintained no personal ties with the dictator and kept themselves free of governmental responsibilities. The press—and, especially, the journalist Aristides Bastidas—played an important role in the execution of this "distance advising."

Bastidas highlighted researchers' needs and aspirations in his writings. Even if the immediate success of this sort of distance advising was sparse and rare—dictators, more often than not, are impermeable to citizens' opinions—it was, at least, useful to disclose research activities for the first time and to capture the public interest in science.

Humberto Fernández Morán, a medical researcher, advised and persuaded the dictator to create, in 1954, a large research institution. As a result, the Venezuelan Institute of Neurology and Brain Research (IVNIC) was born, with Fernández Morán as its first director. He was later to become Minister of Education during the final week of the dictatorship.

DEMOCRACY AND SCIENCE IN VENEZUELA (1958-PRESENT)

January 1958 saw the birth of the present democratic period. The gestation period of the Venezuelan Institute of Scientific Research (IVIC) and the Central University's Faculty of Sciences were started that year.

The process leading to the creation of IVIC originated in 1958. De Venanzi advised Carlos Luis González, Minister of Health of the government "Junta" then replacing the dictator, that he should remove from office the man who had served as Director of IVNIC under the dictatorship. De Venanzi also suggested a replacement: Marcel Roche.

The new government appointed a commission, headed by Roche, to evaluate IVNIC. De Venanzi returned to the university where he became Principal and created the first Faculty of Sciences. That same year, most of the Institute of Medical Research's former scientists moved to IVNIC. Both the new director and the new IVNIC researchers advised the government to transform IVNIC into a new research institution, devoted not only to neurology, but also to medicine, biology, chemistry, physics and mathematics.

By the end of 1958, a university professor and lawyer, Edgar Sanabria, was appointed President of the government Junta. He had the task of leading the country's transition from dictatorship to democracy and of deciding IVNIC's fate. His brother, Antonio Sanabria, a university professor of medicine and former visiting scientist at the Institute of Medical Research, advised him to create IVIC. The government Junta decreed IVNIC's suppression and IVIC's creation on January 9, 1959. According to this decree, IVIC's functions included—among others—advising the national government on science and technology (S&T).

A PARENTHESIS: THE CURRENT VENEZUELAN POLITICAL SYSTEM

In order to understand the evolution of advising on science policy since 1959, I will summarize the dynamics of bipartisan government in Venezuela.

By popular mandate, the two main political parties have alternated in power since 1959. The following Presidents have alternated in that position: Social Democrat Rómulo Betancourt (1959–1964), Social Democrat Raúl Leoni (1964–1969), Christian Democrat Rafael Caldera (1969–1974), Social Democrat Carlos Andrés Pérez (1974–1979), Christian Democrat Luis Herrera Campins (1979–1984), Social Democrat Jaime Lusinchi (1984–1989), and Social Democrat Carlos Andrés Pérez (1989–1994), who was re-elected.

ADVISING AGENCIES UNDER DEMOCRATIC GOVERNMENTS

Marcel Roche led IVIC during the Betancourt and Leoni Administrations. Once the Leoni Administration ended in March 1969, President Caldera appointed Marcel Roche President of the newly created National Council for Scientific and Technological Research (CONICIT) and appointed me as Director of IVIC. One of the roles common to CONICIT and IVIC is adviser to the government.

THE NATIONAL COUNCIL FOR SCIENTIFIC AND TECHNOLOGICAL RESEARCH (CONICIT) AS AN ADVISORY AGENCY

After several years of study, in 1968, Congress passed a statute establishing the National Council for Scientific and Technological Research (CONICIT), a legally autonomous institute accountable to the Presidency through CORDI-PLAN, the Planning and Coordination Central Office of the President of the Republic. As in the case of IVIC, CONICIT was proposed by a group of scientists, but this time with the participation of persons linked to the industrial sector.

Congress consulted persons in the fields of science, higher education, industry and politics. CONICIT was designed as the national government's consulting and financing agency for science and technology. Congress decided that the Council of CONICIT should consist of twenty-one representatives from different institutions. It had a technical rather than a political character. Since its creation, it has organized programs for science development by allocating funds to postgraduate studies and research programs.

Raúl Leoni ordered the statute's implementation at the end of 1968. The process to appoint CONICIT's first administrators took so much time that appointments were not made until 1969 by the newly elected President Caldera. CONICIT began its activities under the leadership of Marcel Roche.

One of the first things that President Caldera asked CONICIT to do was to advise his government on the preparation of the chapter on science and technology of the national development plan to be carried out during his administration. The final version of the plan was subsequently prepared by a CORDI-PLAN team led by sociologist Maritza Izaguirre.

THE VENEZUELAN INSTITUTE OF SCIENTIFIC RESEARCH (IVIC) AS AN ADVISORY AGENCY

IVIC is essentially a research institution which covers several fields of science. In addition, as indicated, its functions include advice to the national government on S&T. I will summarize my experience as IVIC's Director (1969–1974).

The most frequent advising consisted of consultations regarding some projects requiring the institute's services and/or technical assistance. Gradually, a considerable degree of confidence and, mainly, credibility developed regarding IVIC's technical results and recommendations. To cope with the growing demand, the Technological Center was created within IVIC.

Another form of advising required, especially from the director, had to do with some aspects of national science policy and international scientific cooperation. These consultations came mainly from CORDIPLAN. Many of IVIC's suggestions were incorporated into the first chapter on S&T included in the national development plan.

Finally, there were frequent meetings with the President of the Republic. President Caldera visited IVIC's headquarters periodically during his administration. The President was then deeply interested in IVIC, and this favored the development of the institution. Evidence of this was the creation of the Technological Center; the Petroleum and Petrochemistry Center; the Engineering Center; the Center for Advanced Studies, which established the first formal curriculum for graduate courses in science at the master's and doctoral levels; the Latin American Biology Center, and the beginnings of the International Ecology Center, the last two conceived for international cooperation.

Some of these centers were to give rise, in the succeeding ten years, to new scientific institutions, such as INTEVEP (the research and development institute of the nationalized oil companies), the Institute of Engineering, and the International Institute of Advanced Studies (IDEA).

MINISTERS OF STATE TO ESTABLISH A LINK BETWEEN THE PRESIDENT AND SCIENTIFIC INSTITUTIONS

Seeking permanent contact with scientific institutions, President Caldera appointed, in 1972, Rodolfo José Cárdenas, a lawyer, an active politician of the party in power, and a person interested in science, as Minister of State for Youth, Science, and Cultural Affairs. His role with respect to science was to act as a link between the President and the scientific community. Later, in 1973, President Caldera created the Integration Commission of the Scientific and Technological System (SISTECIT), chaired by the minister. The vice president of SISTECIT was the President of CONICIT, Miguel Layrisse, a medical researcher himself and a university professor. One of SISTECIT's tasks was to try to consolidate a budget for the sector. SISTECIT was short-lived; it existed only until the end of that Presidential term.

The next President of the Republic, Carlos Andrés Pérez, appointed, toward the end of his term, historian and politician Jose Luis Salcedo Bastardo as Minister of State for Cultural, Scientific and Technological Affairs. He was expected to link the President with the scientific institutions.

THE MINISTER OF STATE FOR SCIENCE AND TECHNOLOGY: A PERSONAL EXPERIENCE

In 1979, the new President of the Republic, Luis Herrera Campins, decided, from the very beginning of his administration, that a scientific researcher should be appointed to the position of Minister of State for Science and Technology. I occupied that position during his five-year Presidential term. Since this is obviously the kind of Presidential advising that I know best, I will go into some details.

We began by agreeing upon priorities. Throughout his five-year term, we made the necessary adjustments. Priorities were as follows:

- To study the most convenient system of coordination and to develop research institutions without obstructing their formal ties with their corresponding ministries;
- To encourage research in the provinces;
- To develop high-quality basic research and oriented and applied research in priority areas, such as health, agriculture and engineering; and
- To develop a new institution for international scientific cooperation and to reinforce those already existing.

Research Coordination and Development

In order to coordinate and develop institutions in this sector, the Cabinet Council decided that the Minister of State for S&T should participate in the economic and in the educational, scientific and cultural Cabinets. Each Cabinet sector studied some specific topics and prepared suggestions to be finally submitted to the weekly meetings held by the whole Cabinet Council. With the same objective in mind, the presidents and directors of the main scientific institutions had weekly meetings with me to discuss the needs and aspirations of their institutions.

Seeking a more permanent basis for the coordination and development of scientific institutions, an *ad hoc* committee was set up to study the convenience of creating a Minister of S&T with portfolio, *i.e.*, fully endowed with statewide powers. Having heard different opinions and received advice from other agencies, including UNESCO's Science Policy Office, the committee advised:

- The creation of a permanent ministerial office for science and technology, headed by a Minister of State, the new office to form a part of the Ministry of the Secretariat of the Presidency of the Republic;
- To entrust this office with the coordination of the sector; and
- Following UNESCO's advice, to participate in the budgetary allocation of funds to the different scientific institutions. This was the so-called "double-key padlock," which meant that each institution obtained its budget granted by both the minister directly responsible for the scientific institution involved and the Minister of State for Science and Technology. Furthermore, budgets could not be modified without the Minister of State's approval.

During the Herrera Campins Administration, the double-key padlock proved successful, thanks to the voluntary cooperation of the ministers responsible for some of the important agencies for S&T development and research centers. The President's support for this proposal proved to be essential.

In order to coordinate the S&T sector, to participate in the sector's planning, and to prepare the annual budget for the scientific institutions, the S&T office within the Ministry of the Secretariat was created. In addition, a Commission of Science and Technology Policy, with similar purposes, was also created in 1982 by Presidential decree. This commission was chaired by the Minister of State and included CORDIPLAN's Minister, the President of CONICIT, one representative from the Economic Cabinet, and one representative from the Educational, Scientific and Cultural Cabinet.

The creation of this commission met a guarded reception from the S&T Commission of the National Congress and from CONICIT, both of whom felt that their planning functions were being bypassed. As a result, the final draft of the commission's decree was adjusted to meet CONICIT's technical opinion, seeking to fortify both the Congressional Commission and CONICIT. In the final two years of President Herrera Campins's office, we managed to create a budget for S&T as a sector. The protocabinet lasted only until the end of that Presidential term (1984).

Research Regionalization

In order to achieve the second objective, *i.e.,* research development in the provinces, two types of actions were taken. On the one hand, in regions where science activities were relatively less developed, institutions devoted to research in areas of particular interest to those regions were located with the participation of regional development corporations. On the other hand, in regions showing a higher relative development in science and technology activities, foundations were created to promote research with the participation of regional development corporations, higher education and research institutions in the area, CONICIT, and the Minister of State's Office. These foundations, called FUNDACITE, are appropriate organizations to foster research at the regional level and an effective way to stimulate the participation of different sectors in the promotion of science and technology in developing countries.

Sectoral Development of Research

Regarding the third objective, *i.e.*, development of top-quality basic research and oriented and applied research in priority areas, efforts focused—on the one hand—on giving support to basic research institutions and—on the other hand—to increasing the technological research infrastructure that only rarely existed. As a result, two new foundations, the Institute of Engineering and the Fund for Technological Innovation (FINTEC) were created.

International Scientific Cooperation

The last objective was certainly one of the aspects that we developed the most. This objective became a reality when, in 1979, the International Institute of Advanced Studies (IDEA) was created. This institute was organized as a joint foundation with state and private participation, open to cooperation through international organizations and devoted to top-level research and education by means of international workshops and intensive training courses. In addition, since its creation, IDEA has been the headquarters for several international organizations, such as the Latin American Academy of Sciences (ACAL), the COSTED Regional Secretariat for Latin America of the International Council of Scientific Unions (ICSU), and the Simón Bolivar International Center for Scientific Cooperation, created by a Venezuela-UNESCO agreement. Moreover, ACAL has signed cooperation agreements with the Third World Academy of Sciences (TWAS) and UNESCO.

RECENT MINISTERS/PRESIDENTS OF THE NATIONAL COUNCIL FOR SCIENTIFIC AND TECHNOLOGICAL RESEARCH (CONICIT)

Once the term of President Herrera Campins concluded in 1984, a new government headed by President Lusinchi appointed Luis Carbonell, a medical researcher, as Minister of State/President of CONICIT. It is too soon to determine whether it was convenient to merge the position of Minister of State for S&T with the post of President of CONICIT.

The new minister was to have both a larger administrative apparatus and a considerable budget. During the period, Congress granted extraordinary economic powers to the President of the Republic. This allowed a reform of the legal status of the joint foundations with state and private participation, so that all that had received, upon their creation, significant state contributions were compelled to become state foundations.

The President of the Republic was then entitled to freely appoint and remove their authorities, and the majority of the members of their councils were to be government appointments. The foundations created during the Herrera Campins Administration were mainly affected by this resolution. A year or so later, President Lusinchi appointed a medical researcher, Tulio Arends, as the new Minister of State/President of CONICIT.

In February 1989, a new President took office. The elected President, Carlos Andrés Pérez, appointed a sociologist, Dulce Arnao de Uzcátegui, as Minister of State/President of CONICIT. The new minister has announced plans to foster research, to create a corporation for technological development, and to restart regionalization and international cooperation programs.

Minister Arnao de Uzcátegui has created an advisory committee, gathering all the scientists who have occupied the positions of ministers in the sector or presidents of CONICIT. The first committee meeting, held in June 1989, identified the most serious problems in the sector, on that occasion, I highlighted the importance of the brain-drain that has started to affect our country. In February of 1990, the creation of a National System for the Promotion of the Research Scientist was being studied by CONICIT to restrain the brain-drain at present. The document containing this proposal has been reviewed by the advisory comittiee, and some recommendations have been made.

FINAL CONSIDERATIONS

Several years have elapsed since I was Minister of State for Science and Technology, yet I still believe that the permanent S&T Ministerial Office, the Minister of State for S&T as adviser and promoter, the "double-key padlock" budgetary system, and the Commission on S&T Policy are all useful proposals for developing countries. (It should be noted that this office had a staff of only six to eight persons.)

In my view, the tasks of the Minister of State for S&T in a developing country are the following:

- To advise the President on policy issues that are specific to the science and technology sector;
- To develop a national policy, plan and budget for the promotion of S&T with the cooperation of CONICIT and the various ministries;
- To promote and coordinate research and other S&T activities; and
- To promote international and scientific cooperation.

On the other hand, the technical evaluation and funding of specific research programs, the establishment and administration of high-level training programs for human resources in the sector, and the technical advising to the Office of the Minister of State in the preparation of the national plan and budget for the S&T sector pertains to CONICIT.

Because we have frequently seen that some science and technology development programs have been interrupted when power has been constitutionally transferred from one President to another, we need a national framework for science and technology based on the overall consent of the various political and scientific groups. The aim is the institutionalization of science policy in order to resist the changes in government. For this reason, I believe that the recently created advisory committee, which gathers the past Ministers of State and Presidents of CONICIT, is the body which should be expected to offer the sector the political stability and continuity needed. If the science and technology sector is to grow, it must begin to learn from its own experience.

ACKNOWLEDGEMENTS

The author wishes to thank Luis Castro Leiva, Gloria M. Villegas, Walewska Lemoine, Guillermo Cardoza and Oscar Silva-Alvarez for their critical readings of this manuscript, and Irene Delgado for her secretarial assistance.

Science and Technology Advising to the Government(s) in Yugoslavia

Vlastimir Matejić

THE SOCIALIST FEDERAL REPUBLIC OF YUGOSLAVIA *(Sociajalistička Fed-erativna Republika Jugoslavija) was founded in 1963 and has been under a collegial Presidency since 1971. Its present constitution was adopted in 1974. The country's land area is 98,766 square miles, and its estimated population in 1989 was 23,732,000. The official languages are Serbo-Croatian, Slovenian and Macedonian, among others.*

Science and technology advising to the government in Yugoslavia has never been the subject of a comprehensive study and thus this essay will describe only the approach used and the findings of the author.

The starting point is the fact that systematic science and technology advising to the government has never been institutionalized for any length of time. That is to say, practically everything that could be called science and technology advising has been done in a short-term and institutionally unpredictable manner.

All federal and state governments, however, have long recognized the need for science and technology advice, but have never taken the steps necessary for institutionalizing this activity. No one has actually been against it or, to put it another way, many have expressed their interest in and willingness to have such advice, but that has not happened yet in an organized, institutionalized, reliable and responsible way.

The key objective here is to describe and explain the reasons for such a contradictory state, and to analyze some of the features of science and technology advising which are becoming more and more a part of the parliamentary and government decision-making process.

THE CONCEPTUAL FRAMEWORK

The framework of this essay is based on the following claims and findings concerning the subject. First, the science and technology advice that has occurred in government(s) in Yugoslavia has been, in the strictest sense, in response to the governments' needs for these services—no more, no less.

Vlastimir Matejić is a member of the Commission for Science of the Federal Parliament, and a member of the Committee for Science and University Education of the State Government of Serbia. He is also Yugoslav delegate to the OECD Committee for Science and Technology Policy. Dr. Matejić is head of the Science and Technology Policy Research Center at the Institute Mihajlo Pupin, Belgrade, and Professor in the electrical engineering department at the University of Belgrade.

Second, the structure, scope and degree of permanency of these services are determined by the structural features of the government(s) and by the ideological-political-governmental perceptions of the social, economic, technological and overall developmental problems and the concepts for their resolution.

Third, the quality of science and technology advice is determined equally with the governments' needs and expectations and the behavioral features of those from the science and technology community who have supplied the advice.

THE STRUCTURE OF THE GOVERNMENTAL SYSTEM

Yugoslavia is a federal country with a very decentralized parliamentary and governmental system. It is a federation, and each state has its own parliament and government. The relation between a parliament and its government is specific in the sense that the government is only the executive board of the parliament. This relationship is crucial to the understanding of the state of science and technology advising, on the one hand, and to the synthesizing of the appropriately institutionalized system of this advising, on the other.

The important feature of such a structure is that a great deal of power and responsibility is allocated to the state (republic) and even to the local-level parliaments and their governments. In addition to this, Yugoslavia is a multinational country, decentralized primarily on the ethnic criterion. Science policy has been, for the past two decades, separate from the federal government's responsibility because science is considered as a part of the national (ethnic) cultural heritage and is thus under the responsibility of state governments.

Technological development and the resolution of its social, economic and other impacts is generally ascribed to the economic agents—producers and their associations—with some emerging influence of governments, including federal, during recent years. The relationship between the governments in Yugoslavia and science and technology issues, problems and policies is particularly specific and has been shaped by many factors, starting with those determined by ideology and rather unsuccessful attempts to develop a new type of relationship between science and the other elements of society and ending with the actual level of the scientific and economic development of the country and the ongoing crisis situation.

PARLIAMENTS' AND GOVERNMENTS' NEEDS FOR ADVICE

The needs for advice are generated by the federal and state parliaments, their governments, and their departments—the three levels of rather stable structure of the needs. The intensity of those needs has passed through several typical stages, but a sharp increase in this intensity occurred during the 1980s. The structures of the problems and areas to which these needs have been addressed are as follows.

The first and prevailing revealed needs of the federal and state parliaments and governments for science and technology advice are mostly in economic policy problems and issues. The second type of need is caused by the general political and governmental preparation for radical economic reforms. Here again the focus is on the change in economic institutions and development policies and actions in accordance with those changes. Science and technology advice, in the strictest sense, has not been needed up until now for the design of such changes. While a certain minimum of scientific and technological problems and issues could not be bypassed in the design of economic policies and reforms, this has been the subject matter of science and technology advice to the government.

The exception to the above needs of the government is the nuclear energy issue, which has been, from its very beginnings, under the strong stewardship of the federal government.

Governmental departments—and this is particularly true of the federal government—have advisory bodies or, at least, places for establishing them, which are designed so as to supply the departments with expert advice. This is particularly true of the federal and state planning offices. The needs for science and technology advice on the departmental level are revealed usually in an *ad hoc* manner, since they are actually the need for urgent consulting on specific problems. It is rather unjustified to consider these instances as needs for science and technology advice in a proper sense.

State governments express, mostly through the activities of their departments, some needs for science and technology advice in the fields of science and education, utilization of scientific and technological potentials for economic development, the transfer of technology, space communication, the brain-drain, and other problems.

In summary, the needs for science and technology advice to the federal and state governments and parliaments in Yugoslavia are steadily developing, but are restricted so far to the economic policy issues, mostly expressed *ad hoc* or urgent and unpredictable, and thus difficult to plan. The nuclear energy situation has been an explanation.

The factors that can be used to explain these features of governmental need for science and technology advice are the following. First, the political philosophy of socioeconomic development has not appropriately considered the role of science and technology for estimating other factors, such as natural resources, the labor supply, the labor-managed economic system, and similar issues. The governments did follow this philosophy.

Second, due to this philosophy, governments frequently wanted and more or less clearly expressed the need for "wishful advising," *i.e.*, they wanted advice to prove the validity of intended or already decided and undertaken decisions.

Third, whenever governments needed objective science and technology advice, they expected the advice to somehow guarantee the outcome of the implementation of their proposed projects. This expectation led to either hesitation on the part of the scientific community to offer advice or to the reduction of advice for the content of which responsibility can be taken. In both cases, a great many of the proper needs for science and technology advice are not satisfied.

GOVERNMENT DECISION-MAKING

In a nonprivate economy, the government is very much involved in economic and business decisions, particularly in the allocation of investments and price regulation. In Yugoslavia, governments have made many important economic decisions for which science and technology advice was necessary, particularly in regard to the construction of large industrial firms and complexes. In most— if not all—of these cases, those needs have been expressed after a certain political preference to a specific solution has been formulated, so that the main task of the science and technology advisers has been to justify this (political) preference, eventually to suggest some harmless modifications, and to take care of technical problems that may be encountered in the implementation.

Politicians and officials might have had some of the "scientific" consultations before the preference to a specific solution is revealed. Such consultancy can hardly be called science and technology advice.

The outcomes of these situations, among other things, have been such failures that the decision-makers claim that they are finished with science and technology advising. The case of radical reform of the educational system in Yugoslavia, the negative consequences of which are still very obvious, is of great—if not the utmost—historical signficance. This reform was brought about by politicians and government with some advisory justification from a minor part of the scientific community and contrary to strong warnings from a greater part of that same community. This illustrates that, as long as those who want only predetermined science advice govern the policy, it is likely that they will not express any other kinds of advising needs, simply because they prefer advice which meets their own plans.

A second circumstance concerns the real importance and influence of science and technology advice in cases of divergent interests in society. This is exactly the problem that Yugoslavia has been facing for a very long time because, given conflicts of interests and a decentralized system, each multicriterial (multidimensional) problem becomes political to the extent that scientific judgments are of minor importance and little influence. This can be illustrated by two examples.

While the federal government is responsible for the less-developed areas, the main problem is to define the criteria and decision and judgment rules for classifying a region as developed (which gives aid) or undeveloped (which receives financial support). This issue can be considered as a typical case in which science advising is relevant, but can become political to the extent that it is very difficult to make classification improvements on a scientific basis.

The second example is the research system itself. As previously noted, the Yugoslav scientific system consists of practically independent subsystems so that the whole network is fragmented and inefficient. The scientific community has reacted against this situation many times, backing up its advice with many facts. Due to the strong politicization of this issue, however, its solution has remained independent of science advice to government.

As regards the actual situation and its probable future development, for many reasons—but mostly because the developmental power of some factors has been exhausted, political, parliamentary and governmental attention to science and technology has increased. Thus, from the beginning of the 1980s, political and governmental assessors and decision-makers have started looking for science advice; this has brought about several important developments.

First, as has been mentioned, each government has an advisory council in which scientists and other experts perform science and technology advising more and more frequently. Second, the previous federal government introduced the Federal Council for Science and Technology. Along the same lines, after a long period of time, the federal parliament approved the strategy for the technological development of the country, which is still the only approved federal strategy.

Under this strategy, a Federal Fund was created for the promotion of the technological development of the country which amounts to up to 0.15% of the Gross National Product. The federal government is structured so as to influence the scientific and technological development of the country in a direction which yields the utmost in economic growth and social development.

The Federal Secretariat for Development is structured to oversee science and technology, developmental planning, and environmental protection. All these activities and government policies are influenced more and more by science and technology advice. Along these lines, forthcoming federal research projects were designed that should lay out the "scientific bases for the economic and social development of the country."

THE ORGANIZATIONAL FORMS OF ADVICE

There is no permanent science and technology advisory mechanism in the strictest sense for any field or purpose in the federal and state governments of Yugoslavia. The only exception to this has been, for some time, the federal government's Commission for Nuclear Energy. This commission is composed of the heads of the principal departments of the federal government, the heads of the state governments, and representatives of the research institutes in nuclear technology, etc., and chaired by the President of the federal government. It did not, however, perform—due to the structure of its membership—real science and technology advising.

From an organizational point of view, science and technology advising to the government(s) in Yugoslavia is done through the following channels:

- Reports on projects prepared by independent research institutes or universities, these projects being defined so as to cover the specific advising needs of the government and financed by the government;
- Temporarily established groups of scientists and other experts for advising the government;
- Commissions appointed by government through the advisory councils of its department for a whole term; these commissions have mixed memberships from scientists to politicians to industrial managers; and
- A single scientist, expert or a small group of the same who have personal relationships with those who are seeking advice.

Where the scientific content of advice is concerned, the most promising of the above methods are the first and the last. The potentials of these organized forms, however, in supplying scientific content have been only partially explored for reasons which shall be discussed later.

The main characteristics of the above forms are as follows. First, none of the forms is permanent, except the third, whose membership composition and duties make it marginally competent to offer science and technology advice. The lack of permanency causes a lack of scientific standards and the absence of a necessary scientific discipline in the advisory process. As a consequence, advising becomes *ad hoc* and an intellectually voluntary activity.

Second, the research under contract to the government, in cases where there are strong expectations and prejudices on the part of the users of the advice, decreases the intellectual independence of the research institutions and forces them to look for findings and advice that the government hopes to obtain. This leads to a decreased use of the knowledge base for research and to a lack of full objectivity in research findings. The research institutions are forced into such behavior by the users' expectations and by the way these expectations are translated into behavior because the institutions are dependent upon the governments' financial resources. To clarify this point, it should be mentioned that the Yugoslav research system is financed through contracts for end users, *i.e.,* there is no state funding of scientific research except the earlier cited Federal Fund for the promotion of technological development.

During the past four years, the federal parliament has established the Commission for Science to deal with the problems of science and technology development and related matters. The commission has the power and the responsibility to participate in policy matters, the adoption of new laws, and approval of new economic and other measures as they pertain to science and technology. The commission is composed of delegates from the various federal parliamentary bodies from all federal units and from the scientific community. The structure of the delegation is such that—for many agenda items—the commission has the professional credibility and authority to deal with them. Thus the Commission for Science is the federal parliament's science and technology advisory body.

The Commission for the Protection of the Environment serves a similar purpose for the federal parliament but in environmental matters only. During the past few years, this commission has raised many specific questions concerning environmental protection, among which one about nuclear energy resulted in a ban on nuclear energy station construction.

These two commissions have pointed up the necessity for the institutionalization of technology assessment in the federal parliament. The approval of such a proposal is under consideration. A quick study would produce the finding that, for the time being, science and technology advising is more developed and more appropriately institutionalized in the federal parliament than in the federal government. Taking into account policy decision-making and the relationship between the parliament and government in Yugoslavia, this finding should be considered as a development in the right direction.

INFLUENCES ON DECISION-MAKING AND EFFECTIVENESS

The systemic characteristics of science and technology advising to the government of Yugoslavia point to the conclusion that such advice has not, for a very long time, been a very positive influence on governmental decisions, policies, and program formulation. The qualification "positive influence" is used to point out that most of the real influence of science and technology advising has been used as a welcome back-up for already shaped and selected decisions and programs. Such use of science and technology advice is merely a formality and, according to stronger standards, could be qualified as a negative influence. There have, however, been some positive cases, of which science and technology advice on defense issues is one.

If effectiveness is considered in the sense of comparison between cost and effort, on one hand, and the effects of the use of advising, on the other, the following can be concluded.

During the past twenty years, the federal government has allocated and spent so little on science and technology advice that the ratio of *effect:cost* is numerically substantial because the value of the denominator is so small. If one considers the ratio of *effects:efforts* made by those who have given advice to the government, the numerical value of the ratio is very low. Put another way, a small amount of money is spent for science advising, but rather a lot of voluntary work by scientists and other experts has gone into it. This is a consequence of, first, political and governmental underestimation of the importance of and need for science and technology advice and, second, of the willingness of the research community to serve social needs through advising the government.

CONCLUSION

During the 1960s and 1970s, the Yugoslav governments and other influential institutions did not pay appropriate attention to science and technology and their potential for economic growth and social development. Only this can explain the fact that, during the whole history of non-aligned movement in which Yugoslavia has played an important role, science and technology issues have not been on the agenda. Along the same lines, the governmental and political attitude toward science and technology offers an explanation of how and why the Yugoslav economy came to a crisis.

Some positive changes in this area have occurred in recent years: governmental concern with the environment, the adoption of a federal strategy for technological development, and actions to change the system of research financing with a bigger role for the government(s), to mention only a few of the more promising positive signs.

Clearly, these developments are not yet sufficient evidence that science and technology advising to the government will be performed properly in the near future, but they are necessary beginning actions toward a new approach to many policy problems which parliaments and governments in Yugoslavia will deal with while leaning on the policy politically announced as ''science-based development of society.''

Index